Heath Mathematics

Walter E. Rucker · Clyde A. Dilley · David W. Lowry

HEATH

D. C. Heath and Company
Lexington, Massachusetts Toronto

Contributing Authors Edward Manfre, Beth Andrini, Larry Chrystal: 20–21, 40–41, 42–43, 90–91, 106–107, 110–111, 120–121, 146–147, 164–165, 166–167, 200–201, 232–233, 234–235.

Illustrations Leo Abbett/Catharine Bennett/Chris Czernota/Nancy Evers/Linda Strauss Edwards/Judy Filippo/Diane Jaquith/True Kelley/Kay Life/Sally Mavor/Yoshi Miyaki/Cheryl Kirk Noll/Lynn Titleman/John Wallner. Computer Art: Lynn Titleman.

Photography Jonathan Barkan: 213; Fredrik D. Bodin: 170, 171; A. James Casner: 65, 101, 123, 127, 244, 251; John Coletti: 141 (right); Jeffrey Mark Dunn: 230, 231; Jerry Howard/Margarite Bradley: 94 (left), 95, 162 (top and left) 209 (left and right), 296; Paul Johnson: 19, 94 (right), 141 (left), 168, 194, 278, 282; Lou Jones: 14, 196, 197; Tom Magno: 1, 69, 80, 81, 157, 158, 160, 263, 309, 329; Mike Malyszko: 48, 49, 142, 143, 145, 152, 337; Kim Massie/Rainbow: 215; Ned McCormick: title page; Julie O'Neil: 24–25, 31, 59, 144 (top), 189, 206, 336, 342, 345; Palmer/Brilliant: 237, 257; Frank Siteman/Stock, Boston: 173; Deidra Delano Stead: 89, 192, 241, 267, 271, 307, 316, 321; © Dennis Stock/Magnum Photos, Inc.: 35; John Urban: 28, 64, 131, 144 (bottom), 274, 293, 308.

Cover Bruce Terzian, Designer
Ned McCormick, Photographer

Published simultaneously in Canada.

Printed in the United States of America.

International Standard Book Number: 0-669-16037-7

5 6 7 8 9 0

Contents

1

Addition and Subtraction Facts

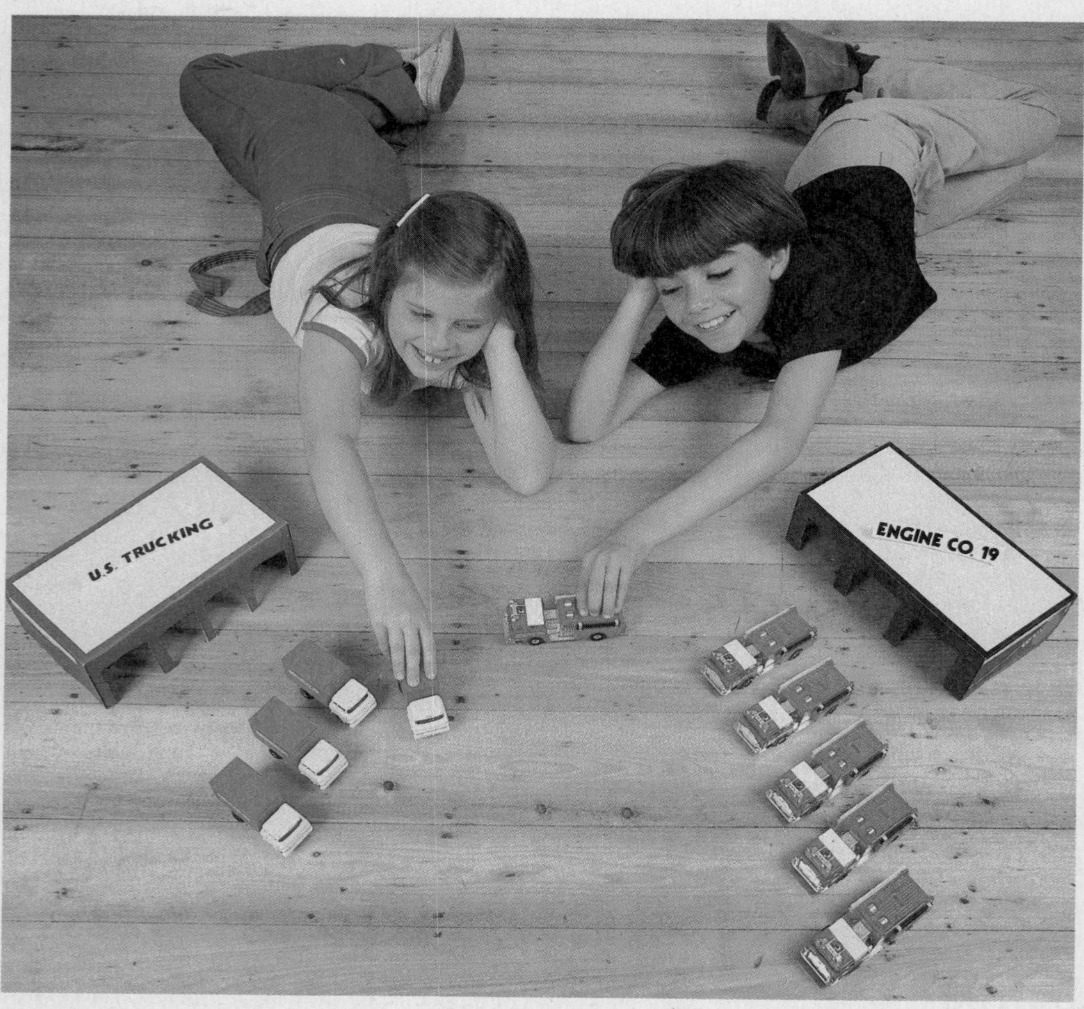

Can Lisa and Tony fit all the trucks in the two garages?

Name ______________________________

Addition facts

EXERCISES

Add.

1. 3 + 2 = 5

2. 0 + 4 = 4

3. 3 + 4 = 7

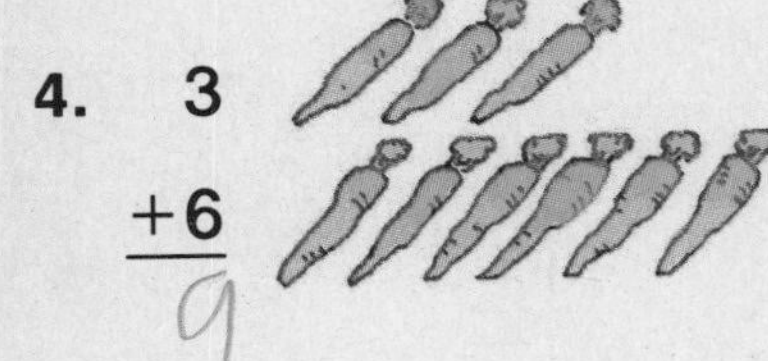

4. 3 + 6 = 9

5. 1 + 4 = 5

6. 2 + 6 = 8

7. 1 + 5 = 6

8. 5 + 4 = 9

9. 3 + 3 = 6

10. 3 + 7 = 10

11. 4 + 2 = 6

12. 2 + 5 = 7

13. $4 + 4$

14. $6 + 4$

15. $4 + 5$

Give each sum.

16. $0 + 2$	17. $4 + 3$	18. $0 + 0$	19. $3 + 1$	20. $6 + 1$	21. $1 + 2$
22. $2 + 7$	23. $1 + 4$	24. $3 + 5$	25. $1 + 1$	26. $5 + 4$	27. $0 + 7$
28. $4 + 6$	29. $8 + 2$	30. $2 + 4$	31. $0 + 5$	32. $5 + 5$	33. $5 + 2$
34. $6 + 4$	35. $6 + 2$	36. $5 + 1$	37. $0 + 1$	38. $2 + 3$	39. $1 + 8$
40. $2 + 2$	41. $6 + 3$	42. $1 + 6$	43. $7 + 3$	44. $1 + 7$	45. $1 + 9$

Use the numbers to write an addition fact. Put a check by each addend. Put a circle around the sum.

46.

47.

48.
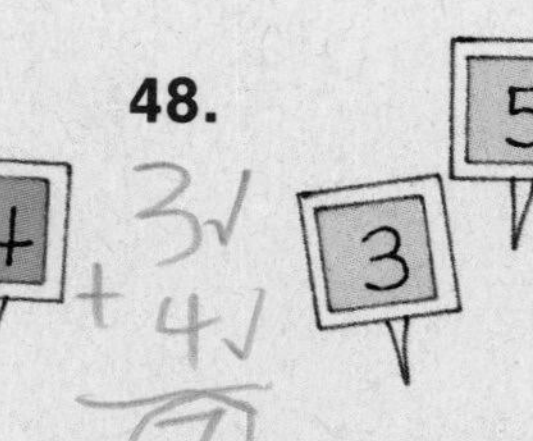

49.

Name Matin #

Properties of addition

The Order Property of Addition
I can change the order of the addends without changing the sum.
4
+5
9
5
+4
9

The Adding 0 Property
If I add any number and 0, I get the number.
8
+0
8

EXERCISES

Give each sum.

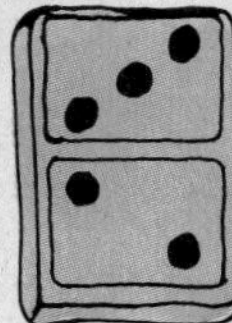

1. $3 + 2 =$ [5]
2. $2 + 3 =$ [5]
3. $6 + 4 =$ [10]
4. $4 + 6 =$ [10]

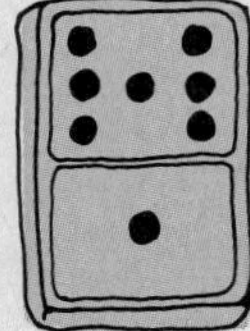

5. $7 + 1 =$ [8]
6. $1 + 7 =$ [8]
7. $5 + 3 =$ [8]
8. $3 + 5 =$ [8]

9. $6 + 2 =$ [8]
10. $2 + 6 =$ [8]
11. $7 + 3 =$ [10]
12. $3 + 7 =$ [10]
13. $2 + 0 =$ [2]
14. $0 + 2 =$ [2]

15. $8 + 2 =$ [10]
16. $2 + 8 =$ [10]
17. $9 + 1 =$ [10]
18. $1 + 9 =$ [10]
19. $7 + 0 =$ [7]
20. $0 + 7 =$ [7]

21. $5 + 1 =$ [6]
22. $1 + 5 =$ [6]
23. $9 + 0 =$ [9]
24. $0 + 9 =$ [9]
25. $6 + 3 =$ [9]
26. $3 + 6 =$ [9]

Add.

27. $\begin{array}{r}3\\+0\\\hline\end{array}$	28. $\begin{array}{r}4\\+1\\\hline\end{array}$	29. $\begin{array}{r}1\\+2\\\hline\end{array}$	30. $\begin{array}{r}8\\+0\\\hline\end{array}$
31. $\begin{array}{r}0\\+0\\\hline\end{array}$	32. $\begin{array}{r}8\\+1\\\hline\end{array}$	33. $\begin{array}{r}0\\+8\\\hline\end{array}$	34. $\begin{array}{r}3\\+7\\\hline\end{array}$
35. $\begin{array}{r}2\\+2\\\hline\end{array}$	36. $\begin{array}{r}1\\+1\\\hline\end{array}$	37. $\begin{array}{r}2\\+5\\\hline\end{array}$	38. $\begin{array}{r}2\\+1\\\hline\end{array}$
39. $\begin{array}{r}0\\+5\\\hline\end{array}$	40. $\begin{array}{r}2\\+4\\\hline\end{array}$	41. $\begin{array}{r}6\\+0\\\hline\end{array}$	42. $\begin{array}{r}3\\+1\\\hline\end{array}$
43. $\begin{array}{r}0\\+6\\\hline\end{array}$	44. $\begin{array}{r}5\\+4\\\hline\end{array}$	45. $\begin{array}{r}5\\+5\\\hline\end{array}$	46. $\begin{array}{r}3\\+4\\\hline\end{array}$
47. $\begin{array}{r}6\\+1\\\hline\end{array}$	48. $\begin{array}{r}1\\+8\\\hline\end{array}$	49. $\begin{array}{r}4\\+2\\\hline\end{array}$	50. $\begin{array}{r}0\\+3\\\hline\end{array}$
51. $\begin{array}{r}1\\+6\\\hline\end{array}$	52. $\begin{array}{r}4\\+4\\\hline\end{array}$	53. $\begin{array}{r}3\\+3\\\hline\end{array}$	54. $\begin{array}{r}7\\+2\\\hline\end{array}$
55. $\begin{array}{r}4\\+3\\\hline\end{array}$	56. $\begin{array}{r}4\\+5\\\hline\end{array}$	57. $\begin{array}{r}2\\+7\\\hline\end{array}$	58. $\begin{array}{r}1\\+6\\\hline\end{array}$
59. $\begin{array}{r}5\\+5\\\hline\end{array}$	60. $\begin{array}{r}5\\+4\\\hline\end{array}$	61. $\begin{array}{r}9\\+0\\\hline\end{array}$	62. $\begin{array}{r}3\\+6\\\hline\end{array}$

Challenge!

Who am I?

63. If you add me to 3, you get 8. ____

64. If you add me to 6, you get 10. ____

65. If you add me to 9, you get 9. ____

66. If you add me to myself, you get 6. ____

Name Matin #2

Sums to 18

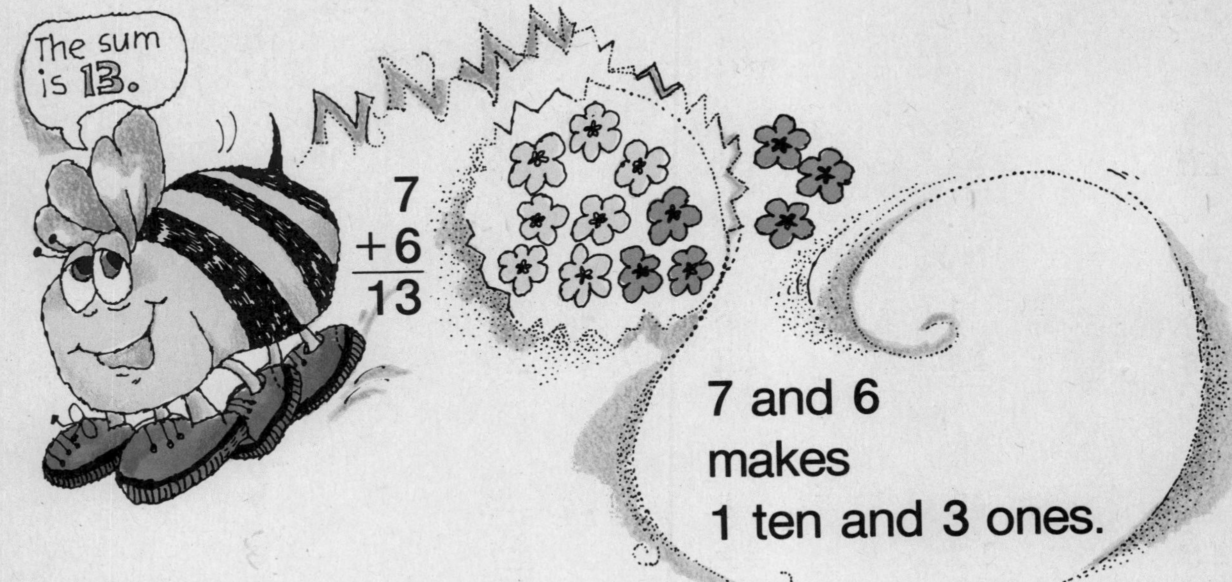
The sum is 13.
7
+6
13
7 and 6
makes
1 ten and 3 ones.

EXERCISES

Give each sum.

1. 6 + 5 = 11

2. 8 + 4 = 12

3. 8 + 3 = 11

4. 9 + 9 = 18

5. 7 + 6 = 13

6. 8 + 8 = 16

7. 8 + 7 = 15

8. 7 + 8 = 15

9. 7 + 4 = 11

10. 4 + 7 = 11

11. 8 + 5 = 13

12. 5 + 8 = 13

13. 8 + 6 = 14

14. 6 + 8 = 14

15. 9 + 8 = 17

16. 8 + 9 = 17

17. 9 + 6 = 15

18. 6 + 9 = 15

19. 9 + 5 = 14

20. 5 + 9 = 14

21. 9 + 7 = 16

22. 7 + 9 = 16

23. 7 + 5 = 12

24. 5 + 7 = 12

Add.

25. $\begin{array}{r} 8 \\ +7 \\ \hline \end{array}$ 26. $\begin{array}{r} 9 \\ +4 \\ \hline \end{array}$ 27. $\begin{array}{r} 8 \\ +3 \\ \hline \end{array}$ 28. $\begin{array}{r} 6 \\ +9 \\ \hline \end{array}$

29. $\begin{array}{r} 5 \\ +6 \\ \hline \end{array}$ 30. $\begin{array}{r} 9 \\ +5 \\ \hline \end{array}$ 31. $\begin{array}{r} 7 \\ +6 \\ \hline \end{array}$ 32. $\begin{array}{r} 6 \\ +8 \\ \hline \end{array}$

33. $\begin{array}{r} 9 \\ +6 \\ \hline \end{array}$ 34. $\begin{array}{r} 9 \\ +3 \\ \hline \end{array}$ 35. $\begin{array}{r} 6 \\ +6 \\ \hline \end{array}$ 36. $\begin{array}{r} 4 \\ +9 \\ \hline \end{array}$

37. $\begin{array}{r} 7 \\ +8 \\ \hline \end{array}$ 38. $\begin{array}{r} 9 \\ +7 \\ \hline \end{array}$ 39. $\begin{array}{r} 5 \\ +7 \\ \hline \end{array}$ 40. $\begin{array}{r} 7 \\ +7 \\ \hline \end{array}$

41. $\begin{array}{r} 8 \\ +6 \\ \hline \end{array}$ 42. $\begin{array}{r} 8 \\ +8 \\ \hline \end{array}$ 43. $\begin{array}{r} 6 \\ +7 \\ \hline \end{array}$ 44. $\begin{array}{r} 4 \\ +7 \\ \hline \end{array}$

45. $\begin{array}{r} 5 \\ +8 \\ \hline \end{array}$ 46. $\begin{array}{r} 9 \\ +9 \\ \hline \end{array}$ 47. $\begin{array}{r} 4 \\ +8 \\ \hline \end{array}$ 48. $\begin{array}{r} 3 \\ +8 \\ \hline \end{array}$

49. $\begin{array}{r} 5 \\ +6 \\ \hline \end{array}$ 50. $\begin{array}{r} 9 \\ +4 \\ \hline \end{array}$ 51. $\begin{array}{r} 8 \\ +3 \\ \hline \end{array}$ 52. $\begin{array}{r} 6 \\ +4 \\ \hline \end{array}$

53. $\begin{array}{r} 9 \\ +5 \\ \hline \end{array}$ 54. $\begin{array}{r} 2 \\ +8 \\ \hline \end{array}$ 55. $\begin{array}{r} 7 \\ +9 \\ \hline \end{array}$ 56. $\begin{array}{r} 2 \\ +9 \\ \hline \end{array}$

57. $\begin{array}{r} 8 \\ +9 \\ \hline \end{array}$ 58. $\begin{array}{r} 3 \\ +9 \\ \hline \end{array}$ 59. $\begin{array}{r} 5 \\ +9 \\ \hline \end{array}$ 60. $\begin{array}{r} 9 \\ +8 \\ \hline \end{array}$

Mental Math

Use the shortcut to find each sum.

Sometimes I use a double to find another sum. The sum is 1 more than 12.

61. $\begin{array}{r} 6 \\ +7 \\ \hline \end{array}$ ($\begin{array}{r} 6 \\ +6 \\ \hline 12 \end{array}$)

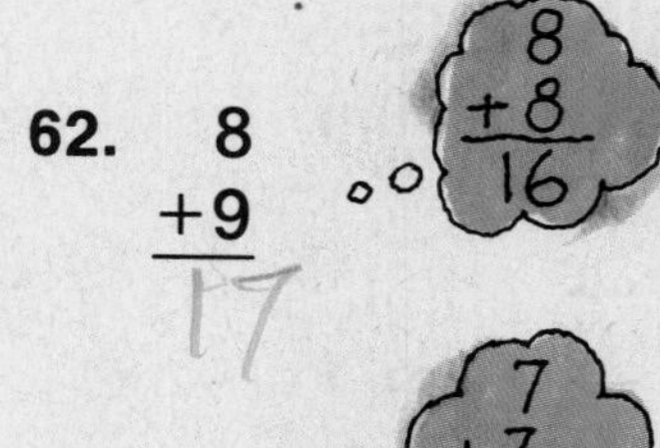

62. $\begin{array}{r} 8 \\ +9 \\ \hline \end{array}$

63. $\begin{array}{r} 7 \\ +8 \\ \hline \end{array}$ ($\begin{array}{r} 7 \\ +7 \\ \hline 14 \end{array}$)

64. $\begin{array}{r} 4 \\ +5 \\ \hline \end{array}$

65. $\begin{array}{r} 8 \\ +7 \\ \hline \end{array}$

66. $\begin{array}{r} 5 \\ +6 \\ \hline \end{array}$

Name Matin #2

Addition equations

You can write addition in equation form, too.

We read the equation as "8 plus 5 equals 13."

EXERCISES

Give each sum.

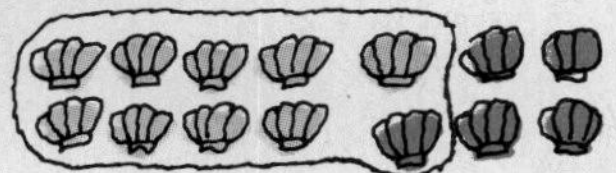

1. 9 + 5 = 14 **2.** 6 + 7 = 13 **3.** 8 + 3 = 11

4. 9 + 6 = 15 **5.** 6 + 9 = 15 **6.** 8 + 8 = 16

7. 5 + 6 = 11 **8.** 8 + 4 = 12 **9.** 5 + 8 = 13

10. 7 + 9 = 16 **11.** 6 + 6 = 12 **12.** 8 + 9 = 17

13. 7 + 8 = 15 **14.** 4 + 8 = 12 **15.** 9 + 4 = 13

16. 7 + 7 = 14 **17.** 9 + 8 = 17 **18.** 8 + 7 = 15

19. 9 + 7 = 16 **20.** 8 + 6 = 14 **21.** 5 + 9 = 14

22. 9 + 3 = 12 **23.** 6 + 9 = 15 **24.** 9 + 9 = 18

Give each sum.

25. 4 + 7 = ____
26. 8 + 4 = ____
27. 7 + 7 = ____
28. 6 + 9 = ____
29. 9 + 2 = ____
30. 8 + 7 = ____
31. 6 + 6 = ____
32. 8 + 5 = ____
33. 9 + 3 = ____
34. 5 + 9 = ____
35. 7 + 8 = ____
36. 5 + 8 = ____
37. 9 + 4 = ____
38. 2 + 9 = ____
39. 8 + 6 = ____
40. 8 + 9 = ____
41. 9 + 6 = ____
42. 8 + 3 = ____
43. 7 + 4 = ____
44. 4 + 8 = ____
45. 9 + 7 = ____
46. 9 + 5 = ____
47. 3 + 8 = ____
48. 6 + 7 = ____
49. 9 + 8 = ____
50. 6 + 8 = ____
51. 3 + 9 = ____
52. 7 + 6 = ____
53. 5 + 7 = ____
54. 4 + 9 = ____
55. 9 + 9 = ____
56. 8 + 8 = ____
57. 7 + 9 = ____

Challenge!

Add across. Add down.

58.

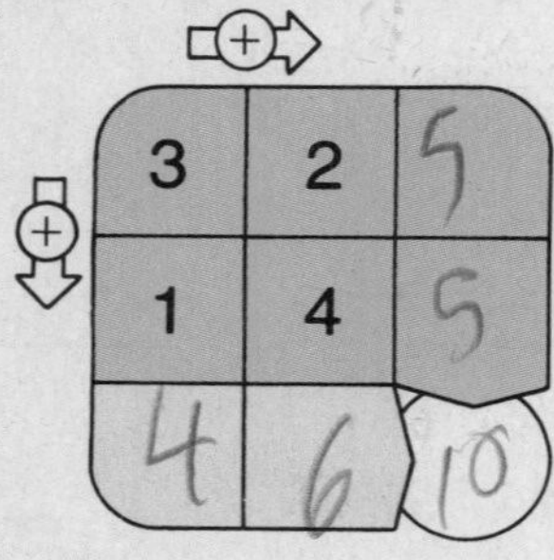

59.

7	1	
2	3	

60.

4	3	
5	3	

Name Matin #2

Missing addends

EXERCISES

How many cars are in the box?

1. 3 + 1 = 4
in all

2. 5 + 2 = 7
in all

3. 2 + 6 = 8
in all

4. 3 + 6 = 9
in all

5. 5 + 5 = 10
in all

6. 2 + 4 = 6
in all

Give each missing addend.

7. 5 + ____ = 11
8. 6 + ____ = 12
9. 8 + ____ = 11

10. 3 + ____ = 11
11. 9 + ____ = 16
12. 7 + ____ = 16

13. 8 + ____ = 16
14. 6 + ____ = 11
15. 9 + ____ = 14

16. 7 + ____ = 15
17. 7 + ____ = 14
18. 9 + ____ = 17

19. 8 + ____ = 14
20. 8 + ____ = 17
21. 8 + ____ = 15

22. 9 + ____ = 18
23. 6 + ____ = 15
24. 7 + ____ = 16

25. ____ + 4 = 11
26. ____ + 5 = 13
27. ____ + 9 = 12

28. ____ + 9 = 13
29. ____ + 6 = 11
30. ____ + 8 = 16

31. ____ + 5 = 14
32. ____ + 8 = 12
33. ____ + 7 = 15

34. ____ + 8 = 11
35. ____ + 7 = 16
36. ____ + 7 = 11

37. ____ + 7 = 12
38. ____ + 9 = 11
39. ____ + 9 = 18

Challenge!

Complete.

40.

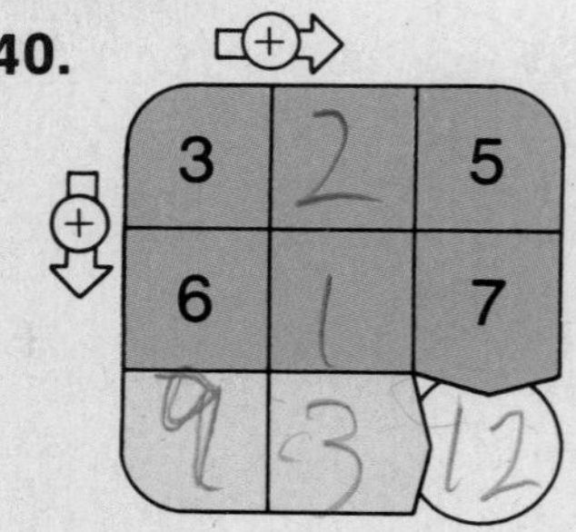

41.

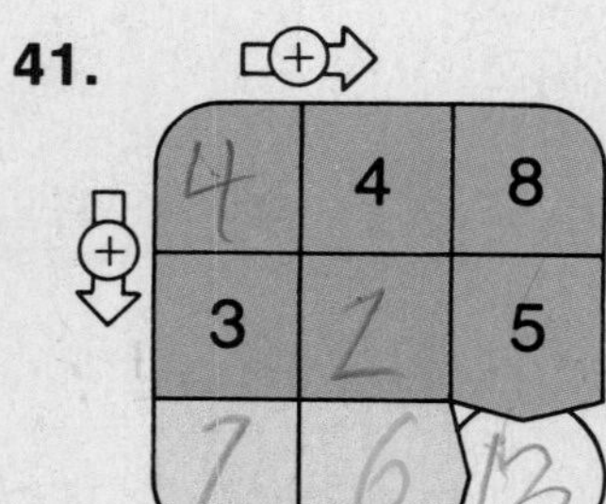

42.

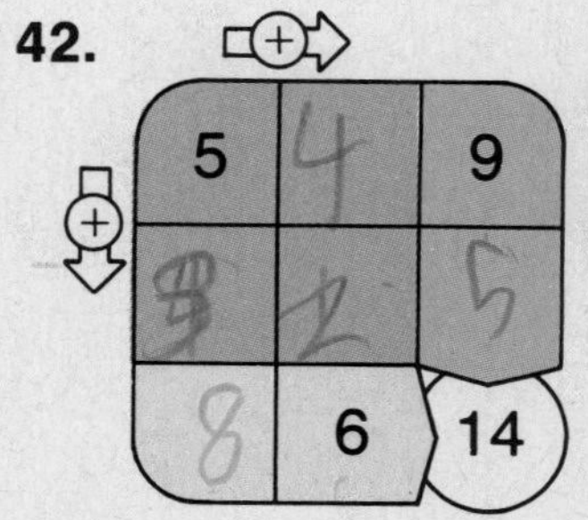

Name ______________________________

Three addends

You can add numbers in any order and get the same sum.

3 (7)	3	3
4	4 (9)	4 (8)
+5	+5	+5
12	12	12

EXERCISES

Add.

1. 4 5 +4	**2.** 6 1 +8	**3.** 7 2 +6	**4.** 2 2 +6	**5.** 4 4 +3	**6.** 7 0 +5
7. 5 1 +5	**8.** 6 2 +8	**9.** 5 2 +9	**10.** 2 3 +6	**11.** 6 3 +9	**12.** 1 4 +6
13. 8 1 +9	**14.** 5 2 +8	**15.** 5 4 +7	**16.** 2 5 +7	**17.** 0 6 +8	**18.** 4 2 +8
19. 5 3 +7	**20.** 2 7 +4	**21.** 1 5 +9	**22.** 2 4 +9	**23.** 1 6 +5	**24.** 3 5 +6
25. 3 6 +7	**26.** 3 4 +9	**27.** 2 6 +7	**28.** 4 3 +8	**29.** 1 8 +7	**30.** 3 3 +7

Mental Math

Use the shortcut to find each sum.

31.	**32.**	**33.**	**34.**
5	6	2	4
3	3	7	6
+5	+7	+8	+5
13 (10 + 3)			

35.	**36.**	**37.**	**38.**
3	5	4	6
6	4	6	3
+7	+5	+7	+4

Add. ***Hint:*** **First look for 10.**

39.	**40.**	**41.**	**42.**	**43.**
5	6	7	4	8
2	3	2	6	1
+8	+7	+3	+3	+9

44.	**45.**	**46.**	**47.**	**48.**
3	1	1	3	3
4	7	6	7	5
+7	+5	+3	+3	+6

49.	**50.**	**51.**	**52.**	**53.**
2	3	3	5	7
8	6	5	3	1
+6	+9	+7	+4	+3

Challenge!

What could have been on each addition fact card?

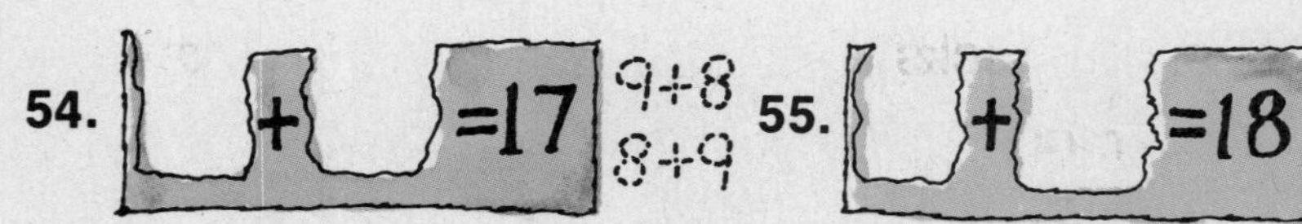

57. ☐ + ☐ =14

58. ☐ + ☐ =15

Name ____________________

Problem Solving

Tables and graphs

EXERCISES

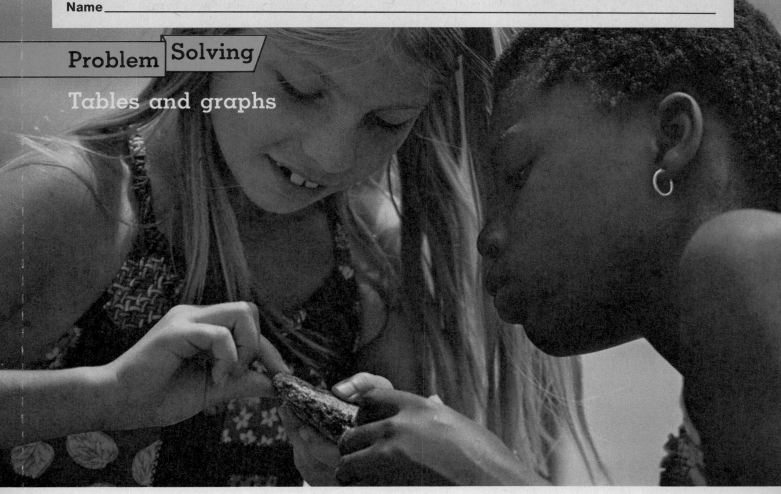

Name	Alex	Terry	Elsa	Sarah	Paige	Katy	Bill	Luis
Rocks found	7	6	8	7	4	5	9	8

1. How many rocks did Terry find? __________

2. How many rocks did Katy find? __________

3. Who found the most? __________

4. Who found the fewest? __________

5. Who found six rocks? __________

6. Who found seven rocks? __________

7. Who found more, Sarah or Paige? __________

8. Who found fewer, Alex or Luis? __________

9. How many children found more than seven? __________

10. How many children found fewer than seven? __________

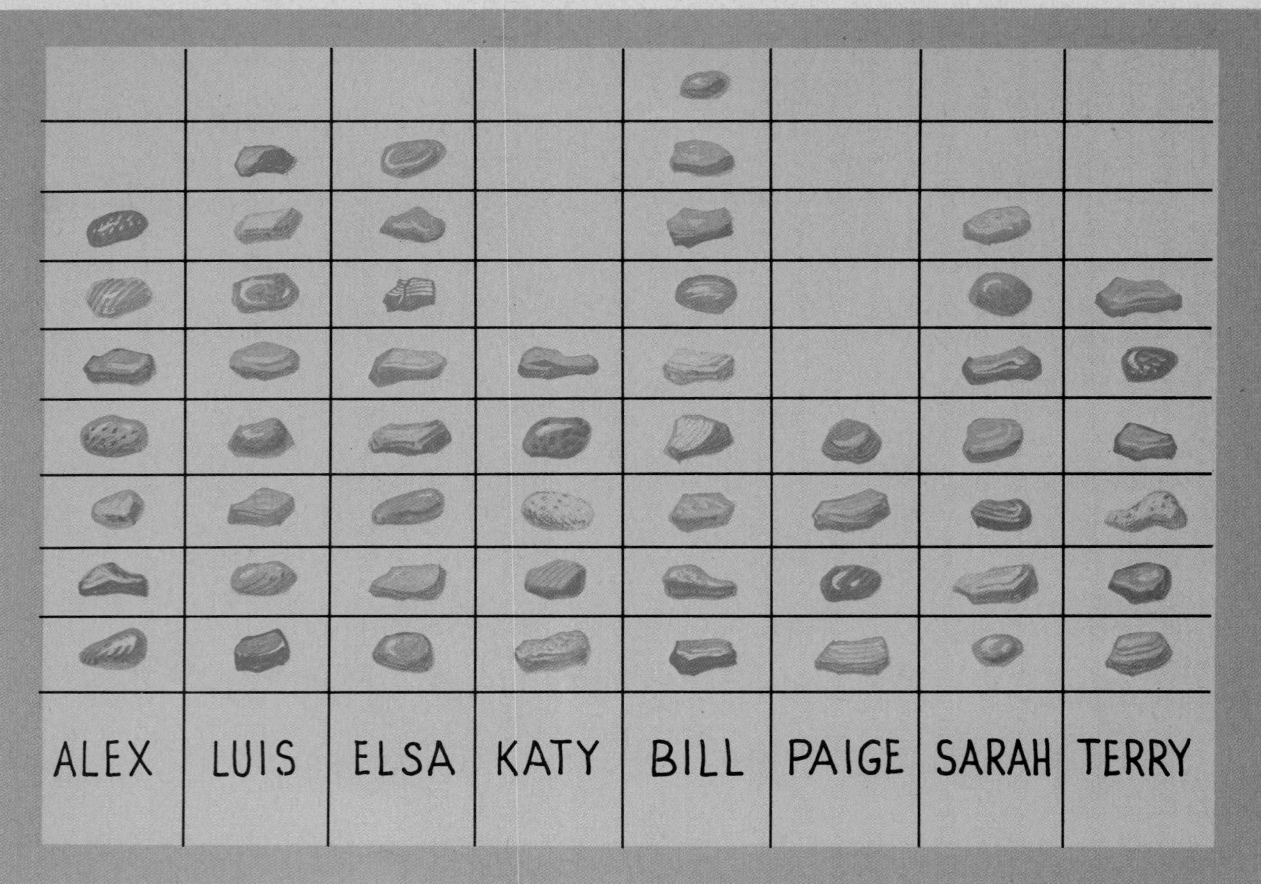

Complete.

11. Luis found 8.

    Katy found 5.

    Together they found 13.

12. Bill found ______.

    Elsa found ______.

    Together they found ______.

13. Alex found ______.

    Terry found ______.

    Together they found ______.

14. Paige found ______.

    Sarah found ______.

    Together they found ______.

★ 15. Katy found ______.

    Paige found ______.

    Sarah found ______.

    Together they found ______.

★ 16. Terry found ______.

    Paige found ______.

    Luis found ______.

    Together they found ______.

Name ____________________

Subtraction facts

EXERCISES

Subtract.

1. $\begin{array}{r} 5 \\ -3 \\ \hline \end{array}$

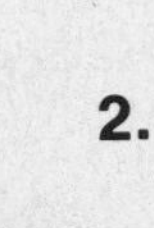

2. $\begin{array}{r} 6 \\ -2 \\ \hline \end{array}$

3. $\begin{array}{r} 8 \\ -3 \\ \hline \end{array}$

4. $\begin{array}{r} 5 \\ -2 \\ \hline \end{array}$

5. $\begin{array}{r} 5 \\ -0 \\ \hline \end{array}$

6. $\begin{array}{r} 4 \\ -4 \\ \hline \end{array}$

7. $\begin{array}{r} 10 \\ -1 \\ \hline \end{array}$ **8.** $\begin{array}{r} 6 \\ -6 \\ \hline \end{array}$ **9.** $\begin{array}{r} 9 \\ -5 \\ \hline \end{array}$ **10.** $\begin{array}{r} 6 \\ -3 \\ \hline \end{array}$ **11.** $\begin{array}{r} 8 \\ -4 \\ \hline \end{array}$ **12.** $\begin{array}{r} 9 \\ -6 \\ \hline \end{array}$

13. $\begin{array}{r} 7 \\ -6 \\ \hline \end{array}$ **14.** $\begin{array}{r} 8 \\ -5 \\ \hline \end{array}$ **15.** $\begin{array}{r} 8 \\ -1 \\ \hline \end{array}$ **16.** $\begin{array}{r} 10 \\ -2 \\ \hline \end{array}$ **17.** $\begin{array}{r} 8 \\ -2 \\ \hline \end{array}$ **18.** $\begin{array}{r} 10 \\ -3 \\ \hline \end{array}$

19. $\begin{array}{r} 9 \\ -2 \\ \hline \end{array}$ **20.** $\begin{array}{r} 10 \\ -4 \\ \hline \end{array}$ **21.** $\begin{array}{r} 9 \\ -9 \\ \hline \end{array}$ **22.** $\begin{array}{r} 7 \\ -3 \\ \hline \end{array}$ **23.** $\begin{array}{r} 10 \\ -5 \\ \hline \end{array}$ **24.** $\begin{array}{r} 9 \\ -8 \\ \hline \end{array}$

Give each difference.

25. $2 - 0$	26. $3 - 3$	27. $10 - 2$	28. $6 - 0$
29. $4 - 2$	30. $10 - 3$	31. $7 - 5$	32. $10 - 5$
33. $5 - 4$	34. $8 - 6$	35. $6 - 3$	36. $9 - 8$
37. $9 - 2$	38. $8 - 5$	39. $5 - 3$	40. $8 - 8$
41. $10 - 6$	42. $7 - 4$	43. $6 - 4$	44. $10 - 7$
45. $10 - 4$	46. $9 - 4$	47. $5 - 2$	48. $8 - 3$
49. $9 - 5$	50. $7 - 3$	51. $9 - 7$	52. $6 - 2$
53. $5 - 4$	54. $9 - 6$	55. $8 - 1$	56. $7 - 2$
57. $6 - 5$	58. $10 - 8$	59. $8 - 4$	60. $9 - 3$

Challenge!

Who am I?

61. ______

If you subtract me from 9, you get 4.

62. ______

If you subtract me from 10, you get 7.

63. ______

If you subtract me from 6, you get 6.

64. ______

If you subtract me from myself, you get 0.

Name ____________________

Addition and subtraction

Addition and subtraction are related.

EXERCISES

Give each family of facts.

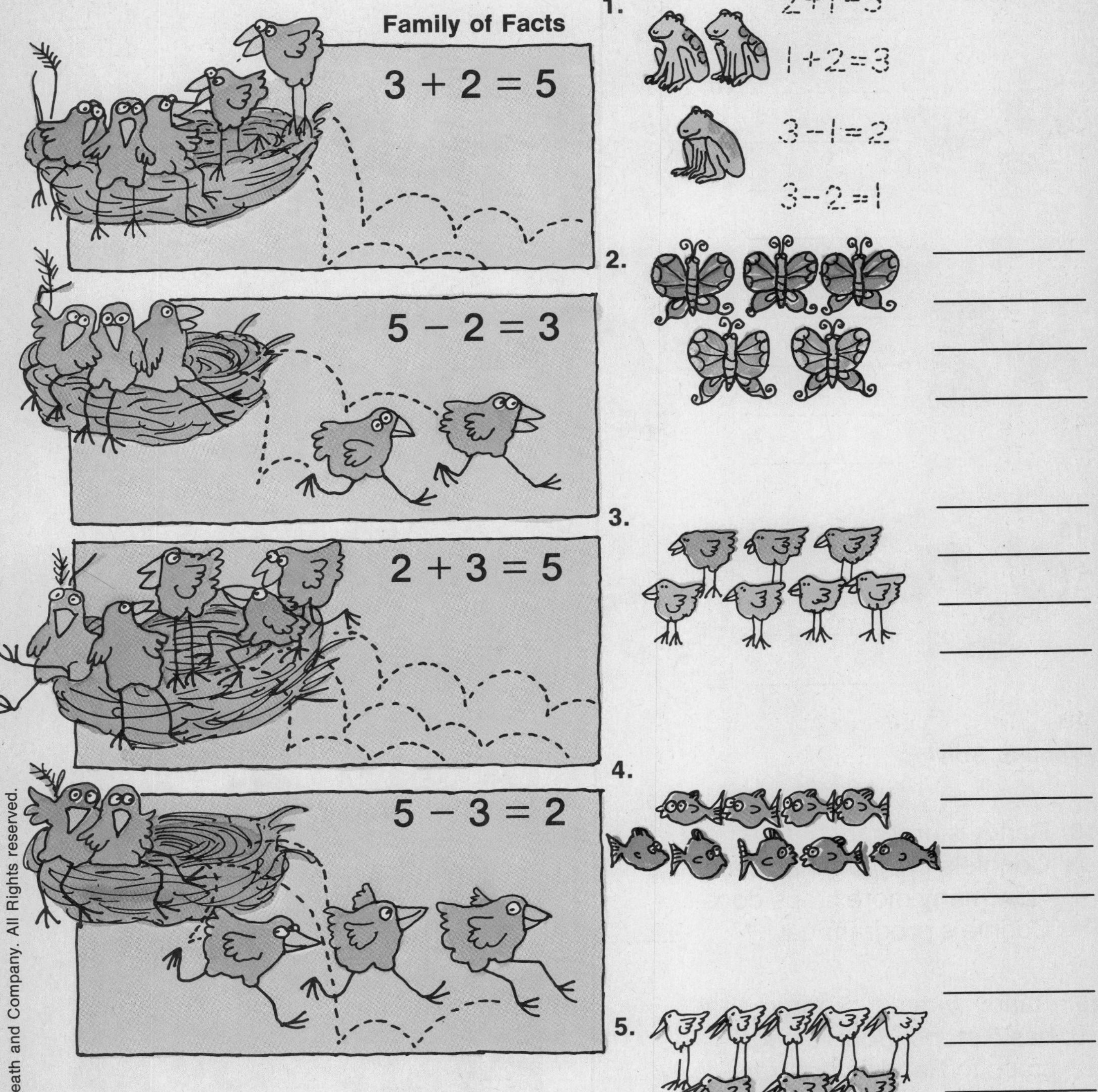

1. 2+1=3, 1+2=3, 3−1=2, 3−2=1

2. ____ ____ ____ ____

3. ____ ____ ____ ____

4. ____ ____ ____ ____

5. ____ ____ ____ ____

Use the numbers. Write two addition equations and two subtraction equations.

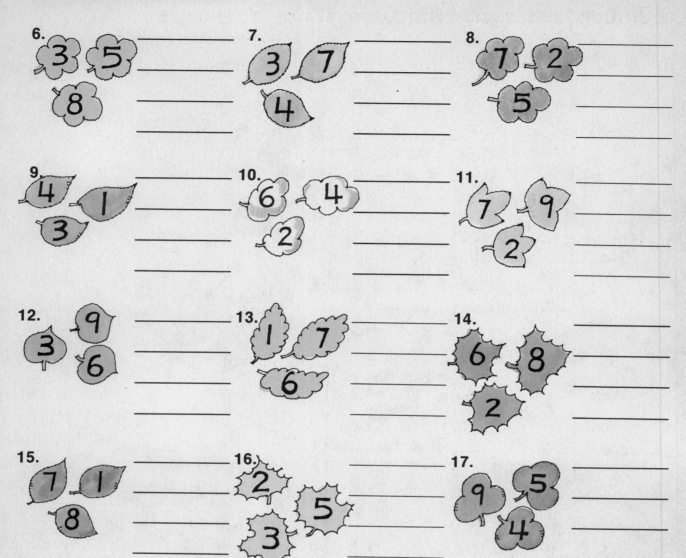

6. 3 5 8 ______ ______ ______ ______

7. 3 7 4 ______ ______ ______ ______

8. 7 2 5 ______ ______ ______ ______

9. 4 1 3 ______ ______ ______ ______

10. 6 4 2 ______ ______ ______ ______

11. 7 9 2 ______ ______ ______ ______

12. 9 3 6 ______ ______ ______ ______

13. 1 7 6 ______ ______ ______ ______

14. 6 8 2 ______ ______ ______ ______

15. 7 1 8 ______ ______ ______ ______

16. 2 5 3 ______ ______ ______ ______

17. 9 5 4 ______ ______ ______ ______

Problem Solving

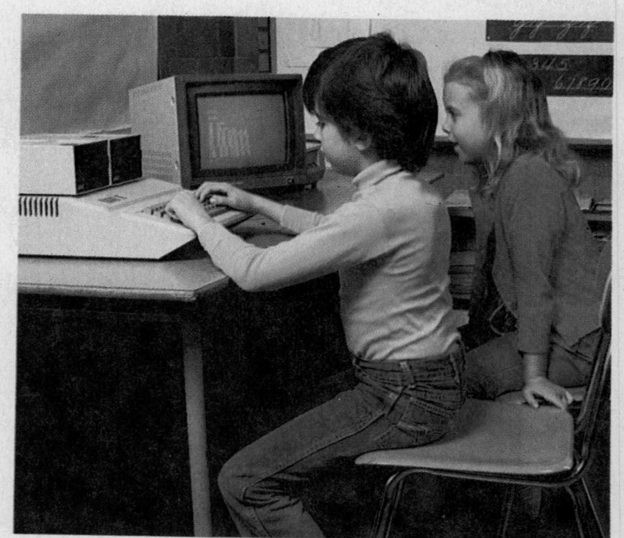

18. Randy's program has 4 steps. Connie's program has 6 steps. How many more steps does Connie's program have? ______

19. Randy writes a program that has 5 steps. Connie adds 3 steps to Randy's program. How many steps does Randy's program have now? ______

Name ____

Exploring addition and subtraction

Problem A	Laura has 16 counters. If she takes away 7 counters, how many will she have left?

Problem B	Sam has 7 counters. How many more does he need to have 16 counters?

In this lesson, you will explore how problems like these are alike. Work in groups. Get 18 counters and a cup. Record your answers on a separate sheet of paper if you need more space.

1. Act out Problem A:
Put 16 counters on the desk.
Cover 7 counters with the cup.
Count how many are left.

______

2. Act out Problem B:
Put 7 counters on the desk.
Drop counters in the cup until you reach 16.
Count how many are in the cup.

______

3. Look at these number sentences:

16 − 7 = _?_ 7 + _?_ = 16

Think and talk about these questions:

a. Which number sentence can you solve from what you did in exercise 1? Why?

____

b. Which number sentence can you solve from what you did in exercise 2? Why?

____

c. Can you think of other ways to act out 7 + _?_ = 16?

d. Can you think of other ways to act out 16 − 7 = _?_?

4. What do you notice about your answers to
$16 - 7 = \underline{?}$ and $7 + \underline{?} = 16$?

____

5. What do you think will happen when you solve each of these pairs of number sentences? Test your guess by acting these out with your counters. What happens?

a. $15 - 8 =$ ______ $8 +$ ______ $= 15$

b. $12 - 4 =$ ______ $4 +$ ______ $= 12$

c. $10 - 3 =$ ______ $3 +$ ______ $= 10$

d. $17 - 9 =$ ______ $9 +$ ______ $= 17$

6. Write a related number sentence.

a. $13 - 6 =$ ______ ______________

b. $6 +$ ______ $= 11$ ______________

c. $14 - 8 =$ ______ ______________

d. $18 - 9 =$ ______ ______________

e. $5 +$ ______ $= 13$ ______________

f. How did you come up with your number sentences?

g. Solve your number sentences. What did you discover with the pairs of number sentences?

____

h. Why do you think this happened?

7. Use a calculator to make pairs of number sentences with larger numbers.

a. ______________ ______________

b. ______________ ______________

Name ____________________

Subtraction facts

You can subtract by taking away.

$12 - 3 = \underline{9}$

Read as "12 minus 3 equals 9."

You can subtract by finding a missing addend.

$11 - 4 = \underline{7}$

Read as "11 minus 4 equals 7."

EXERCISES

Subtract.

1. $12 - 5 = \underline{7}$

2. $11 - 5 =$ ____

3. $13 - 4 =$ ____

4. $12 - 7 =$ ____

5. $13 - 8 =$ ____

6. $11 - 9 =$ ____

7. $12 - 8 =$ ____

8. $13 - 6 =$ ____

9. $12 - 6 =$ ____

10. $17 - 8 =$ ____

11. $16 - 8 =$ ____

12. $15 - 9 =$ ____

13. $14 - 8 =$ ____

14. $11 - 8 =$ ____

15. $17 - 9 =$ ____

16. $14 - 9 =$ ____

17. $16 - 7 =$ ____

18. $15 - 8 =$ ____

19. $11 - 6 =$ ____

20. $15 - 7 =$ ____

21. $11 - 7 =$ ____

22. $15 - 6 =$ ____

23. $18 - 9 =$ ____

24. $16 - 9 =$ ____

Subtract.

25. 11 − 5 = _____ 26. 13 − 7 = _____ 27. 15 − 6 = _____

28. 14 − 8 = _____ 29. 11 − 6 = _____ 30. 12 − 6 = _____

31. 11 − 2 = _____ 32. 13 − 8 = _____ 33. 13 − 6 = _____

34. 14 − 7 = _____ 35. 12 − 7 = _____ 36. 15 − 8 = _____

37. 12 − 5 = _____ 38. 18 − 9 = _____ 39. 11 − 4 = _____

40. 15 − 9 = _____ 41. 11 − 7 = _____ 42. 14 − 6 = _____

43. 12 − 4 = _____ 44. 14 − 5 = _____ 45. 16 − 8 = _____

46. 16 − 7 = _____ 47. 11 − 9 = _____ 48. 12 − 8 = _____

49. 12 − 3 = _____ 50. 13 − 5 = _____ 51. 11 − 3 = _____

52. 17 − 8 = _____ 53. 12 − 9 = _____ 54. 13 − 9 = _____

Mental Math **Use each shortcut.**

To add 9, I sometimes add 10 and then subtract 1.

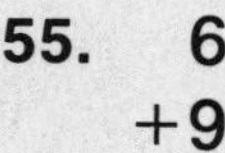

55. $\begin{array}{r} 6 \\ +9 \\ \hline \end{array}$ 56. $\begin{array}{r} 9 \\ +9 \\ \hline \end{array}$ 57. $\begin{array}{r} 8 \\ +9 \\ \hline \end{array}$ 58. $\begin{array}{r} 7 \\ +9 \\ \hline \end{array}$

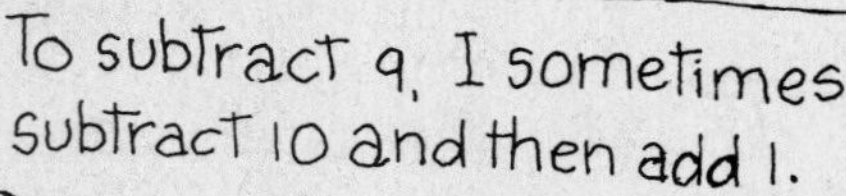

To subtract 9, I sometimes subtract 10 and then add 1.

59. $\begin{array}{r} 15 \\ -9 \\ \hline \end{array}$ 60. $\begin{array}{r} 18 \\ -9 \\ \hline \end{array}$ 61. $\begin{array}{r} 16 \\ -9 \\ \hline \end{array}$ 62. $\begin{array}{r} 17 \\ -9 \\ \hline \end{array}$

Name ____________________

Problem Solving

Planning what to do

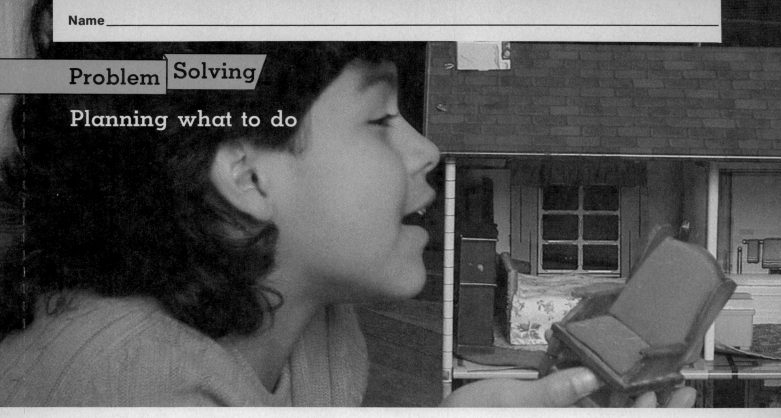

How will you solve the problem?
Will you add or subtract?

There were 4 little chairs.
There were 5 big chairs.
How many chairs were there?

Bill had 8 tables.
He gave Mary 5 tables.
How many did he have then?

Bill made 6 lamps.
Jan made 4 lamps.
How many more did Bill make?

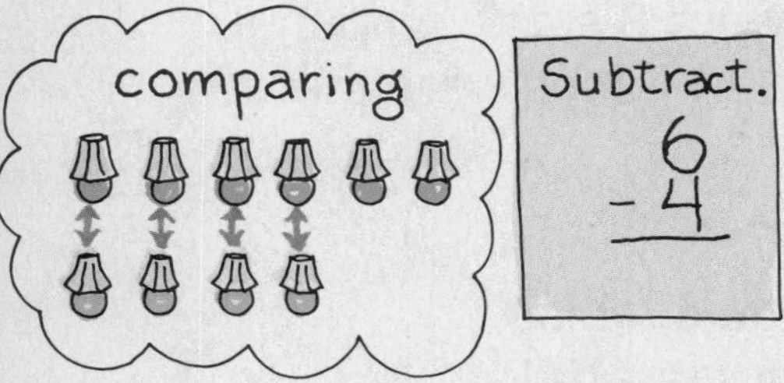

Mary had 3 rugs.
Jan gave her some more rugs.
Then Mary had 7 rugs.
How many rugs did Jan give Mary?

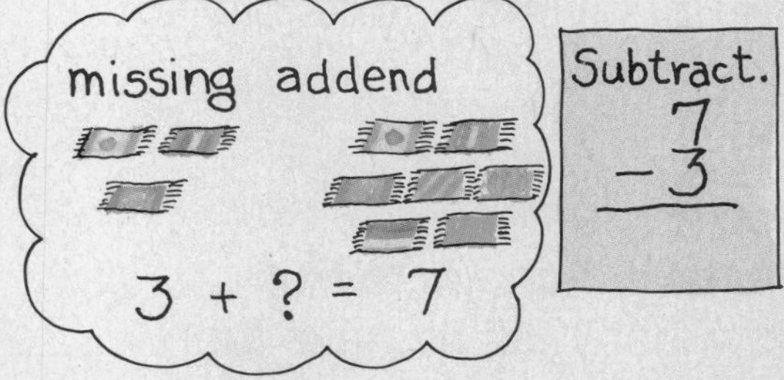

EXERCISES

How will you solve the problem?
Add or subtract?

1. There were 7 big lamps.
   There were 3 small lamps.
   How many more big lamps
   were there? ______

2. Ann had 4 chairs.
   She bought some more chairs.
   Then she had 6 chairs.
   How many chairs did she buy?
   ______

3. Jan made 9 tables.
   Bill made 7 tables.
   How many fewer tables did
   Bill make? ______

4. Mary had 8 pictures.
   She lost 3 pictures.
   How many did she have then?
   ______

5. John had 5 forks.
   Ruth had 8 forks.
   How many more forks did
   Ruth have? ______

6. There were 7 big lamps.
   There were 3 small lamps.
   How many lamps were there?
   ______

7. Bob had 9 chairs.
   He gave 3 chairs to Ruth.
   How many did he have then? ______

8. Bill made 8 tables.
   2 tables were red.
   How many were not red? ______

Name ____________________

Problem Solving Three-step method

These steps can help you solve problems.

1. Study the problem until you understand it.

2. Plan what to do and do it.

3. Answer the question and check your answer.

There were 8 animal masks and 4 clown masks. How many masks were there in all?

Add.
$$\begin{array}{r} 8 \\ +\ 4 \\ \hline 12 \end{array}$$

Answer: There were 12 masks in all.

EXERCISES

Solve.

1. Juan brought 14 bags. The class used 5 bags. How many bags did he have left? _______

2. Jill used 9 blue ribbons. She used 6 red ribbons. How many ribbons did she use in all? _______

3. Bob had 8 ribbons. He bought 8 more ribbons. How many ribbons did he have then? _______

4. One class made 16 masks. 8 masks were clowns. How many were not clowns? _______

5. 13 masks had hair. 6 masks had red hair. How many masks had hair that was not red? _______

6. Karen made 9 masks. 4 masks had whiskers. How many did not have whiskers? _______

7. 8 boys and 7 girls won prizes. How many children won prizes? _______

★ 8. Don used 7 bags. Mary used 9 bags. Who used fewer bags? _______ How many fewer? _______

Name ___

Problem Solving Money

1 penny

1 cent

1¢

1 nickel

5 cents

5¢

1 dime

10 cents

10¢

EXERCISES

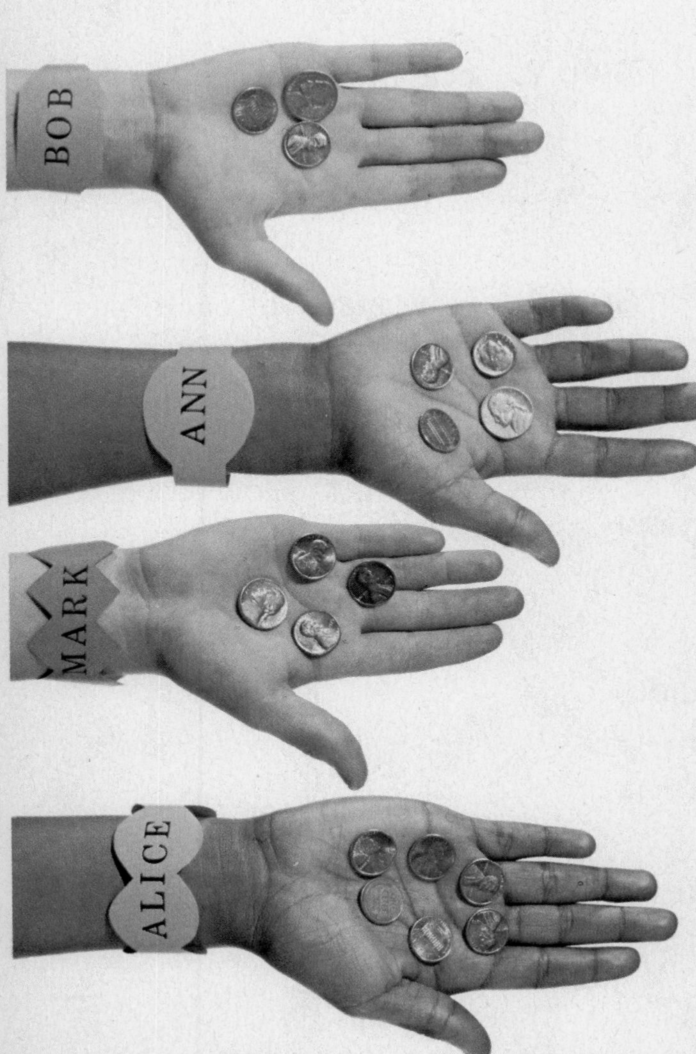

1. How many pennies does Bob have? ___
2. How many nickels does Mark have? ___
3. Who has a dime? ___
4. How much do Bob and Mark have together? ___
5. How much do Alice and Bob have together? ___
6. Who has more money, Mark or Alice? ___
7. How much more money does Ann have than Mark? ___
8. How much more money does Ann have than Bob? ___
9. Who has the least money? ___
10. Who has the most money? ___

Problem Solving Drawing a picture

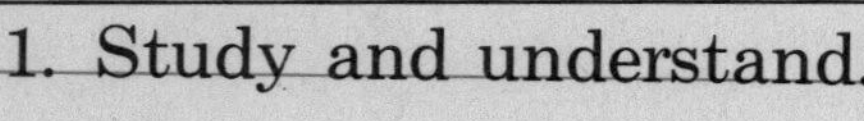

1. Study and understand.
2. Plan and do.
3. Answer and check.

You can solve the problem by drawing a picture.

The zoo sells red balloons, green balloons, and yellow balloons. Sarah buys some balloons. How many of each color does she have?

Clues:
- She has 5 balloons in all.
- She has 3 red balloons.
- She has at least 1 of each color.

Step 1. She has 5 balloons.
Hint: Draw 5 balloons.

Step 2. She had 3 red balloons.
Hint: Color 3 red.

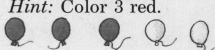

Step 3. Color the rest of the balloons.
Hint: 1 has to be green and 1 has to be yellow. Why?

Step 4. How many of each color does she have?
Hint: Look at Step 3.

Answer: Sarah has 1 green balloon, 1 yellow balloon, and 3 red balloons.

EXERCISES

There are red balloons, green balloons, and yellow balloons. Every child has at least 1 of each color.

Solve by drawing a picture. Use crayons.

1. How many of each color does Dave have?
Clues:
- There are 6 in all.
- 4 are red.

2. How many of each color does Maria have?
Clues:
- There are 5 in all.
- There are 3 red ones.

Name ________________________________

Chapter Checkup

Give each sum. [pages 2–13]

1. $\begin{array}{r} 3 \\ +4 \\ \hline \end{array}$
2. $\begin{array}{r} 4 \\ +4 \\ \hline \end{array}$
3. $\begin{array}{r} 3 \\ +6 \\ \hline \end{array}$
4. $\begin{array}{r} 6 \\ +4 \\ \hline \end{array}$
5. $\begin{array}{r} 0 \\ +6 \\ \hline \end{array}$
6. $\begin{array}{r} 4 \\ +5 \\ \hline \end{array}$
7. $\begin{array}{r} 6 \\ +5 \\ \hline \end{array}$
8. $\begin{array}{r} 7 \\ +7 \\ \hline \end{array}$
9. $\begin{array}{r} 8 \\ +7 \\ \hline \end{array}$
10. $\begin{array}{r} 4 \\ +8 \\ \hline \end{array}$
11. $\begin{array}{r} 8 \\ +9 \\ \hline \end{array}$
12. $\begin{array}{r} 9 \\ +4 \\ \hline \end{array}$
13. $\begin{array}{r} 8 \\ +8 \\ \hline \end{array}$
14. $\begin{array}{r} 5 \\ +7 \\ \hline \end{array}$
15. $\begin{array}{r} 9 \\ +9 \\ \hline \end{array}$
16. $\begin{array}{r} 9 \\ +8 \\ \hline \end{array}$
17. $\begin{array}{r} 6 \\ +6 \\ \hline \end{array}$
18. $\begin{array}{r} 7 \\ +9 \\ \hline \end{array}$

Give each difference. [pages 16–23]

19. $\begin{array}{r} 12 \\ -5 \\ \hline \end{array}$
20. $\begin{array}{r} 7 \\ -0 \\ \hline \end{array}$
21. $\begin{array}{r} 8 \\ -4 \\ \hline \end{array}$
22. $\begin{array}{r} 9 \\ -4 \\ \hline \end{array}$
23. $\begin{array}{r} 8 \\ -8 \\ \hline \end{array}$
24. $\begin{array}{r} 10 \\ -6 \\ \hline \end{array}$
25. $\begin{array}{r} 15 \\ -6 \\ \hline \end{array}$
26. $\begin{array}{r} 15 \\ -8 \\ \hline \end{array}$
27. $\begin{array}{r} 11 \\ -8 \\ \hline \end{array}$
28. $\begin{array}{r} 17 \\ -8 \\ \hline \end{array}$
29. $\begin{array}{r} 13 \\ -8 \\ \hline \end{array}$
30. $\begin{array}{r} 12 \\ -9 \\ \hline \end{array}$
31. $\begin{array}{r} 16 \\ -8 \\ \hline \end{array}$
32. $\begin{array}{r} 17 \\ -9 \\ \hline \end{array}$
33. $\begin{array}{r} 11 \\ -6 \\ \hline \end{array}$
34. $\begin{array}{r} 16 \\ -7 \\ \hline \end{array}$
35. $\begin{array}{r} 13 \\ -9 \\ \hline \end{array}$
36. $\begin{array}{r} 14 \\ -7 \\ \hline \end{array}$

Solve. [pages 14–15, 24–29]

37. Jerry had 6 bottles.
He found 9 bottles.
How many bottles did
he have then? ________

38. Beth had 16 boxes.
She lost 9 boxes.
How many boxes did
she have then? ________

Chapter Project

ORDERING ADDENDS

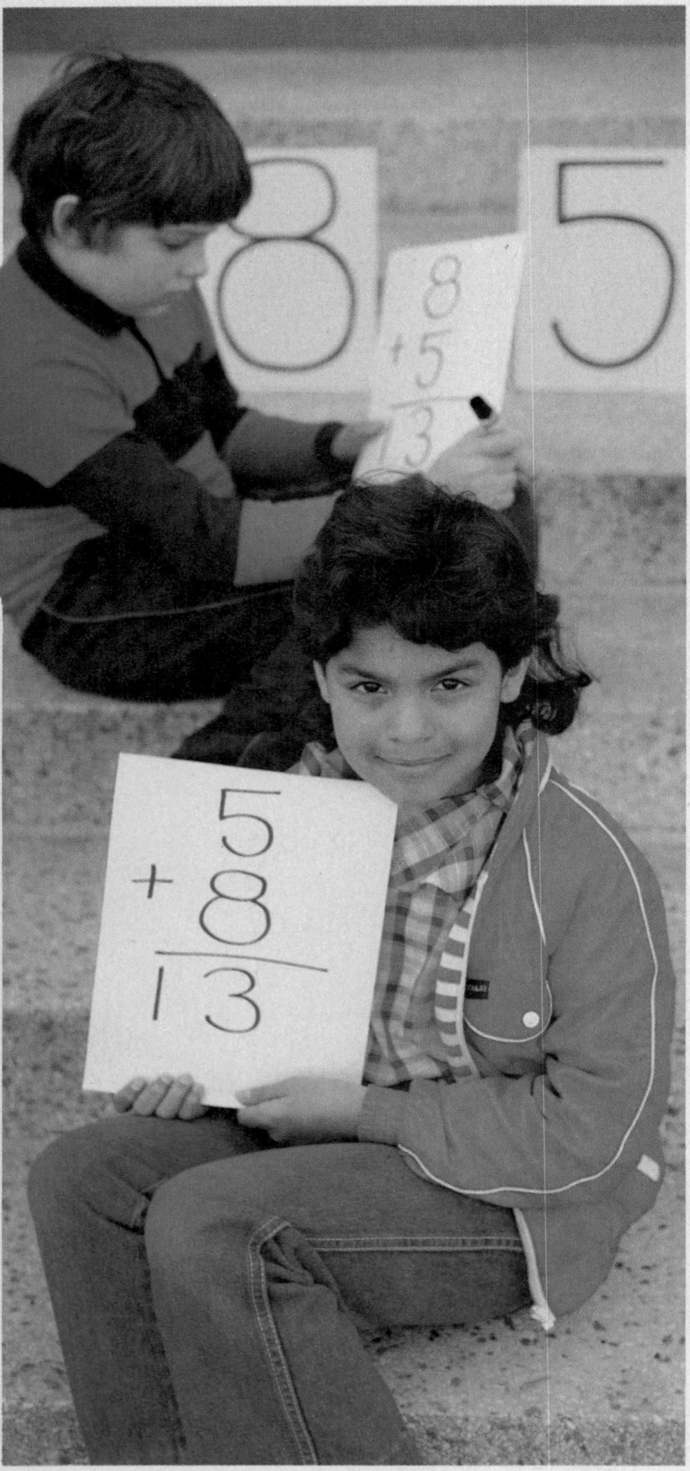

You can order 2 addends in 2 ways.

1. Make these number cards.

Use your cards to see how many ways you can order 3 addends.

2. Make these number cards.

Use your cards to see how many ways you can order 4 addends.

Name ____________________

Chapter Review

Give each sum.

1. $7 + 0$	**2.** $5 + 4$	**3.** $2 + 6$	**4.** $4 + 6$	**5.** $3 + 8$	**6.** $8 + 8$
7. $7 + 9$	**8.** $5 + 9$	**9.** $7 + 8$	**10.** $6 + 6$	**11.** $9 + 9$	**12.** $5 + 8$
13. $9 + 4$	**14.** $8 + 9$	**15.** $2 + 9$	**16.** $6 + 8$	**17.** $4 + 8$	**18.** $9 + 6$

Give each difference.

19. $7 - 0$	**20.** $9 - 5$	**21.** $8 - 8$	**22.** $10 - 3$	**23.** $9 - 6$	**24.** $8 - 5$
25. $15 - 6$	**26.** $11 - 6$	**27.** $17 - 9$	**28.** $12 - 3$	**29.** $15 - 7$	**30.** $18 - 9$
31. $16 - 8$	**32.** $12 - 4$	**33.** $14 - 5$	**34.** $11 - 4$	**35.** $16 - 7$	**36.** $13 - 8$

Chapter Challenge

MAGIC TRIANGLES

1. Add the numbers along each side.

Did you get the same sum? ________
When the sums are the same, the triangle is magic.

3
8 7
4 2
6 5 1 9

2. Is this a magic triangle? ________
Hint: Add the numbers along each side.

3. Is this a magic triangle? ________

Name ________________________________

Cumulative Checkup

STANDARDIZED FORMAT

Give the correct letter.

1. Add.

$$\begin{array}{r} 5 \\ +3 \\ \hline \end{array}$$

   a. 7
   b. 2
   c. 8
   d. none of these

2. Add.
   9 + 8

   a. 17
   b. 1
   c. 16
   d. none of these

3. In 8 + 5 = 13, 13 is called the

   a. sum
   b. addend
   c. difference
   d. none of these

4. Complete.
   3 + ? = 8

   a. 11
   b. 5
   c. 6
   d. none of these

5. Add.

$$\begin{array}{r} 5 \\ 3 \\ +9 \\ \hline \end{array}$$

   a. 17
   b. 18
   c. 16
   d. none of these

6. Subtract.

$$\begin{array}{r} 10 \\ -7 \\ \hline \end{array}$$

   a. 2
   b. 4
   c. 5
   d. none of these

7. Subtract.
   16 − 7

   a. 8
   b. 7
   c. 9
   d. none of these

8. In 14 − 6 = 8, 8 is called the

   a. sum
   b. difference
   c. addend
   d. none of these

9. How much money?
   1 nickel
   3 pennies

   a. 4¢
   b. 12¢
   c. 8¢
   d. none of these

10. Which has the greatest sum?

    a. 6 + 9
    b. 7 + 9
    c. 8 + 8
    d. 9 + 8

11. Had 9 pennies. Found 6 pennies. How many pennies in all?

    a. 3 b. 16
    c. 15 d. none of these

12. Carl had 8 buttons. He gave Judy 3 of them. How many did he have then?

    a. 5 b. 6
    c. 11 d. 12

2

Place Value

Some of these birds will fly more than 925 miles to reach their winter home.

Name ____________________

Ordinal numbers

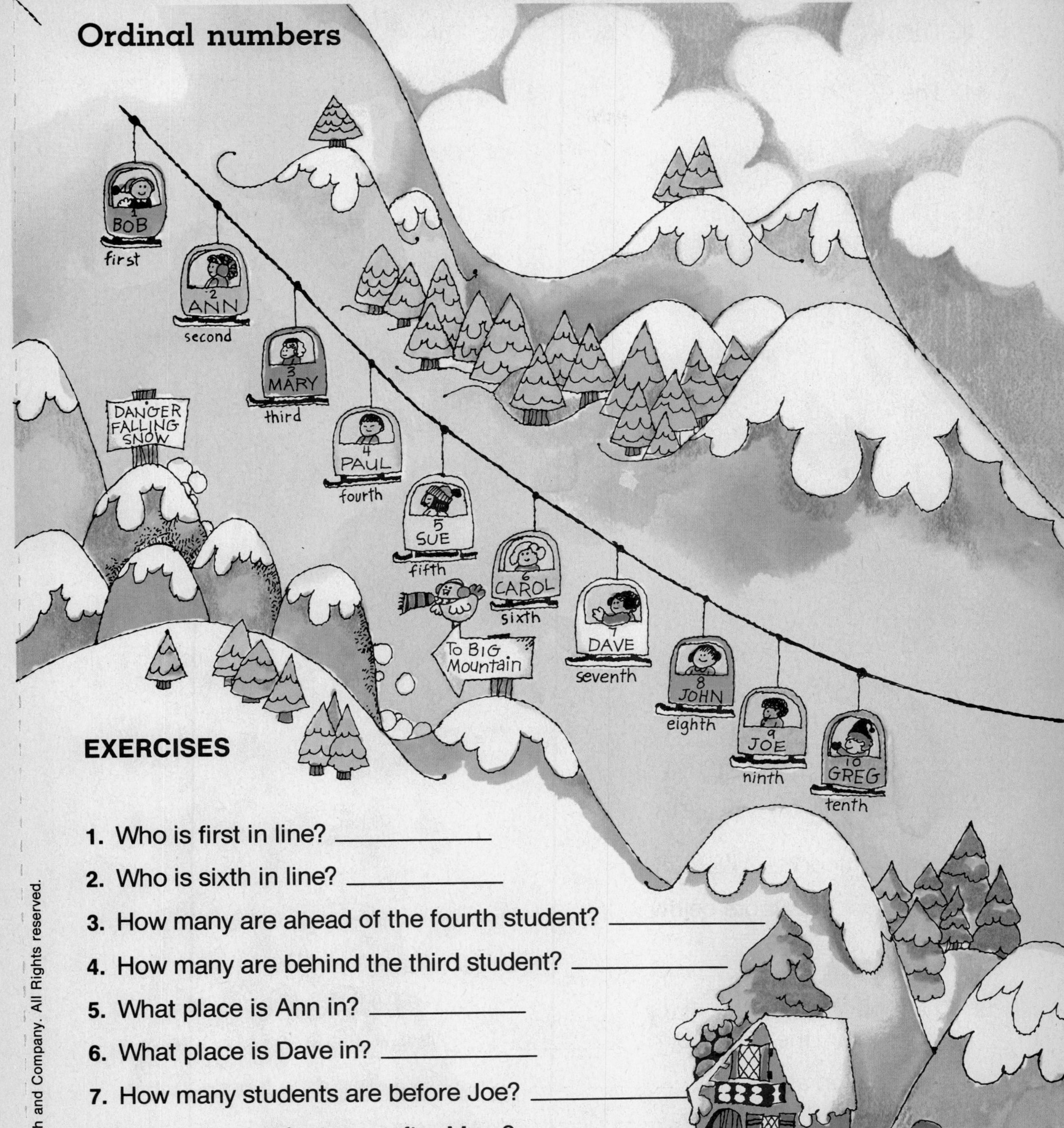

EXERCISES

1. Who is first in line? ____________
2. Who is sixth in line? ____________
3. How many are ahead of the fourth student? ____________
4. How many are behind the third student? ____________
5. What place is Ann in? ____________
6. What place is Dave in? ____________
7. How many students are before Joe? ____________
8. How many students are after Mary? ____________

Complete.

9. The is eighth.

10. The is ________.

11. The is ________.

12. The is ________.

13. The is ________.

14. The is ________.

15. The ________ is ninth.

16. The ________ is tenth.

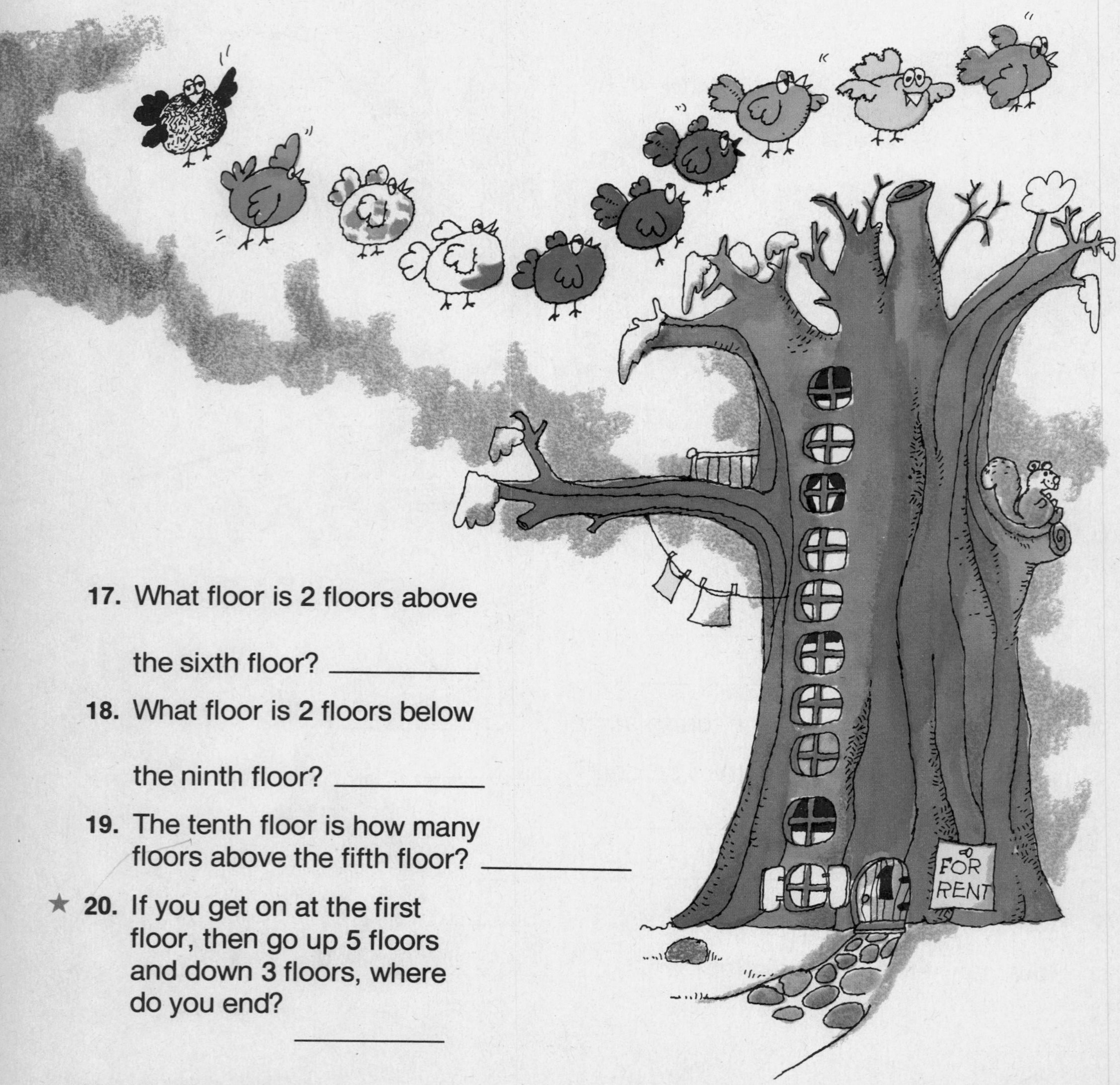

17. What floor is 2 floors above the sixth floor? ________

18. What floor is 2 floors below the ninth floor? ________

19. The tenth floor is how many floors above the fifth floor? ________

★ 20. If you get on at the first floor, then go up 5 floors and down 3 floors, where do you end?

____

Name ________________________________

Tens and ones

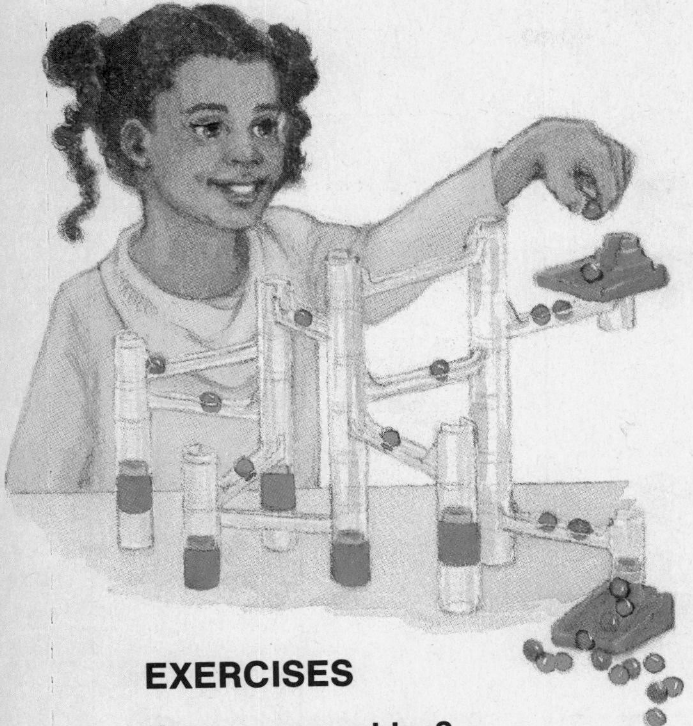

We use the **digits**

0, 1, 2, 3, 4, 5, 6, 7, 8, 9

to write about larger numbers.

Here are three ways to write about the number of marbles:

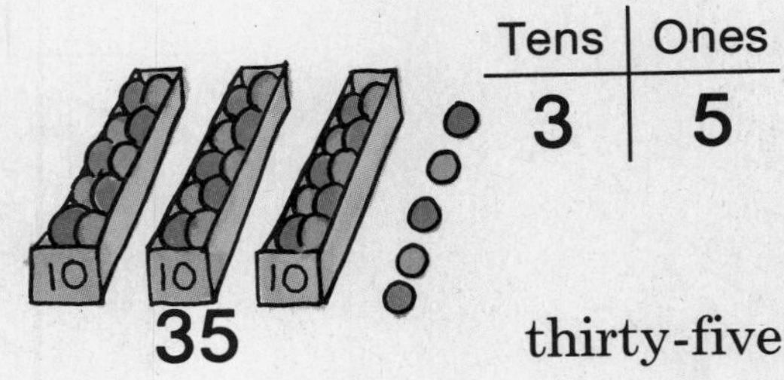

Tens	Ones
3	5

35

thirty-five

EXERCISES

How many marbles?

1. ________

2.  ________

3. 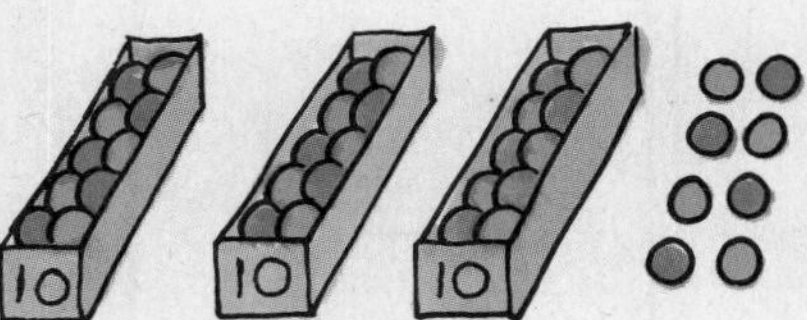 ________

4.  ________

5. 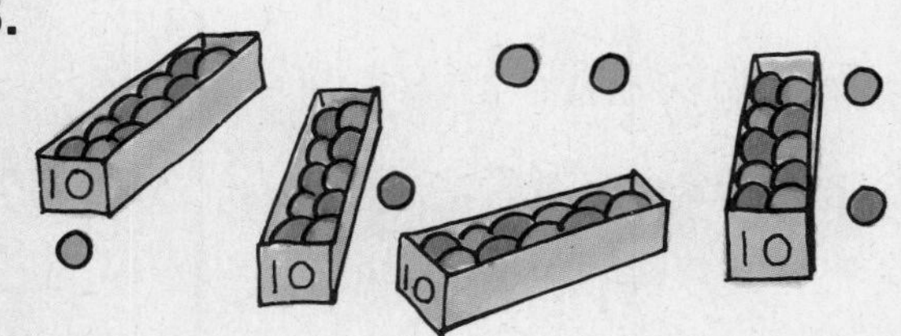 ________

6. 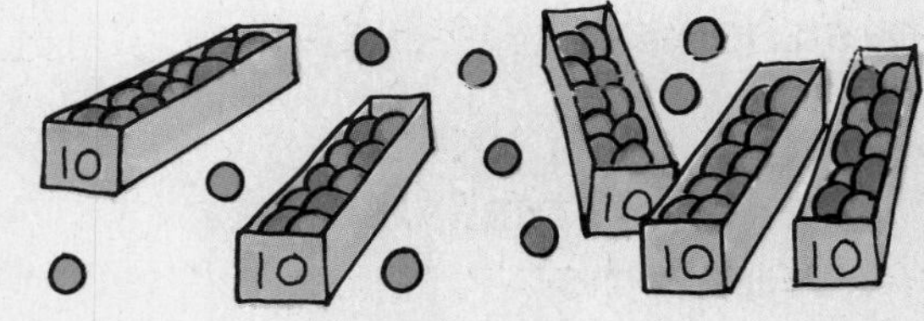 ________

How many marbles?

7.

______

8.

______

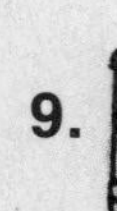

9.

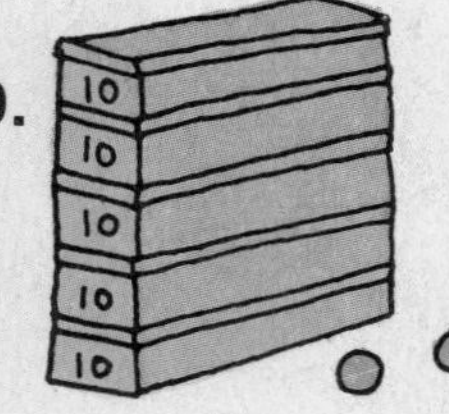

______

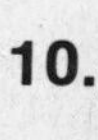

10.

______

11.

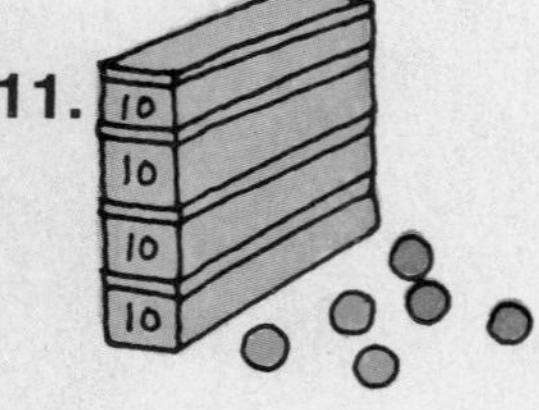

12.

Write the number.

13. forty-seven ______
14. seventy-four ______
15. fifty-six ______
16. sixty-five ______
17. ninety-three ______
18. thirty-nine ______
19. eighty-two ______
20. twenty-eight ______

Problem Solving—drawing a picture

21. Joan has red marbles, blue marbles, and green marbles. How many of each color does she have?

Clues:

- She has 12 marbles in all.
- 7 are not red.
- She has one more blue marble than green marbles.

KEEPING SKILLS SHARP

1. $7 + 5$
2. $7 + 4$
3. $6 + 5$
4. $7 + 7$
5. $5 + 8$
6. $8 + 7$
7. $4 + 8$
8. $8 + 8$
9. $6 + 6$
10. $9 + 4$
11. $8 + 9$
12. $8 + 6$
13. $9 + 5$
14. $3 + 8$
15. $6 + 9$
16. $9 + 9$
17. $6 + 7$
18. $7 + 9$

Name ____________________

Hundreds, tens, ones

Work in groups.
Get squared paper and scissors.
Record your answers on a separate sheet of paper if you need more space.

PART A

1. Take a sheet of squared paper. How many squares do you think are on 1 sheet? Estimate. Write your estimate.

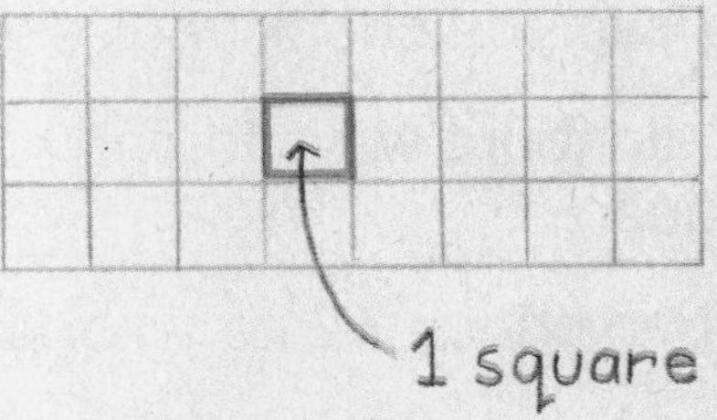

   ____

2. How did you estimate? How did others in your group estimate?
3. How can you check your estimate? Try different ways. Write your answers.
4. Try this way to check:
   a. Cut out as many hundreds as you can. The hundreds square should be 10 squares long and 10 squares wide.
   b. From the pieces that are left, cut out as many tens as you can.
   c. Then, from the pieces left, cut out as many ones as you can.
   d. Group ones to make tens.
   e. Group tens to make hundreds.

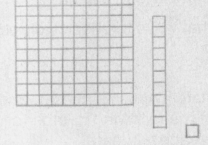

5. How many squares did you cut in all? Write your answer.

   ____

6. Compare your answer with your estimate.
   a. What ways to estimate worked best?
   b. What ways to check worked best?

PART B

7. Take another sheet of squared paper. Estimate how many squares you think are on:

   a. $\frac{1}{2}$ sheet ________ b. $\frac{1}{4}$ sheet ________ c. 2 sheets ________

   Write each estimate.

   d. How did you make your estimates?

   e. What ways did others use?

8. How can you check your estimates?

   a. Talk about ways to find how many squares.

   b. Then check. Write your answers.

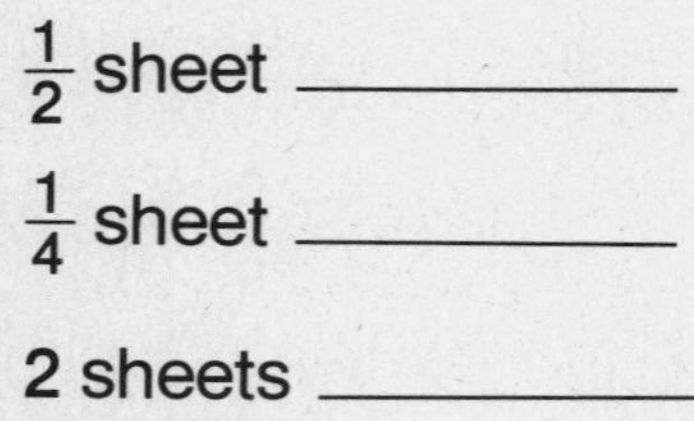

$\frac{1}{2}$ sheet ________

$\frac{1}{4}$ sheet ________

2 sheets ________

9. Compare your answers with your estimates.

   a. What ways to estimate worked best?

   b. What ways to check worked best?

PART C

10. Estimate if you will need 1, 2, or 3 sheets to get the following number of squares. Write each estimate.

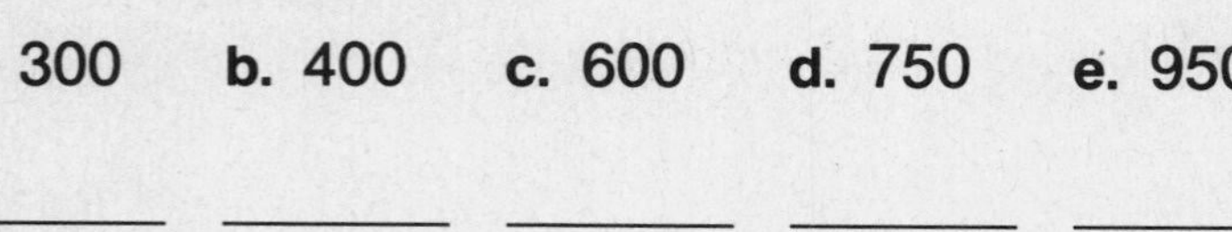

a. 300 b. 400 c. 600 d. 750 e. 950

________ ________ ________ ________ ________

   f. What ways did your group estimate?

11. Talk about ways to check your estimates. Then check.

    a. ________ b. ________ c. ________ d. ________ e. ________

12. Compare your answers with your estimates.

Name ___

Counting and estimating

Work in groups.
Record your answers on a separate sheet of paper if you need more space.

PART A

1. Look at the handprint on page 43. How many squares do you think are in the handprint? Make a guess. Write it down. Compare the guesses in your group.

   Guess: ___

2. Make an estimate by counting. (Parts of squares can add up to a whole square.) Write down your estimate. Try to think of ways to help your group estimate.

   Estimate: ___

3. Compare your guess and your estimate. What happened? Why? Compare with the other students in your group.

4. Compare your group's estimates with the estimates of other groups. Are they all the same? What happened? Why?

PART B

5. Trace both of your hands on squared paper. How many squares do you think are in your two handprints? Make a guess and write it down.

   Guess: ___

6. Make an estimate by counting. Write down your estimate. Help others in your group to make estimates. Compare the guesses and estimates in your group.

   Estimate: ___

7. Compare sizes of handprints.

PART C

Think and talk about these questions.

8. What can you tell about the age of the person who made the handprint on page 43? How can you tell?

9. How can you use what you know about your handprint to estimate the number of squares you have in one footprint?

10. Why doesn't it make sense to give exact answers to questions 8 and 9?

Name ____________________

Comparing numbers

35 comes before 40.

35 < 40

35 is less than 40

41 comes after 34.

41 > 34

41 is greater than 34

EXERCISES

< or >?
is less than **is greater than**

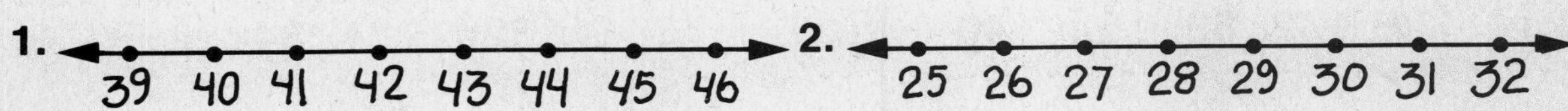

46 ◯ 40

25 ◯ 31

3. 35 ◯ 36
4. 48 ◯ 35
5. 36 ◯ 42
6. 45 ◯ 38
7. 37 ◯ 43
8. 43 ◯ 34
9. 57 ◯ 60
10. 40 ◯ 37
11. 80 ◯ 90
12. 99 ◯ 86
13. 58 ◯ 77
14. 66 ◯ 47

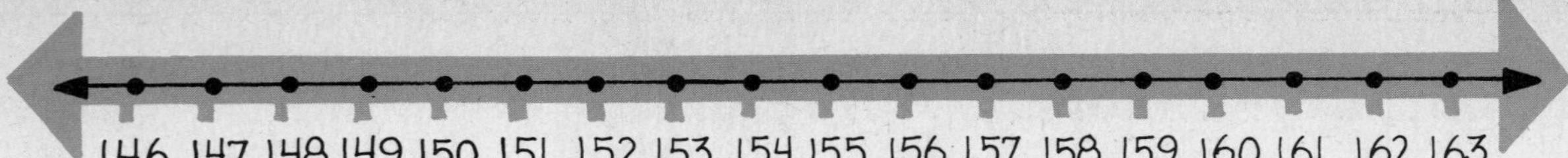

148 comes before 152.

$148 < 152$

161 comes after 158.

$161 > 158$

$<$ or $>$?

15. 148 ◯ 157 **16.** 153 ◯ 146 **17.** 151 ◯ 155

18. 152 ◯ 163 **19.** 185 ◯ 162 **20.** 151 ◯ 173

21. 120 ◯ 117 **22.** 160 ◯ 185 **23.** 190 ◯ 189

24. 190 ◯ 191 **25.** 187 ◯ 165 **26.** 189 ◯ 198

Order from least to greatest.

27. 123, 74, 96 ____________

28. 130, 108, 153 ____________

29. 167, 211, 198 ____________

30. 132, 83, 152, 140 ____________

31. 326, 284, 341, 299 ____________

Problem Solving

32. Jack is 28 years old.
Jill is 52 years old.

Who is older? __________

33. Joe is 153 centimeters tall.
Ken is 163 centimeters tall.

Who is taller? __________

34. Rover is 45 centimeters tall.
Duke is 53 centimeters tall.

Which dog is shorter? __________

35. Martha scored 116 points.
Charles scored 114 points.

Who scored more? __________

36. Sandy read 123 pages.
Dennis read 142 pages.

Who read more? __________

Name ______________________________

Counting by 10 and by 100

You can think about bars of 10 to count by 10.

Count by 10.

10 20 30 40 50 60

Count by 10. Start at 80.

80 90 100 110

EXERCISES

Count by 10.
Give the next three numbers.

1. 50 ______
2. 80 ______
3. 90 ______
4. 130 ______
5. 160 ______
6. 120 ______
7. 460 ______
8. 340 ______
9. 820 ______
10. 720 ______
11. 610 ______
12. 450 ______
13. 180 ______
14. 200 ______
15. 190 ______
16. 570 ______
17. 690 ______
18. 490 ______
19. 890 ______
20. 770 ______

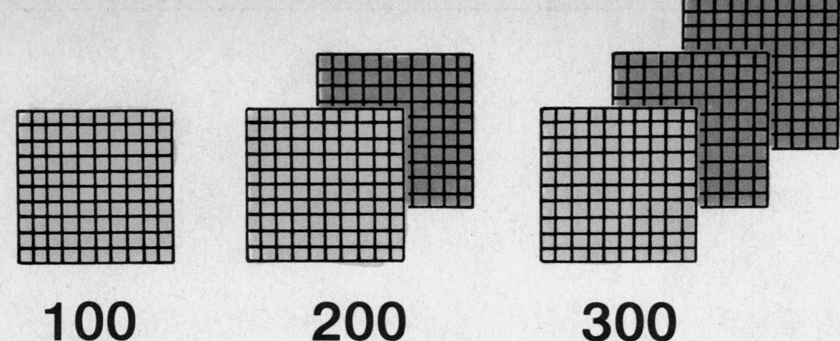

Count by 100.
Give the next two numbers.

21. 100 ________

22. 500 ________

23. 400 ________

24. 300 ________

25. 200 ________

26. 600 ________

Carol used 10 cubes to make 1 dog.

Ken used 30 cubes to make 3 dogs.

Problem Solving

27. Mary made 4 dogs.
How many cubes did she use? ________

28. Ricardo made 7 dogs.
How many cubes did he use? ________

★ **29.** Kevin made 6 dogs.
John made 3 dogs.
How many cubes did they use in all? ________

KEEPING SKILLS SHARP

Give each missing addend.

1. 6 + ____ = 9

2. 8 + ____ = 8

3. 7 + ____ = 12

4. 3 + ____ = 10

5. 9 + ____ = 14

6. 4 + ____ = 12

7. 8 + ____ = 15

8. 5 + ____ = 10

9. 6 + ____ = 14

10. 6 + ____ = 11

11. 5 + ____ = 13

12. 8 + ____ = 17

13. 9 + ____ = 11

14. 6 + ____ = 15

15. 7 + ____ = 16

16. 6 + ____ = 13

17. 9 + ____ = 18

Name ____________________

Dollars

1 dollar
$1
100 cents
100¢

1 dime

10 cents
10¢

1 penny

1 cent
1¢

A dot is used between the dollars and cents.

$2.43

Read as "two dollars and forty-three cents."

EXERCISES

Match.

1. 

______

a. 

2. 

______

b. 

3. 

______

c. 

How much money?

4.

5.

6.

7.

8.

9.

10.

11.

Name ____________________

Rounding

Sometimes numbers are rounded to the nearest ten.

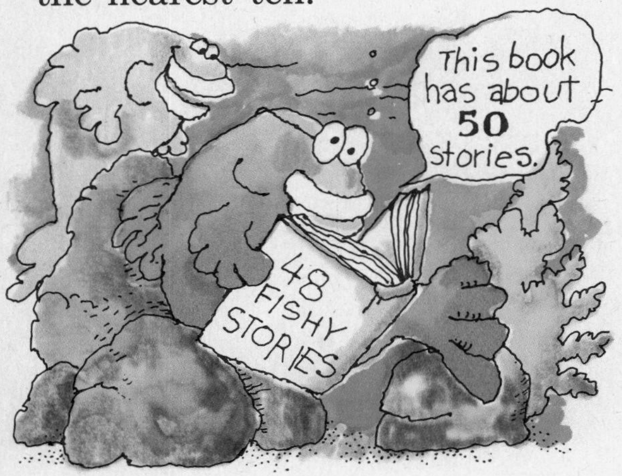

Round **87** to the nearest ten.

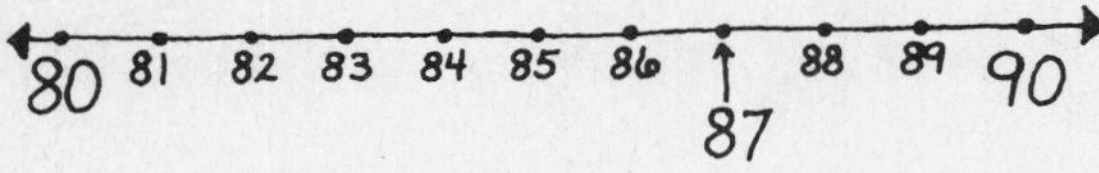

87 is between **80** and **90**.

It is nearer **90**.
So, round up to **90**.

Round **43** to the nearest ten.

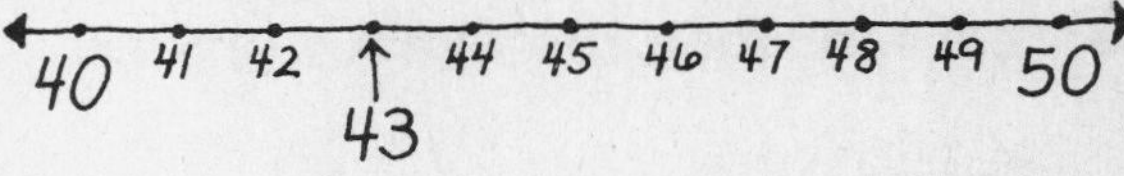

43 is between **40** and **50**.

It is nearer **40**.
So, round down to **40**.

Round **65** to the nearest ten.

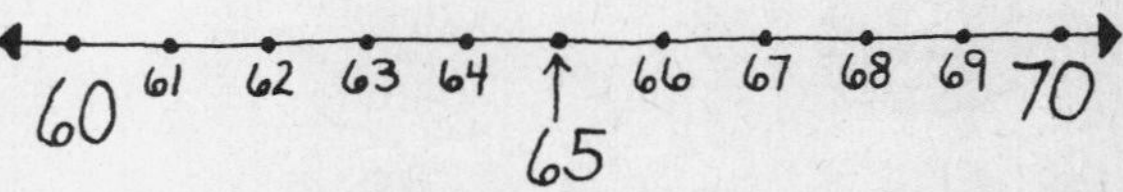

65 is halfway between **60** and **70**.

When a number is halfway between two numbers, round to the larger number.

So, round **65** up to **70**.

EXERCISES

Round to the nearest ten.

40 41 42 43 44 45 46 47 48 49 50

1. 44 ____ **2.** 47 ____ **3.** 41 ____ **4.** 45 ____

70 71 72 73 74 75 76 77 78 79 80

5. 77 ____ **6.** 73 ____ **7.** 75 ____ **8.** 78 ____

9. 18 ____ **10.** 54 ____ **11.** 89 ____ **12.** 25 ____

13. 39 ____ **14.** 62 ____ **15.** 37 ____ **16.** 85 ____

17. 12 ____ **18.** 55 ____ **19.** 7 ____ **20.** 19 ____

Challenge!

The exact number was rounded to the nearest ten. Pick the exact number.

21. 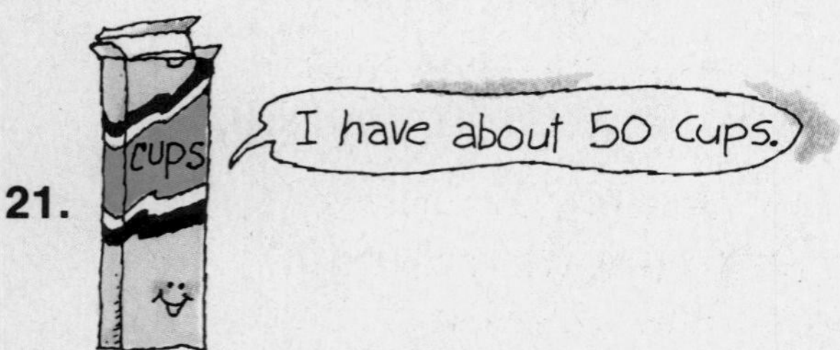
CUPS
I have about 50 cups.

a. 44 cups **b.** 47 cups **c.** 56 cups

22. 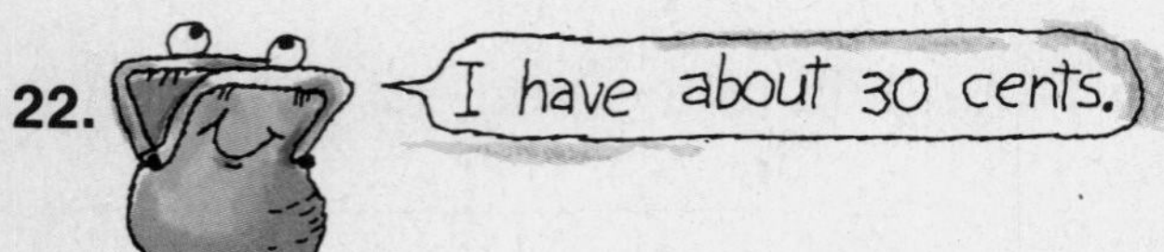
I have about 30 cents.

a. 50¢ **b.** 19¢ **c.** 32¢

23. 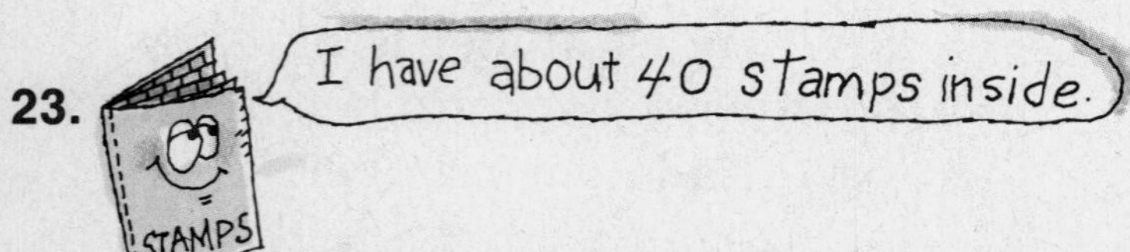
I have about 40 stamps inside.
STAMPS

a. 37 stamps **b.** 48 stamps **c.** 51 stamps

KEEPING SKILLS SHARP

1. $\begin{array}{r} 3 \\ 3 \\ +5 \\ \hline \end{array}$ **2.** $\begin{array}{r} 2 \\ 1 \\ +5 \\ \hline \end{array}$

3. $\begin{array}{r} 4 \\ 3 \\ +5 \\ \hline \end{array}$ **4.** $\begin{array}{r} 3 \\ 4 \\ +5 \\ \hline \end{array}$

5. $\begin{array}{r} 2 \\ 6 \\ +8 \\ \hline \end{array}$ **6.** $\begin{array}{r} 7 \\ 2 \\ +8 \\ \hline \end{array}$

7. $\begin{array}{r} 8 \\ 0 \\ +5 \\ \hline \end{array}$ **8.** $\begin{array}{r} 6 \\ 3 \\ +5 \\ \hline \end{array}$

9. $\begin{array}{r} 4 \\ 4 \\ +4 \\ \hline \end{array}$ **10.** $\begin{array}{r} 5 \\ 3 \\ +9 \\ \hline \end{array}$

11. $\begin{array}{r} 1 \\ 7 \\ +7 \\ \hline \end{array}$ **12.** $\begin{array}{r} 2 \\ 6 \\ +9 \\ \hline \end{array}$

13. $\begin{array}{r} 5 \\ 4 \\ +9 \\ \hline \end{array}$ **14.** $\begin{array}{r} 2 \\ 6 \\ +8 \\ \hline \end{array}$

Name

Rounding

There are about 500 fish in the tank.
512 fish

These examples show how to round a number to the nearest hundred.

Round **378** to the nearest hundred.

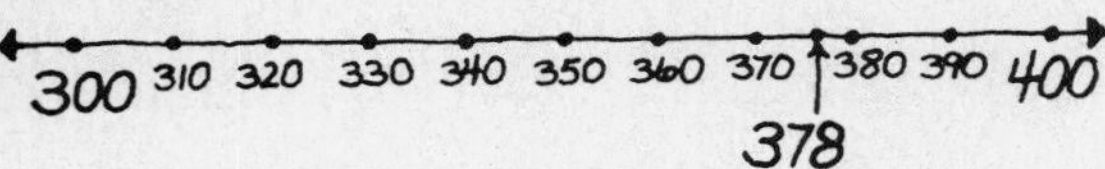

378 is between **300** and **400.**
It is nearer **400**.
So, round up to **400**.

Round **650** to the nearest hundred.

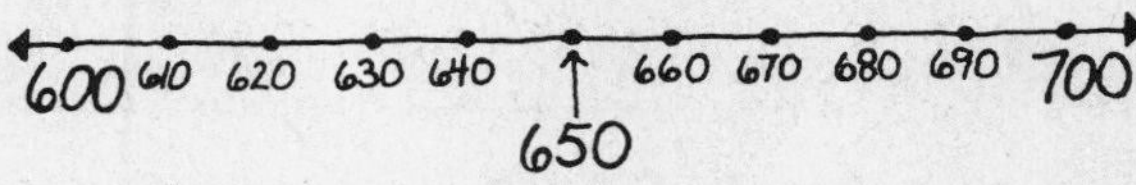

650 is between **600** and **700**.

When a number is halfway between two numbers, round to the larger number.

So, round up to **700**.

To round money to the nearest dollar, look at the cents.

Round **$.50** or more up to the next dollar.

$.89 is more than **$.50**.
So, round up to **$5.00**.

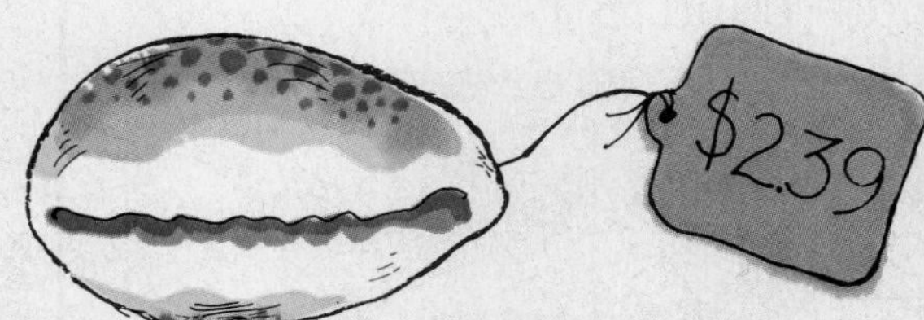

$.39 is less than **$.50**.
So, round down to **$2.00**.

EXERCISES

Round to the nearest hundred.

1. 740 ____	**2.** 380 ____	**3.** 210 ____	**4.** 570 ____	**5.** 891 ____
6. 852 ____	**7.** 650 ____	**8.** 249 ____	**9.** 450 ____	**10.** 382 ____
11. 607 ____	**12.** 842 ____	**13.** 445 ____	**14.** 593 ____	**15.** 911 ____
16. 503 ____	**17.** 344 ____	**18.** 837 ____	**19.** 250 ____	**20.** 735 ____
21. 120 ____	**22.** 460 ____	**23.** 349 ____	**24.** 116 ____	**25.** 781 ____
26. 901 ____	**27.** 381 ____	**28.** 97 ____	**29.** 732 ____	**30.** 50 ____

Round to the nearest dollar.

31. \$1.99 ____	**32.** \$2.47 ____	**33.** \$1.13 ____	**34.** \$1.54 ____	**35.** \$2.73 ____
36. \$2.39 ____	**37.** \$4.68 ____	**38.** \$3.19 ____	**39.** \$4.09 ____	**40.** \$6.71 ____
41. \$7.08 ____	**42.** \$5.25 ____	**43.** \$3.24 ____	**44.** \$5.62 ____	**45.** \$8.32 ____
46. \$9.29 ____	**47.** \$6.50 ____	**48.** \$4.45 ____	**49.** \$7.75 ____	**50.** \$6.09 ____
51. \$3.50 ____	**52.** \$9.49 ____	**53.** \$8.85 ____	**54.** \$2.79 ____	**55.** \$4.50 ____
56. \$.79 ____	**57.** \$7.77 ____	**58.** \$.50 ____	**59.** \$4.56 ____	**60.** \$8.06 ____

Challenge!

Guess my number.

61. My number is the greatest number you can round to the nearest hundred and get 300. ____

62. My number is the smallest number you can round to the nearest hundred and get 800. ____

63. My number is the greatest number you can round to the nearest hundred and get 600. ____

Name ____________________

Thousands

When you put 10 hundreds together, you get 1 thousand.

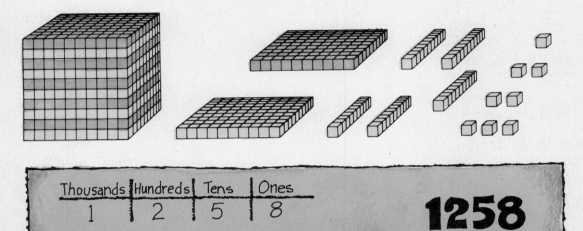

Thousands	Hundreds	Tens	Ones
1	2	5	8

1258

One thousand two hundred fifty-eight

EXERCISES

How many blocks?

1.

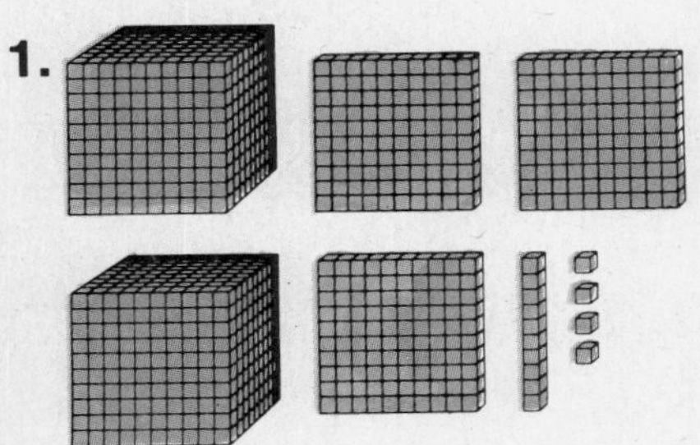

____

2.

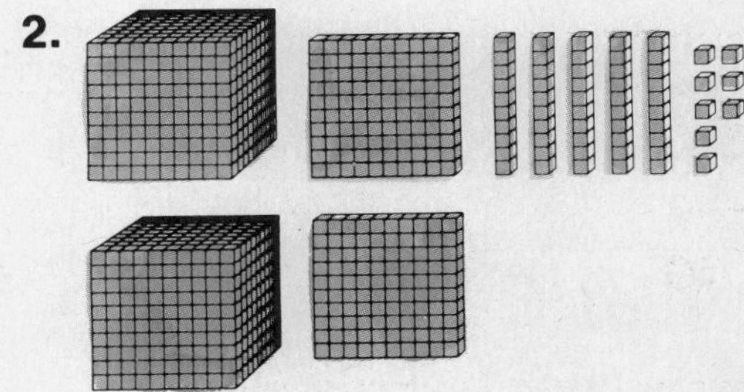

____

3.

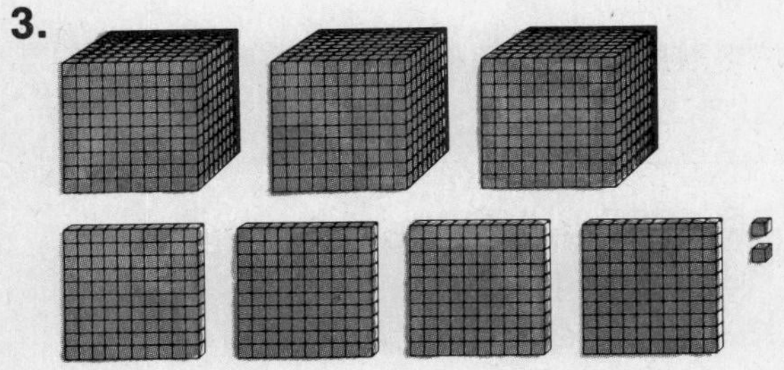

____

4.

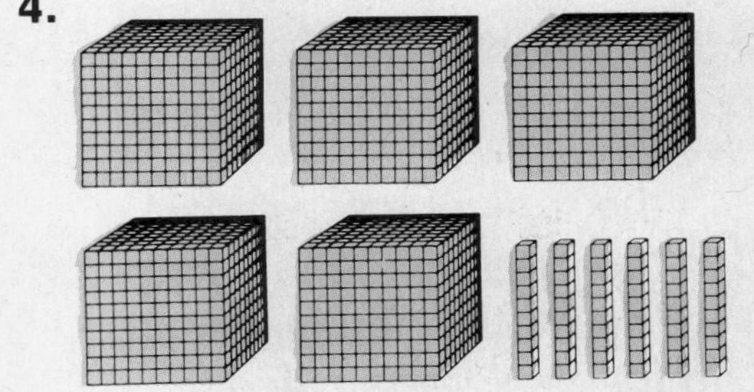

____

Write each number.

5. 4 thousands, 3 hundreds, 8 tens, 5 ones ______
6. 9 thousands, 6 hundreds, 4 tens, 6 ones ______
7. 5 thousands, 0 hundreds, 5 tens, 2 ones ______
8. 2 thousands, 7 hundreds, 0 tens, 0 ones ______
9. 6 thousands, 3 hundreds, 0 tens, 2 ones ______
10. 8 thousands, 0 hundreds, 5 tens, 2 ones ______

Count.

Give the next three numbers.

11. 1235

12. 4561	13. 5678	14. 6000	15. 3019
______	______	______	______
16. 7598	17. 8799	18. 3998	19. 8999
______	______	______	______
20. 7563	21. 8739	22. 2099	23. 2999
______	______	______	______

Challenge!

Give the number that has

24. 5 in the ones place
 2 in the hundreds place
 8 in the thousands place
 3 in the tens place

 ______

25. 6 in the hundreds place
 3 in the tens place
 0 in the ones place
 7 in the thousands place

 ______

26. 3 in the tens place
 6 in the ones place
 1 in the thousands place
 5 in the hundreds place

 ______

27. 9 in the ones place
 3 in the thousands place
 8 in the hundreds place
 7 in the tens place

 ______

Name ____________

More about thoughts

EXERCISES

Read.

1. 3274
2. 5186
3. 7294
4. 3185
5. 5784
6. 7854
7. 8457
8. 4758
9. 5204
10. 6203
11. 5206
12. 3825
13. 3720
14. 5960
15. 3140
16. 7180
17. 5037
18. 2086
19. 3027
20. 9011

Write each number.

21. six thousand two hundred ninety-three ____________
22. five thousand four hundred sixty-one ____________
23. eight thousand seven hundred eleven ____________
24. four thousand three hundred six ____________
25. four thousand two hundred ____________
26. three thousand forty ____________
27. seven thousand ____________
28. seven thousand nine ____________

Give the value of the red digit.

29. 61**4**0 ______ 30. **3**281 ______ 31. **5**731 ______

32. 3**4**96 ______ 33. 781**4** ______ 34. 80**6**1 ______

35. **1**728 ______ 36. 620**5** ______ 37. 333**3** ______

38. 33**3**3 ______ 39. 3**3**33 ______ 40. **3**333 ______

Give the next three numbers.

41. 1243 ______ 42. 1608 ______ 43. 1748 ______

44. 1499 ______ 45. 2949 ______ 46. 1098 ______

47. 6999 ______ 48. 4608 ______ 49. 2709 ______

Give the number that comes before and the number that comes after.

50. 1458 ______ 51. 2069 ______ 52. 3470 ______

53. 1600 ______ 54. 1080 ______ 55. 5910 ______

56. 1100 ______ 57. 1799 ______ 58. 1000 ______

Challenge!

Give the total score.

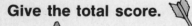

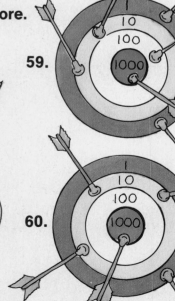

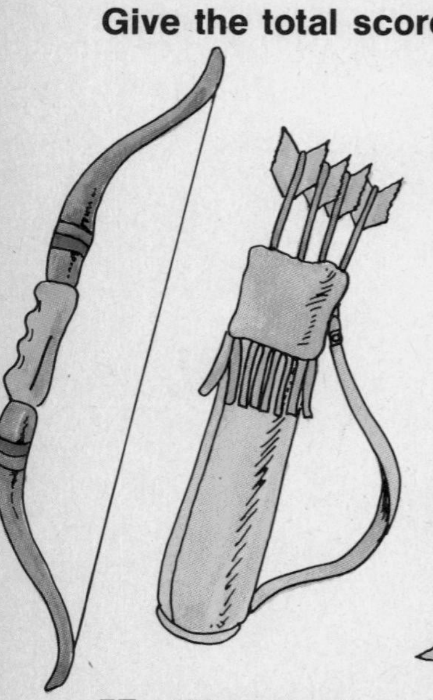

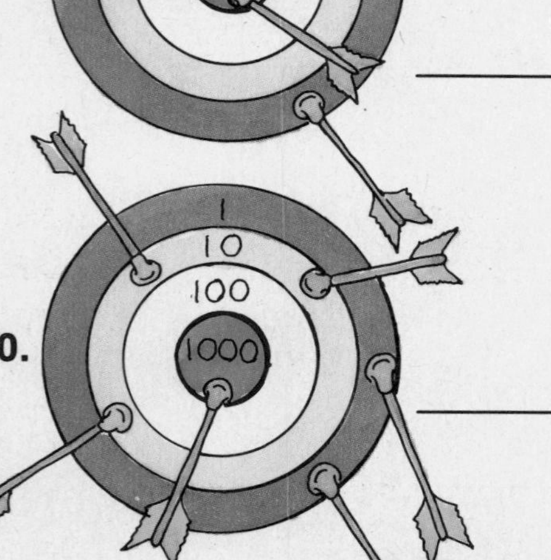

59. ______

60. ______

KEEPING SKILLS SHARP

1. 13 − 8	2. 14 − 7
3. 12 − 4	4. 15 − 9
5. 14 − 5	6. 17 − 8
7. 16 − 8	8. 11 − 8
9. 13 − 9	10. 18 − 9
11. 12 − 3	12. 12 − 5
13. 11 − 4	14. 17 − 9
15. 15 − 7	16. 14 − 6
17. 13 − 6	18. 16 − 7

Name ____________________

Comparing numbers

Which number is greater?

2432 > 2351
is greater than

2351 < 2432
is less than

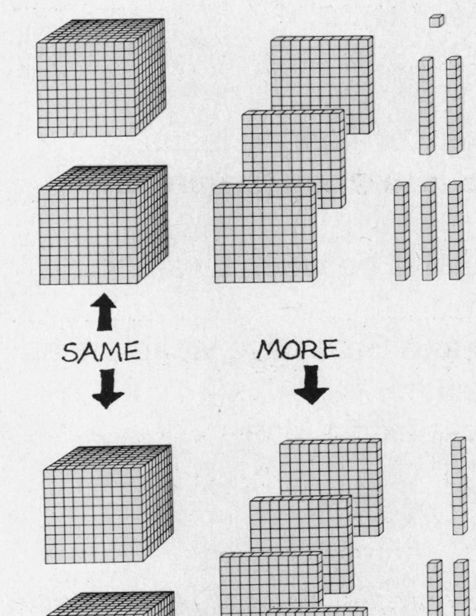

EXERCISES

< or >?
is less than **is greater than**

1. 5382 ◯ 6382	2. 4821 ◯ 2834	3. 6423 ◯ 6504
4. 9806 ◯ 9527	5. 4391 ◯ 4267	6. 8347 ◯ 8601
7. 5984 ◯ 5979	8. 6728 ◯ 6718	9. 7456 ◯ 7470
10. 8293 ◯ 8261	11. 2582 ◯ 2538	12. 7595 ◯ 7593
13. 9643 ◯ 9640	14. 3512 ◯ 3514	15. 1010 ◯ 1001

Challenge!

Who am I?

16. 

I am 1000 greater than 4368.

____

17. 

____

Problem Solving Logical reasoning

Study the clues.
Name each child.

Clues:

- Lisa is not wearing jeans.
- Terry is wearing glasses and a hat.
- Manuel is between Lisa and Terry.
- Alan and Beth have jackets that are alike.
- Lee is next to Alan.

1.

2.

3.

4.

5.

6.

Name ____________________

Ten thousands

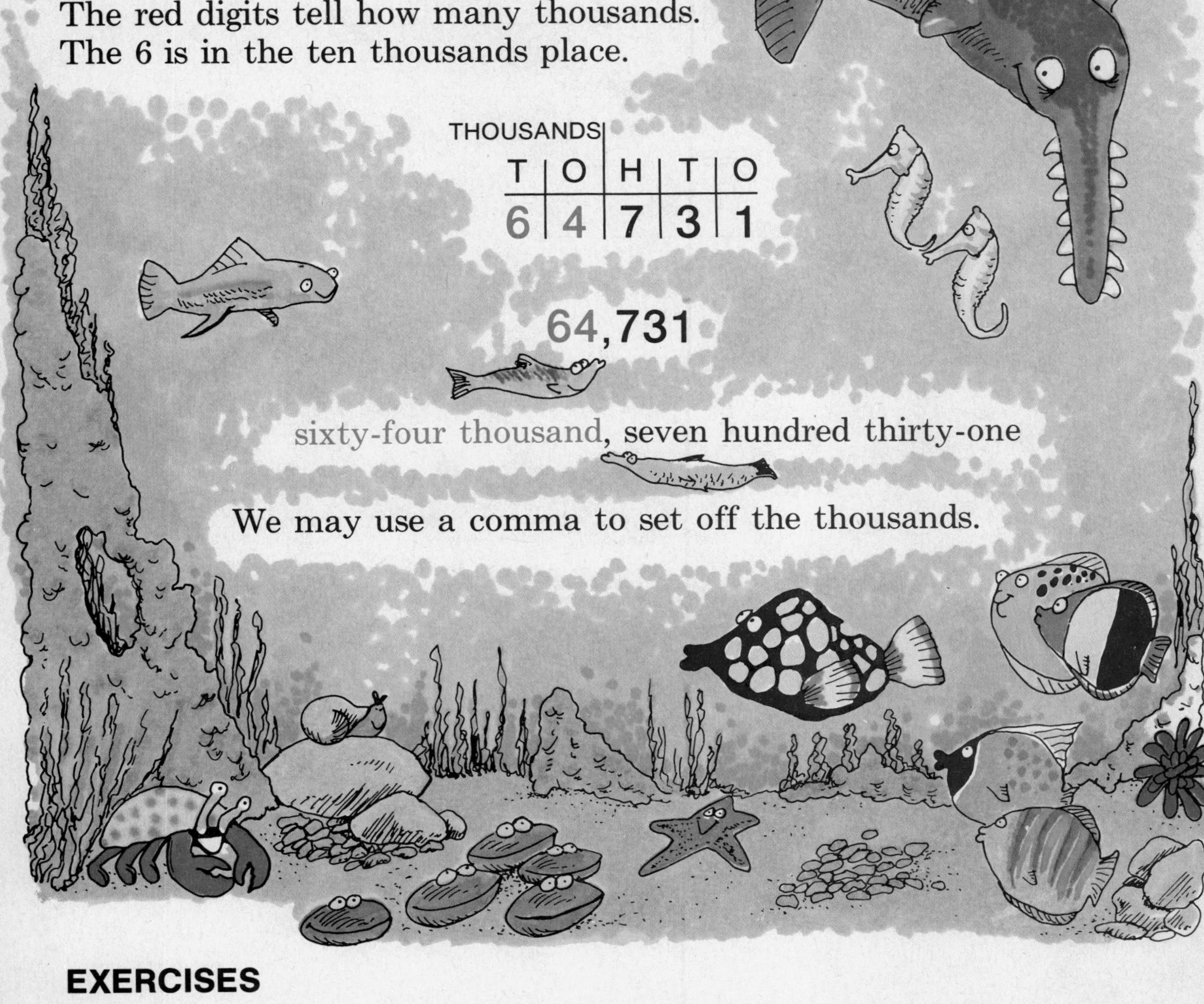

The red digits tell how many thousands.
The 6 is in the ten thousands place.

THOUSANDS				
T	O	H	T	O
6	4	7	3	1

64,731

sixty-four thousand, seven hundred thirty-one

We may use a comma to set off the thousands.

EXERCISES

Read.

1. The deepest place in any ocean is 36,198 feet deep.
2. People have gone down 35,800 feet into the ocean.
3. The whale shark is the largest fish. The largest whale sharks weigh about 38,000 pounds.
4. Some fish can go down as far as 24,600 feet into the ocean.
5. The Pacific Ocean is about 11,000 miles wide.
6. There are about 12,000 blue whales in the world.

Write the number.

7. twenty-one thousand ____________
8. fifty-six thousand ____________
9. seventy thousand ____________
10. eleven thousand ____________
11. thirty-four thousand, one hundred sixty-four ____________
12. forty-five thousand, six hundred thirty-seven ____________
13. one thousand four hundred sixteen ____________
14. thirty thousand, eight hundred ____________

Count.
Write the next three numbers.

15. **16,345**

16. **27,563** ____________ ____________

17. **48,358** ____________ ____________

18. **63,298** ____________ ____________

19. **72,499** ____________ ____________

20. **84,000** ____________ ____________

21. **10,378** ____________ ____________

★ **22.** **16,999** ____________ ____________

★ **23.** **29,998** ____________ ____________

Challenge!

The table has been cut apart.
Write the number.

24.

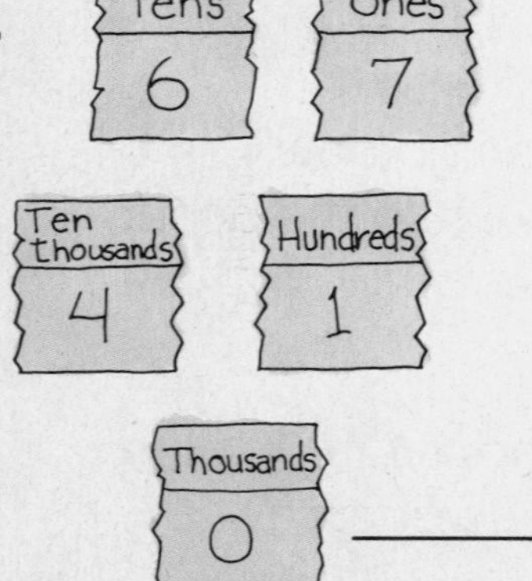

____

25.

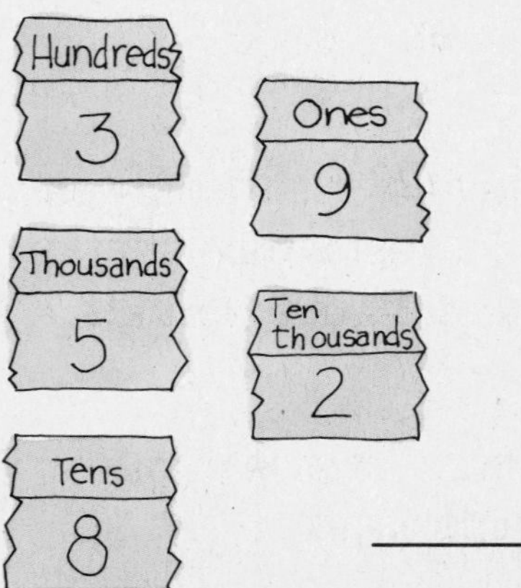

____

Name ______________________________

Hundred thousands

THOUSANDS					
H	T	O	H	T	O
3	7	4	5	3	6

374,536

three hundred seventy-four thousand, five hundred thirty-six

The red digits tell how many thousands. We may use a comma to set off the thousands.

EXERCISES

Read.

1. The distance around the middle of the earth is about 25,000 miles.

2. The moon is about 250,000 miles from the earth.

3. The Saturn Five can put a load weighing 222,000 pounds into orbit around the earth.

4. To travel from the earth to the moon, a spaceship must reach a speed of 24,500 miles per hour.

5. Neil Armstrong and Buzz Aldrin landed on the moon July 20, 1969.

Write the number.

6. forty-two thousand ____________
7. three hundred thousand ____________
8. five hundred fifty thousand ____________
9. seven hundred forty-two thousand ____________
10. two hundred twelve thousand, three hundred ____________
11. five hundred sixty-two thousand, four hundred eighty ____________
12. twenty-one thousand, five hundred sixty-two ____________

★ **Write the numbers and put in commas.**

13. 47321

7 8 9 ÷
4 5 6 ×
1 2 3 −
0 · = +

____

14. 85941

____

15. 67321

____

16. 92406

____

17. 235784

____

18. 834156

____

19. 27000

____

20. 400000

____

21. 500302

____

22. 986591

____

23. 843259

____

Name ______________________________

Chapter Checkup

Write the number. [pages 38–41, 54–57, 60–63]

1.

Tens	Ones
3	6

______

2.

Hundreds	Tens	Ones
5	2	3

______

3.

Thousands	Hundreds	Tens	Ones
4	0	1	7

______

4. sixty-two ______

5. three hundred eighty ______

6. two hundred eleven ______

7. five hundred nine ______

8. one thousand two hundred sixty-five ______

9. five thousand forty ______

10. nine thousand two hundred seven ______

< or >? [pages 42–45, 58]

< is less than **> is greater than**

11. 89 ◯ 69

12. 281 ◯ 316

13. 360 ◯ 342

14. 3516 ◯ 3543

15. 3824 ◯ 3915

16. 8516 ◯ 8507

How much money? [pages 48–49]

17.

______

18.

______

Round. [pages 50–53]

19. 73 to the nearest ten. ______

20. 47 to the nearest ten. ______

21. 207 to the nearest hundred. ______

22. $3.57 to the nearest dollar. ______

Chapter Project

MAKING A TABLE

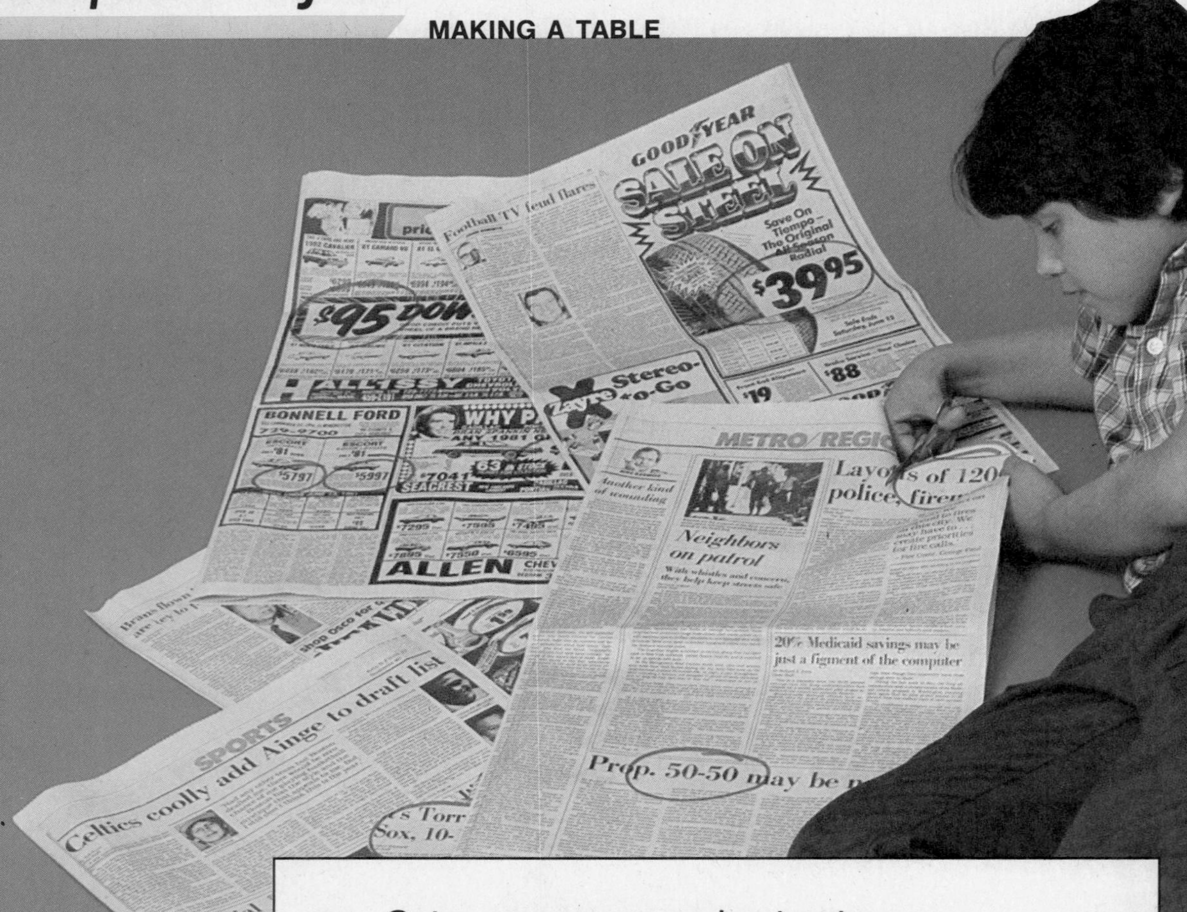

1. Get a newspaper and cut out some number facts.
2. Make a table like the one below.
3. Put your facts in the right boxes.

0–9	
10–99	79¢
100–999	
1000–9999	$5797 1200
Greater than 9999	

Name ____________________

Chapter Review

How many blocks?

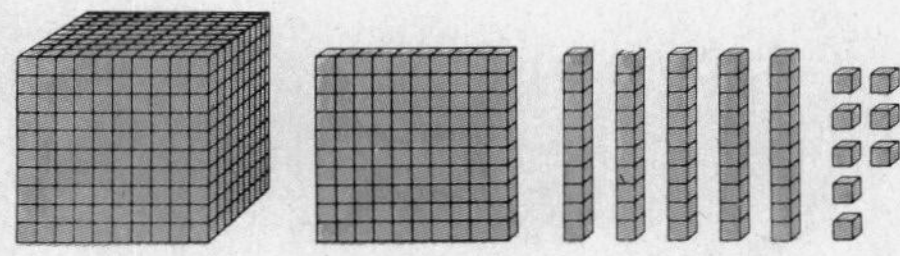

1. ______

2. ______

3. ______

4. ______

5. ______

6. ______

< or >?

is less than **is greater than**

7. 83 ◯ 79

8. 139 ◯ 143

9. 59 ◯ 39	**10.** 80 ◯ 93	**11.** 171 ◯ 206
12. 234 ◯ 243	**13.** 329 ◯ 300	**14.** 430 ◯ 445
15. 1200 ◯ 1300	**16.** 2000 ◯ 1800	**17.** 2436 ◯ 2430

Round to the nearest ten.

18. 73 ______	**19.** 78 ______	**20.** 74 ______	**21.** 76 ______	**22.** 75 ______
23. 82 ______	**24.** 67 ______	**25.** 54 ______	**26.** 35 ______	**27.** 41 ______

Round to the nearest hundred.

28. 730 ______	**29.** 781 ______	**30.** 743 ______	**31.** 762 ______	**32.** 754 ______
33. 826 ______	**34.** 673 ______	**35.** 548 ______	**36.** 350 ______	**37.** 419 ______

Chapter Challenge

PLACE-VALUE PUZZLES

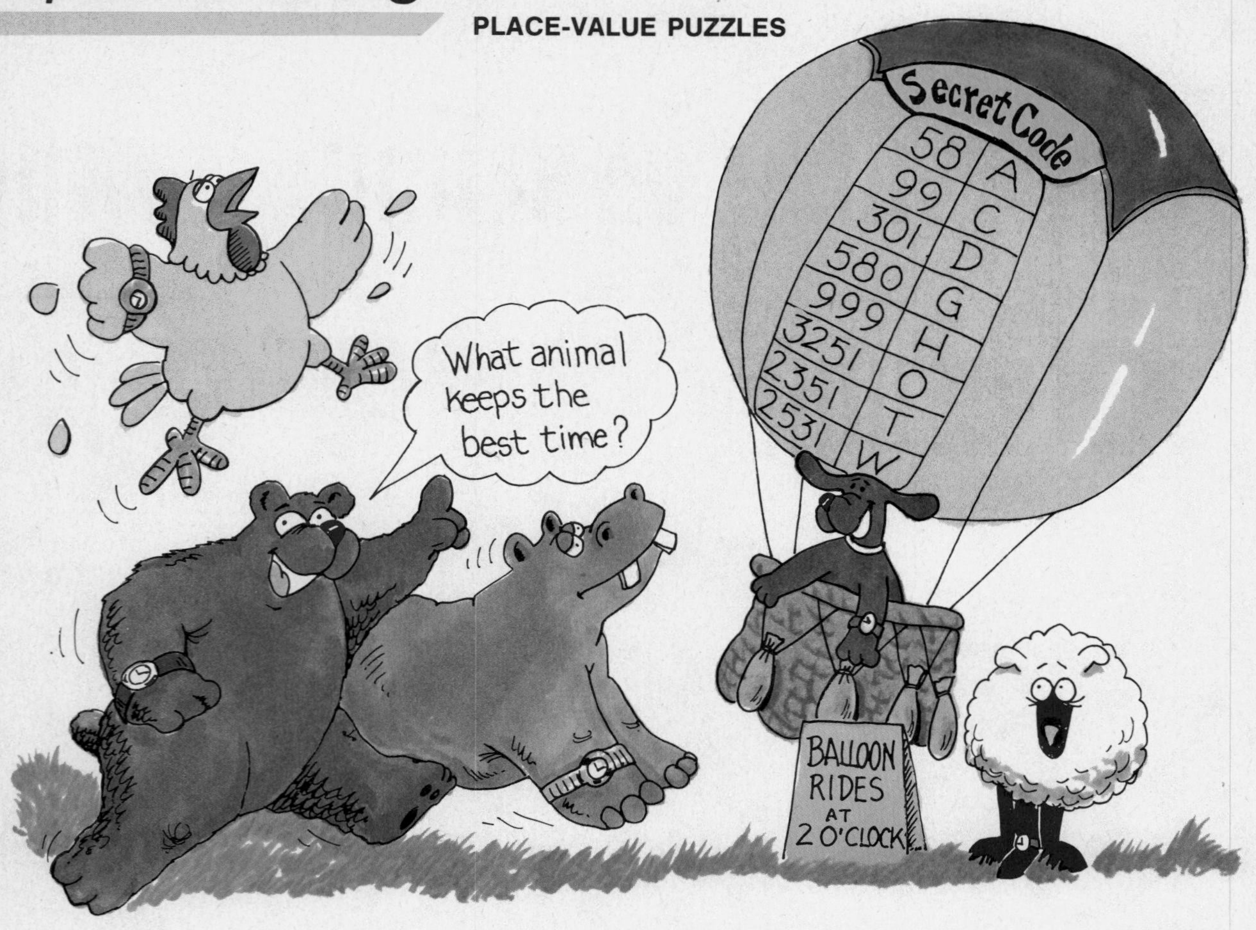

First give the number.
Then give the letter.
What number is

1. 10 less than 68?
2. 2 thousands, 5 hundreds, 3 tens, and 1 one?
3. 20 greater than 38?
4. 100 less than 2451?
5. 1 less than 100?
6. 1 less than 1000?
7. 2 thousands less than 2301?
8. 3 hundreds greater than 2951?
9. 2 thousands less than 2580?

	NUMBER	LETTER
1.	58	A
2.		
3.		
4.		
5.		
6.		
7.		
8.		
9.		

Name ____________________

Cumulative Checkup

STANDARDIZED FORMAT

Give the correct letter.

1. Add.

$$\begin{array}{r} 2 \\ 5 \\ +9 \\ \hline \end{array}$$

a. 16
b. 15
c. 14
d. 17

2. Subtract.

$$\begin{array}{r} 14 \\ -9 \\ \hline \end{array}$$

a. 4
b. 3
c. 6
d. none of these

3. How much money?
2 dimes
2 nickels
3 pennies

a. 24¢ **b.** 28¢
c. 33¢ **d.** 43¢

4. What letter is seventh in this word?

NUMERAL

a. L
b. R
c. A
d. E

5. Which number is smallest?

a. sixty-four
b. forty-six
c. forty-eight
d. fifty

6. What number is 10 more than 78?

a. 79
b. 178
c. 68
d. 88

7. What number is 1 less than 170?

a. 169
b. 171
c. 179
d. none of these

8. 76 rounded to the nearest ten is

a. 70
b. 77
c. 80
d. 100

9. Six thousand four hundred four is

a. 6440
b. 6400
c. 6044
d. 6404

10. Which number is greatest?

a. 5683
b. 5671
c. 5684
d. 5646

11. How much money?
1 dollar
3 dimes
4 pennies

a. \$1.34 **b.** \$1.54
c. \$1.70 **d.** \$1.52

12. Beverly had 7 apples. Patrick had 5 apples. How many more did Beverly have?

a. 3 **b.** 2
c. 13 **d.** 12

3

Addition

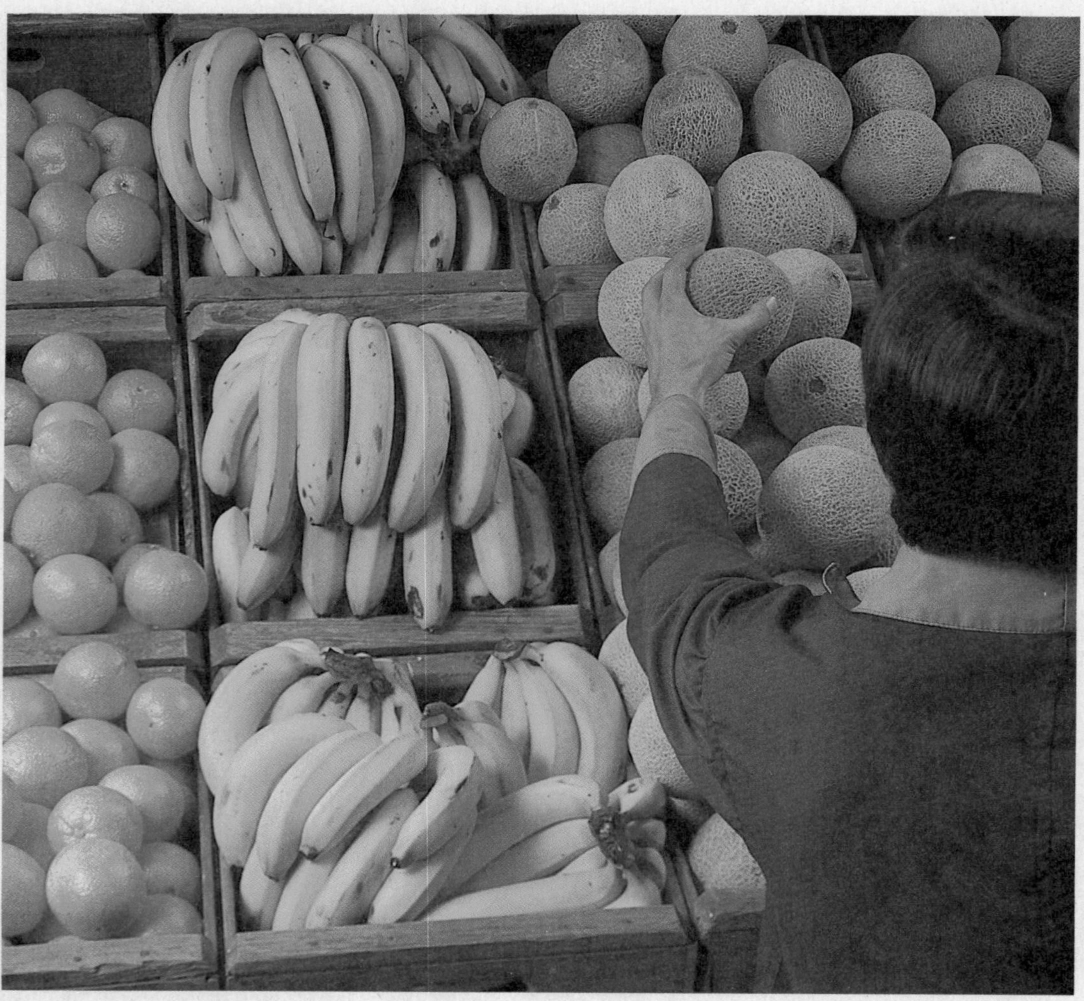

Eric uses wooden boxes to display cantaloupes. He put 38 cantaloupes in one box and 44 in another box. How many cantaloupes did he display?

Name ____________________

READY OR NOT?

1. 4 +5	2. 5 +8	3. 7 +8	4. 5 +6	5. 7 +7	6. 6 +6
7. 9 +8	8. 0 +8	9. 4 +8	10. 1 +7	11. 6 +0	12. 6 +7
13. 2 +7	14. 7 +9	15. 9 +4	16. 5 +9	17. 8 +8	18. 3 +7
19. 9 +6	20. 6 +8	21. 4 +6	22. 9 +9	23. 3 +8	24. 3 +9

Adding 2-digit numbers

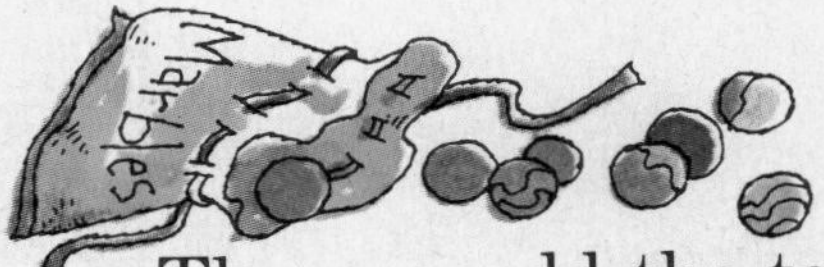

To find the sum, first we add the ones.

Tens	Ones
3	5
+2	3
	8

Then we add the tens.

Tens	Ones
3	5
+2	3
5	8

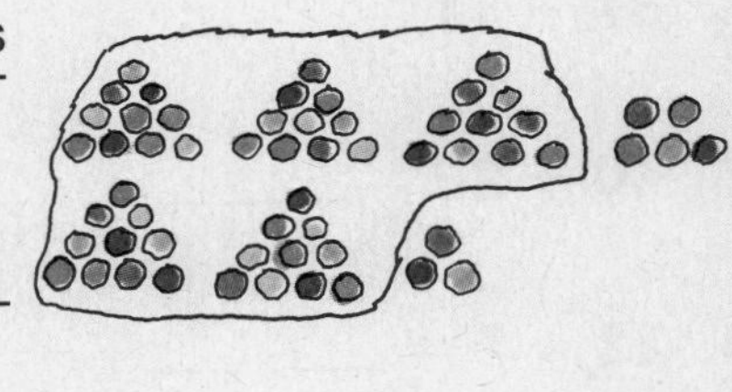

There are 58 marbles in all.

EXERCISES

Add.

1. 24 +21

2. 22 +36

3. 30 +25

4. 62 + 21	5. 63 + 22	6. 12 + 30	7. 32 + 32	8. 51 + 16
9. 43 + 22	10. 57 + 32	11. 21 + 70	12. 35 + 41	13. 49 + 50
14. 32 + 5	15. 43 + 4	16. 21 + 7	17. 34 + 5	18. 40 + 9

19. 53 + 21 = ______

53
+21
74

20. 35 + 14 = ______

35
+14

21. 14 + 35 = ______ 22. 51 + 45 = ______ 23. 45 + 51 = ______

24. 37 + 41 = ______ 25. 25 + 62 = ______ 26. 53 + 26 = ______

27. 40 + 28 = ______ 28. 26 + 71 = ______ 29. 54 + 14 = ______

30. 23 + 2 = ______ 31. 51 + 6 = ______ 32. 9 + 70 = ______

Challenge!

Add across. Add down.

33.

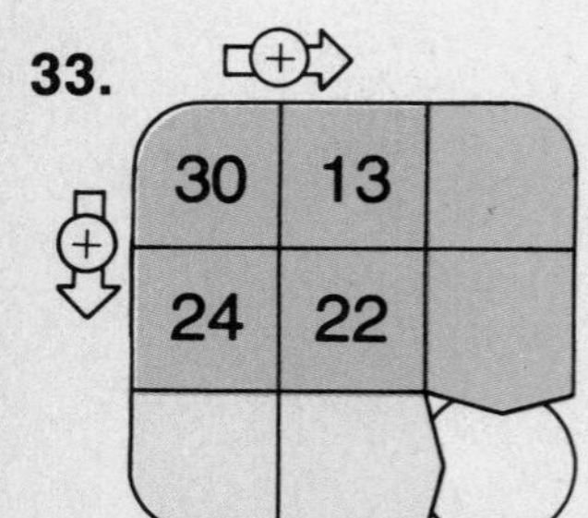

34.

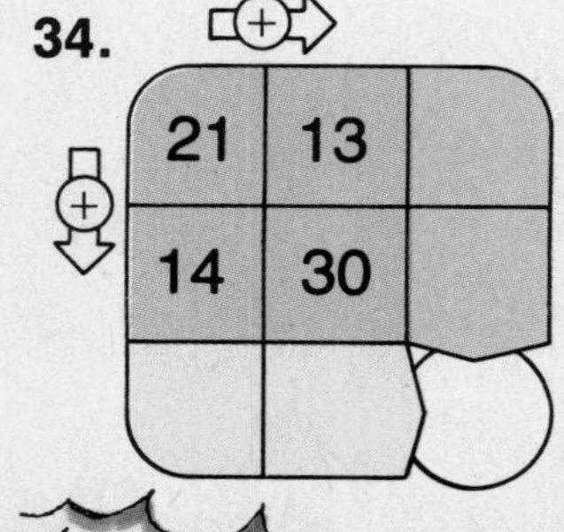

Name ______________________________

Adding with regrouping

Add ones.

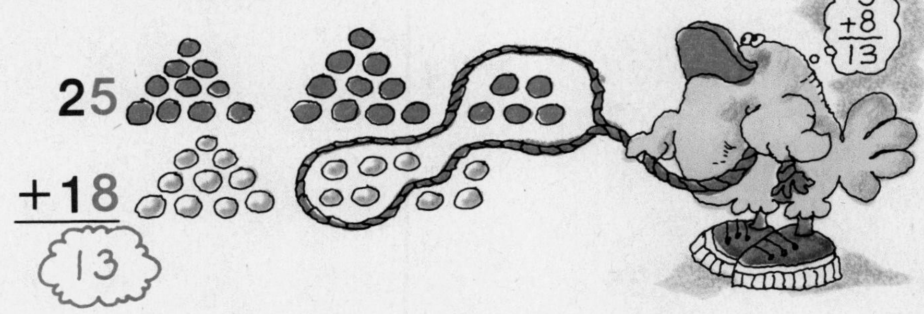

Regroup.

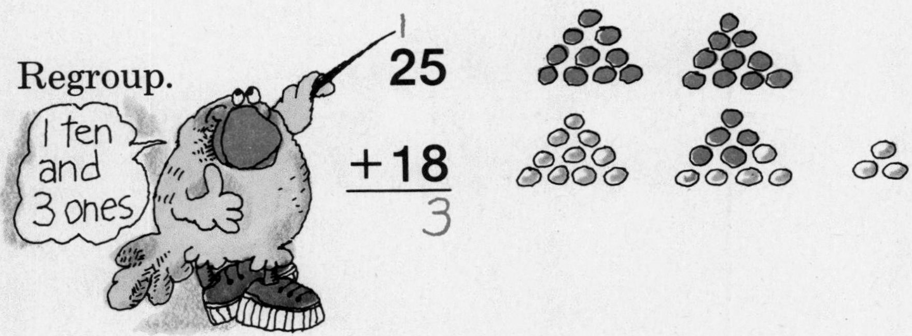

Add tens.

The **total** number of eggs is 43.

EXERCISES

Give the total.

1. 28 + 24

2. 35 + 29

3. 38 + 23

4. 36 + 38

5. 55 + 38

6. 45 + 19

7. 57 + 26

8. 42 + 36

9. 25 + 55

10. 47 + 7

11. 26 + 43

12. 62 + 29

13. 27 + 27

14. 66 + 25

15. 56 + 17

16. 35 + 28

17. 63 + 28

18. 53 + 8

19. 39 + 20

20. 41 + 29

21. 43 + 6

22. 67 + 32

23. 37 + 18

24. 48 + 48

25. 46 + 16 = _______

26. 38 + 7 = _______

27. 29 + 17 = _______

28. 54 + 8 = _______

29. 6 + 77 = _______

30. 49 + 36 = _______

31. 64 + 27 = _______

32. 55 + 30 = _______

Mental Math

Use the shortcut.

To add 9, I can add 10 and subtract 1.
SHORTCUT

33. 47 + 9 = _______

34. 58 + 9 = _______

35. 65 + 9 = _______

36. 37 + 9 = _______

37. 73 + 9 = _______

38. 84 + 9 = _______

Name ______________________________

Adding—regrouping tens

Add ones.

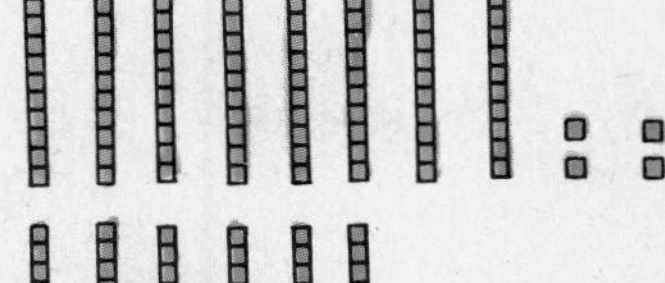

$$\begin{array}{r} 84 \\ +63 \\ \hline 7 \end{array}$$

Add tens.

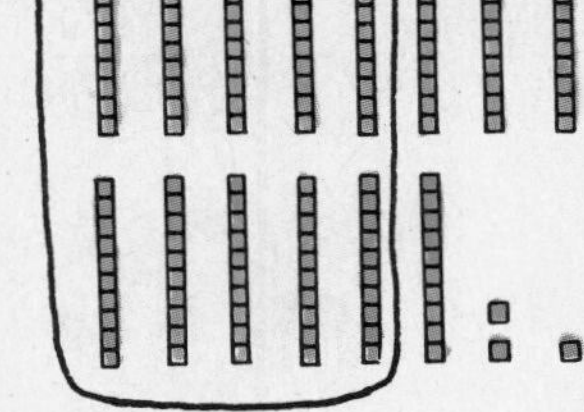

$$\begin{array}{r} 84 \\ +63 \\ \hline 7 \end{array}$$

$$\begin{array}{r} 84 \\ +63 \\ \hline 147 \end{array}$$

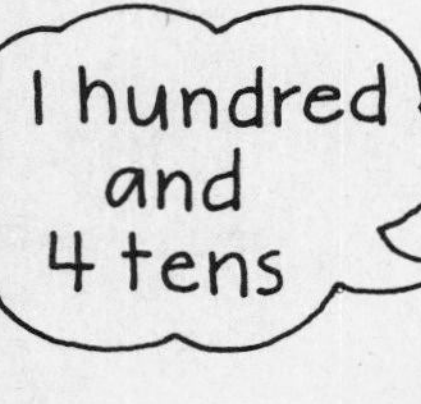

EXERCISES

Add.

1. $\begin{array}{r} 65 \\ +53 \\ \hline \end{array}$

2. $\begin{array}{r} 72 \\ +55 \\ \hline \end{array}$

3. $\begin{array}{r} 74 \\ +65 \\ \hline \end{array}$

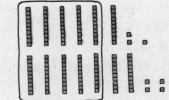

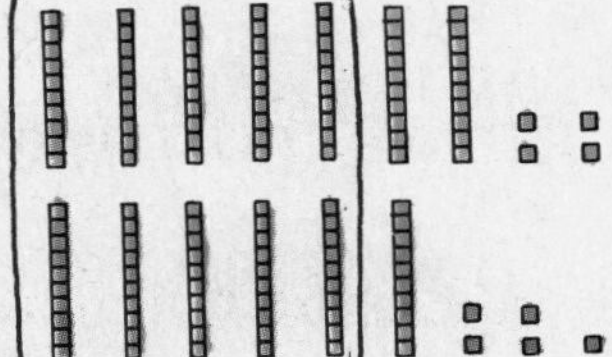

4. $\begin{array}{r} 63 \\ +75 \\ \hline \end{array}$

5. 56 + 83	6. 49 + 70	7. 68 + 51	8. 85 + 73	9. 95 + 82
10. 67 + 53	11. 67 + 55	12. 87 + 78	13. 65 + 36	14. 83 + 59
15. 86 + 28	16. 97 + 48	17. 78 + 83	18. 68 + 17	19. 88 + 75
	20. $.84 + .59 = $1.43	21. $.99 + .38	22. $.75 + .22	23. $.69 + .56
	24. $.64 + .28	25. $.76 + .19	26. $.59 + .95	27. $.98 + .74
	28. $.85 + .28	29. $.75 + .53	30. $.80 + .70	31. $.96 + .19

Adding money is like adding whole numbers.

Challenge!

Solve.

32. Gordon bought two of these treats at the circus. He spent $.85 in all. Which two treats did he buy?

____

33. Althea bought two of these treats. She spent a total of $1.05. Which two treats did she buy?

____

Name ______________________________

Problem Solving Money

→ Menu ←

Hamburger..	$.85
Superburger.	$.99
Hot Dog...	$.65
Salad....	$.49
Soup.....	$.35
Shake....	$.68
Large Milk.	$.37
Small Milk.	$.26

EXERCISES

Give the total price.

1.  ____________

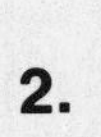

2.   ____________

3.  ____________

4. 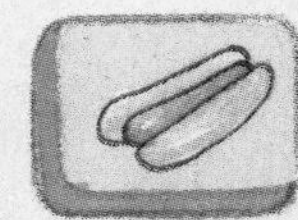  ____________

5.   ____________

6. ____________

7. ____________

8.   ____________

Solve.

9. Jan bought 1 hamburger and 1 large milk. How much did she spend? _______

10. Will bought 2 hot dogs. How much did he spend? _______

11. Pretend you have $1.35. Do you have enough money to buy
    - a. 1 hamburger and 1 hot dog? _______
    - b. 1 hot dog and 1 large milk? _______
    - c. 1 superburger and 1 small milk? _______
    - d. 1 salad and 1 shake? _______
    - e. 2 hot dogs? _______
    - f. 2 shakes? _______
    - ★ g. 3 soups? _______
    - ★ h. 2 salads and 1 shake? _______
    - ★ i. 1 superburger and 2 small milks? _______

12. Pretend you have $1.50. Do you have enough money to buy
    - a. 1 superburger and 1 shake? _______
    - b. 1 hamburger and 1 soup? _______
    - c. 1 hot dog and 1 shake? _______
    - d. 1 hot dog and 1 salad? _______
    - e. 2 hamburgers? _______
    - f. 2 salads? _______
    - ★ g. 3 large milks? _______
    - ★ h. 2 hot dogs and 1 small milk? _______
    - ★ i. 1 superburger and 2 small milks? _______

Problem Solving—logical reasoning

13. Together John and Greg ordered 1 hamburger, 1 hot dog, 1 shake, and 1 large milk. What did each boy eat?

    Clues:
    - Each boy had 1 sandwich and 1 drink.
    - John did not eat the hamburger.
    - Greg did not drink the shake.

    ____

14. Together Maria and Ruth ordered 1 superburger, 1 hot dog, 1 salad, 1 shake, and 1 small milk. What did each girl eat?

    Clues:
    - Each girl ate 3 foods.
    - Maria did not eat the superburger or drink the milk.
    - They shared the salad.

    ____

Name ____________________

More than 2 addends

Add ones.

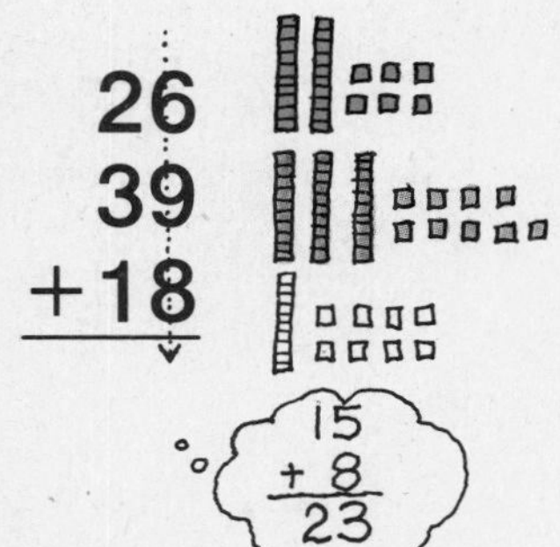

Regroup.

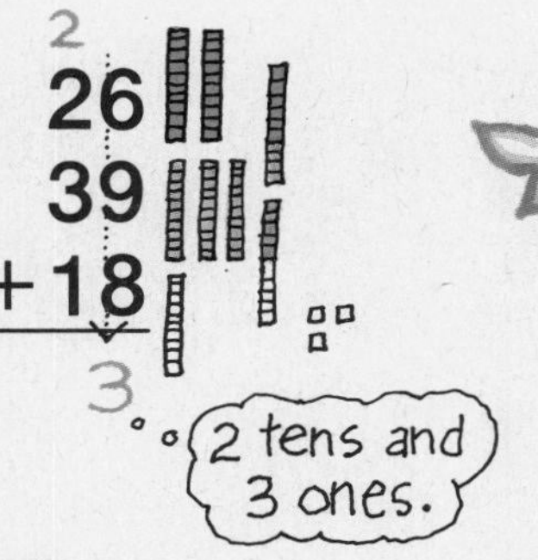

Add tens.

2
26
39
+18
83

Now let's check our work. We can check addition by adding from bottom to top.

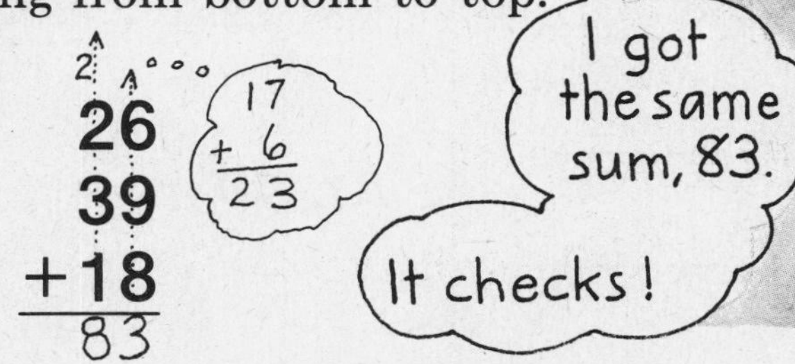

EXERCISES

Give each sum.

			Check
1.	28 17 +25 ↓	**2.**	28 17 +25 ↑
3.	45 29 +15 ↓	**4.**	45 29 +15 ↑
5.	43 29 +38 ↓	**6.**	43 29 +38 ↑
7.	36 48 +29 ↓	**8.**	36 48 +29 ↑
9.	46 58 +37 ↓	**10.**	46 58 +37 ↑
11.	39 48 +56 ↓	**12.**	39 48 +56 ↑

Add.

13. 26 + 37 + 49

14. 35 + 56 + 28

15. 59 + 74 + 86

16. 53 + 29 + 68

17. 16 + 21 + 29 + 35

18. 47 + 56 + 66 + 27

19. 27 + 39 + 48 + 55

20. 49 + 26 + 67 + 38

21. 46 + 57 + 29 + 28 ________

22. 45 + 64 + 38 + 16 ________

23. 54 + 38 + 9 + 17 ________

24. 25 + 65 + 18 + 7 ________

Mental Math

SHORTCUT
To add 18, I add 20 and subtract 2.

Use the shortcut.

25. 47 + 18 = ________

26. 53 + 18 = ________

27. 68 + 18 = ________

28. 59 + 18 = ________

29. 37 + 18 = ________

30. 75 + 18 = ________

31. 63 + 18 = ________

32. 39 + 18 = ________

KEEPING SKILLS SHARP

1. 16 − 8
2. 9 − 6
3. 14 − 8
4. 13 − 8
5. 15 − 8
6. 17 − 9
7. 12 − 6
8. 12 − 9
9. 11 − 4
10. 18 − 9
11. 8 − 8
12. 13 − 9
13. 13 − 7
14. 17 − 8
15. 10 − 8
16. 14 − 7
17. 10 − 3
18. 15 − 6

Name ____

Adding 3-digit numbers

Add ones and regroup.	Add tens.	Add hundreds.
1 334 +249 3	1 334 +249 83	1 334 +249 583

EXERCISES

Give each sum.

1. 327 +456	**2.** 214 +328	**3.** 326 +252	**4.** 226 +443	**5.** 418 +226
6. 459 +216	**7.** 524 +329	**8.** 238 +401	**9.** 406 +357	**10.** 308 +178
11. 352 +531	**12.** 238 +406	**13.** 468 +317	**14.** 342 +342	**15.** 526 +269
16. 469 +319	**17.** 254 +439	**18.** 306 +582	**19.** 529 +101	**20.** 348 +317

Problem Solving

21. How many tickets did the first grade sell? ________

22. How many tickets did the third grade sell? ________

23. How many tickets did the fourth grade sell? ________

24. Did the second grade sell fewer than 200 tickets? ________

25. Who sold more tickets, the fifth grade or the sixth grade? ________

Puppet Show

Tickets Sold	First Week	Second Week
First Grade	123	105
Second Grade	96	89
Third Grade	108	95
Fourth Grade	119	125
Fifth Grade	98	98
Sixth Grade	89	105

Name ______________________________

Addition—regrouping tens

Add ones.

```
  263
+ 584
    7
```

Add tens.

```
  263
+ 584
  147
```

Regroup.

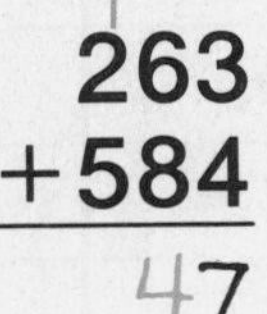

```
   1
  263
+ 584
   47
```

Add hundreds.

```
   1
  263
  584
  847
```

EXERCISES

Add.

1. 354 + 281	**2.** 562 + 253	**3.** 293 + 483	**4.** 570 + 246	**5.** 392 + 165
6. 546 + 237	**7.** 444 + 393	**8.** 637 + 358	**9.** 453 + 274	**10.** 275 + 321
11. 406 + 27	**12.** 524 + 93	**13.** 49 + 107	**14.** 87 + 462	**15.** 178 + 12
16. $3.88 + 4.21	**17.** $4.07 + 2.32	**18.** $5.04 + 1.77	**19.** $2.18 + 1.91	**20.** $5.46 + 2.93

21. 256 + 371 = ______

22. 583 + 195 = ______

23. 666 + 73 = ______

24. 85 + 307 = ______

25. 94 + 524 = ______

26. 477 + 182 = ______

27. 51 + 63 + 45 = ______

28. 326 + 81 + 140 = ______

Complete these tables.

Add 43.

29.	65	108
30.	93	
31.	174	
32.	126	
33.	594	

Add 356.

34.	293	
35.	182	
36.	327	
37.	460	
38.	271	

Problem Solving

39. Tumbling Tim did 43 flips in the afternoon show and 29 flips in the evening show.

How many flips did he do in all? ______

40. Tumbling Tina gave 15 shows in one week. 9 of the shows were at night. How many shows were not at night? ______

41. Tina climbed 23 steps to the low swing. She climbed 48 more steps to the high swing. How many steps did she take to get to the high swing? ______

42. Tim practiced 152 minutes on Monday and 239 minutes on Tuesday. How many minutes did he practice in all? ______

KEEPING SKILLS SHARP

Round to the nearest ten.

1. 26 ______
2. 31 ______
3. 45 ______
4. 48 ______
5. 53 ______
6. 56 ______
7. 74 ______
8. 62 ______
9. 93 ______
10. 95 ______

Round to the nearest hundred.

11. 108 ______
12. 128 ______
13. 153 ______
14. 247 ______
15. 285 ______
16. 295 ______
17. 332 ______
18. 476 ______
19. 534 ______
20. 593 ______
21. 628 ______
22. 914 ______
23. 806 ______
24. 799 ______

Name

Adding—regrouping ones and tens

Add ones.

$$\begin{array}{r} 285 \\ +376 \\ \hline \end{array}$$

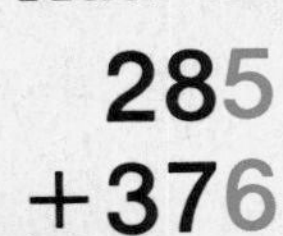

Regroup.

$$\begin{array}{r} {}^{1} \\ 285 \\ +376 \\ \hline 1 \end{array}$$

Add tens.

$$\begin{array}{r} {}^{1} \\ 285 \\ +376 \\ \hline 1 \end{array}$$

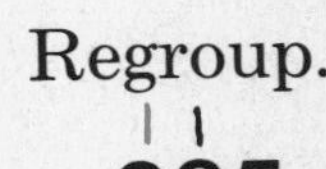

Regroup.

$$\begin{array}{r} {}^{1\,1} \\ 285 \\ +376 \\ \hline 61 \end{array}$$

Add hundreds.

$$\begin{array}{r} {}^{1\,1} \\ 285 \\ +376 \\ \hline 661 \end{array}$$

EXERCISES

Add.

1. 295 + 376	**2.** 378 + 256	**3.** 467 + 384	**4.** 275 + 468	**5.** 593 + 247
6. 384 + 229	**7.** 508 + 296	**8.** 352 + 580	**9.** 392 + 341	**10.** 524 + 168
11. 395 + 271	**12.** 458 + 458	**13.** 729 + 158	**14.** 476 + 258	**15.** 258 + 476

16. \$5.92 +3.24

17. \$7.59 +2.16

18. \$3.88 +4.56

19. \$2.97 +6.29

20. \$3.46 +5.32

21. 153 68 +53

22. 253 24 +145

23. 138 54 +95

24. 536 129 +43

25. 206 58 +8

26. 316 208 54 +19

27. 158 74 130 +87

28. 156 241 58 +267

29. 374 29 162 +6

30. 593 106 86 +7

Complete.

31.

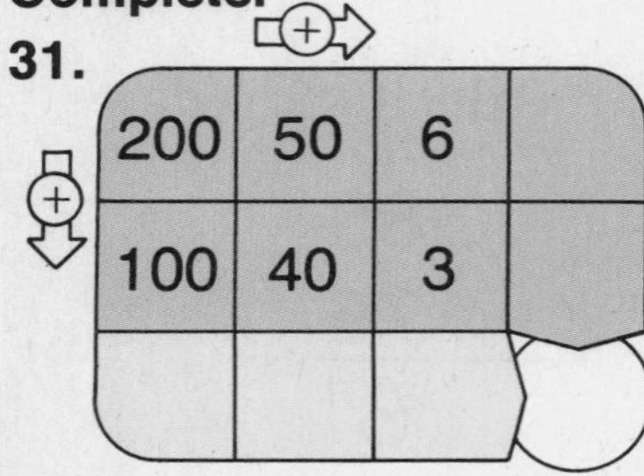

32.

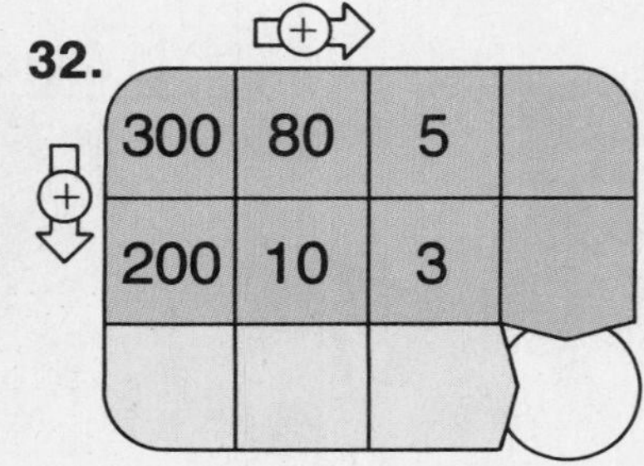

33.

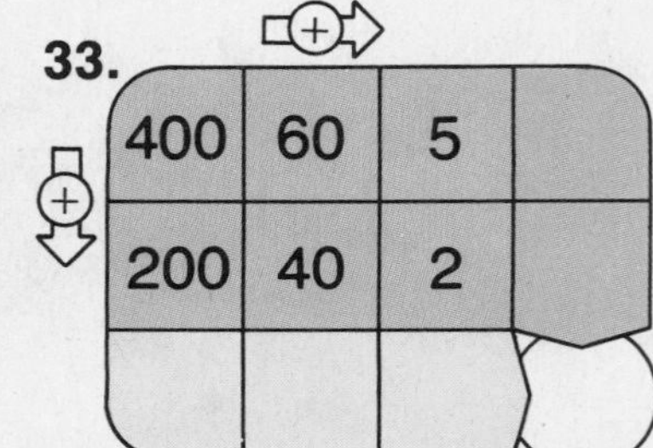

Challenge!

Find the missing digit.

34. 52 +243 = 764

35. 3 4 +452 = 756

36. 326 +14 = 473

37. 4 2 +184 = 616

38. 21 +315 = 533

39. 75 +286 = 761

Name ______________________________

Adding—regrouping ones, tens, and hundreds

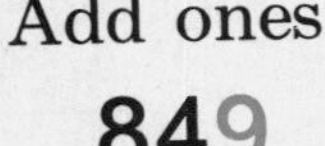

Add ones.

$$\begin{array}{r} 849 \\ +276 \\ \hline 15 \end{array}$$

Regroup.

$$\begin{array}{r} \overset{1}{8}49 \\ +276 \\ \hline 5 \end{array}$$

Add tens.

$$\begin{array}{r} 849 \\ +276 \\ \hline 12\,5 \end{array}$$

Regroup.

$$\begin{array}{r} 849 \\ +276 \\ \hline 25 \end{array}$$

Add hundreds.

$$\begin{array}{r} 849 \\ +276 \\ \hline 1125 \end{array}$$

I thousand and I hundred.

EXERCISES

Add.

1. 524 + 960	**2.** 613 + 821	**3.** 752 + 654	**4.** 829 + 374	**5.** 456 + 597
6. 729 + 308	**7.** 835 + 214	**8.** 653 + 378	**9.** 514 + 795	**10.** 953 + 689
11. 695 + 546	**12.** 747 + 859	**13.** 513 + 358	**14.** 829 + 173	**15.** 382 + 956

16. 584 + 592

17. 959 + 386

18. 626 + 958

19. 846 + 759

20. 758 + 279

21. 738 + 497

22. 675 + 386

23. 890 + 278

24. 853 + 589

25. 629 + 296

26. $7.52 + 6.51

27. $2.59 + 9.58

28. $9.14 + 7.59

29. $3.74 + 6.80

30. $8.29 + 3.58

31. 829 + 370 = ______

32. 596 + 748 = ______

33. 785 + 391 = ______

34. 593 + 278 = ______

35. 605 + 597 = ______

36. 665 + 487 = ______

37. $8.56 + $8.56 = ______

38. $9.58 + $7.96 = ______

Problem Solving

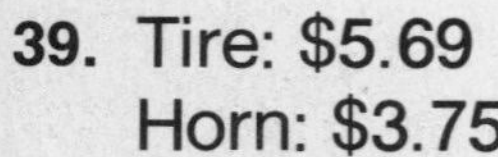

39. Tire: $5.69
Horn: $3.75
How much for both? ______

★ 40. Bicycle: $92.50
Light: $4.59
How much for both? ______

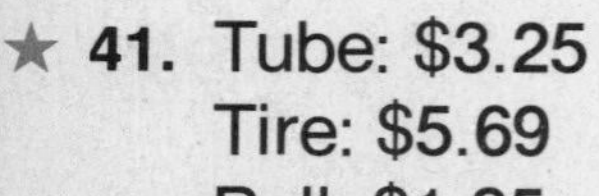

★ 41. Tube: $3.25
Tire: $5.69
Bell: $1.85
How much for all? ______

Name ____________________

Estimating sums

Sometimes you do not need an exact answer. Then you can **estimate**.

One way to estimate a sum is to round each addend.

To estimate this sum:

$$\begin{array}{r} 29 \\ +54 \\ \hline \end{array} \quad \begin{array}{l} \text{round to} \\ \text{round to} \end{array} \quad \begin{array}{r} 30 \\ +50 \\ \hline 80 \end{array}$$

The sum is about 80.

To estimate this sum:

$$\begin{array}{r} 227 \\ +584 \\ \hline \end{array} \quad \begin{array}{l} \text{round to} \\ \text{round to} \end{array} \quad \begin{array}{r} 200 \\ +600 \\ \hline 800 \end{array}$$

The sum is about 800.

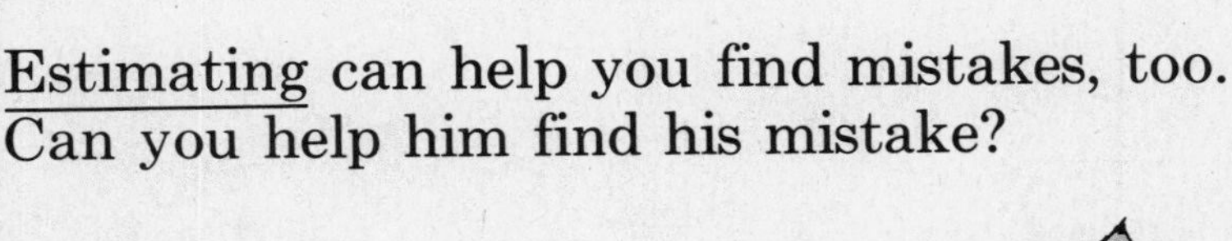

Estimating can help you find mistakes, too.
Can you help him find his mistake?

40+20=60
The answer should be around 60. I must have made a mistake.
37
+18
45

EXERCISES

Round to the nearest ten.
Estimate each sum.

1. $\begin{array}{r} 48 \\ +17 \\ \hline \end{array}$	**2.** $\begin{array}{r} 39 \\ +49 \\ \hline \end{array}$	**3.** $\begin{array}{r} 52 \\ +21 \\ \hline \end{array}$	**4.** $\begin{array}{r} 63 \\ +17 \\ \hline \end{array}$	**5.** $\begin{array}{r} 74 \\ +15 \\ \hline \end{array}$
6. $\begin{array}{r} 39 \\ +38 \\ \hline \end{array}$	**7.** $\begin{array}{r} 42 \\ +27 \\ \hline \end{array}$	**8.** $\begin{array}{r} 51 \\ +38 \\ \hline \end{array}$	**9.** $\begin{array}{r} 42 \\ +59 \\ \hline \end{array}$	**10.** $\begin{array}{r} 37 \\ +63 \\ \hline \end{array}$

Round to the nearest hundred.
Estimate each sum.

11. $\begin{array}{r} 327 \\ +318 \\ \hline \end{array}$	**12.** $\begin{array}{r} 219 \\ +478 \\ \hline \end{array}$	**13.** $\begin{array}{r} 421 \\ +308 \\ \hline \end{array}$	**14.** $\begin{array}{r} 524 \\ +389 \\ \hline \end{array}$	**15.** $\begin{array}{r} 275 \\ +190 \\ \hline \end{array}$

Which sum is greater?

1.

H	T	O
3	8	5
6	5	9

10 4 4

H	T	O
5	3	6
5	8	9

2.

H	T	O
7	4	3
8	5	9

H	T	O
7	5	8
9	3	4

3.

H	T	O
9	6	7
5	3	8

H	T	O
7	9	3
6	8	5

4.

H	T	O
7	4	8
6	5	9

H	T	O
6	9	5
8	7	4

Play the game.

H	T	O

1. Draw a table like this one.
2. As your teacher picks a card, write the digit in any place in your table.
3. After six digits have been picked, add your numbers.
4. The player who gets the greatest sum wins!

Name ____________________

Problem Solving Using a chart

Admission	
Adult	$3.00
Children (under 12)	1.75
Rides	
Bumper cars	1.00
Ferris wheel	.75
Merry-go-round	.75
Mousetrap	.50
Parachute	1.25
Pony ride	.50
Roller coaster	1.50

Work in groups. Use a calculator to help you. Record your answers on a separate sheet of paper.

1. Write a story about what rides you would go on if you had $5.00 to spend on a field trip to a carnival. Tell how much you would spend and how much you would have left. In each group, compare and discuss each story.
2. If you had $10.00, would you have enough money for admission and to ride each ride once?
3. Sue spent exactly $5.00 on rides. As you answer the following questions, keep a record of your answers.
   a. What combination of rides could she have gone on?
   b. How many different combinations did your group find?
   c. What different ways did you use to help you find the answers?

4. Find another group and compare your answers to exercise 3.

5. Suppose Ed had $5.00 to spend on rides. He went on the same ride over and over until nothing was left.
   a. Which rides could he have gone on to do that?
   b. How many times could he go on each of those rides over and over?
   c. How did you find the answer? Discuss.

6. Together Kyle and Colin bought seven tickets. One was for the Ferris wheel, two for the pony ride, one for the bumper cars, two for the mousetrap, and one for the parachute. What did each boy ride? Use the clues to find the answer.

   Clues:
   - Neither boy went on a ride twice.
   - Colin went on four rides.
   - In all, Colin's rides cost **50¢** more than Kyle's.

7. Make up your own problem with clues about the carnival rides.

Name ____________________

Adding larger numbers

Large numbers can be added in the same way as smaller numbers.

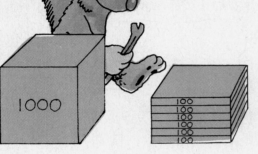

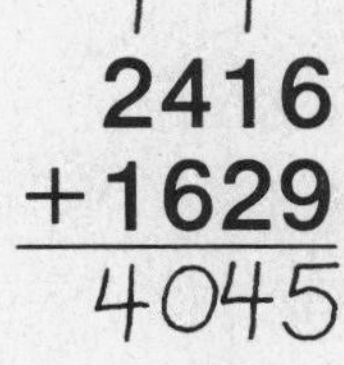

EXERCISES

Add.

1. 3278 + 4125	**2.** 7463 + 1282	**3.** 5067 + 3543	**4.** 3333 + 1586
5. 2654 + 3528	**6.** 3614 + 2537	**7.** 2579 + 5426	**8.** 5426 + 2579
9. 2718 + 3295	**10.** 5583 + 2978	**11.** 4729 + 4873	**12.** 5979 + 3864

13. 5785 + 2336 = ______

14. 6157 + 1289 = ______

15. 3859 + 4675 = ______

16. 2856 + 2344 = ______

17. 7825 + 358 = ______

18. 3650 + 799 = ______

19. 5368 + 754 = ______

20. 526 + 4859 = ______

21. 7218 + 1395 = ________ 22. 6284 + 2593 = ________

23. 4706 + 395 = ________ 24. 467 + 2953 = ________

Challenge!

Find the two wrong answers.
Correct them.

25. 1000 more than the sum of 2168 and 3042 equals

______

26. 100 more than the sum of 3745 and 1782 equals

______

27. 10 more than the sum of 3666 and 333 equals

4099

______

28. 20 more than the double of 4537 equals

9094

______

KEEPING SKILLS SHARP

Write the number.

1. fifty-six __________
2. ninety __________
3. one hundred three __________
4. one hundred sixty-seven __________
5. two thousand three hundred __________
6. five thousand forty-six __________
7. four thousand one hundred forty __________
8. six thousand two hundred eleven __________
9. nine thousand two hundred fifteen __________
10. eight thousand five __________

Name ____________________

Problem Solving Using data

Mrs. Barnes, the coach, uses a computer to keep records for each class. The computer screen shows the students' records.

BOUNCES WITHOUT MISSING

NAME	FIRST TRY	SECOND TRY	THIRD TRY
ALICE	37	32	27
CARMEN	49	30	28
ELENA	19	51	52
GRACE	44	38	27
JOHN	28	35	46
LORI	29	50	43
MANDY	40	43	31
RICARDO	50	42	30

Solve.

1. How many bounces did Alice get on her
   a. first try? ________
   b. second try? ________
   c. third try? ________

2. Who had the most bounces on the
   a. first try? ________
   b. second try? ________
   c. third try? ________

3. Who had more bounces on their second try than on their first try? ________

4. What was the total of Lori's first and second tries? ________

5. What was the total number of bounces for Alice? ________

6. What was the total number of bounces for Carmen? ________

7. Who had the greater total, Alice or Carmen? ________

8. What was John's total? ________

9. What was Elena's total? ________

10. Who had the greater total, John or Elena? ________

★ 11. Who had the greater total, Grace or Mandy? ________

★ 12. Who had the greatest total? ________

★ 13. Who had the lowest total? ________

★ 14. How many had a greater total than Ricardo? ________

Name ____________________

Chapter Checkup

Give each sum. [pages 70–75, 78–80, 82–87, 89, 92–93]

1. $\begin{array}{r} 56 \\ +28 \\ \hline \end{array}$

2. $\begin{array}{r} 37 \\ +6 \\ \hline \end{array}$

3. $\begin{array}{r} 76 \\ +35 \\ \hline \end{array}$

4. $\begin{array}{r} 84 \\ +76 \\ \hline \end{array}$

5. $\begin{array}{r} 59 \\ +57 \\ \hline \end{array}$

6. $\begin{array}{r} 25 \\ 38 \\ +29 \\ \hline \end{array}$

7. $\begin{array}{r} 42 \\ 18 \\ +6 \\ \hline \end{array}$

8. $\begin{array}{r} 59 \\ 7 \\ +26 \\ \hline \end{array}$

9. $\begin{array}{r} 25 \\ 53 \\ +18 \\ \hline \end{array}$

10. $\begin{array}{r} 29 \\ 30 \\ +31 \\ \hline \end{array}$

11. $\begin{array}{r} 352 \\ +594 \\ \hline \end{array}$

12. $\begin{array}{r} 635 \\ +281 \\ \hline \end{array}$

13. $\begin{array}{r} 734 \\ +586 \\ \hline \end{array}$

14. $\begin{array}{r} 598 \\ +275 \\ \hline \end{array}$

15. $\begin{array}{r} 659 \\ +748 \\ \hline \end{array}$

16. 23 + 36 = ______

17. 58 + 29 = ______

18. 159 + 283 = ______

19. 325 + 875 = ______

Estimate each sum. [page 88]

20. $\begin{array}{r} 47 \\ +39 \\ \hline \end{array}$

21. $\begin{array}{r} 52 \\ +67 \\ \hline \end{array}$

22. $\begin{array}{r} 327 \\ +188 \\ \hline \end{array}$

Give the total price. [pages 76–77, 81, 90–91, 94–95]

23.

______

24.

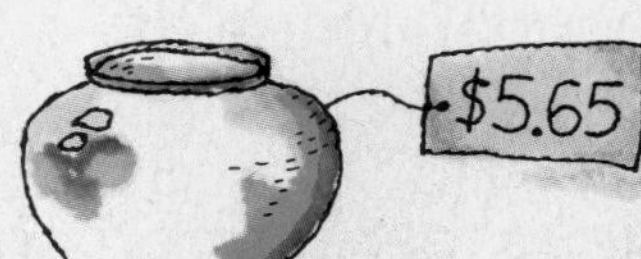

______

Chapter Project

MAKING A GRAPH

1. Get two blocks and number the sides 1 through 6.
2. Get a piece of graph paper and put the numbers 2 through 12 at the bottom.
3. Roll your blocks and graph the sum of the "up" numbers.
4. Do step 3 about 50 times.
5. Tell some things that your graph shows.

Name ______________________________

Chapter Review

REGROUP 10 ONES FOR 1 TEN

$$\begin{array}{r} \scriptstyle 1 \\ 45 \\ +27 \\ \hline 72 \end{array}$$

REGROUP ONES AND TENS

$$\begin{array}{r} \scriptstyle 1 \\ 68 \\ +59 \\ \hline 127 \end{array}$$

REGROUP 20 ONES FOR 2 TENS

$$\begin{array}{r} \scriptstyle 2 \\ 35 \\ 28 \\ +39 \\ \hline 102 \end{array}$$

REGROUP ONES AND TENS

$$\begin{array}{r} \scriptstyle 11 \\ 395 \\ +246 \\ \hline 641 \end{array}$$

REGROUP ONES, TENS, AND HUNDREDS

$$\begin{array}{r} \scriptstyle 11 \\ 578 \\ +943 \\ \hline 1521 \end{array}$$

Add.

1. $\begin{array}{r} 53 \\ +21 \\ \hline \end{array}$ **2.** $\begin{array}{r} 74 \\ +15 \\ \hline \end{array}$ **3.** $\begin{array}{r} 61 \\ +6 \\ \hline \end{array}$

4. $\begin{array}{r} 36 \\ +28 \\ \hline \end{array}$ **5.** $\begin{array}{r} 47 \\ +7 \\ \hline \end{array}$ **6.** $\begin{array}{r} 18 \\ +65 \\ \hline \end{array}$

7. $\begin{array}{r} 59 \\ +68 \\ \hline \end{array}$ **8.** $\begin{array}{r} 74 \\ +36 \\ \hline \end{array}$ **9.** $\begin{array}{r} 65 \\ +57 \\ \hline \end{array}$

10. $\begin{array}{r} 49 \\ 13 \\ +28 \\ \hline \end{array}$ **11.** $\begin{array}{r} 36 \\ 29 \\ +18 \\ \hline \end{array}$ **12.** $\begin{array}{r} 27 \\ 59 \\ +8 \\ \hline \end{array}$

13. $\begin{array}{r} 259 \\ +386 \\ \hline \end{array}$ **14.** $\begin{array}{r} 758 \\ +165 \\ \hline \end{array}$ **15.** $\begin{array}{r} 387 \\ +546 \\ \hline \end{array}$

16. $\begin{array}{r} 674 \\ +829 \\ \hline \end{array}$ **17.** $\begin{array}{r} 253 \\ +978 \\ \hline \end{array}$ **18.** $\begin{array}{r} 768 \\ +697 \\ \hline \end{array}$

Chapter Challenge

MAGIC SQUARES

This is a magic square because all the sums are the same.

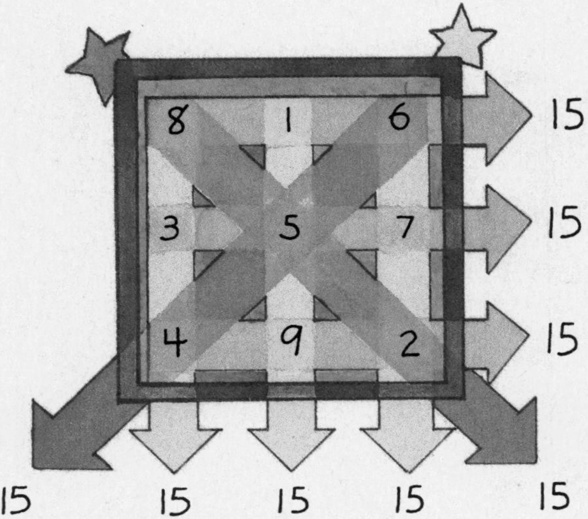

Are these magic squares?

1.

16	2	12
6	10	14
8	18	4

______

2.

80	10	60
30	50	70
40	90	20

______

3.

30	23	28
25	27	29
26	31	24

______

4.

27	31	24
25	26	29
30	23	28

______

5. Start with the magic square at the top of the page. Make a new square by adding 10 to each number.

18	11	16
13		

Do you get a magic square? ______

Name ____________________

Cumulative Checkup

STANDARDIZED FORMAT

Give the correct letter.

1. Add.

$$\begin{array}{r} 9 \\ +8 \\ \hline \end{array}$$

a. 16
b. 17
c. 18
d. 15

2. Complete.
6 + ? = 9

a. 15
b. 13
c. 14
d. none of these

3. Subtract.

$$\begin{array}{r} 16 \\ -7 \\ \hline \end{array}$$

a. 9
b. 7
c. 8
d. none of these

4. How much money?
2 dimes
3 nickels
3 pennies

a. 34¢ **b.** 42¢
c. 43¢ **d.** 38¢

5. The 8 in 583 stands for

a. 8 ones
b. 8 hundreds
c. 8 tens
d. none of these

6. 342 rounded to the nearest hundred is

a. 340
b. 350
c. 400
d. 300

7. In 7958, which digit is in the thousands place?

a. 8
b. 9
c. 7
d. 5

8. Which is the most money?

a. $2.56
b. $1.65
c. $2.65
d. $1.56

9. Add.
38 + 27

a. 65
b. 55
c. 75
d. none of these

10. Add.

$$\begin{array}{r} 659 \\ +245 \\ \hline \end{array}$$

a. 894
b. 804
c. 904
d. none of these

11. Milk: $.35
Hot dog: $.85
What is the total price?

a. $.50 **b.** $1.10
c. $1.20 **d.** none of these

12. 48 boys
37 girls
How many children?

a. 11 **b.** 75
c. 85 **d.** none of these

4

Subtraction

Maria had 20 baby teeth. She has lost 5 of them. How many baby teeth does she have left?

Name ____

READY OR NOT?

1. $\begin{array}{r} 14 \\ -6 \\ \hline \end{array}$
2. $\begin{array}{r} 13 \\ -9 \\ \hline \end{array}$
3. $\begin{array}{r} 15 \\ -6 \\ \hline \end{array}$
4. $\begin{array}{r} 9 \\ -9 \\ \hline \end{array}$
5. $\begin{array}{r} 14 \\ -7 \\ \hline \end{array}$
6. $\begin{array}{r} 16 \\ -8 \\ \hline \end{array}$
7. $\begin{array}{r} 11 \\ -9 \\ \hline \end{array}$
8. $\begin{array}{r} 17 \\ -9 \\ \hline \end{array}$
9. $\begin{array}{r} 11 \\ -8 \\ \hline \end{array}$
10. $\begin{array}{r} 18 \\ -9 \\ \hline \end{array}$
11. $\begin{array}{r} 12 \\ -9 \\ \hline \end{array}$
12. $\begin{array}{r} 10 \\ -6 \\ \hline \end{array}$

Subtracting 2-digit numbers

To find the difference, we first subtract the ones.

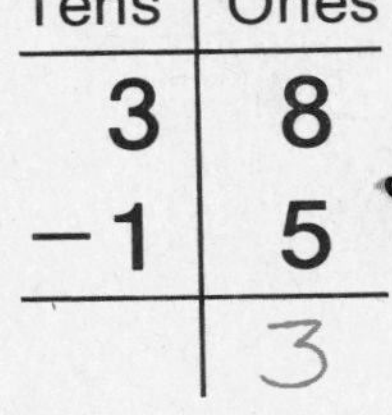

Tens	Ones
3	8
−1	5
	3

Then we subtract the tens.

Tens	Ones
3	8
−1	5
2	3

There are 23 eggs left.

EXERCISES

Subtract.

1. $\begin{array}{r} 36 \\ -12 \\ \hline \end{array}$
2. $\begin{array}{r} 39 \\ -16 \\ \hline \end{array}$
3. $\begin{array}{r} 43 \\ -20 \\ \hline \end{array}$

4. $\begin{array}{r} 48 \\ -23 \\ \hline \end{array}$

5. $\begin{array}{r} 47 \\ -15 \\ \hline \end{array}$

6. $\begin{array}{r} 38 \\ -16 \\ \hline \end{array}$

7. $\begin{array}{r} 59 \\ -25 \\ \hline \end{array}$

8. $\begin{array}{r} 28 \\ -25 \\ \hline \end{array}$

9. $\begin{array}{r} 59 \\ -35 \\ \hline \end{array}$

10. $\begin{array}{r} 39 \\ -29 \\ \hline \end{array}$

11. $\begin{array}{r} 57 \\ -52 \\ \hline \end{array}$

12. $\begin{array}{r} 65 \\ -11 \\ \hline \end{array}$

13. $\begin{array}{r} 60 \\ -10 \\ \hline \end{array}$

14. $\begin{array}{r} 46 \\ -15 \\ \hline \end{array}$

15. $\begin{array}{r} 79 \\ -63 \\ \hline \end{array}$

16. $\begin{array}{r} 44 \\ -12 \\ \hline \end{array}$

17. $\begin{array}{r} 77 \\ -71 \\ \hline \end{array}$

18. $\begin{array}{r} 53 \\ -32 \\ \hline \end{array}$

19. $\begin{array}{r} 85 \\ -45 \\ \hline \end{array}$

20. $\begin{array}{r} 86 \\ -53 \\ \hline \end{array}$

21. $\begin{array}{r} 65 \\ -40 \\ \hline \end{array}$

22. $\begin{array}{r} 56 \\ -21 \\ \hline \end{array}$

23. $\begin{array}{r} 74 \\ -74 \\ \hline \end{array}$

24. $\begin{array}{r} 75 \\ -31 \\ \hline \end{array}$

25. $\begin{array}{r} 88 \\ -46 \\ \hline \end{array}$

26. $\begin{array}{r} 69 \\ -25 \\ \hline \end{array}$

27. $\begin{array}{r} 78 \\ -63 \\ \hline \end{array}$

28. $\begin{array}{r} 96 \\ -30 \\ \hline \end{array}$

29. 68 − 24 = ________

30. 80 − 20 = ________

31. 95 − 25 = ________

32. 76 − 33 = ________

33. 87 − 45 = ________

Challenge!

Give the key (+ or −) you would push to get the answer.

34. 28 ☐ 13 ☐ 12 = 29

35. 48 ☐ 25 ☐ 31 = 54

36. 49 ☐ 14 ☐ 32 = 95

37. 68 ☐ 21 ☐ 25 = 22

38. 77 ☐ 52 ☐ 43 = 68

(one hundred three) 103

Name ______________________________

Subtracting with regrouping

When there are not enough ones, you have to regroup.

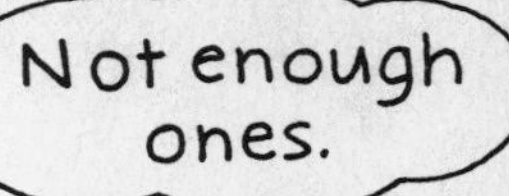

$$\begin{array}{r} 32 \\ -15 \\ \hline \end{array}$$

$$\begin{array}{r} {\scriptstyle 2\ 12} \\ \not{3}\not{2} \\ -15 \\ \hline \end{array}$$

$$\begin{array}{r} {\scriptstyle 2\ 12} \\ \not{3}\not{2} \\ -15 \\ \hline 17 \end{array}$$

EXERCISES

Do you have to regroup?
Yes or no?

1. $\begin{array}{r} 64 \\ -32 \\ \hline \end{array}$ ______
2. $\begin{array}{r} 64 \\ -34 \\ \hline \end{array}$ ______
3. $\begin{array}{r} 64 \\ -35 \\ \hline \end{array}$ ______
4. $\begin{array}{r} 70 \\ -25 \\ \hline \end{array}$ ______
5. $\begin{array}{r} 34 \\ -29 \\ \hline \end{array}$ ______
6. $\begin{array}{r} 47 \\ -21 \\ \hline \end{array}$ ______
7. $\begin{array}{r} 85 \\ -34 \\ \hline \end{array}$ ______
8. $\begin{array}{r} 76 \\ -49 \\ \hline \end{array}$ ______
9. $\begin{array}{r} 56 \\ -18 \\ \hline \end{array}$ ______
10. $\begin{array}{r} 93 \\ -19 \\ \hline \end{array}$ ______

Subtract.

11. $\begin{array}{r} 31 \\ -18 \\ \hline \end{array}$

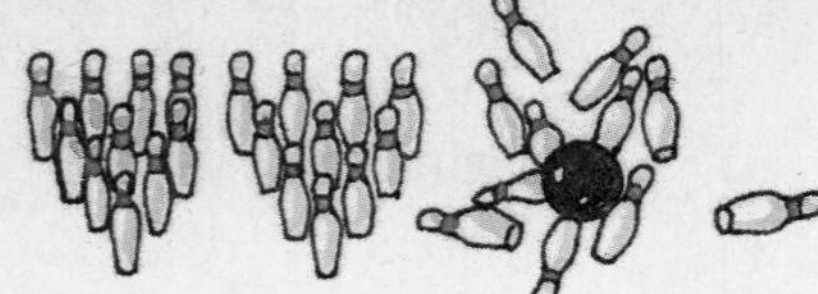

12. $\begin{array}{r} 33 \\ -15 \\ \hline \end{array}$

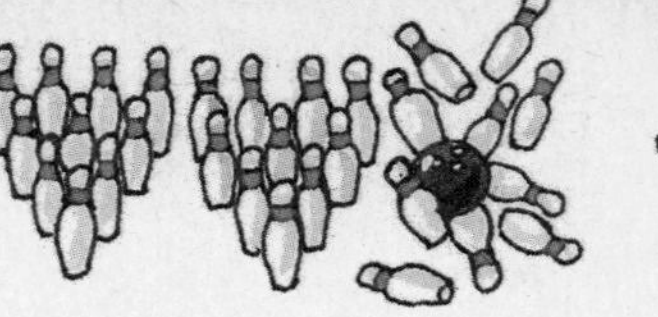

13. $\begin{array}{r} 44 \\ -19 \\ \hline \end{array}$

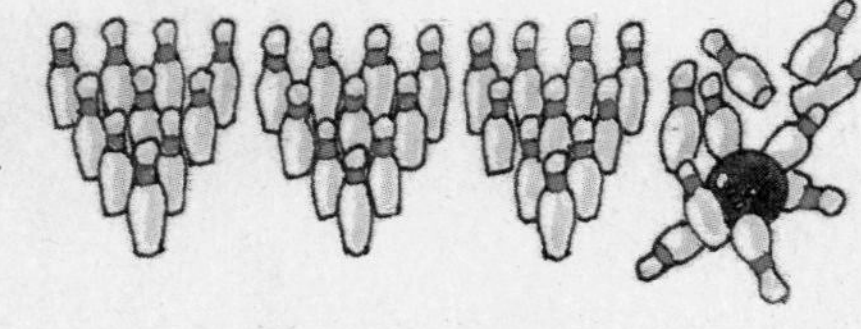

14. $\begin{array}{r} 45 \\ -28 \\ \hline \end{array}$

15. $\begin{array}{r} 50 \\ -32 \\ \hline \end{array}$ 16. $\begin{array}{r} 33 \\ -12 \\ \hline \end{array}$ 17. $\begin{array}{r} 41 \\ -23 \\ \hline \end{array}$ 18. $\begin{array}{r} 74 \\ -58 \\ \hline \end{array}$ 19. $\begin{array}{r} 62 \\ -31 \\ \hline \end{array}$

20. $\begin{array}{r} 65 \\ -18 \\ \hline \end{array}$ 21. $\begin{array}{r} 54 \\ -45 \\ \hline \end{array}$ 22. $\begin{array}{r} 82 \\ -25 \\ \hline \end{array}$ 23. $\begin{array}{r} 51 \\ -46 \\ \hline \end{array}$ 24. $\begin{array}{r} 90 \\ -42 \\ \hline \end{array}$

25. $\begin{array}{r} 64 \\ -32 \\ \hline \end{array}$ 26. $\begin{array}{r} 81 \\ -26 \\ \hline \end{array}$ 27. $\begin{array}{r} 52 \\ -39 \\ \hline \end{array}$ 28. $\begin{array}{r} 42 \\ -16 \\ \hline \end{array}$ 29. $\begin{array}{r} 50 \\ -35 \\ \hline \end{array}$

30. $\begin{array}{r} 40 \\ -18 \\ \hline \end{array}$ 31. $\begin{array}{r} 53 \\ -36 \\ \hline \end{array}$ 32. $\begin{array}{r} 70 \\ -49 \\ \hline \end{array}$ 33. $\begin{array}{r} 43 \\ -21 \\ \hline \end{array}$ 34. $\begin{array}{r} 44 \\ -32 \\ \hline \end{array}$

35. $\begin{array}{r} 80 \\ -35 \\ \hline \end{array}$ 36. $\begin{array}{r} 63 \\ -22 \\ \hline \end{array}$ 37. $\begin{array}{r} 71 \\ -65 \\ \hline \end{array}$ 38. $\begin{array}{r} 80 \\ -63 \\ \hline \end{array}$ 39. $\begin{array}{r} 61 \\ -58 \\ \hline \end{array}$

To subtract 9, I can subtract 10 and then add 1.
Shortcut

Mental Math

Use the shortcut.

40. 66 − 9 = ________ 41. 45 − 9 = ________

42. 53 − 9 = ________ 43. 91 − 9 = ________

44. 72 − 9 = ________ 45. 80 − 9 = ________

Name ____________________

Addition and subtraction

Work in pairs.
Record your answers on a separate sheet of paper.
Get a set of base ten blocks and a calculator.
Each partner makes a chart like this:

My number	Partner's number	Problem and sum	Sum minus partner's number

1. You and your partner each pick a number between 10 and 50, and each write it in the first column of your own chart. Write your partner's number in the second column of your chart.

2. Each partner shows the number with base-ten blocks.

   Here is how Kathy wrote her number and her partner Bill's number on her chart:

Kathy's chart

My number	Partner's number
46	35

Kathy shows her number with blocks.

Here is how Bill wrote his number and Kathy's number on his chart:

Bill's chart

My number	Partner's number
35	46

Bill shows his number with blocks.

3. Put both sets of blocks together and write the problem and sum in the third column. (Remember to regroup.)

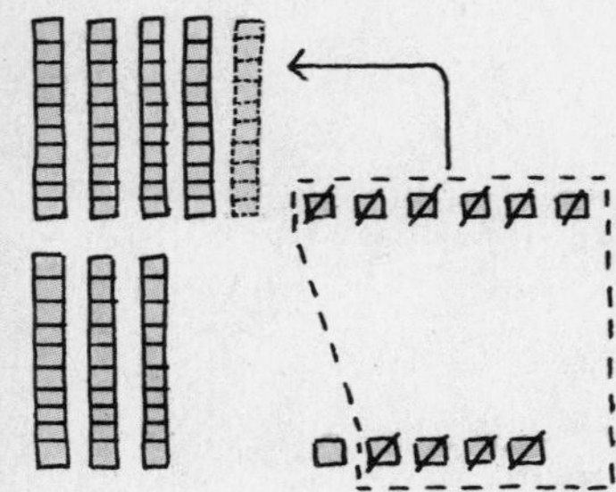

Kathy's chart

My number	Partner's number	Problem and sum	Sum minus partner's number
46	35	46 + 35 = 81	

4. Use the base ten blocks to subtract your partner's number from the sum. (Remember to regroup.)

5. Write the problem and the answer in the fourth column.

Kathy's chart

My number	Partner's number	Problem and sum	Sum minus partner's number
46	35	46 + 35 = 81	81 − 35 = 46

6. Repeat exercises 1 through 5 with 3 new pairs of numbers. Continue to fill in the chart.

7. Use a calculator to try this with larger numbers.

8. Compare the numbers on your chart with the numbers on your partner's chart.

   a. What do you notice about the numbers in column three? Why do you think this happens? Will this always happen?

   b. What do you notice about the numbers in column four? Why do you think this happens? Will this always happen?

Name ______________________________

Subtracting 3-digit numbers

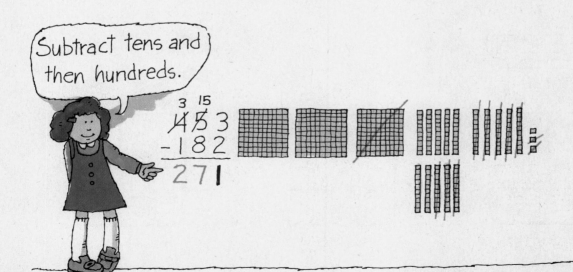

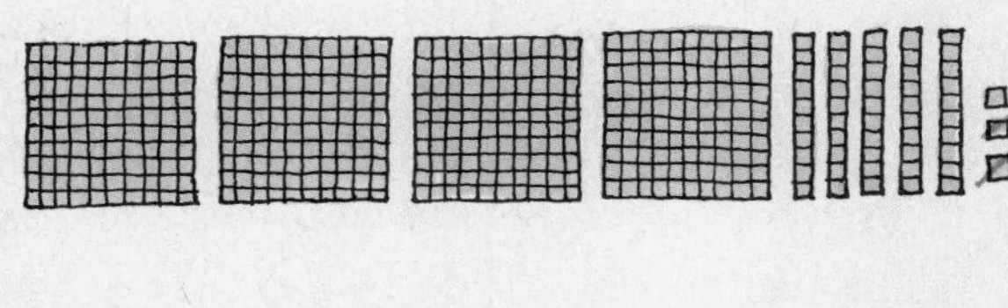

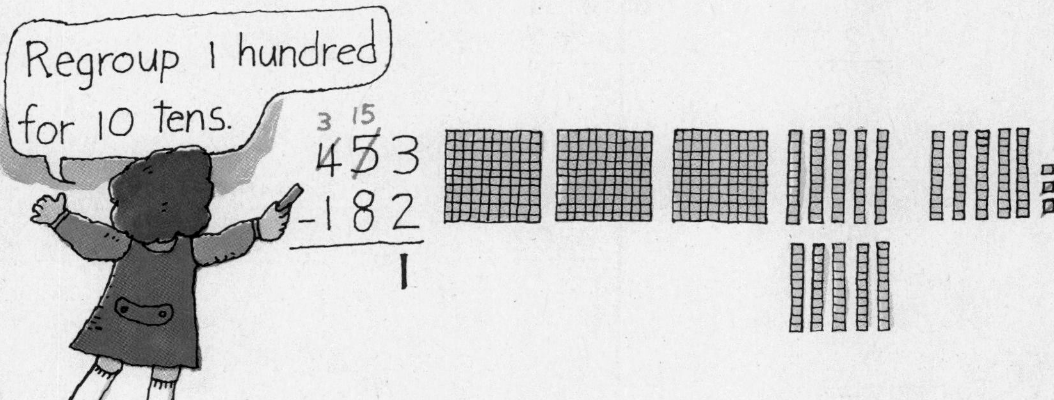

Regroup 1 hundred for 10 tens.
3 15
453
-182
1

Subtract tens and then hundreds.

3 15
453
-182
271

EXERCISES

Subtract.

1. 538 −213	2. 827 −301	3. 658 −283	4. 742 −592	5. 553 −172
6. 757 −166	7. 926 −315	8. 608 −246	9. 591 −300	10. 826 −256
11. 718 −52	12. 655 −85	13. 529 −46	14. 658 −73	15. 704 −91
16. \$5.67 −3.18	17. \$6.23 −2.09	18. \$7.40 −3.28	19. \$9.58 −6.29	20. \$6.25 −5.09
21. \$6.92 −6.58	22. \$7.29 −6.84	23. \$6.08 −4.92	24. \$8.67 −7.59	25. \$5.63 −4.91

26. 819 − 306 = ________

27. 729 − 508 = ________

28. 952 − 372 = ________

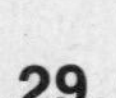

Challenge!

Find a way to push each marked key once to get the answer.

29.

____

30.

____

31.

____

Name

Problem Solving Using a bar graph

Work in groups. Get squared paper.
Record your answers on a separate sheet of paper.
Students in a class at the Apple Tree School were polled. They were asked to tell their favorite sport to play, color, subject, sport to watch, fruit, pizza, and pet. The results of the poll are shown.

Sport to play		Color		Subject	
Baseball	9	Blue	9	Reading	5
Soccer	7	Red	8	Math	7
Swimming	3	Green	3	Spelling	6
Ice skating	2	Yellow	4	Social studies	1
Roller skating	3	Orange	1	Science	3
Football	4	Purple	3	Language	2
Other	2	Other	2	Other	6

Sport to watch		Fruit		Pizza	
Soccer	2	Apple	10	Plain	7
Gymnastics	2	Orange	8	Sausage	6
Football	8	Banana	5	Mushroom	1
Baseball	9	Peach	2	Pepperoni	2
Hockey	4	Pear	1	Onion	5
Basketball	4	Plum	1	Meatball	1
Other	1	Other	3	Other	8

One group showed their results on a bar graph.

Pet	
Cat	7
Dog	9
Gerbil	4
Turtle	2
Bird	1
Fish	3
Other	4

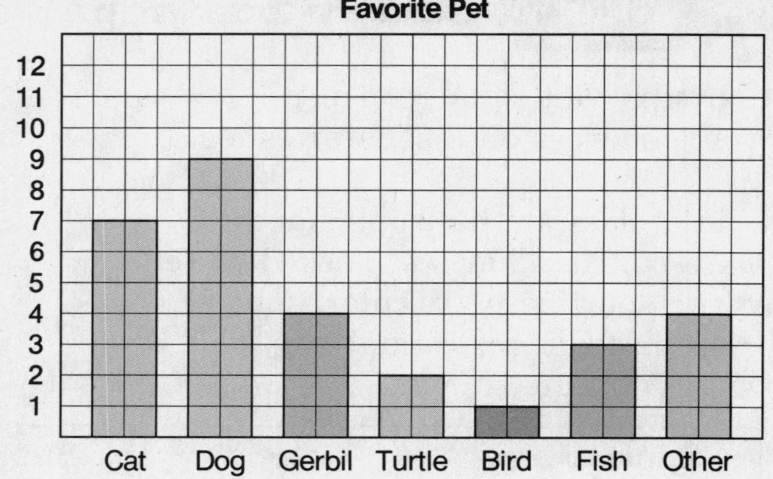

1. Graph the results of one of the items polled on page 110. Make a graph like the one shown above.

2. Now poll the students in your class on the same favorite as the graph you made. Make another graph showing the results of your poll.

3. Compare the Apple Tree School graph and your class graph. Which poll had more students? How can you tell?

4. Do you think the results from either graph would be similar to the results in another class? Why or why not?

5. Do you think the results from either graph would be similar to the results in other classes in the United States? Why or why not?

6. Did the three most popular categories in your class graph make up more than half the votes? Was the same true for the Apple Tree School graph?
   a. What strategy did your group use to answer these questions?
   b. Compare your strategy with that of one other group.
   c. Which strategy worked better?

Name ______________________________

Subtracting 3-digit numbers

Sometimes you have to regroup more than once.

Not enough ones.

$$\begin{array}{r} 542 \\ -277 \\ \hline \end{array}$$

Regroup.

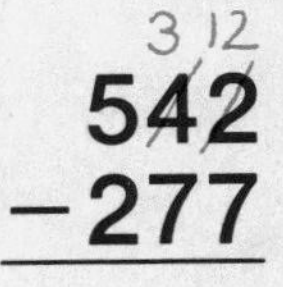

$$\begin{array}{r} {\scriptstyle 3\ 12} \\ 5\not{4}\not{2} \\ -277 \\ \hline \end{array}$$

Subtract ones.

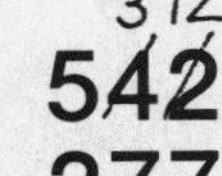

$$\begin{array}{r} {\scriptstyle 3\ 12} \\ 5\not{4}\not{2} \\ -277 \\ \hline 5 \end{array}$$

Regroup.

$$\begin{array}{r} {\scriptstyle 13} \\ {\scriptstyle 4\ \not{3}\ 12} \\ \not{5}\not{4}\not{2} \\ -277 \\ \hline 5 \end{array}$$

Subtract tens.

$$\begin{array}{r} {\scriptstyle 13} \\ {\scriptstyle 4\ \not{3}\ 12} \\ \not{5}\not{4}\not{2} \\ -277 \\ \hline 65 \end{array}$$

Subtract hundreds.

$$\begin{array}{r} {\scriptstyle 13} \\ {\scriptstyle 4\ \not{3}\ 12} \\ \not{5}\not{4}\not{2} \\ -277 \\ \hline 265 \end{array}$$

Water Hole

EXERCISES

Subtract.

1. 346 − 159	**2.** 437 − 289	**3.** 520 − 157	**4.** 638 − 349	**5.** 725 − 558
6. 836 − 597	**7.** 952 − 386	**8.** 735 − 259	**9.** 943 − 478	**10.** 525 − 269

11. 762 −348	**12.** 403 −152	**13.** 571 −329	**14.** 629 −252	**15.** 629 −375
16. 558 −269	**17.** 856 −589	**18.** 482 −194	**19.** 946 −379	**20.** 754 −596
21. 418 −302	**22.** 629 −461	**23.** 753 −48	**24.** 666 −283	**25.** 726 −489

Problem Solving

26. How much do the boxes weigh together? ________

27. How much heavier is the yellow box? ________

KEEPING SKILLS SHARP

Round to the nearest ten.

1. 73 ______	**2.** 78 ______	**3.** 75 ______	**4.** 94 ______	**5.** 97 ______
6. 42 ______	**7.** 38 ______	**8.** 16 ______	**9.** 25 ______	**10.** 8 ______

Round to the nearest hundred.

11. 740 ______	**12.** 793 ______	**13.** 750 ______	**14.** 509 ______	**15.** 581 ______
16. 913 ______	**17.** 821 ______	**18.** 763 ______	**19.** 550 ______	**20.** 847 ______

Name

Subtracting 3-digit numbers

Sometimes you will need to regroup twice before subtracting ones.

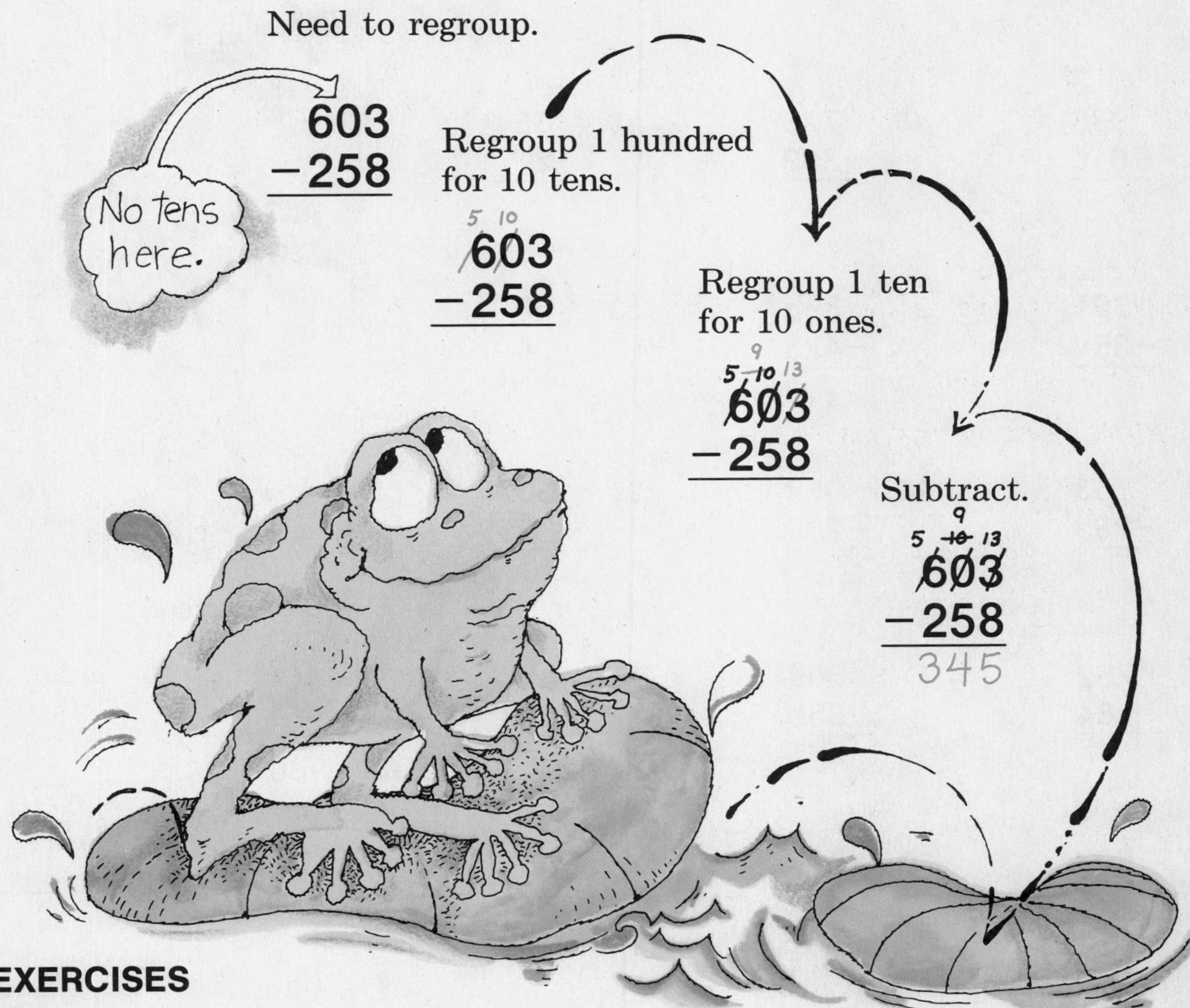

Need to regroup.
603
−258
No tens here.
Regroup 1 hundred for 10 tens.
5 10
603
−258
Regroup 1 ten for 10 ones.
9
5 10 13
603
−258
Subtract.
9
5 10 13
603
−258
345

EXERCISES

Subtract.

1. 801 − 348

2. 702 − 275

3. 605 − 368

4. 403 − 125

5. 304 − 256

6. 906 − 719

7. 801 − 357

8. 700 − 269

9. 603 − 348

10. 500 − 329

11. $594 - 211$

12. $628 - 319$

13. $605 - 453$

14. $725 - 438$

15. $403 - 248$

16. $301 - 158$

17. $935 - 616$

18. $728 - 359$

19. $654 - 277$

20. $701 - 358$

21. $896 - 423$

22. $604 - 241$

23. $753 - 289$

24. $653 - 289$

25. $507 - 358$

26. $752 - 84$

27. $609 - 258$

28. $358 - 299$

29. $802 - 246$

30. $746 - 358$

31. $501 - 216$

32. $563 - 467$

33. $900 - 527$

34. $489 - 325$

35. $634 - 349$

36. $873 - 496$

37. $958 - 659$

Mental Math

To subtract 28, I subtract 30 and then add 2.
SHORTCUT

Use the shortcut.

38. 70 − 28 = ________

39. 60 − 28 = ________

40. 90 − 28 = ________

41. 100 − 28 = ________

42. 150 − 28 = ________

43. 170 − 28 = ________

44. 260 − 28 = ________

45. 350 − 28 = ________

Name ____________________

Practice

EXERCISES

Subtract.

1.	655 −138	**2.**	172 −27	**3.**	503 −434	**4.**	312 −9	**5.**	409 −53
6.	140 −124	**7.**	631 −44	**8.**	913 −272	**9.**	240 −18	**10.**	601 −7
11.	830 −7	**12.**	147 −64	**13.**	500 −9	**14.**	200 −137	**15.**	872 −91
16.	768 −282	**17.**	391 −165	**18.**	586 −28	**19.**	404 −8	**20.**	153 −59
21.	804 −411	**22.**	147 −64	**23.**	702 −296	**24.**	310 −91		
25.	916 −99	**26.**	627 −162	**27.**	852 −36				

Add or subtract.

28.	341 −127	**29.**	701 −685	**30.**	437 +114	**31.**	690 −34	**32.**	743 +96
33.	195 +743	**34.**	512 −82	**35.**	493 +8	**36.**	734 +419	**37.**	336 −182

Problem Solving Acting it out

1. Study and understand.	You can solve the problem by acting it out with play money.
2. Plan and do.	
3. Answer and check.	

Jane had 5 dollars. She earned 3 dollars. Then she spent 2 dollars. She got 4 dollars for her birthday. How many dollars did she have then?

Step 1. Jane had 5 dollars. *Hint:* Put down 5 dollars.

Step 2. She earned 3 dollars. *Hint:* Put down 3 more dollars.

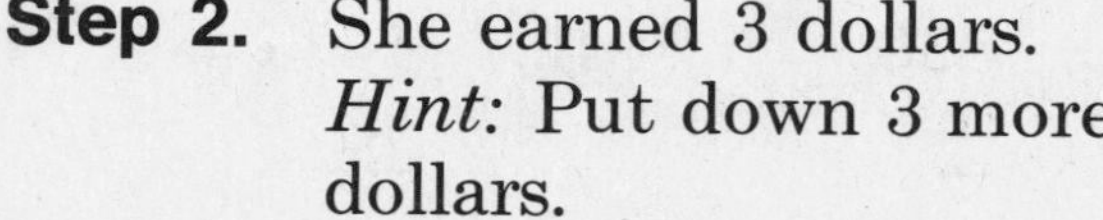

Step 3. Then she spent 2 dollars. *Hint:* Take away 2 dollars.

Step 4. Then she got 4 dollars for her birthday. *Hint:* Put down 4 dollars.

How many dollars did she have?

Answer: Jane had 10 dollars.

EXERCISES

Solve by acting it out.
Use play money or slips of paper.

1. Carlos had 8 dollars. He earned 3 dollars. Then he spent 4 dollars for a book and 5 dollars for a toy. How many dollars did he have then? ____________

★ 2. Karen had 6 dollars. She earned 3 dollars. She bought a jump rope for 4 dollars. After she lost some money, she had 3 dollars left. How many dollars did she lose? ____________

Name ______________________________

Estimating differences

You can use rounding to help estimate a difference. An estimate can help you find mistakes.

Each number is rounded to the nearest ten.

79	rounds to	80
−23	rounds to	−20
		60

Each number is rounded to the nearest hundred.

598	rounds to	600
−223	rounds to	−200
		400

The difference is about 60.

The difference is about 400.

EXERCISES

Round to the nearest ten.
Estimate each difference.

1. 92 − 28
2. 87 − 46
3. 63 − 31
4. 74 − 20
5. 93 − 62
6. 59 − 15
7. 74 − 23
8. 58 − 37
9. 65 − 49
10. 94 − 27

Round to the nearest hundred.
Estimate each difference.

11. 598 − 326
12. 614 − 195
13. 874 − 229
14. 769 − 255
15. 893 − 374
16. 808 − 299
17. 701 − 519
18. 902 − 385
19. 500 − 218
20. 900 − 196

Add or subtract. Estimate to check your work.

21. $584 + 326$

22. $584 - 326$

23. $715 + 482$

24. $715 - 482$

25. $623 + 587$

26. $623 - 487$

27. $906 + 758$

28. $906 - 758$

29. $596 + 379$

30. $729 - 583$

31. $648 + 856$

32. $593 - 407$

33. $753 - 278$

34. $651 - 384$

35. $906 + 539$

36. $537 - 288 =$ ________

37. $653 + 249 =$ ________

38. $706 + 816 =$ ________

39. $903 - 775 =$ ________

Problem Solving

40. Who sold the most tickets? ________

41. How many tickets did Anita and Brian sell together? ________

42. How many tickets did Carl, David, and Jeanne sell together? ________

43. How many more tickets did Susan sell than Anita? ________

44. How many more tickets did David sell than Wilma? ________

Gymnastics Show

Name	Tickets Sold
Anita	46
Brian	38
Carl	53
David	76
Jeanne	59
Mike	35
Susan	68
Wilma	47

Name ______________________________

Estimation

Work in groups. Get crayons and string. Complete the following steps for each problem:

Have each member of the group make an estimate.

Talk about how you made your estimates.

Do each activity and find the answer.

Compare the answer with your estimates.

1. a. How many crayons can one person in the group hold in one hand?

   Estimate: ______ *Answer:* ______

   b. How many crayons can the same person hold in two hands?

   Estimate: ______ *Answer:* ______

3. a. Pick a person in your group. How many times can the person tap the right foot in ten seconds?

   Estimate: ______ *Answer:* ______

   b. How many times can the person tap the left foot in ten seconds?

   Estimate: ______ *Answer:* ______

5. Think about the activities you just did. Answer these questions:

   a. Compare your estimates for parts a and b in activities 1 to 4.

   b. Which estimate was closer? Why?

2. a. How many walking steps will it take one person in the group to cross the room?

   Estimate: ______ *Answer:* ______

   b. How many walking steps will it take the same person in the group to cross the room in the other direction?

   Estimate: ______ *Answer:* ______

4. a. Pick a person in your group. Cut a length of string the same as the person's height. How many times would that person's foot fit along the length of the string?

   Estimate: ______ *Answer:* ______

   b. Try this activity above with another person in your group.

   Estimate: ______ *Answer:* ______

Estimating in different situations

Work in groups.
Record your answers on a separate sheet of paper.
Read each problem and discuss these questions:

Would estimation be useful in the situation?

How close would your estimate need to be?

Would it be better if your estimate were too high or too low? Would it matter?

How would you estimate? What information would you need?

Could you get an exact answer if you needed one?

1. The teacher sends you to the art room to get rolled paper to cover the bulletin board. The entire roll of paper is too heavy to carry back to the classroom. How much rolled paper will you bring back to the classroom?

2. You are asked to bring math books for 35 students from the storage room to the classroom. How many students do you need to make only one trip?

3. You need napkins for 38 people. If 8 napkins come in a package, how many packages will you buy?

4. You are going to plant flowers along your school fence, which is 45 feet long. If the flowers should be about 8 inches apart, how many flowers do you need?

5. You are going to help bake 6 dozen cookies for the school bake sale. How long will it take you?

Name ____________________

Problem Solving Two-step problems

Sometimes you have to do 2 steps to solve a problem.

Carol bought a puzzle for $1.53 and a ball for $2.29. She gave the clerk $5. How much change did she get?

Step 1. Add to find the total cost of the puzzle and the ball.

$$\begin{array}{r} \$1.53 \\ +2.29 \\ \hline \$3.82 \end{array}$$

Step 2. Subtract to find the change.

$$\begin{array}{r} \$5.00 \\ -3.82 \\ \hline \$1.18 \end{array}$$

Answer: Carol got $1.18 in change.

EXERCISES

Solve these two-step problems.

1. José bought an airplane for $2.06 and a coloring book for $.89. He gave the clerk $3. How much change did he get? ________

2. Lisa had $2.50. She wanted to buy a yo-yo for $1.29 and a truck for $1.58. How much more money did she need? ________

3. Christine built a model airplane in 15 hours. Donald built a model truck in 9 hours and a model car in 8 hours. How much longer did it take Donald to build his models?

____

4. Karen wanted to buy 2 teddy bears. A teddy bear costs $3.25. She had $5.75. How much more did she need?

____

5. Bill bought an airplane for $1.98 and a car for $1.39. Carl bought a boat for $1.75. How much more did Bill spend?

____

6. Jan bought 2 coloring books for $.98 each. Barbara bought a ball for $1.57. How much less did Barbara spend?

____

★ 7. An airplane costs 98¢. A truck costs 19¢ less than the airplane. A car costs 10¢ less than the truck. How much does the car cost? ________

★ 8. A truck costs 39¢. An airplane costs 10¢ more than the truck. How much do they cost together? ________

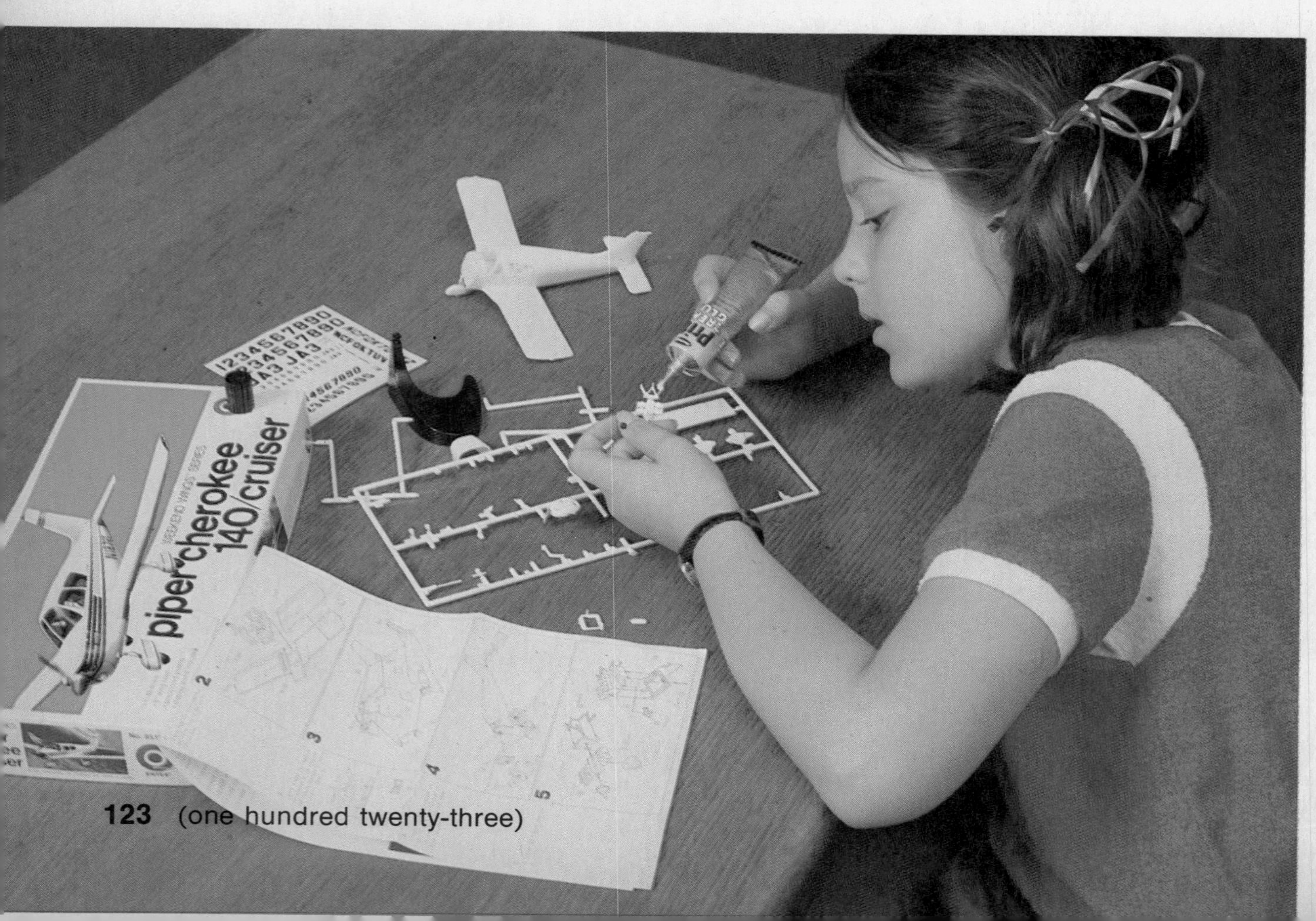

Name ______________________________

Subtracting 4-digit numbers

Regroup 1 ten for 10 ones.
Subtract ones.

Regroup 1 hundred for 10 tens.
Subtract tens.

Regroup 1 thousand for 10 hundreds.
Subtract hundreds.

Subtract thousands.

EXERCISES

Subtract.

1. 8973 − 2546
2. 6543 − 2170
3. 5432 − 1856
4. 7345 − 2286
5. 9386 − 2559
6. 6258 − 2079
7. 5763 − 1694
8. 3940 − 1583
9. 9637 − 2749
10. 7635 − 3958
11. 5824 − 1786
12. 8863 − 4597
13. 7593 − 6650
14. 2473 − 1278
15. 8812 − 3960
16. 6813 − 1796

17. $\begin{array}{r} 7128 \\ -3452 \\ \hline \end{array}$

18. $\begin{array}{r} 9604 \\ -2358 \\ \hline \end{array}$

19. $\begin{array}{r} 8300 \\ -2564 \\ \hline \end{array}$

20. $\begin{array}{r} 4674 \\ -1295 \\ \hline \end{array}$

21. $\begin{array}{r} 5963 \\ -2874 \\ \hline \end{array}$

22. $\begin{array}{r} 6208 \\ -3169 \\ \hline \end{array}$

23. $\begin{array}{r} 5342 \\ -2658 \\ \hline \end{array}$

24. $\begin{array}{r} 9375 \\ -4897 \\ \hline \end{array}$

Give the end number.

KEEPING SKILLS SHARP

Bonita did these problems on her calculator. Three are wrong. Estimate to find the wrong answers.

1. 291 + 406   897   ______
2. 512 + 183   695   ______
3. 421 + 308   729   ______
4. 475 + 192   567   ______
5. 627 + 184   911   ______
6. 616 + 215   831   ______

Name ________________________________

Chapter Checkup

Give each difference. [pages 102–109, 112–116, 124–125]

1. $\begin{array}{r} 59 \\ -23 \\ \hline \end{array}$ 2. $\begin{array}{r} 92 \\ -38 \\ \hline \end{array}$ 3. $\begin{array}{r} 75 \\ -49 \\ \hline \end{array}$ 4. $\begin{array}{r} 709 \\ -254 \\ \hline \end{array}$ 5. $\begin{array}{r} 842 \\ -290 \\ \hline \end{array}$

6. $\begin{array}{r} 524 \\ -458 \\ \hline \end{array}$ 7. $\begin{array}{r} 752 \\ -275 \\ \hline \end{array}$ 8. $\begin{array}{r} 835 \\ -368 \\ \hline \end{array}$ 9. $\begin{array}{r} 621 \\ -459 \\ \hline \end{array}$ 10. $\begin{array}{r} 920 \\ -275 \\ \hline \end{array}$

11. $\begin{array}{r} 504 \\ -375 \\ \hline \end{array}$ 12. $\begin{array}{r} 306 \\ -169 \\ \hline \end{array}$ 13. $\begin{array}{r} 400 \\ -358 \\ \hline \end{array}$ 14. $\begin{array}{r} 702 \\ -465 \\ \hline \end{array}$ 15. $\begin{array}{r} 801 \\ -397 \\ \hline \end{array}$

16. 68 − 42 = ________ 17. 92 − 57 = ________

18. 721 − 347 = ________ 19. 815 − 456 = ________

20. 902 − 529 = ________ 21. 401 − 357 = ________

Estimate each difference. [pages 118–121]

22. $\begin{array}{r} 91 \\ -67 \\ \hline \end{array}$ 23. $\begin{array}{r} 142 \\ -88 \\ \hline \end{array}$ 24. $\begin{array}{r} 703 \\ -494 \\ \hline \end{array}$

Solve. [pages 110–111, 117, 120–123]

25. How many more crackers are in the larger box? ________

26. How much more does the larger box cost? ________

Chapter Project

COLLECTING DATA

1. List all the children in your class.
2. Next to each name, write the age of the child.
3. Add all the ages. This is your **class life sum.**
4. What will your class life sum be 1 year from now?
5. What was your class life sum 1 year ago?
6. What was your class life sum 3 years ago?
7. What was your class life sum 5 years ago?

Name ________________

Chapter Review

REGROUP 1 TEN FOR 10 ONES

REGROUP 1 TEN FOR 10 ONES

REGROUP 1 HUNDRED FOR 10 TENS

REGROUP TWICE

REGROUP TWICE

Subtract.

1. 78 − 24
2. 69 − 35
3. 98 − 43

Example: 52 − 23 = 29

4. 63 − 38
5. 82 − 45
6. 90 − 67

Example: 643 − 228 = 415

7. 562 − 349
8. 780 − 259
9. 865 − 457

Example: 548 − 352 = 196

10. 748 − 392
11. 926 − 451
12. 837 − 263

Example: 725 − 256 = 469

13. 523 − 258
14. 735 − 386
15. 947 − 268

Example: 701 − 345 = 356

16. 804 − 259
17. 602 − 354
18. 500 − 276

Chapter Challenge

MISSING ADDENDS

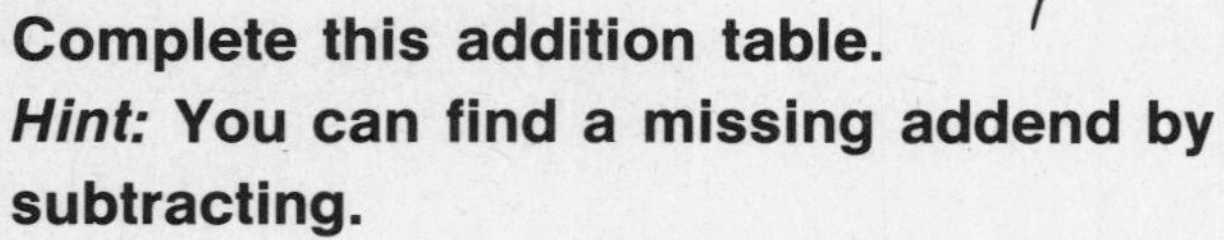

Complete this addition table.
Hint: **You can find a missing addend by subtracting.**

+	58	93				408
94	152			233		
		160	226			
185						
			586			
658					1194	
						784

Name ____________________

Cumulative Checkup

STANDARDIZED FORMAT

Give the correct letter.

1. In 5 + 8 = 13, 13 is called the

- **a.** addend
- **b.** difference
- **c.** sum
- **d.** none of these

2. Complete.
5 + ? = 8

- **a.** 13
- **b.** 3
- **c.** 14
- **d.** none of these

3. Add.

$$\begin{array}{r} 6 \\ 2 \\ +9 \\ \hline \end{array}$$

- **a.** 17
- **b.** 18
- **c.** 16
- **d.** 15

4. Five hundred nine is

- **a.** 509
- **b.** 590
- **c.** 905
- **d.** none of these

5. In 3896, what digit is in the hundreds place?

- **a.** 6
- **b.** 8
- **c.** 9
- **d.** 3

6. Which number is 10 more than 136?

- **a.** 126
- **b.** 236
- **c.** 137
- **d.** 146

7. Which totals $1.56?

- **a.** 1 dollar and 6 dimes
- **b.** 5 dimes and 6 pennies
- **c.** 1 dollar, 6 dimes, and 5 pennies
- **d.** none of these

8. Add.

$$\begin{array}{r} 73 \\ 68 \\ +95 \\ \hline \end{array}$$

- **a.** 236
- **b.** 226
- **c.** 235
- **d.** 237

9. Add.

$$\begin{array}{r} 5829 \\ +3648 \\ \hline \end{array}$$

- **a.** 9467
- **b.** 8467
- **c.** 9477
- **d.** none of these

10. Subtract.

$$\begin{array}{r} 716 \\ -493 \\ \hline \end{array}$$

- **a.** 323
- **b.** 383
- **c.** 223
- **d.** 283

11. Barry had 23 stamps. He bought 18 more stamps. How many did he have then?

- **a.** 5
- **b.** 15
- **c.** 41
- **d.** none of these

12. Jan had $.58. She wanted to buy a model car for $.95. How much more money did she need?

- **a.** $1.53
- **b.** $.43
- **c.** $.33
- **d.** none of these

5

Time and Money

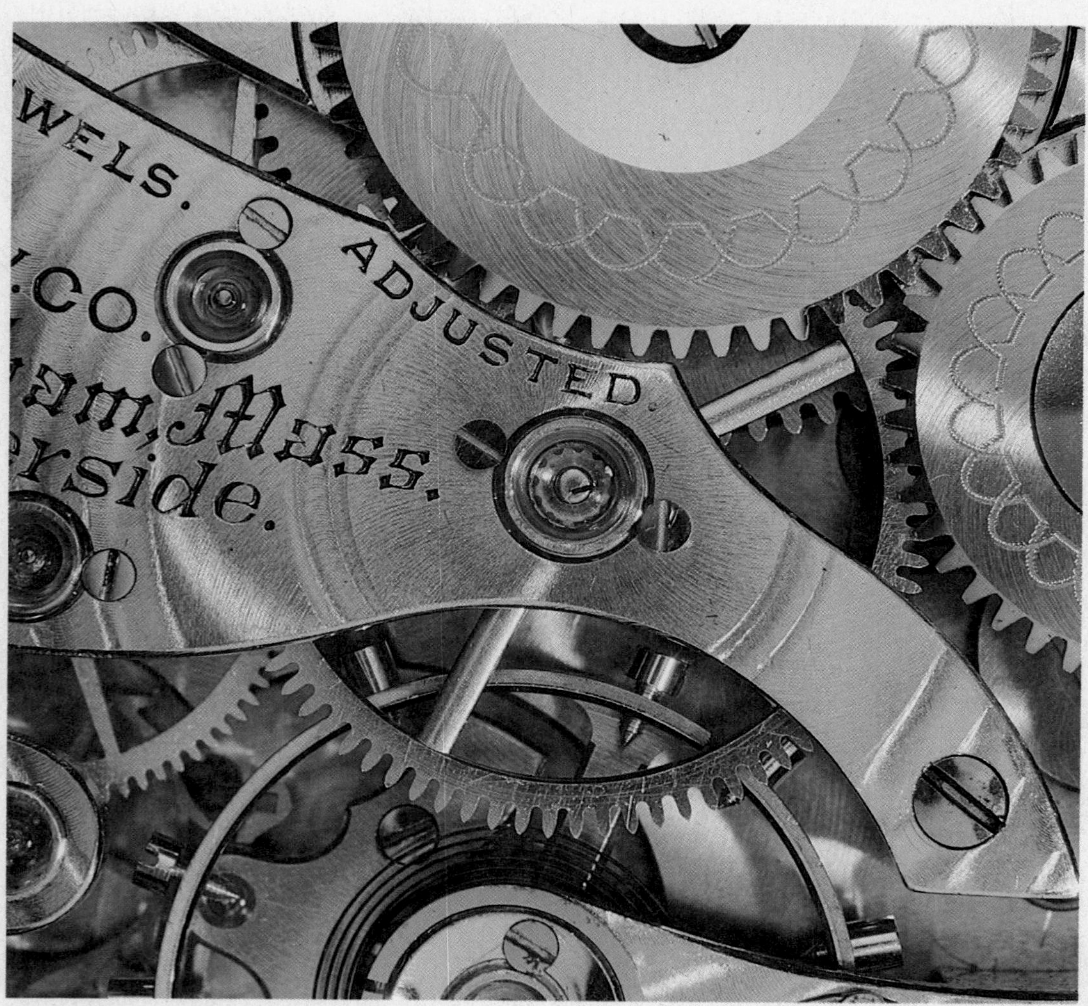

If the clock in the picture is wound tight, it will run 6 hours longer than a full day. How many hours will the clock run?

Name ____________________

Hour and half hour

The short hand is the hour hand.
The long hand is the minute hand.

These two clocks both show 4:00.
We read 4:00 as "four o'clock."

These two clocks both show 8:30.
We read 8:30 as "eight-thirty."

EXERCISES

Give the time.

1.  ________

2.  ________

3.  ________

4.  ________

5.  ________

6.  ________

7.  ________

8.  ________

9.  ________

Give the time.

10. one hour later than

____

11. one hour earlier than

____

12. two hours earlier than

____

13. one hour earlier than

____

14. two hours later than

____

15. one hour later than

____

Complete.

	Time in	Baking time	Time out
16.	7:00	1 hour	
17.	8:00	2 hours	
18.	9:30	2 hours	
19.	10:30	1 hour	
20.	2:30	2 hours	
★ **21.**	3:30		5:30
★ **22.**		2 hours	7:30

Name ____________________

Minutes

The time is 9:10
or
10 minutes after 9 o'clock.

The time is 6:25
or
25 minutes after 6 o'clock.

The time is 3:50
or
50 minutes after 3 o'clock.

EXERCISES

Give each time.

1.  ________

2.  ________

3.  ________

4.  ________

5.  ________

6.  ________

7.  ________

8.  ________

9.  ________

10.  ________

11.  ________

12.  ________

Match.

13.  ____

a. 10 minutes after 7

14.  ____

b. 50 minutes after 6

15.  ____

c. 7:50

16.  ____

d. 6:10

KEEPING SKILLS SHARP

Round to the nearest ten.

1. 77 ________
2. 83 ________
3. 95 ________
4. 46 ________
5. 83 ________
6. 67 ________

Round to the nearest hundred.

7. 241 ________
8. 695 ________
9. 850 ________
10. 627 ________
11. 344 ________
12. 784 ________

Name ________________________________

Minutes

There are 60 minutes in 1 hour.

7:08

2:33

9:58

Times in the second half of each hour are often given in another way.

The time is 4:50
or
10 minutes *before* 5 o'clock.

The time is 9:39
or
21 minutes *before* 10 o'clock.

EXERCISES

Give each time.

1.  8:06

2.  ________

3. ________

4. 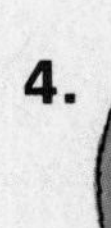  ________

5.  ________

6.  ________

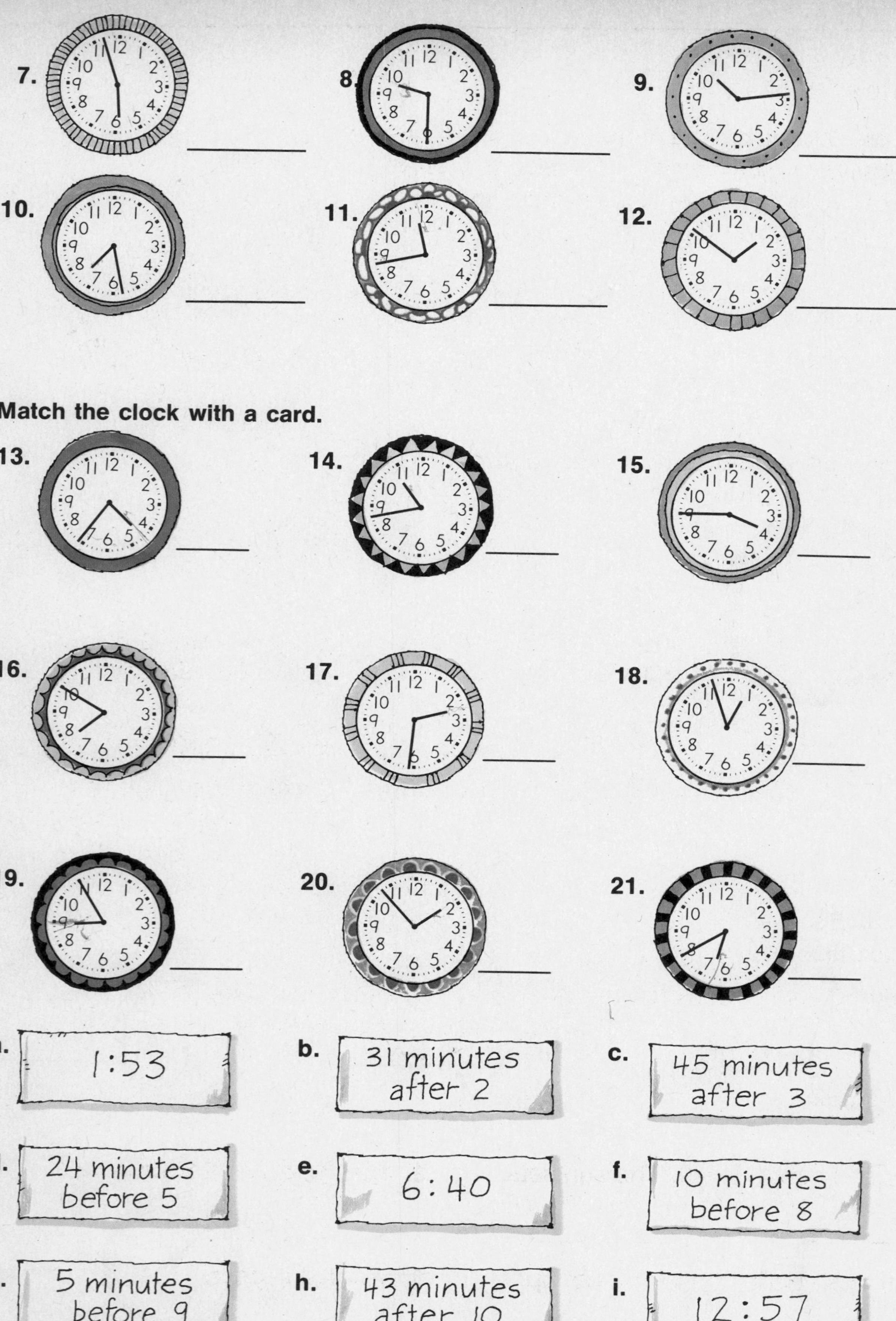

Match the clock with a card.

a. 1:53

b. 31 minutes after 2

c. 45 minutes after 3

d. 24 minutes before 5

e. 6:40

f. 10 minutes before 8

g. 5 minutes before 9

h. 43 minutes after 10

i. 12:57

Name ____________________

A.M. and P.M.

There are 24 hours in a day.
The hour hand goes around 2 times in a day.
There is an 8 o'clock in the morning and
an 8 o'clock at night.

8:00 A.M.

8:00 P.M.

A.M. is used for times after 12:00 midnight and before 12:00 noon.

P.M. is used for times after 12:00 noon and before 12:00 midnight.

Dolores goes to school
at 8:00 A.M.

Dolores watches TV
at 8:00 P.M.

EXERCISES

A.M. or P.M.?

1. The sun rises. ________

2. The sun sets. ________

3. You get home from school. ________

4. You go to bed. ________

5. You get up. ________

6. You eat supper. ________

Give each time.
Be sure to give A.M. or P.M.

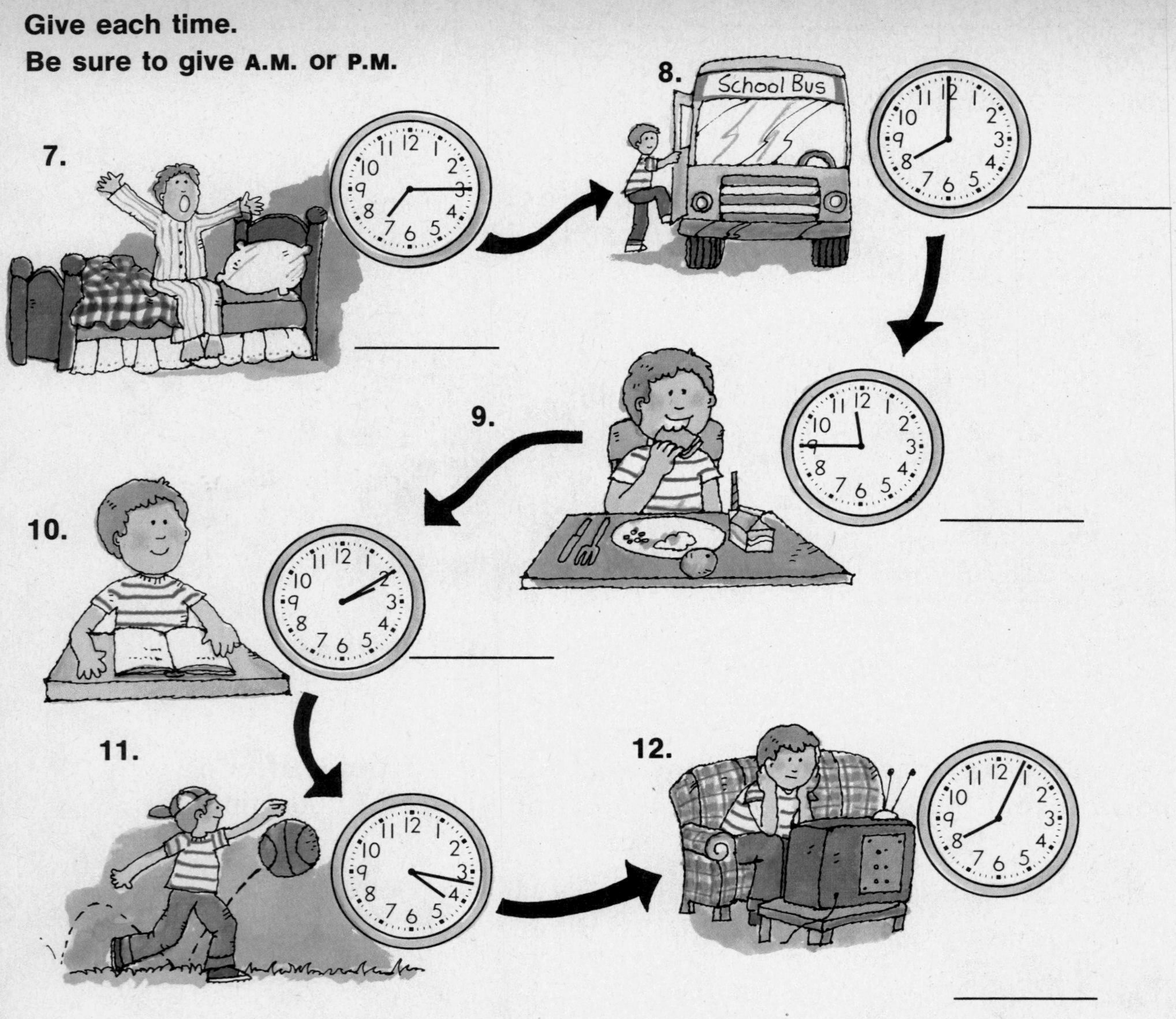

cock-a-dooodle-doooo...

Give each time.
Be sure to give A.M. or P.M.

13. one hour after 12:00 midnight ________

14. three hours after 12:00 midnight ________

15. two hours before 12:00 noon ________

★ **16.** one hour and 20 minutes before midnight ________

★ **17.** two hours and 30 minutes before noon ________

Name ____________________

More about time

Beth and her grandfather are waiting for a train. It is 7:50. The train will come at 8:15. How long will they have to wait?

To find the answer, study these clocks.

Now

When train leaves

They will have to wait a total of 25 minutes.

EXERCISES

Complete.

1. Now: 

   Next train: 2:30

   Waiting time: ________

2. Now: 

   Next train: 3:09

   Waiting time: ________

3. Now: 

   Next train: 5:05

   Waiting time: ________

4. Now: 

   Next train: 6:10

   Waiting time: ________

5. Now:  

   Next train: 7:15

   Waiting time: ________

6. Now: 

   Next train: 1:05

   Waiting time: ________

Computers help us travel

Ticket agents use computers to write tickets and give out seat numbers. A computer also shows arrival and departure times on a screen.

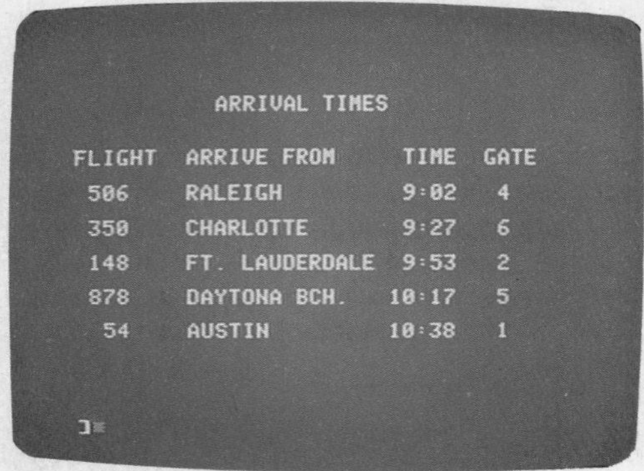

ARRIVAL TIMES

FLIGHT	ARRIVE FROM	TIME	GATE
506	RALEIGH	9:02	4
350	CHARLOTTE	9:27	6
148	FT. LAUDERDALE	9:53	2
878	DAYTONA BCH.	10:17	5
54	AUSTIN	10:38	1

EXERCISES

1. What time does flight 878 arrive? ________
2. What flight arrives at 9:27? ________

How many minutes between these arrival times?

3. Flight 506 and Flight 350 ________
4. Flight 350 and Flight 148 ________
5. Flight 878 and Flight 54 ________
6. ★ Flight 148 and Flight 878 ________
7. ★ Flight 350 and Flight 878 ________
8. ★ Flight 506 and Flight 54 ________

Mental Math

You can find these sums faster by using mental math than by using a calculator.

Think about adding 100 and subtracting.
Shortcut

9. 132 + 99 = ______
10. 134 + 99 = ______
11. 145 + 98 = ______
12. 168 + 97 = ______

Name ______________________________

Money

penny

1¢
$.01

nickel

5¢
$.05

dime

10¢
$.10

quarter

25¢
$.25

half-dollar

50¢
$.50

dollar

100¢
$1.00

EXERCISES

Give the total value in dollars.

1.

______

2.

______

3.

______

4.

______

How much change?

5. 

______

6. 

______

7. 

______

8. 

______

Problem Solving

9. Bill had a half-dollar, a quarter, and 3 pennies. How much did he have in all? ______

10. Joan had 2 quarters. She found a dime and 2 nickels. How much did she have in all? ______

11. Leon had a half-dollar, 2 quarters, and 3 dimes. He spent the half-dollar. How much was left? ______

12. Sarah had a half-dollar and 3 quarters. She spent $.67. How much did she have left? ______

Challenge!

Find the missing input or output.

13. 

	Input	Output
	21	48
a.	16	
b.	19	
c.		54

Name Matin #2

More about money

Clerks work with money. They tell you how much something costs. They also make change.

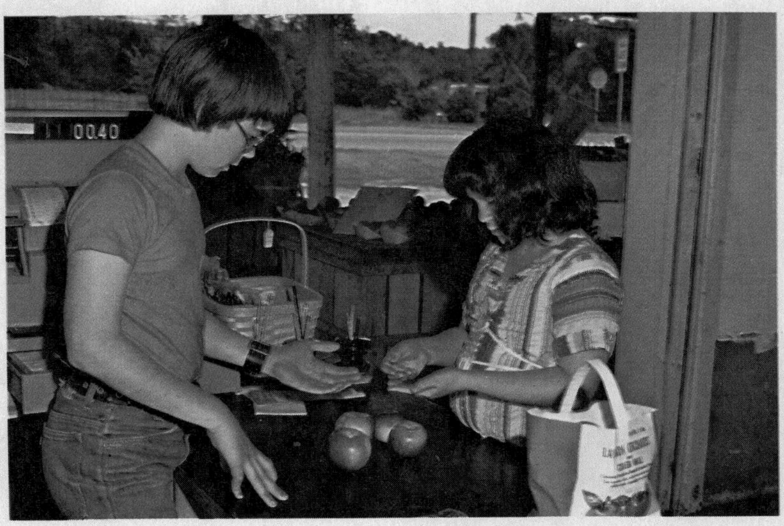

EXERCISES

Tell what coins you would give the clerk.

	You have	You buy	You give the clerk
1.		$.43	half-dollar
2.		$.59	half-dollar quarter
3.		$.85	halfdoller-halfdoller
4.		$1.35	halfdoller-halfdoller quarter-dime

Mark the money you would give the clerk.

5.

6.

7.

8.

9.

10.

Challenge!

Can you tell what is in each bag?

11.

____

12.

____

13.

____

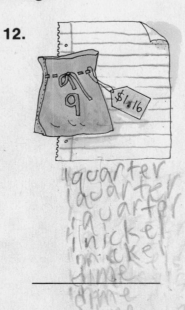

Name ______________________________

Earning and Spending

Work in groups. Get play money (dollars, half-dollars, quarters, nickels, and pennies), 1 number cube, and a marker for each player. Record your answers on a separate sheet of paper.

Money Game Rules:

1. Each player starts with $5.00.
2. Each player takes three turns rolling the number cube and moving on the path on page 147.
3. You will spend or receive money.
4. If you land on a space that tells you to spend money and you don't have enough, you lose a turn.
5. Record each play on your paper.

Example:

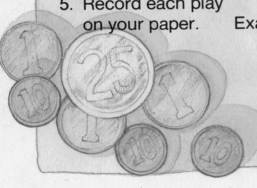

Start:	$5.00
Receive:	+2.25
	7.25
Spend:	−1.50
	5.75
Spend:	−2.75
	3.00

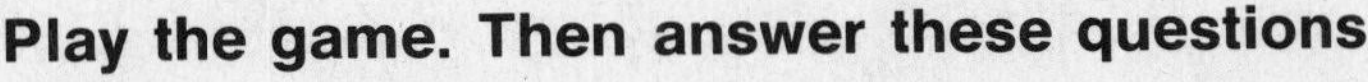

Play the game. Then answer these questions.

1. What is the most money a player can end up with after three turns? What spaces would the player land on?

2. If a player has five turns, what is the most money the player can end up with? What spaces would the player land on?

3. How did your group solve exercises 1 and 2? Compare your way with the way one other group solved these problems.

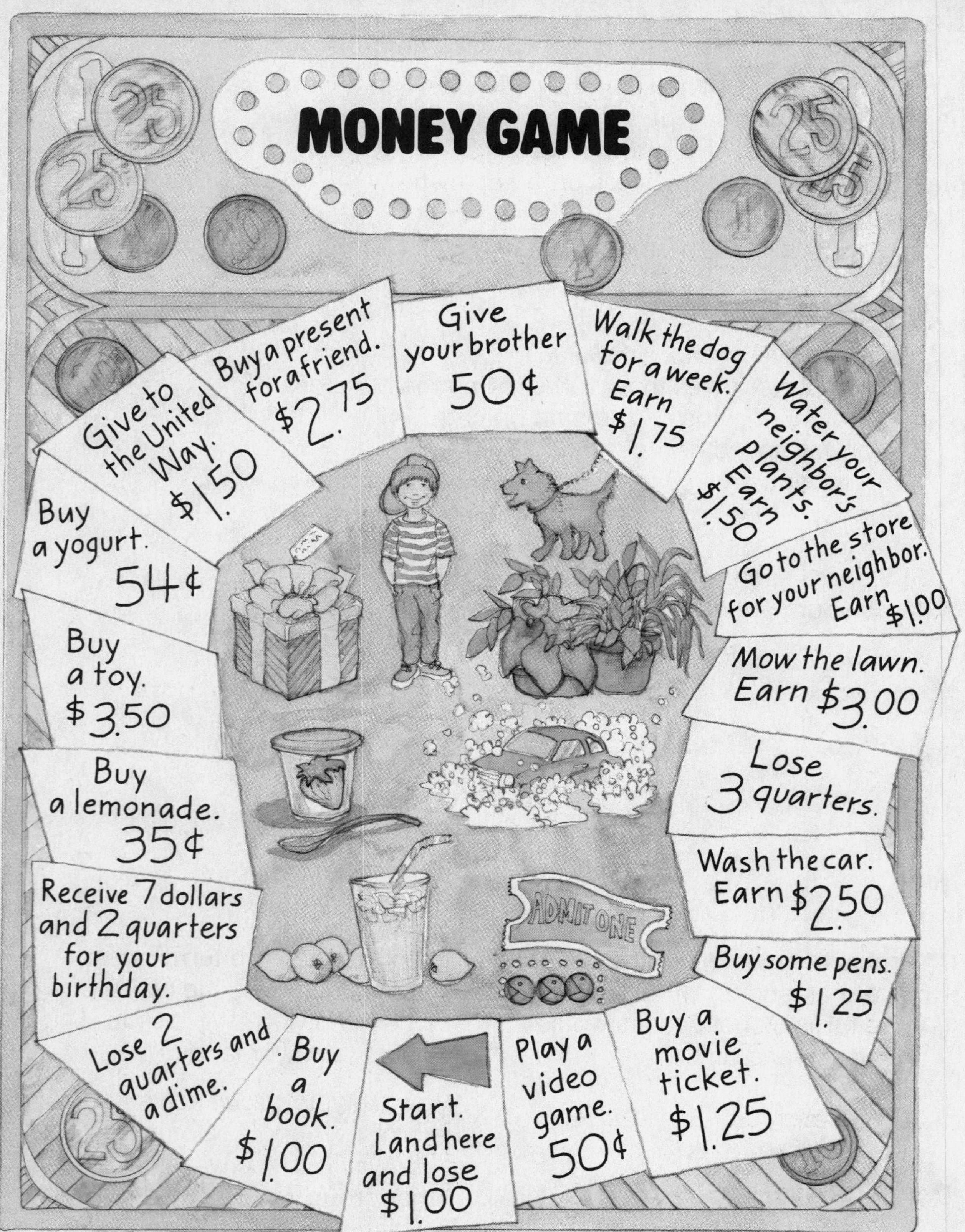
MONEY GAME
Give to the United Way. $1.50
Buy a present for a friend. $2.75
Give your brother 50¢
Walk the dog for a week. Earn $1.75
Water your neighbor's plants. Earn $1.50
Buy a yogurt. 54¢
Go to the store for your neighbor. Earn $1.00
Buy a toy. $3.50
Mow the lawn. Earn $3.00
Lose 3 quarters.
Buy a lemonade. 35¢
Wash the car. Earn $2.50
Receive 7 dollars and 2 quarters for your birthday.
ADMIT ONE
Buy some pens. $1.25
Lose 2 quarters and a dime.
Buy a book. $1.00
Start. Land here and lose $1.00
Play a video game. 50¢
Buy a movie ticket. $1.25

Name ____________________

Problem Solving Estimating to check

1. Study and understand.
2. Plan and do.
3. Answer and check.

Estimating can help you check your answer.

Jim had $6.04.
He spent $1.95.
How much money did he have left?

Do the arithmetic.

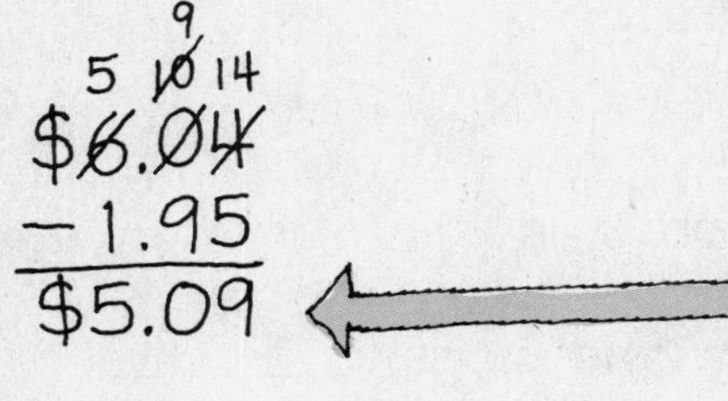

Estimate to check.

$$\begin{array}{r} \$6.00 \\ -2.00 \\ \hline \$4.00 \end{array}$$

My answer is not close to my estimate. I made a mistake. Can you find the mistake?

EXERCISES

Solve. Check by estimating.

1. Driving to Zoo

Before breakfast: 39 miles
After breakfast: 27 miles

How far was it to the zoo?

____

2. Buying Tickets

Adult: $1.95
Child: $.95

How much for 2 adults' tickets and 2 children's tickets?

____

3. Seeing Movies
African animals: 28 minutes
Asian animals: 17 minutes

How long to see both? ________

4. Walking around Zoo
Walk A: 55 minutes
Walk B: 38 minutes
How much longer was Walk A? ________

5. Comparing Weights
Mother elephant: 9000 pounds
Baby elephant: 880 pounds
How much heavier was the mother elephant? ________

6. Comparing Speeds
Horse: 45 miles per hour
Fox: 40 miles per hour
How much faster was the horse? ________

7. Comparing Heights
Mother giraffe: 17 feet
Baby giraffe: 6 feet
How much taller was the mother? ________

8. Comparing Ages
Oldest turtle: 147 years
Youngest turtle: 9 years
What was the difference in age? ________

9. Eating Lunch
Milk shake: $.90
Hot dog: $.85
How much for 1 milk shake and 2 hot dogs? ________

10. Eating Lunch
Had: $1.50
Hot dog: $.85
How much more was needed to buy 2 hot dogs? ________

11. Buying Pictures
Lion: $3.50
Elephant: $2.35

How much for both? ________

12. Buying Zoo Book
Had $4.00
Bought book for $2.25

How much money was left? ________

Name ________________________________

Problem Solving Estimating with money

Solve. Check by estimating.

1. Alex wants to buy 

and 

   How much money does he need? ________

2. Ruth wants to buy  and 

   How much money does she need? ________

3. Carla has $6.00.
   She wants to buy 

   How much money will she have left? ________

4. Tom has $4.50.
   He wants to buy 

   How much money will he have left? ________

5. How much more does  cost than  ?

   ____

6. How much more do  cost than  ?

   ____

7. Terry wants to buy and

How much money does she need? ________

8. Sarah has $8.54.

She wants to buy

How much money will she have left? ________

9. Robert has $3.88.

He wants to buy

How much more money does he need? ________

10. Janet has $2.63.

She wants to buy

How much more money does she need? ________

★ 11. Mary wants to buy , , and

How much money does she need? ________

★ 12. Larry has $9.00.

He wants to buy and

How much money will he have left? ________

Name ______________________

Chapter Checkup

Give each time. [pages 132–137]

1.  ________

2.  ________

3.  ________

A.M. or P.M.? [pages 138–141]

4. one hour after midnight ________
5. 3:47 in the afternoon ________
6. one hour after 11:30 A.M. ________
7. two hours after 10:30 P.M. ________

Give the total value in dollars. [pages 142–145]

8. 

____

9. 

____

Solve. [pages 143, 146–151]

10. Alex had $3.45. He earned one half-dollar and three dimes. How much did he have then? ________

11. Elaine had $3.08. She spent a dollar and a quarter. How much did she have then? ________

Chapter Project

USING A BAR GRAPH

Mr. Mahoney's class made this graph. It shows what time the students go to bed before a school day.

1. How many go to bed at 8:00? ______
2. How many go to bed before 8:00? ______
3. How many go to bed after 9:00? ______
4. How many students are in the class? ______
5. Make a graph like this for your class.
6. Tell some things about your graph.

Name ______________________________

Chapter Review

Match.

______ 1.

a.

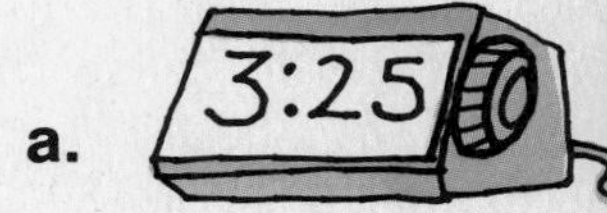

______ 2.

b.

______ 3.

c. 12:16

______ 4.

d.

Give the total value in dollars.

5.

____

6.

____

7. one dollar
two quarters

one dime ______________

8. two dollars
two half-dollars
three dimes

four pennies ______________

Chapter Challenge

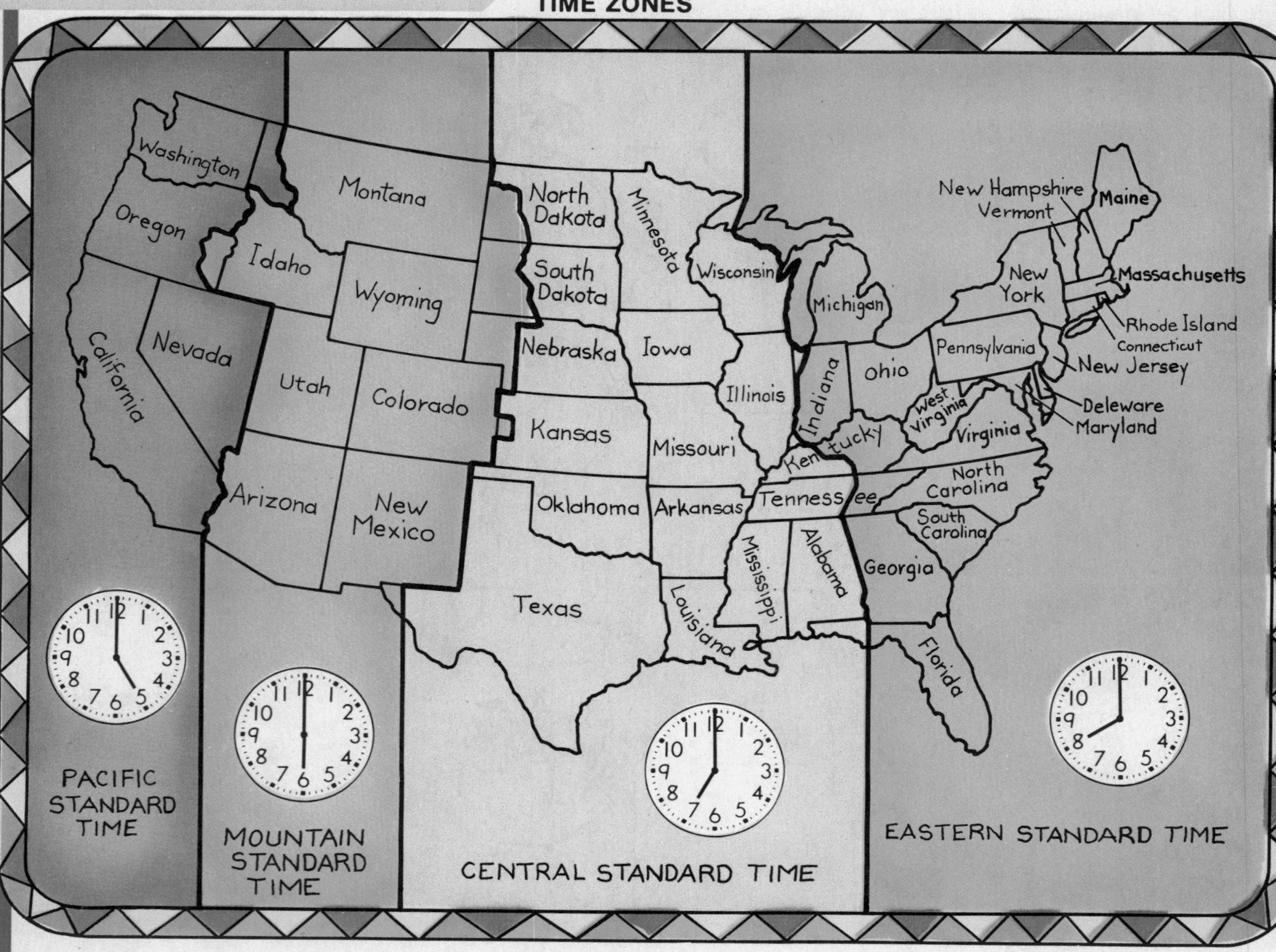

1. It is 5:00 A.M. in California. What time is it in Colorado? _______
2. What time is it in Missouri when it is 3:00 P.M. in Ohio? _______
3. It is 11:00 A.M. in Arizona. What time is it in New York? _______
4. It is 10:00 P.M. in Nevada. What time is it in Maryland? _______
5. When it is noon in Georgia, what time is it in the state of Washington? _______
6. A jet flew from Chicago, Illinois, to New York City. It took 1 hour and 50 minutes. If it left Chicago at 11:45 A.M., what time did it arrive in New York? _______
7. Find out what time zones Alaska and Hawaii are in. _______

Name ____________________

Cumulative Checkup

STANDARDIZED FORMAT

Give the correct letter.

1. In 6 + 4 = 10, 6 is called

a. a sum
b. an addend
c. a difference
d. none of these

2. Add.

$$\begin{array}{r} 3 \\ 5 \\ +6 \\ \hline \end{array}$$

a. 13
b. 15
c. 14
d. 16

3. Which numeral has a 6 in the hundreds place?

a. 346
b. 680
c. 568
d. none of these

4. Which number is the smallest?

a. 3782
b. 3827
c. 3278
d. 3287

5. Add.

$$\begin{array}{r} 37 \\ 29 \\ +48 \\ \hline \end{array}$$

a. 104
b. 94
c. 114
d. 113

6. Add.

$$\begin{array}{r} 368 \\ +249 \\ \hline \end{array}$$

a. 617
b. 507
c. 607
d. none of these

7. Subtract.

$$\begin{array}{r} 800 \\ -347 \\ \hline \end{array}$$

a. 453
b. 563
c. 543
d. 547

8. What time is it?

a. 11:55
b. 12:55
c. 11:00
d. none of these

9. Which time is in the afternoon?

a. noon
b. 2:30 A.M.
c. 4:45 P.M.
d. none of these

10. How much money?
1 dollar
1 half-dollar
2 dimes
1 nickel
3 pennies

a. $1.78
b. $1.83
c. $2.28
d. $2.03

11. 54 red pencils
38 blue pencils
How many more red pencils?

a. 24 **b.** 92
c. 16 **d.** 82

12. Kit had 91¢. She spent 15¢ for a pencil and 19¢ for a pen. How much money did she have left?

a. 76¢ **b.** 57¢
c. 34¢ **d.** 72¢

6

Multiplication Facts through 9×5

Jessica put all her magnets together. She had 9 rows. Each row had 4 magnets. How many magnets did Jessica have?

Name Matin #2

Addition and multiplication

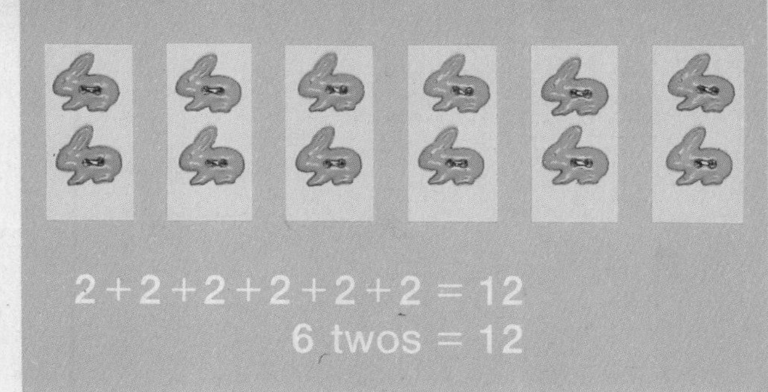

The total number of buttons can be found by adding.

There are 6 sets of two buttons.

EXERCISES

How many?

1. 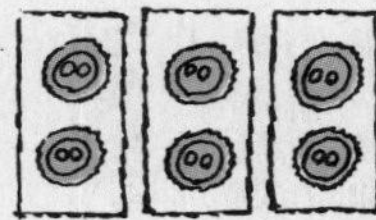

   2 + 2 + 2 = 6

   3 twos = 6

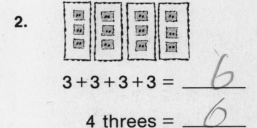

2. 3 + 3 + 3 + 3 = 6

   4 threes = 6

3. 

   4 + 4 + 4 = 12

   3 fours = 12

4. 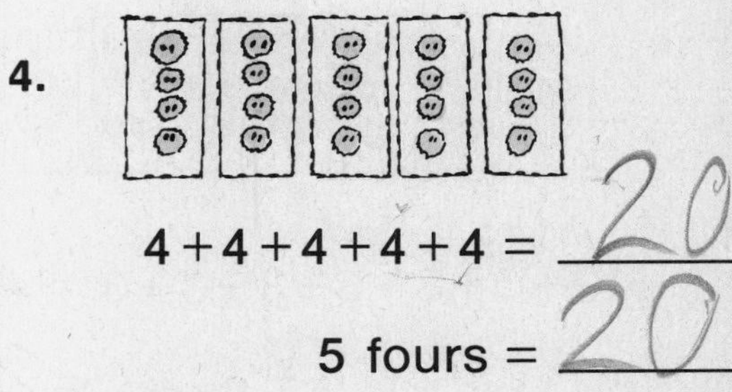

   4 + 4 + 4 + 4 + 4 = 20

   5 fours = 20

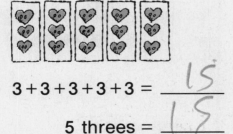

5. 3 + 3 + 3 + 3 + 3 = 15

   5 threes = 15

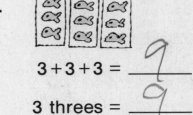

6. 3 + 3 + 3 = 9

   3 threes = 9

How many?

7. 

$3 + 3 + 3 + 3 + 3 + 3 =$ ______

6 threes = ______

8.

$4 + 4 =$ ______

2 fours = ______

9.

$2 + 2 + 2 + 2 + 2 =$ ______

5 twos = ______

10.

$4 + 4 + 4 + 4 + 4 + 4 =$ ______

6 fours = ______

11.

$3 + 3 + 3 + 3 + 3 + 3 + 3 =$ ______

7 threes = ______

12.

$2 + 2 + 2 + 2 =$ ______

4 twos = ______

13.

$4 + 4 + 4 + 4 =$ ______

4 fours = ______

14.

$2 + 2 + 2 + 2 + 2 + 2 + 2 =$ ______

7 twos = ______

Name Matin

2 as a factor

There are 3 sets of two.

$$2 + 2 + 2 = 6$$
$$3 \text{ twos} = 6$$
$$3 \times 2 = 6$$

We can multiply to find the total.

Read this multiplication equation as "three-times two equals six."

1. $1 \times 2 =$ 2

2. $2 \times 2 =$ 4

3.  $3 \times 2 =$ 6

4. $4 \times 2 =$ 8

5. $5 \times 2 =$ 10

6. $6 \times 2 =$ 12

7. $7 \times 2 =$ 14

8. $8 \times 2 =$ 16

9. $9 \times 2 =$ 18

Multiply.

10. 2 in each set
$\times 3$ sets
6 in all

11. 
2 in each set
$\times 5$ sets
10 in all

12. $\begin{array}{r} 2 \\ \times 1 \\ \hline 2 \end{array}$ 13. $\begin{array}{r} 2 \\ \times 2 \\ \hline 4 \end{array}$ 14. $\begin{array}{r} 2 \\ \times 3 \\ \hline 6 \end{array}$ 15. $\begin{array}{r} 2 \\ \times 4 \\ \hline 8 \end{array}$ 16. $\begin{array}{r} 2 \\ \times 5 \\ \hline 10 \end{array}$ 17. $\begin{array}{r} 2 \\ \times 6 \\ \hline 12 \end{array}$

18. $\begin{array}{r} 2 \\ \times 7 \\ \hline 14 \end{array}$ 19. $\begin{array}{r} 2 \\ \times 8 \\ \hline 16 \end{array}$ 20. $\begin{array}{r} 2 \\ \times 9 \\ \hline 18 \end{array}$ 21. $\begin{array}{r} 2 \\ \times 8 \\ \hline 16 \end{array}$ 22. $\begin{array}{r} 2 \\ \times 6 \\ \hline 12 \end{array}$ 23. $\begin{array}{r} 2 \\ \times 2 \\ \hline 4 \end{array}$

24. $\begin{array}{r} 2 \\ \times 4 \\ \hline 8 \end{array}$ 25. $\begin{array}{r} 2 \\ \times 7 \\ \hline 14 \end{array}$ 26. $\begin{array}{r} 2 \\ \times 9 \\ \hline 18 \end{array}$ 27. $\begin{array}{r} 2 \\ \times 5 \\ \hline 10 \end{array}$ 28. $\begin{array}{r} 2 \\ \times 8 \\ \hline 16 \end{array}$ 29. $\begin{array}{r} 2 \\ \times 7 \\ \hline 14 \end{array}$

30. $\begin{array}{r} 2 \\ \times 9 \\ \hline 18 \end{array}$ 31. $\begin{array}{r} 2 \\ \times 3 \\ \hline 6 \end{array}$ 32. $\begin{array}{r} 2 \\ \times 8 \\ \hline 16 \end{array}$ 33. $\begin{array}{r} 2 \\ \times 4 \\ \hline 8 \end{array}$ 34. $\begin{array}{r} 2 \\ \times 1 \\ \hline 2 \end{array}$ 35. $\begin{array}{r} 2 \\ \times 9 \\ \hline 18 \end{array}$

Complete.

36. $\begin{array}{r} 2 \\ \times 1 \\ \hline \end{array}$ $\begin{array}{r} 2 \\ \times 2 \\ \hline \end{array}$ $\begin{array}{r} 2 \\ \times 3 \\ \hline \end{array}$ $\begin{array}{r} 2 \\ \times 4 \\ \hline \end{array}$ $\begin{array}{r} 2 \\ \times 5 \\ \hline \end{array}$

0 1 2 3 [4] 5 [6] 7 [8] 9 [[illegible]]

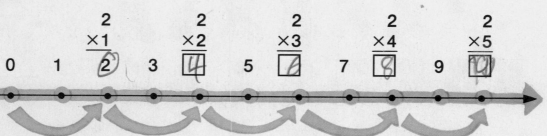

37. Even numbers: 2, 4, 6, 8, 10, 12, 14, 16, 18

38. Odd numbers: 1, 3, 5, 7, 9, 11, 13, 17, 19

Name Matin

3 as a factor

$4 \times 3 = 12$

EXERCISES
Give each product.

1. $1 \times 3 =$ 3
2. $2 \times 3 =$ 6
3. $3 \times 3 =$ 9
4. $4 \times 3 =$ 12
5. $5 \times 3 =$ 15
6. $6 \times 3 =$ 18
7. $7 \times 3 =$ 21
8. $8 \times 3 =$ 24
9. $9 \times 3 =$ 27

Multiply.

10. 

3 in each set
×4 sets
12 in all

11.   

3 in each set
×6 sets
18 in all

12. 3 ×1 3	13. 3 ×2 6	14. 3 ×3 9	15. 3 ×4 12	16. 3 ×5 15	17. 3 ×6 18
18. 3 ×7 21	19. 3 ×8 24	20. 3 ×9 27	21. 2 ×2 4	22. 2 ×4 8	23. 3 ×9 27
24. 2 ×9 18	25. 3 ×1 3	26. 2 ×3 6	27. 2 ×5 10	28. 3 ×6 18	29. 3 ×5 15
30. 3 ×7 21	31. 2 ×1 2	32. 3 ×4 12	33. 2 ×8 16	34. 2 ×7 14	35. 3 ×9 27

Problem Solving

36. There are 3 paintbrushes in each box. There are 8 boxes. How many paintbrushes are there? _______

37. There are 3 paintbrushes in one box. There are 8 paintbrushes in another box. How many paintbrushes are there? _______

38. There are 2 jars of paste on each table. There are 7 tables. How many jars of paste are there? _______

39. There are 2 jars of paste on a desk. On a table there are 7 jars of paste. How many more jars of paste are on the table? _______

40. There are 3 boxes of pencils. There are 6 pencils in each box. How many pencils are there? _______

41. There are 3 pens in a box. There are 6 pens on the desk. How many pens are there? _______

Name ____________________

Multiplication patterns

Work in groups. Get squared paper. Record your answers on a separate sheet of paper if you need more space.

PART A

Look at these rectangles.

1 × 3 = 3

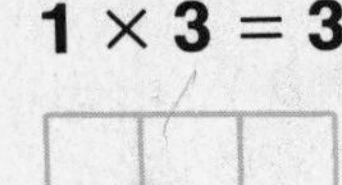

2 × 3 = 6

3 × 3 = 9

1. Draw the next 3 rectangles in the pattern.
2. How many little squares does each rectangle have?
3. Write a multiplication equation for each rectangle you drew.
4. What pattern do you see in the number of squares in each rectangle?
5. Fill in the chart for 4, 5, and 6.

	1	2	3	4	5	6	7	8	9
× 3	3	6	9						

6. If you know that 6 × 3 is 18, how can that help you find what 7 × 3 is?

   How could that have helped you find what 5 × 3 is?

7. Complete the × 3 chart. Draw rectangles to check if you need to.

8.

	1	2	3	4	5	6	7	8	9
× 2									

   a. Fill in your chart for 1, 2, and 3. Do you see a pattern?
   b. Use that pattern to complete the chart.
   c. If you know that 7 × 2 = 14, how could that help you find what 8 × 2 is?

9. Fill in the first two facts.

$2 \times 5 =$ ______

$3 \times 5 =$ ______

$4 \times 5 =$ ______

$5 \times 5 =$ ______

$6 \times 5 =$ ______

a. What do you think 4×5 is? Draw a rectangle to check.
b. What pattern do you see in this list of facts?
c. Use that pattern to figure out the rest of the list. Draw rectangles to check.

10. How can the pattern above help you figure out what 7×5 and 8×5 are? Try it. Did it work?

11. Draw a rectangle to show what 7×6 is.

a. How can this help you find out what 8×6 is?
b. Make an estimate. Check by drawing a rectangle.

PART B

12. Which is larger? Make a guess. Draw rectangles to check.

a. 6×3 or 7×2

b. 3×4 or 2×5

c. 5×6 or 4×7

d. 8×4 or 9×3

e. 7×8 or 6×9

f. 4×7 or 7×4

13. What did you discover when you compared 4×7 with 7×4? Do you think this would happen for 5×8 and 8×5? Draw rectangles to check.

14. Do you think this would happen for any other pairs of numbers? Make up some pairs of numbers. Draw rectangles to check.

15. Compare your answers to exercises 12–14 with those of one other group.

Name ______________________________

Exploring 4 as a factor

Work in groups.
Get squared paper and a calculator.
Record your answers on a separate sheet of paper if you need more space.

$1 \times 2 = 2$

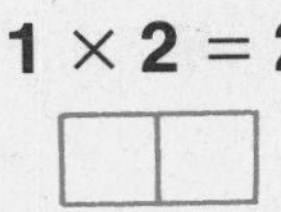

$2 \times 2 = 4$

$3 \times 2 = 6$

$1 \times 4 = 4$

$2 \times 4 = 8$

$3 \times 4 = 12$

PART A

1. Look at the red rectangles. What pattern do you see?

2. Look at the blue rectangles. What pattern do you see?

3. How many squares will the next red rectangle in the pattern have? Write your guess. Draw the rectangle to check.

4. How many squares will the next blue rectangle in the pattern have? Write your guess. Draw the rectangle to check.

5.

	1	2	3	4	5	6	7	8	9
× 2	2	4	6						
× 4	4	8	12						

a. Fill in both rows of the chart for 4, 5, and 6. Draw rectangles when you need to.

b. Compare the two rows of the chart. What patterns do you see?

6. If you can multiply by 2, how can this help you multiply by 4? Make up a rule that tells how to multiply by 4 if you know how to multiply by 2.

7. Test your rule with the rest of the numbers in the chart.
   a. Does your rule work?
   b. Does your rule work for larger numbers? Use a calculator to find out.

PART B

Make 2 teams. Then have each team do these steps:

8. Draw a secret rectangle. Make it between 2 and 9 squares high. Make it either 2, 3, or 4 squares wide. Do not show your rectangle to the other team yet.

9. Get a piece of paper. Use it to cover up part of your secret rectangle. Cover a corner and part of 2 sides. Now show the uncovered part of your rectangle to the other team.

10. Ask the other team to figure out how many squares are in the whole rectangle.

11. Try this activity a few times. Let each team take turns drawing the secret rectangle. Make a new secret rectangle each time.

12. What ways did your team use to figure out how many squares were in the secret rectangles? What ways did the other team use?

Name ________________________________

5 as a factor

2 ☆s have 10 △s.

EXERCISES

Give each product. If you need to, use the picture above.

1. 1 × 5 = ______	**2.** 2 × 5 = ______	**3.** 3 × 5 = ______
4. 4 × 5 = ______	**5.** 5 × 5 = ______	**6.** 6 × 5 = ______
7. 7 × 5 = ______	**8.** 8 × 5 = ______	**9.** 9 × 5 = ______
10. 4 × 5 = ______	**11.** 5 × 5 = ______	**12.** 6 × 5 = ______
13. 8 × 5 = ______	**14.** 9 × 5 = ______	**15.** 1 × 5 = ______
16. 4 × 5 = ______	**17.** 3 × 5 = ______	**18.** 2 × 5 = ______
19. 3 × 5 = ______	**20.** 5 × 5 = ______	**21.** 7 × 5 = ______
22. 8 × 5 = ______	**23.** 6 × 5 = ______	**24.** 9 × 5 = ______

Multiply.

25. 5×1	26. 5×2	27. 5×3	28. 5×4	29. 5×5	30. 5×6
31. 5×7	32. 5×8	33. 5×9	34. 3×7	35. 3×5	36. 4×3
37. 2×9	38. 2×7	39. 4×4	40. 3×4	41. 5×6	42. 4×9
43. 5×7	44. 3×3	45. 5×8	46. 4×6	47. 5×9	48. 3×6
49. 3×8	50. 4×7	51. 4×8	52. 4×5	53. 3×9	54. 5×5

Challenge!

Give the missing number.

55.

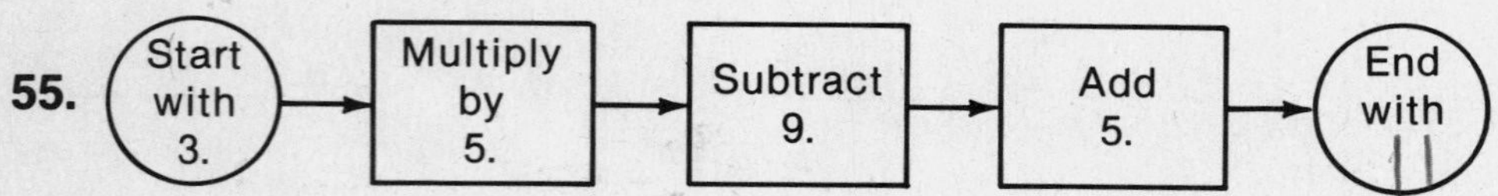
Start with 3.
Multiply by 5.
Subtract 9.
Add 5.
End with

56.

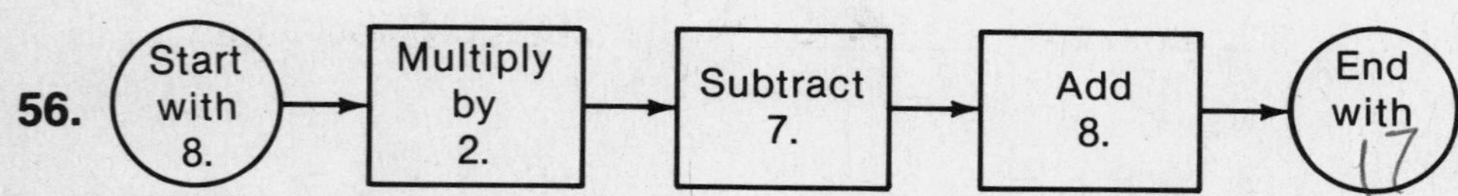
Start with 8.
Multiply by 2.
Subtract 7.
Add 8.
End with

57.

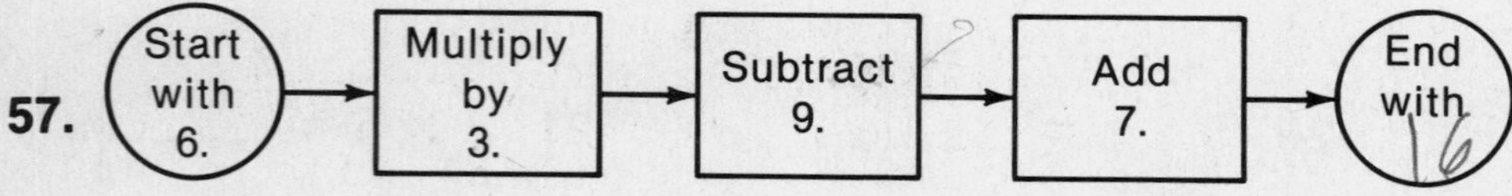
Start with 6.
Multiply by 3.
Subtract 9.
Add 7.
End with

Name ____________________

Problem Solving

Using data

EXERCISES

Complete.

1. 2 [house] cost __6__ ¢.
2. 2 [car] cost __8__ ¢.

3. 4 [umbrella] cost __20__ ¢.
4. 5 [car] cost __20__ ¢.
5. 8 [kite] cost __16__ ¢.
6. 6 [umbrella] cost __30__ ¢.
7. 9 [umbrella] cost __45__ ¢.
8. 8 [car] cost __32__ ¢.
9. 7 [kite] cost __14__ ¢.
10. 7 [umbrella] cost __35__ ¢.
11. 9 [kite] cost __18__ ¢.
12. 8 [house] cost __24__ ¢.

Complete.

13. 4 cost _______ ¢.

14. 6 cost _______ ¢.

15. 5 cost _______ ¢.

16. 8 cost _______ ¢.

17. 9 cost _______ ¢.

18. 7 cost _______ ¢.

19. 6 cost _______ ¢.

20. 9 cost _______ ¢.

Solve.

21. Luis had 50¢.
He bought 9
How much money
did he have left? _______

22. Lisa had 75¢.
She bought 6
How much money
did she have left? _______

★ 23. How much do
4 and 2
cost? _______

★ 24. How much do 8
and 5 cost?
____

Name ____

Problem Solving Too much information

1. Study and understand.
2. Plan and do.
3. Answer and check.

Sometimes there are more facts in the problem than you need.

Popcorn costs 25¢ a bag.
Peanuts cost 30¢ a bag.
How much do 2 bags of peanuts cost?

These facts are needed:
cost 30¢ a bag
2 bags

Answer:
2 bags of peanuts cost 60¢.

EXERCISES

Tell what facts you need. Then solve the problem.

1. There are 12 lions.
There are 15 tigers.
There are 8 elephants.
How many lions and tigers are there in all? ______

2. There are 12 lions.
There are 15 tigers.
There are 8 elephants.
How many more tigers than elephants are there? ______

3. There are 3 lions and 2 tigers in each cage. There are 6 cages. How many lions are there? ______

4. On June 25 the circus came to town. 2307 children and 1948 adults saw the circus. How many people saw the circus? ______

5. There are 8 monkeys in each big cage. There are 5 monkeys in each small cage. There are 4 big cages. There are 3 small cages. How many monkeys are in the big cages? _______

6. There are 8 monkeys in each big cage. There are 5 monkeys in each small cage. There are 4 big cages. There are 3 small cages. How many monkeys are there in all? _______

7. 12 clowns are in the first car. 15 clowns are in the second car. 16 clowns are in the third car. How many more clowns are in the third car than in the first car? _______

8. There were 8 children. Each child ate 2 hot dogs and 3 cookies. How many cookies did they eat in all? _______

9. There were 23 red balloons, 45 blue balloons, and 18 yellow balloons. How many more red balloons were there than yellow balloons? _______

10. There were 50 pink balloons and 43 green balloons. 15 of the green balloons blew away. How many green balloons were left? _______

Name ______

1 and 0 as factors

$2 \times 1 = 2$

$3 \times 0 = 0$

Any number times 1 is the same number.

EXERCISES
Give each product.

1. $1 \times 1 =$ 1

2. $2 \times 1 =$ 2

3. $3 \times 1 =$ 3

4. $4 \times 1 =$ 4

5. $5 \times 1 =$ 5

6. $6 \times 1 =$ 6

7. $7 \times 1 =$ 7

8. $8 \times 1 =$ 8

9. $9 \times 1 =$ 9

Any number times 0 is 0.

10. $1 \times 0 =$ 0

11. $2 \times 0 =$ 0

12. $3 \times 0 =$ 0

13. $4 \times 0 =$ 0

14. $5 \times 0 =$ 0

15. $6 \times 0 =$ 0

16. $7 \times 0 =$ 0

17. $8 \times 0 =$ 0

18. $9 \times 0 =$ 0

Multiply.

19. 4×7	20. 0×1	21. 1×6	22. 3×7	23. 0×6	24. 2×7
25. 1×3	26. 0×9	27. 2×8	28. 3×8	29. 4×8	30. 3×4
31. 1×7	32. 1×2	33. 1×9	34. 2×5	35. 5×9	36. 0×3
37. 2×6	38. 5×6	39. 3×9	40. 5×7	41. 0×8	42. 5×4
43. 3×6	44. 0×7	45. 4×9	46. 0×2	47. 4×5	48. 1×5
49. 4×6	50. 1×1	51. 1×8	52. 2×9	53. 5×8	54. 2×3

KEEPING SKILLS SHARP

Yoshiro did these problems on his calculator. Three are wrong. Estimate to find the wrong answers.

1. 189 + 235 → 424
2. 201 + 496 → 597
3. 284 + 515 → 799
4. 547 + 414 → 1041
5. 695 + 138 → 933
6. 417 + 281 → 698

Name Matán #2

More about multiplication

The Order Property of Multiplication

You can change the order of the factors without changing the product.

$2 \times 4 = 8$ $4 \times 2 = 8$

EXERCISES

Give each product.

1. a. $4 \times 1 =$ 4
   b. $1 \times 4 =$ 4
2. a. $3 \times 0 =$ 0
   b. $0 \times 3 =$ 0
3. a. $5 \times 1 =$ 5
   b. $1 \times 5 =$ 5
4. a. $4 \times 0 =$ 0
   b. $0 \times 4 =$ 0
5. a. $3 \times 1 =$ 3
   b. $1 \times 3 =$ 3
6. a. $6 \times 2 =$ 12
   b. $2 \times 6 =$ 12
7. a. $5 \times 2 =$ 10
   b. $2 \times 5 =$ 10
8. a. $3 \times 2 =$ 6
   b. $2 \times 3 =$ 6
9. a. $9 \times 0 =$ 0
   b. $0 \times 9 =$ 0
10. a. $3 \times 5 =$ 15
    b. $5 \times 3 =$ 15
11. a. $3 \times 4 =$ 12
    b. $4 \times 3 =$ 12
12. a. $4 \times 5 =$ 20
    b. $5 \times 4 =$ 20

Multiply.

13. $\begin{array}{r} 3 \\ \times 5 \\ \hline \end{array}$ 14. $\begin{array}{r} 5 \\ \times 8 \\ \hline \end{array}$ 15. $\begin{array}{r} 5 \\ \times 4 \\ \hline \end{array}$ 16. $\begin{array}{r} 4 \\ \times 4 \\ \hline \end{array}$ 17. $\begin{array}{r} 5 \\ \times 6 \\ \hline \end{array}$ 18. $\begin{array}{r} 5 \\ \times 1 \\ \hline \end{array}$

19. $\begin{array}{r} 4 \\ \times 6 \\ \hline \end{array}$ 20. $\begin{array}{r} 3 \\ \times 7 \\ \hline \end{array}$ 21. $\begin{array}{r} 4 \\ \times 3 \\ \hline \end{array}$ 22. $\begin{array}{r} 3 \\ \times 4 \\ \hline \end{array}$ 23. $\begin{array}{r} 3 \\ \times 9 \\ \hline \end{array}$ 24. $\begin{array}{r} 4 \\ \times 7 \\ \hline \end{array}$

25. $\begin{array}{r} 3 \\ \times 6 \\ \hline \end{array}$ 26. $\begin{array}{r} 5 \\ \times 3 \\ \hline \end{array}$ 27. $\begin{array}{r} 4 \\ \times 8 \\ \hline \end{array}$ 28. $\begin{array}{r} 5 \\ \times 2 \\ \hline \end{array}$ 29. $\begin{array}{r} 5 \\ \times 7 \\ \hline \end{array}$ 30. $\begin{array}{r} 3 \\ \times 3 \\ \hline \end{array}$

How many blocks?

31. 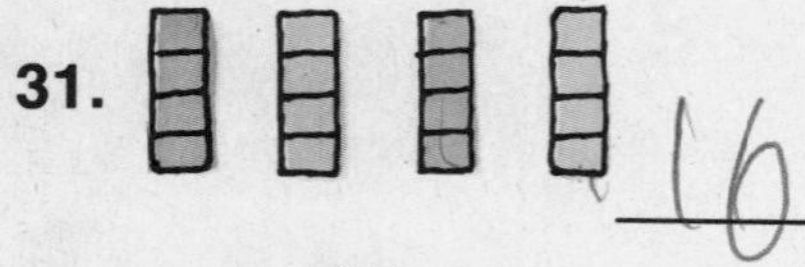 ____

32. 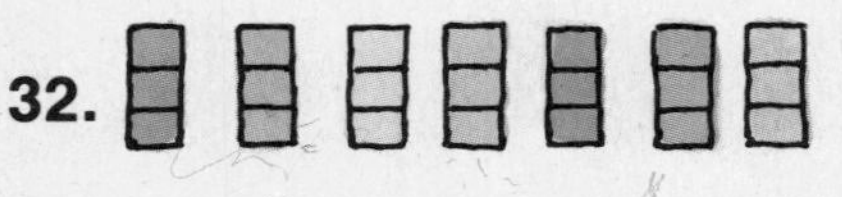 ____

33. 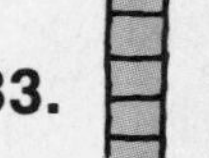 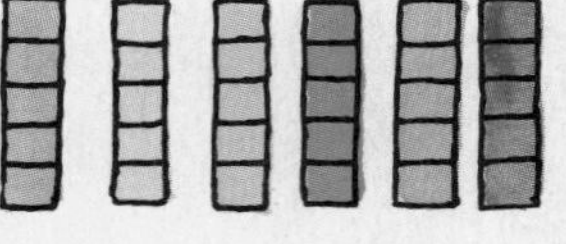 ____

34. 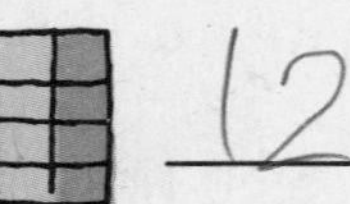 ____

35. 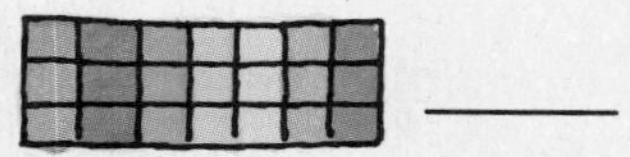 ____

36.  ____

37. 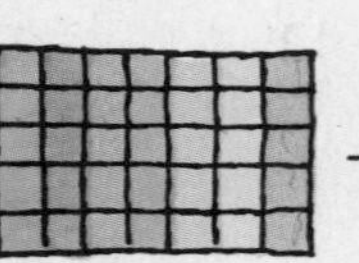 ____

38. 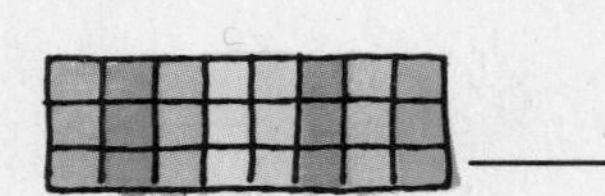 ____

39. 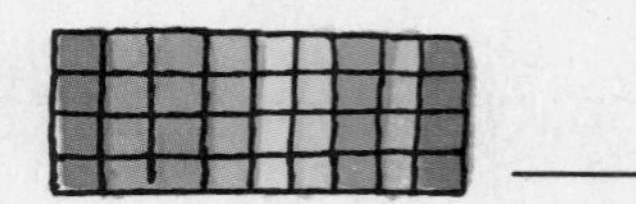 ____

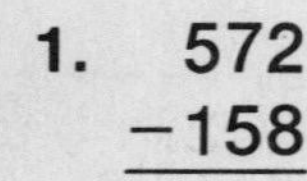

KEEPING SKILLS SHARP

1. $\begin{array}{r} 572 \\ -158 \\ \hline \end{array}$ 2. $\begin{array}{r} 621 \\ -249 \\ \hline \end{array}$ 3. $\begin{array}{r} 430 \\ -228 \\ \hline \end{array}$ 4. $\begin{array}{r} 852 \\ -343 \\ \hline \end{array}$ 5. $\begin{array}{r} 934 \\ -628 \\ \hline \end{array}$

6. $\begin{array}{r} 743 \\ -358 \\ \hline \end{array}$ 7. $\begin{array}{r} 628 \\ -249 \\ \hline \end{array}$ 8. $\begin{array}{r} 413 \\ -179 \\ \hline \end{array}$ 9. $\begin{array}{r} 525 \\ -259 \\ \hline \end{array}$ 10. $\begin{array}{r} 610 \\ -258 \\ \hline \end{array}$

11. $\begin{array}{r} 203 \\ -159 \\ \hline \end{array}$ 12. $\begin{array}{r} 506 \\ -258 \\ \hline \end{array}$ 13. $\begin{array}{r} 703 \\ -375 \\ \hline \end{array}$ 14. $\begin{array}{r} 800 \\ -453 \\ \hline \end{array}$ 15. $\begin{array}{r} 900 \\ -267 \\ \hline \end{array}$

Name Matin #2

Practice

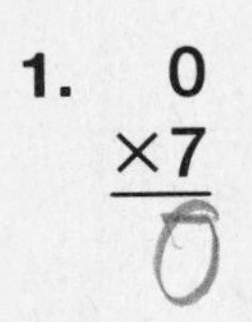

		1. 0×7 = 0	2. 5×5 = 25	3. 3×2 = 6	4. 4×6 = 24
		5. 4×3 = 12	6. 2×3 = 6	7. 5×6 = 30	8. 4×2 = 8
9. 2×2 = 4	10. 5×1 = 5	11. 2×4 = 8	12. 4×7 = 28	13. 3×3 = 9	14. 5×3 = 15
15. 3×4 = 12	16. 0×0 = 0	17. 5×7 = 35	18. 3×6 = 18	19. 4×8 = 32	20. 3×9 = 27
21. 2×7 = 14	22. 3×5 = 15	23. 2×5 = 10	24. 4×5 = 20	25. 5×8 = 40	26. 5×2 = 10
27. 2×1 = 2	28. 5×4 = 20	29. 3×7 = 21	30. 3×1 = 3	31. 4×1 = 4	32. 2×9 = 18
33. 2×6 = 12	34. 4×4 = 16	35. 2×8 = 16	36. 5×9 = 45	37. 3×8 = 24	38. 4×9 = 36

Problem Solving Making a table

1. Study and understand.	*You can solve the problem by making a table.*
2. Plan and do.	
3. Answer and check.	

Terry has 12 stickers. If he gets 2 stickers each day, how many more days will it take him to collect a total of 30 stickers?

Days	Today	1	2	3	4	5	6	7	8	9
Stickers	12	14	16	18	20	22	24	26	28	30

Answer: It will take 9 more days to collect a total of 30 stickers.

EXERCISES

Complete the table to solve the problem.

1. Lisa has 31 stickers. If she gets 3 stickers each day, how long will it take her to collect a total of 46 stickers? ______

Days	Today	1	2	3	4
Stickers	31	34	37	40	43

Solve each problem by making a table.

2. Earl has 24 stickers. If he gives away 3 stickers each day, how many stickers will he have after 5 days? ______

★ 3. Nina has 31 stickers. She gets 3 more stickers each day. Will she have 50 stickers after a week? ______

Name ____________________

Problem Solving / Drawing a picture

1. Study and understand. 2. Plan and do. 3. Answer and check.	*Sometimes it helps to draw a picture or to make a picture in my mind.*

There are 3 boxes of apples.
There are 8 apples in each box.
How many apples are there?

Answer: There are 24 apples.

EXERCISES

Match the picture to the problem.

1. There are 4 boxes of apples.
There are 3 apples in each box.

How many apples are there? ________

a. 

2. There are 4 apples in one box.
There are 3 apples in another box.

How many apples are there? ________

b. 

3. There are 3 boxes of apples.
There are 4 apples in each box.

How many apples are there? ________

c. 

Solve. Draw pictures to help you.

4. There are 8 lemons. There are 5 oranges. How many pieces of fruit are there in all? _______

5. Mike has 5 carrots and 2 tomatoes. How many more carrots does he have? _______

6. John has 5 boxes of oranges. There are 4 oranges in each box. How many oranges does he have in all? _______

7. There are 3 cars. There are 6 trucks. How many more trucks are there? _______

8. Mio has 9¢. Karen has 3¢. How much money do they have in all? _______

9. There are 3 banks. Each bank has 7¢ in it. How much money is there in all? _______

10. Heather had 8¢. She bought an apple that costs 6¢. How much money did she have left?

____

11. Brian bought 5 boxes of apples. Each box had 6 apples in it. How many apples did he buy in all? _______

Challenge!

Tell a story.

Name ______________________________

Problem Solving Reading graphs

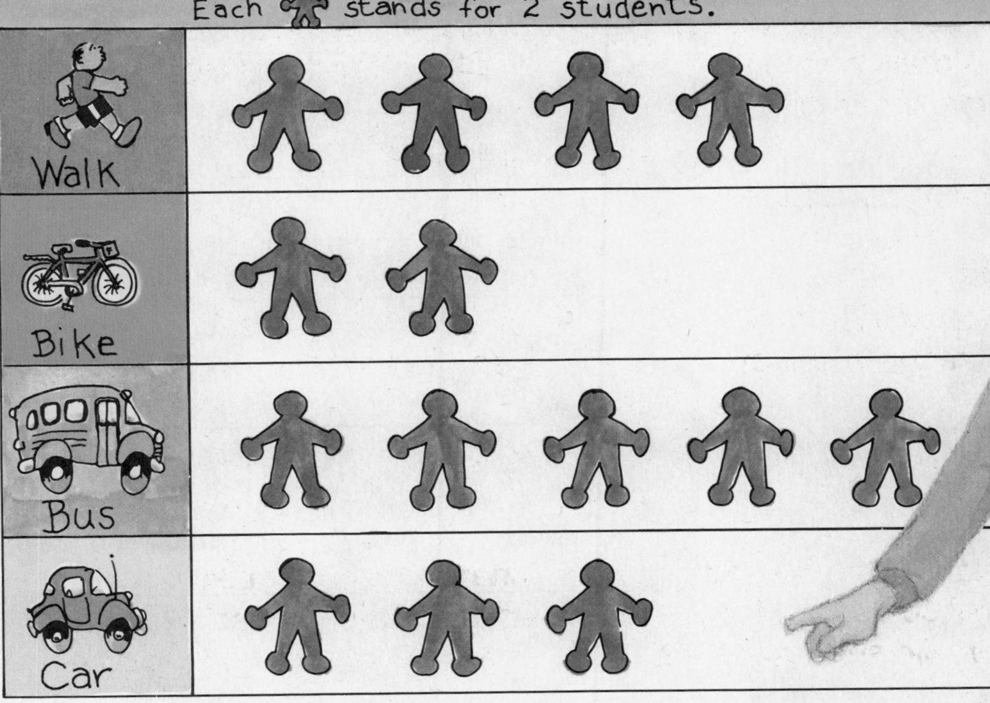
How we come to school
Each stands for 2 students.
Walk
Bike
Bus
Car
The picture graph shows how the students in our class come to school.

EXERCISES

How many students

1. walk? *Hint:*

means 4 × 2.

2. ride a bus? ______

3. ride a bicycle? ______

4. ride in a car? ______

5. How many more students ride a bus than ride a bicycle? ______

6. How many students either walk or ride in a car? ______

★ 7. How many students are in the class? ______

★ 8. How many students do not walk to school? ______

The bar graph shows how many students bought each dinosaur model.

Our Visit to the Dinosaur Museum

Dinosaur models we bought –

10
9
8
7
6
5
4
3
2
1

How many students bought

9.  ? ______

10.  ? ______

11.  ? ______

12.  ? ______

13. Did more students buy  than  ? ______

14. How many more students bought  than  ? ______

15. costs 5¢.
How much did the class spend on  ? ______

16.  costs 7¢.
How much did the class spend on  ? ______

Name Matin #2

Chapter Checkup

Multiply. [pages 158–169, 174–178]

1. 4×2 = 8	2. 2×7 = 14	3. 4×5 = 20	4. 3×7 = 21	5. 5×1 = 5	6. 2×1 = 2
7. 5×2 = 10	8. 3×1 = 3	9. 4×7 = 28	10. 0×5 = 0	11. 3×3 = 9	12. 5×4 = 20
13. 0×8 = 0	14. 0×0 = 0	15. 2×5 = 10	16. 5×9 = 45	17. 2×2 = 4	18. 3×2 = 6
19. 2×4 = 8	20. 5×6 = 30	21. 2×9 = 18	22. 2×3 = 6	23. 4×4 = 16	24. 4×3 = 12
25. 4×6 = 24	26. 3×9 = 27	27. 3×4 = 12	28. 4×9 = 36	29. 2×8 = 16	30. 5×8 = 40

31. $3 \times 5 =$ 15

32. $6 \times 3 =$ 18

33. $7 \times 5 =$ 35

34. $1 \times 3 =$ 3

35. $6 \times 2 =$ 12

36. $4 \times 4 =$ 16

Solve. [pages 163, 170–173, 179–183]

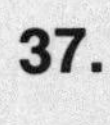

37.   

How many candles? 15

38. 

How many pencils? 20

39. One eraser costs 3¢. How much do 8 erasers cost? 24¢

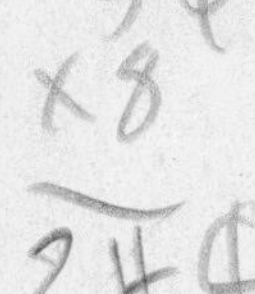

40. One pencil costs 5¢. How much do 7 pencils cost? 35¢

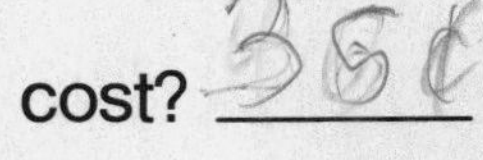

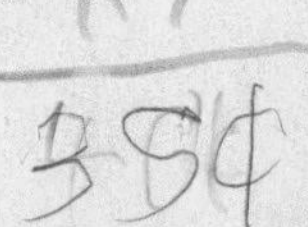

Chapter Project

MAKING A PICTURE GRAPH

Favorite Television Show Each 🯅 stands for 3 friends	
Amazing Animals	🯅 🯅 🯅
Funny People	🯅 🯅 🯅 🯅 🯅
Crazy Cartoons	🯅 🯅 🯅
Super People	🯅
Space Ship Zoom	

1. Make a list of your five favorite television shows.
2. Let some friends see your list. Have them tell which on your list they like best.
3. Make a picture graph. *Hint:* You may want to let 🯅 stand for more than one friend, as in the example.
4. Tell what your graph shows.

Name Matin

Chapter Review

Multiply.

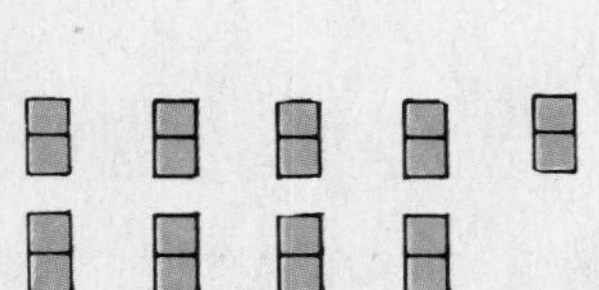

1. 1 × 2 = 2   2. 2 × 2 = 4   3. 3 × 2 = 6

4. 4 × 2 = 8   5. 5 × 2 = 10   6. 6 × 2 = 12

7. 7 × 2 = 14   8. 8 × 2 = 16   9. 9 × 2 = 18

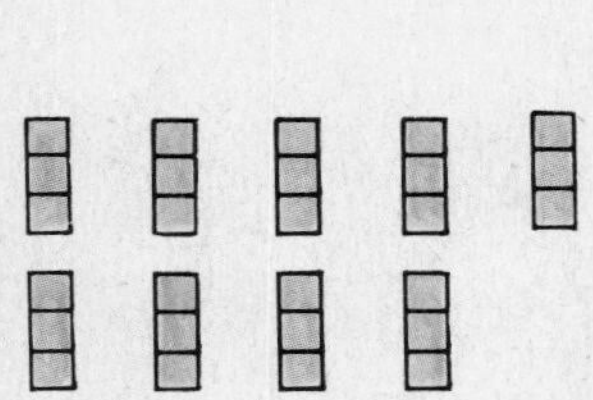

10. 1 × 3 = 3   11. 2 × 3 = 6   12. 3 × 3 = 9

13. 4 × 3 = 16   14. 5 × 3 = 15   15. 6 × 3 = 18

16. 7 × 3 = 21   17. 8 × 3 = 24   18. 9 × 3 = 27

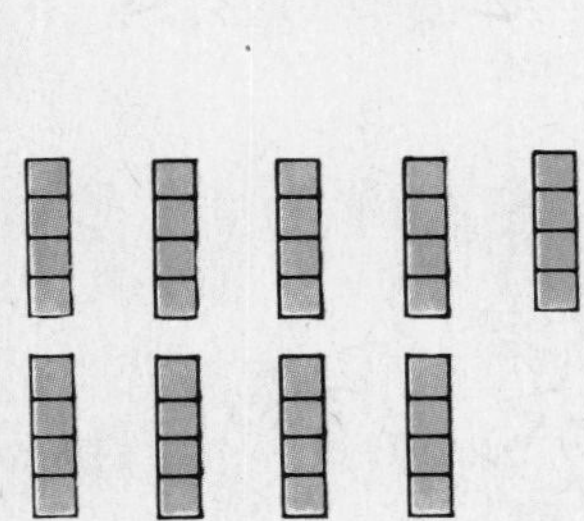

19. 1 × 4 = 4   20. 2 × 4 = 8   21. 3 × 4 = 12

22. 4 × 4 = 16   23. 5 × 4 = 20   24. 6 × 4 = 24

25. 7 × 4 = 28   26. 8 × 4 = 32   27. 9 × 4 = 36

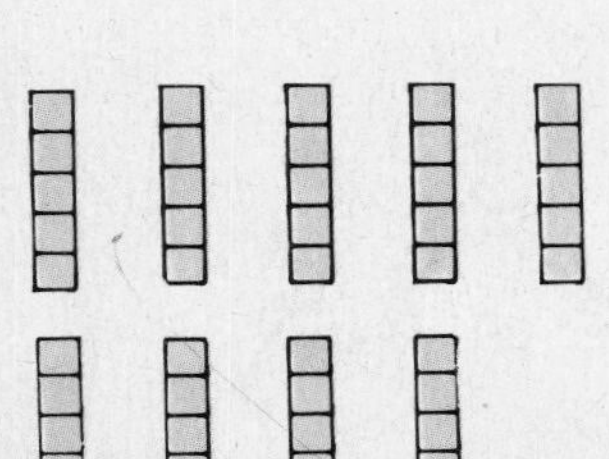

28. 1 × 5 = 5   29. 2 × 5 = 10   30. 3 × 5 = 15

31. 4 × 5 = 20   32. 5 × 5 = 25   33. 6 × 5 = 30

34. 7 × 5 = 35   35. 8 × 5 = 40   36. 9 × 5 = 45

Chapter Challenge

NUMBER PUZZLES

Give the missing numbers.

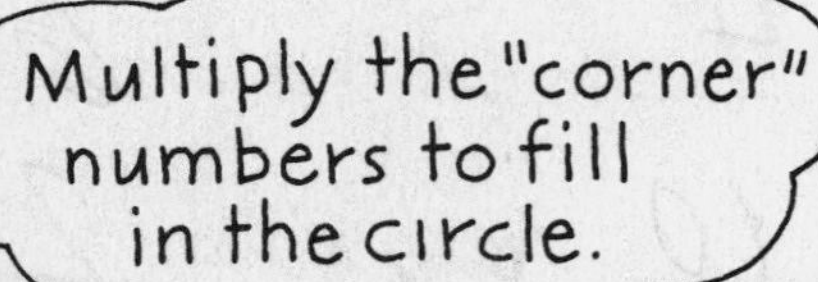

Multiply the "corner" numbers to fill in the circle.

1.

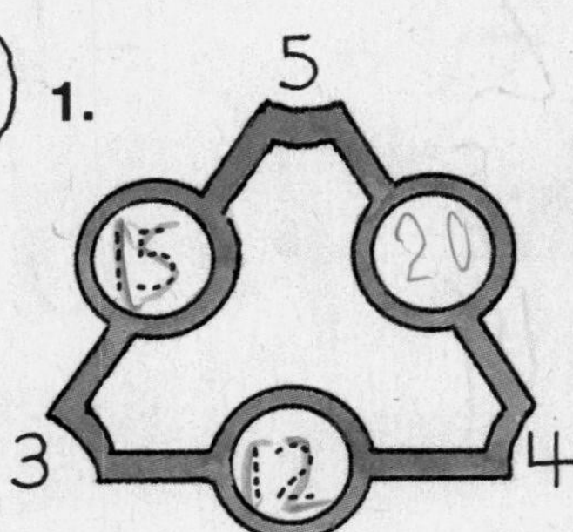

2.

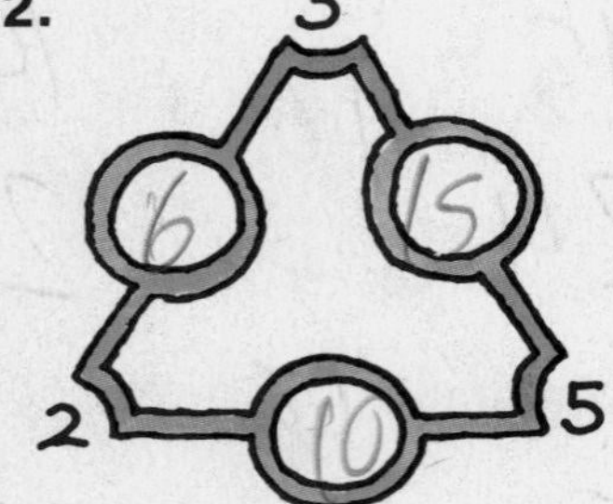

3.

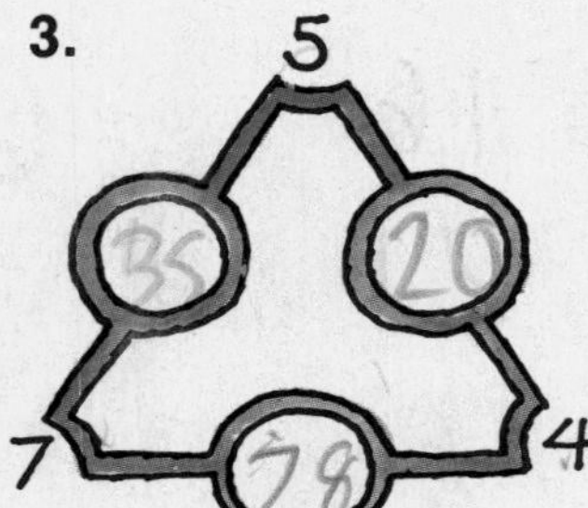

4.

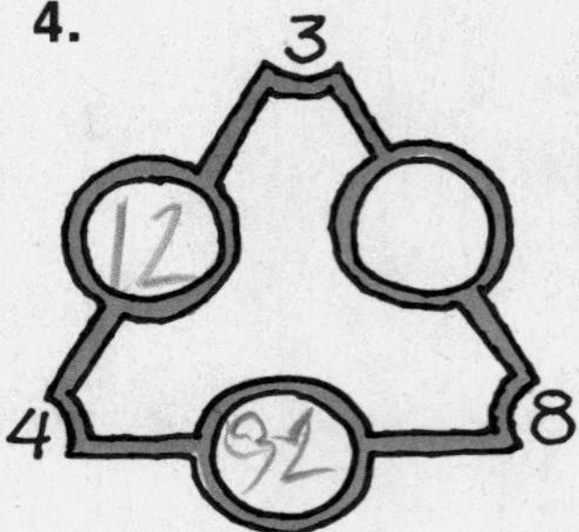

5.

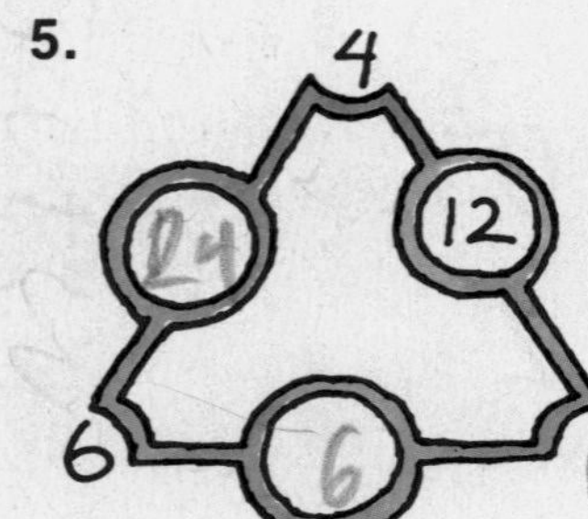

6.

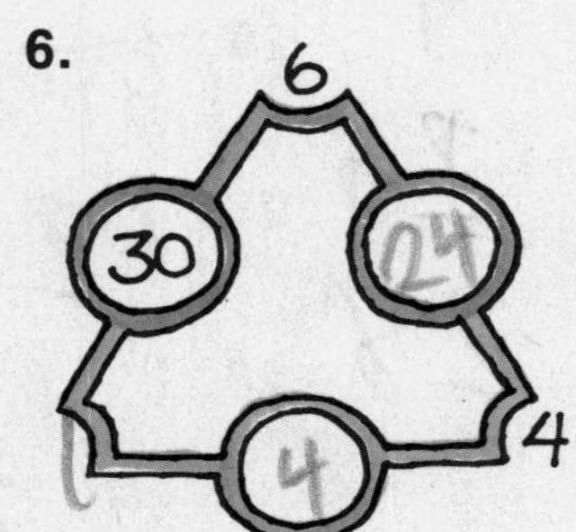

7.

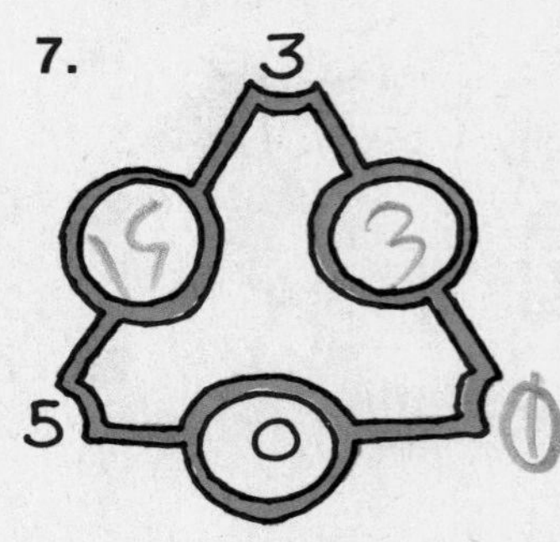

8.

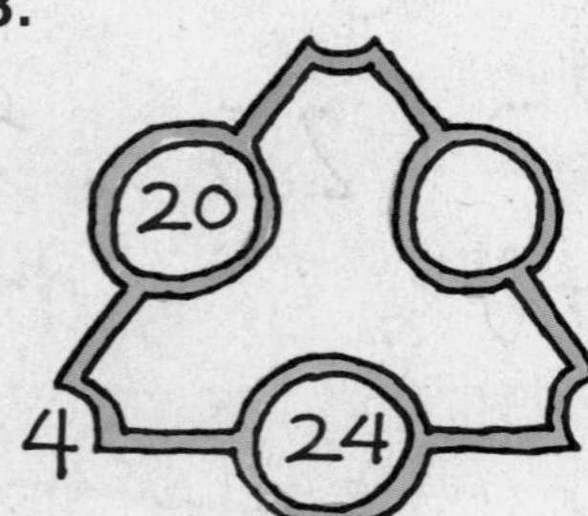

9.

24

32 8

10.

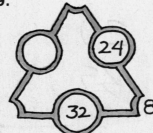

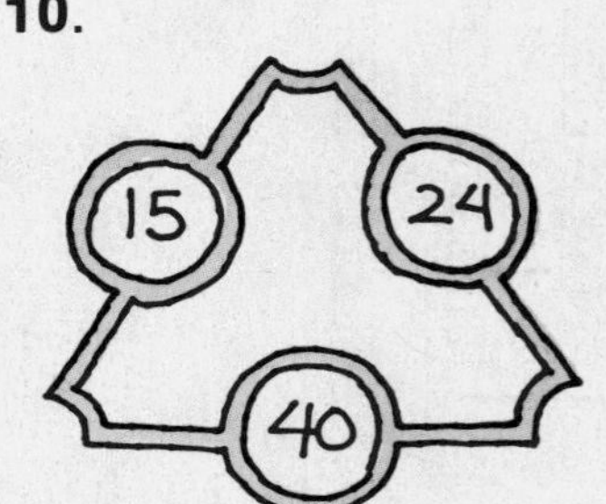

Name ______________________________

Cumulative Checkup

STANDARDIZED FORMAT

Give the correct letter.

1. Complete.
4 + ? = 7

a. 11
b. 5
c. 3
d. none of these

2. In 17 − 9 = 8, 8 is called the

a. sum
b. difference
c. product
d. none of these

3. What number is 10 more than 340?

a. 440
b. 330
c. 400
d. none of these

4. Six hundred five is

a. 650
b. 605
c. 665
d. none of these

5. 66 rounded to the nearest ten is

a. 100
b. 60
c. 70
d. 67

6. Add.

$$\begin{array}{r} 79 \\ 68 \\ +35 \\ \hline \end{array}$$

a. 182
b. 162
c. 172
d. none of these

7. Add.

$$\begin{array}{r} 7691 \\ +1442 \\ \hline \end{array}$$

a. 9143
b. 9133
c. 8033
d. none of these

8. Subtract.

$$\begin{array}{r} 603 \\ -275 \\ \hline \end{array}$$

a. 332
b. 338
c. 328
d. 428

9. How many minutes in one hour?

a. 50
b. 30
c. 100
d. 60

10. How much money?
1 dollar
1 half-dollar
1 dime
1 nickel
2 pennies

a. $1.42
b. $1.67
c. $1.76
d. none of these

11. Multiply.

$$\begin{array}{r} 3 \\ \times 6 \\ \hline \end{array}$$

a. 18
b. 9
c. 24
d. none of these

12. There are 9 pears in one box and 3 pears in another box. How many pears are there?

a. 27 **b.** 12
c. 6 **d.** none of these

7

Division Facts

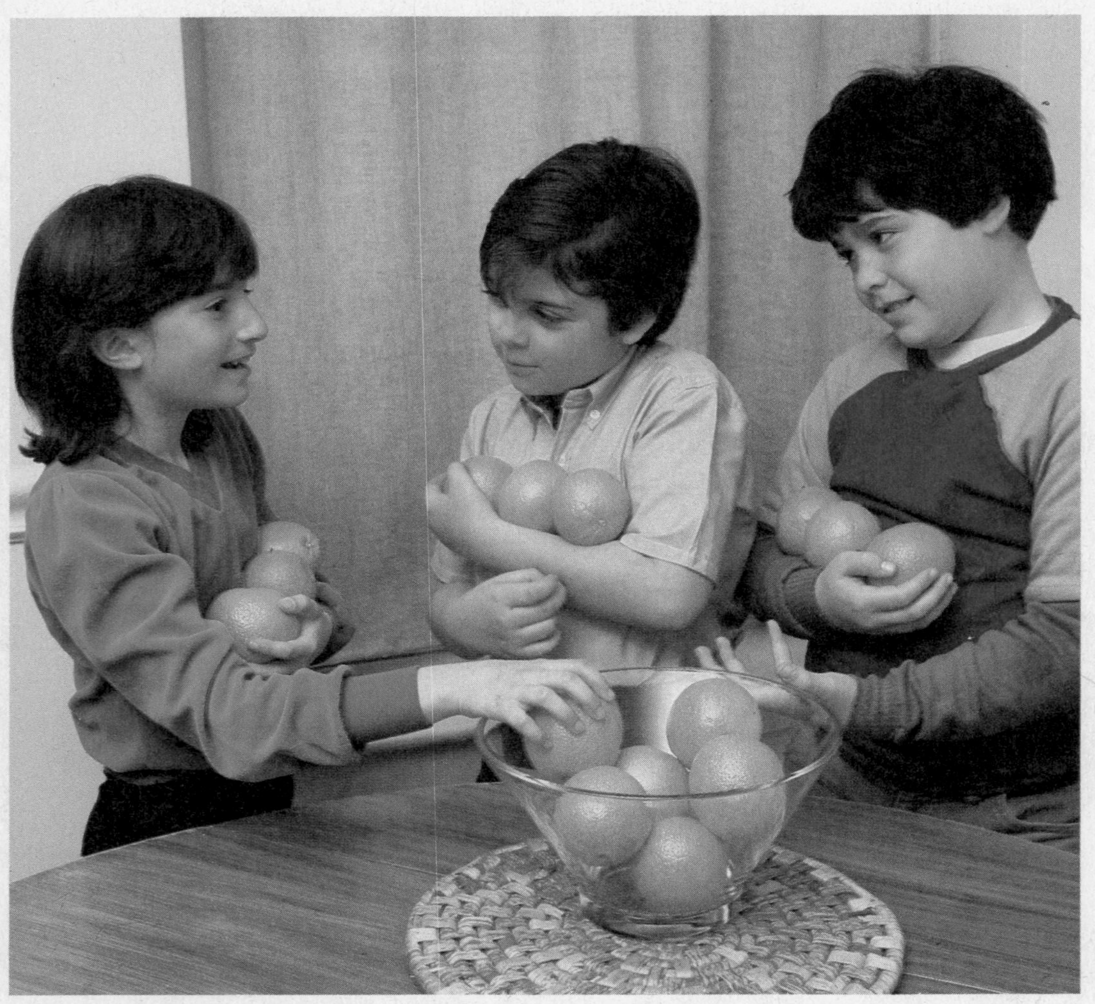

Marcia divided 15 oranges evenly among Tom, Jessie, and herself. How many did each person get?

Name ______________________________

Division

How many
sets of three?

Division equation → 18 ÷ 3 = 6

18	÷	3	=	6
beads in all		beads in each set		sets

18 divided by 3 equals 6.

EXERCISES

1. 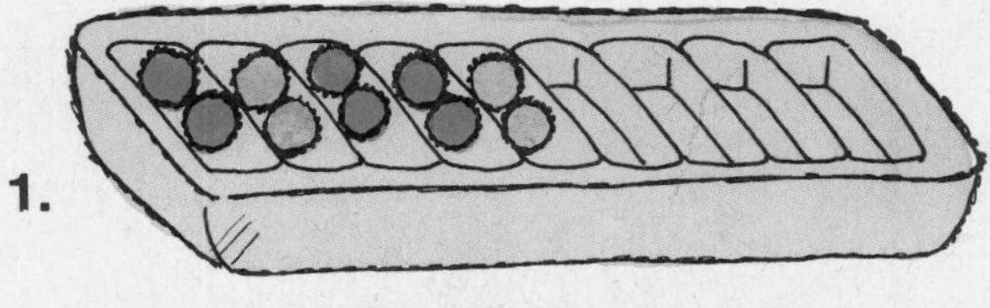

How many twos in 10?

____

2. 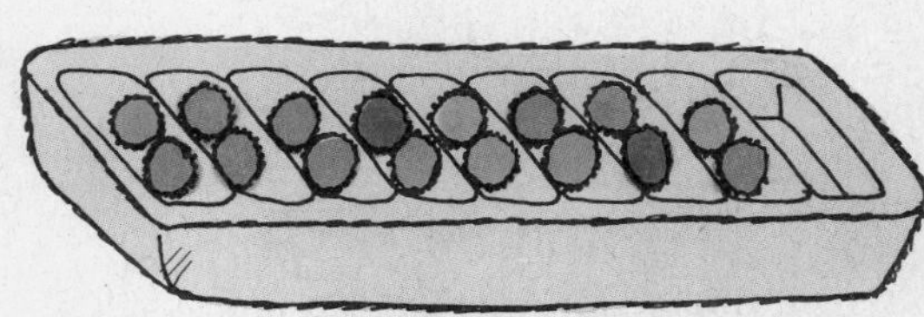

How many twos in 16?

____

3. 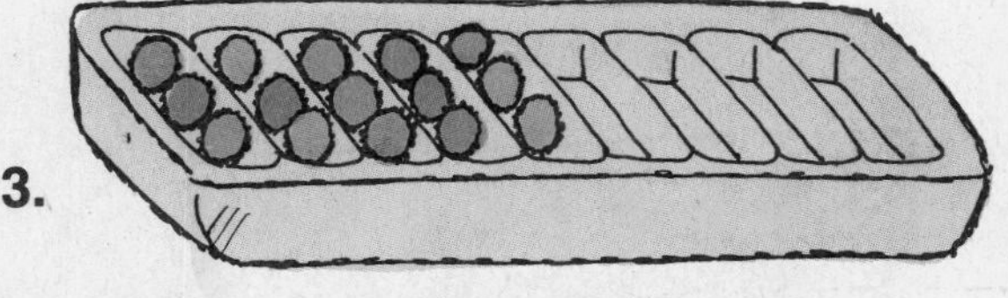

How many threes in 15?

____

4. 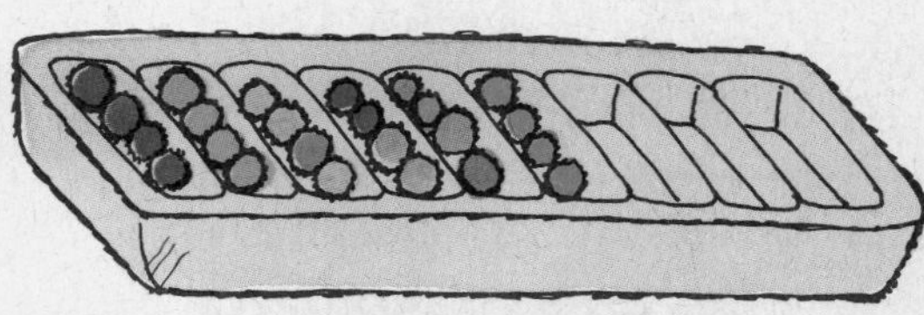

How many fours in 24?

____

Divide.

5. 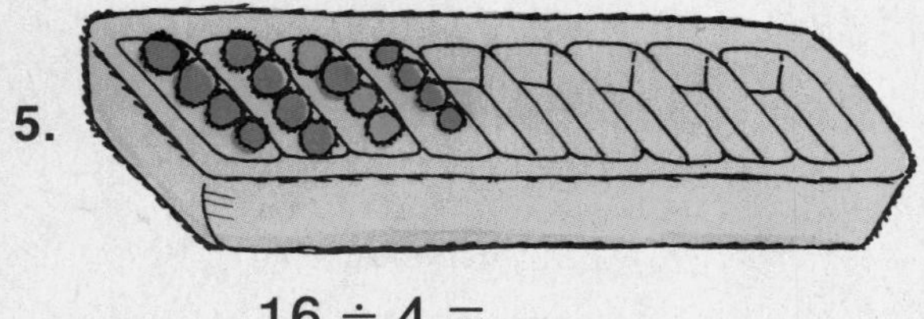

16 ÷ 4 = _____

6. 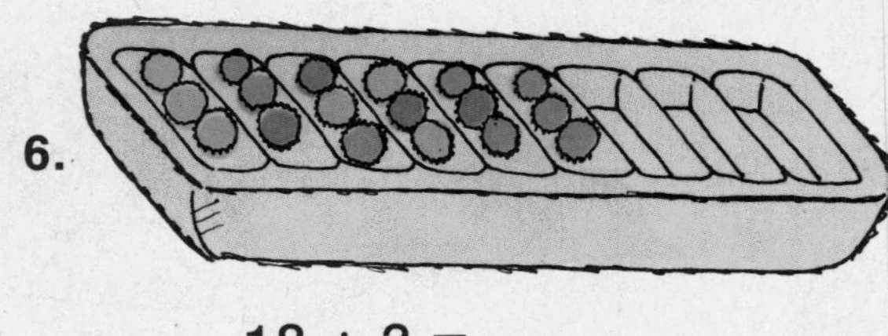

18 ÷ 3 = _____

7. 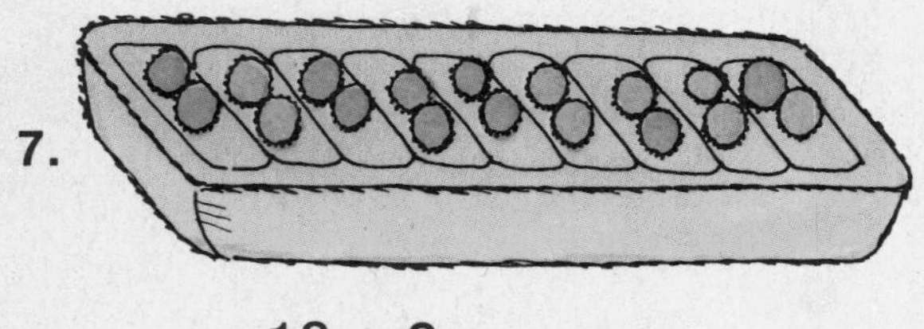

18 ÷ 2 = _____

8. 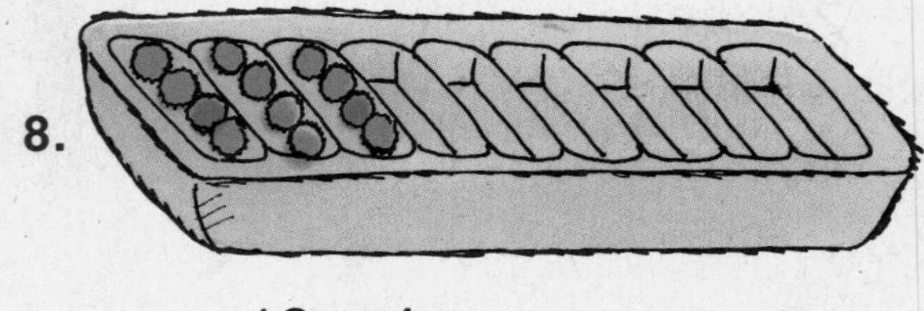

12 ÷ 4 = _____

9. 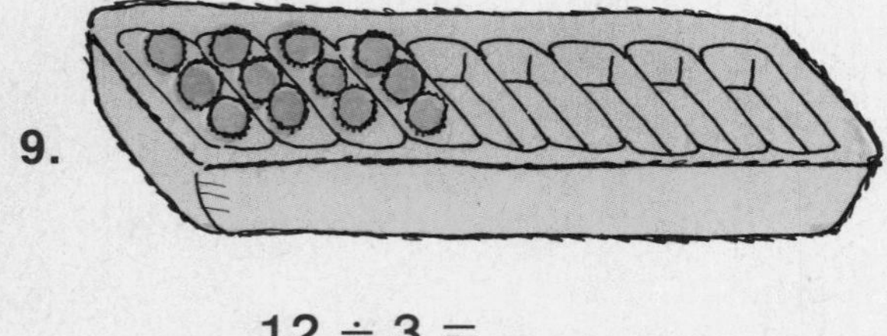

12 ÷ 3 = _____

10. 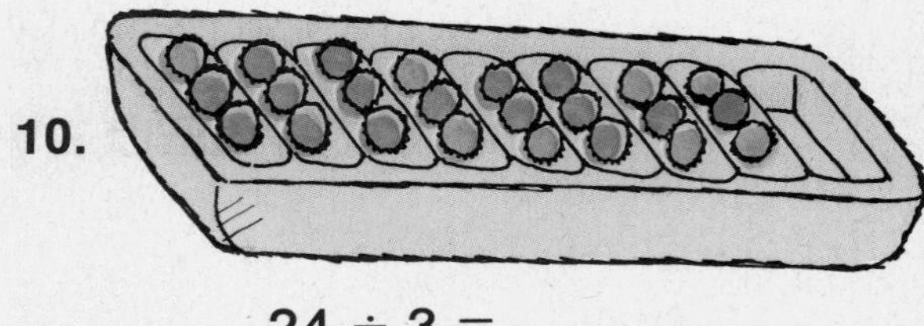

24 ÷ 3 = _____

11.

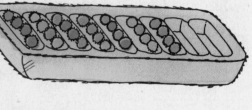

28 ÷ 4 = _____

12. 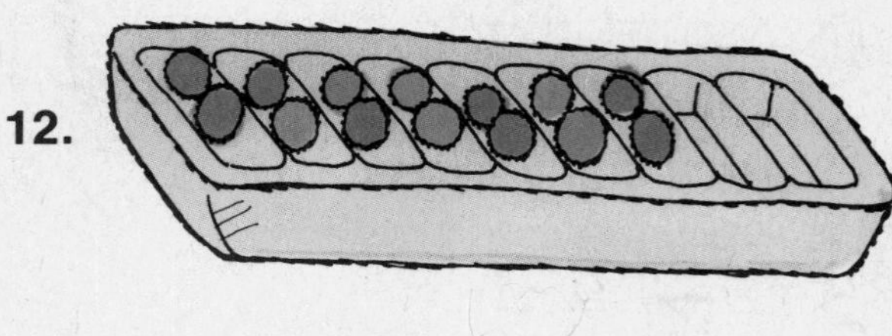

14 ÷ 2 = _____

13. 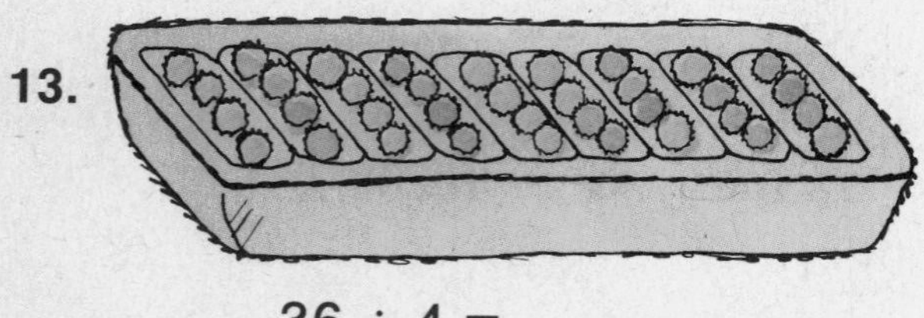

36 ÷ 4 = _____

14. 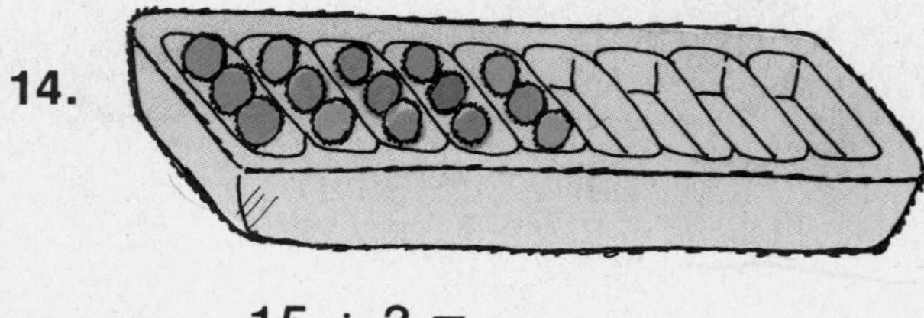

15 ÷ 3 = _____

Name Matin #2

Dividing by 2 and 3

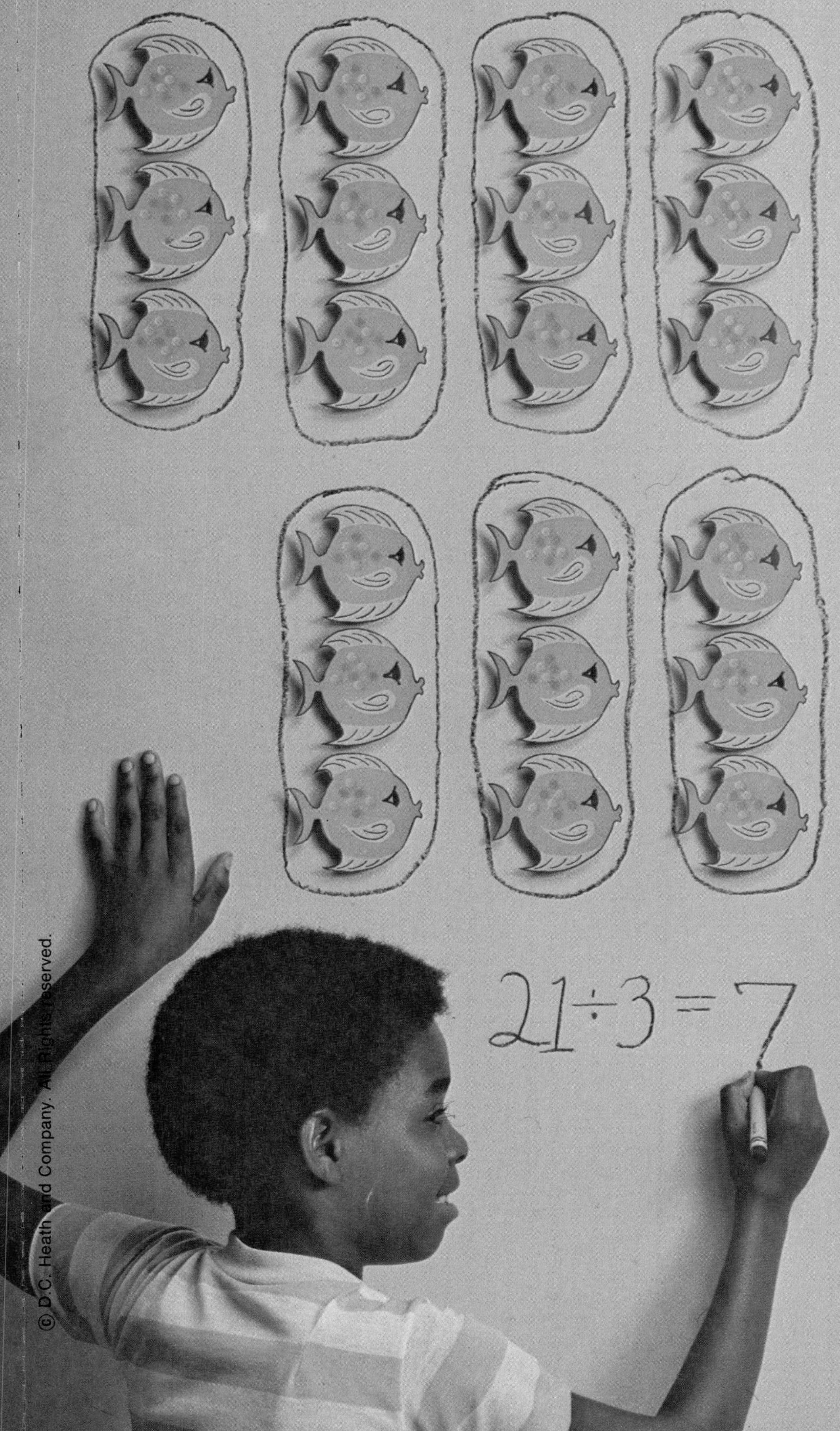

EXERCISES

Divide.

1. 3 ÷ 3 = 1
2. 4 ÷ 2 = 2
3. 6 ÷ 3 = 2
4. 10 ÷ 2 = 5
5. 2 ÷ 2 = 0
6. 18 ÷ 2 = 9
7. 9 ÷ 3 = 3
8. 12 ÷ 3 = 4
9. 8 ÷ 2 = 4
10. 15 ÷ 3 = 5
11. 16 ÷ 2 = 8
12. 24 ÷ 3 = 8
13. 6 ÷ 2 = 3
14. 21 ÷ 3 = 7
15. 18 ÷ 3 = 6
16. 12 ÷ 2 = 6
17. 27 ÷ 3 = 9

18. 6 ÷ 2 = ______ 19. 12 ÷ 3 = ______ 20. 2 ÷ 2 = ______

21. 6 ÷ 3 = ______ 22. 3 ÷ 3 = ______ 23. 16 ÷ 2 = ______

24. 8 ÷ 2 = ______ 25. 4 ÷ 2 = ______ 26. 18 ÷ 3 = ______

27. 18 ÷ 2 = ______ 28. 9 ÷ 3 = ______ 29. 12 ÷ 2 = ______

30. 15 ÷ 3 = ______ 31. 21 ÷ 3 = ______ 32. 10 ÷ 2 = ______

33. 27 ÷ 3 = ______ 34. 14 ÷ 2 = ______ 35. 24 ÷ 3 = ______

Problem Solving

36. There were 15 frogs. There were 3 frogs on each log. How many logs were there? ______

37. There were 16 fish. There were 2 fish in each tank. How many tanks were there? ______

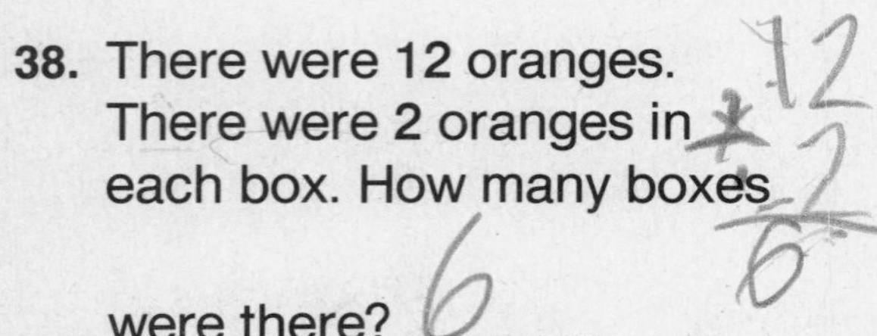

38. There were 12 oranges. There were 2 oranges in each box. How many boxes were there? ______

39. There were 21 apples. There were 3 apples for each basket. How many baskets were there? ______

40. There were 24 rocks. There were 3 rocks for each boy. How many boys were there? ______

41. There were 18 leaves. There were 2 leaves for each girl. How many girls were there? ______

Name ____________________

Dividing by 4 and 5

EXERCISES

Give each quotient.

1. 10 ÷ 5 = ______
2. 4 ÷ 4 = ______
3. 32 ÷ 4 = ______
4. 24 ÷ 4 = ______
5. 5 ÷ 5 = ______
6. 35 ÷ 5 = ______
7. 40 ÷ 5 = ______
8. 20 ÷ 4 ______
9. 20 ÷ 5 = ______
10. 25 ÷ 5 = ______
11. 15 ÷ 5 ______
12. 8 ÷ 4 = ______
13. 12 ÷ 4 = ______
14. 30 ÷ 5 ______
15. 45 ÷ 5 = ______
16. 36 ÷ 4 = ______
17. 16 ÷ 4 = ______
18. 28 ÷ 4 = ______

19. 16 ÷ 4 = ______ **20.** 3 ÷ 3 = ______ **21.** 4 ÷ 2 = ______

22. 6 ÷ 2 = ______ **23.** 10 ÷ 5 = ______ **24.** 5 ÷ 5 = ______

25. 12 ÷ 3 = ______ **26.** 6 ÷ 3 = ______ **27.** 8 ÷ 2 = ______

28. 15 ÷ 5 = ______ **29.** 35 ÷ 5 = ______ **30.** 21 ÷ 3 = ______

31. 10 ÷ 2 = ______ **32.** 20 ÷ 4 = ______ **33.** 12 ÷ 4 = ______

34. 20 ÷ 5 = ______ **35.** 4 ÷ 4 = ______ **36.** 16 ÷ 2 = ______

37. 24 ÷ 4 = ______ **38.** 24 ÷ 3 = ______ **39.** 32 ÷ 4 = ______

40. 14 ÷ 2 = ______ **41.** 25 ÷ 5 = ______ **42.** 15 ÷ 3 = ______

43. 40 ÷ 5 = ______ **44.** 8 ÷ 4 = ______ **45.** 27 ÷ 3 = ______

46. 18 ÷ 3 = ______ **47.** 18 ÷ 2 = ______ **48.** 28 ÷ 4 = ______

49. 36 ÷ 4 = ______ **50.** 30 ÷ 5 = ______ **51.** 45 ÷ 5 = ______

52. 2 ÷ 2 = ______ **53.** 9 ÷ 3 = ______ **54.** 12 ÷ 2 = ______

Challenge!

Find the missing input or output.

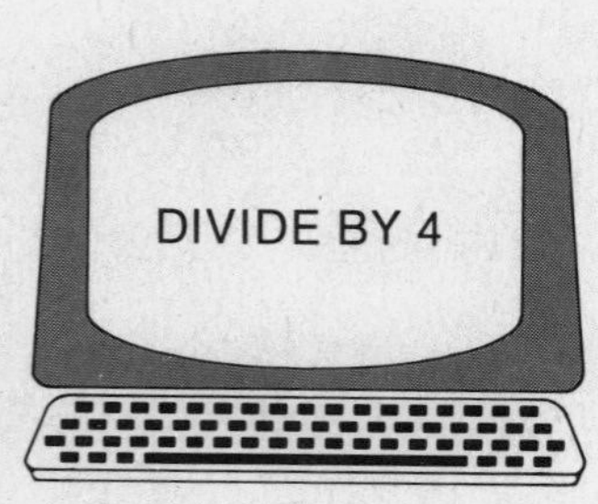

	Input	Output
	16	4
55.	24	
56.	32	
57.		9

Name Matin #2

Problem Solving

Mixed practice

EXERCISES

Solve.

1. They left at 8:30 in the morning and arrived 2 hours later. What time did they arrive? 10:30
   it's 10:30 now

2. They rode the bus 27 miles and walked 4 miles. How far did they travel? ______

3. Ruth's pack weighed 12 pounds. John's pack weighed 11 pounds. How much did the packs weigh together? 23
   it's 23 pounds together

4. Roger's pack weighed 13 pounds. Lauren's pack weighed 9 pounds. How much less did Lauren's pack weigh? ______

5. They saw 23 blue birds and 18 red birds. How many more blue birds than red birds did they see? 5
   there are 5 more bluebirds than red birds.

6. They saw 4 nests. Each nest had 3 eggs. How many eggs did they see? ______

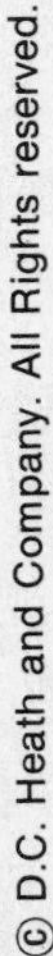

7. They saw 27 ducks swimming and 19 ducks flying. How many ducks did they see?

   ______

8. They stopped to rest at 3:45. They finished resting at 4:20. How long did they rest?

   ______

9. They took 36 hot dogs. There were 4 hot dogs in each package. How many packages did they take?

   ______

10. They took 40 cookies. There were 5 cookies in each package. How many packages did they take?

    ______

11. Each package had 4 rolls. They took 8 packages. How many rolls did they take?

    ______

12. They took 36 hot dogs. They took 8 packages of rolls. Each package had 4 rolls. How many more hot dogs than rolls did they take?

    ______

13. Each package had 2 apples. They took 16 apples. How many packages did they take?

    ______

14. Each package had 5 oranges. They took 45 oranges. How many packages did they take?

    ______

15. They took 45 oranges. They took 16 apples. How many pieces of fruit did they take?

    ______

16. They got home at 8:30 that night. How long were they away? (*Hint:* See exercise 1.)

    ______

Name ____________________

Another way to write division

How many threes in 12?

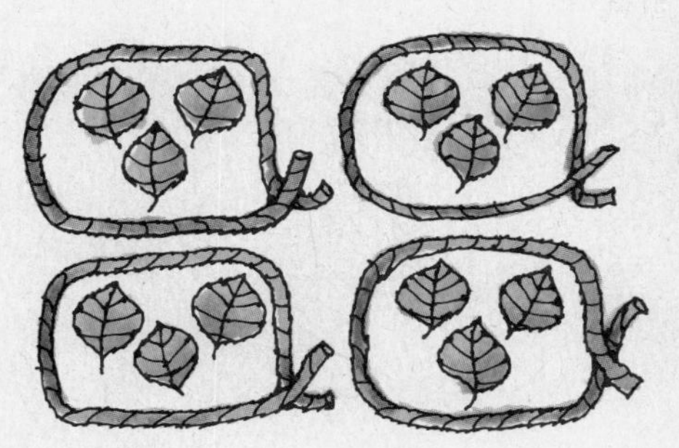

$$3\overline{)12}$$ with 4 written above

4 sets

12 leaves in all

3 leaves in each set

EXERCISES

Divide.

1. 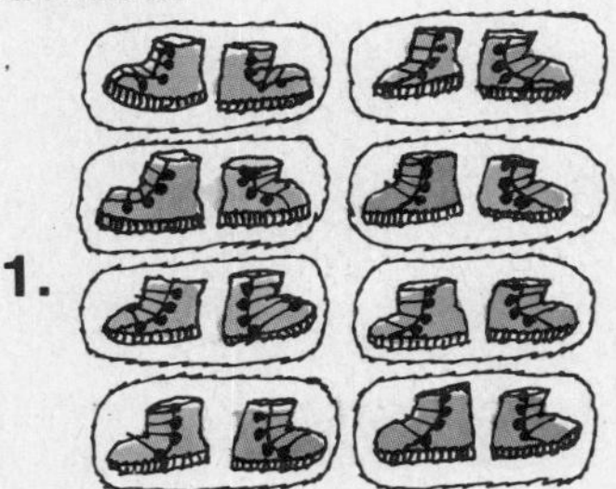 $2\overline{)16}$

2. 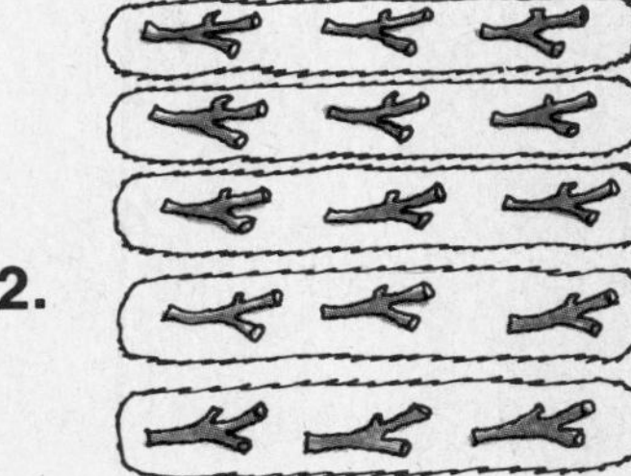 $3\overline{)15}$

3. $4\overline{)12}$

4. $5\overline{)20}$

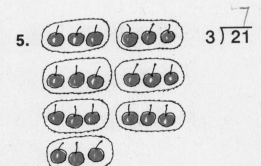

5. $3\overline{)21}$

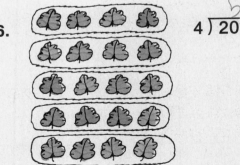

6. $4\overline{)20}$

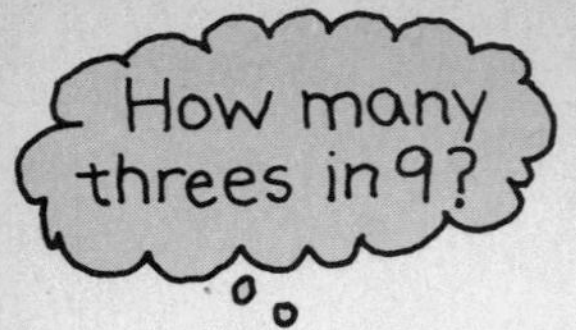

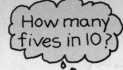

How many twos in 8?

How many fives in 10?

7. 3) 9 8. 2) 8 9. 5) 10

10. 5) 5 11. 2) 10 12. 3) 12

13. 5) 40 14. 4) 24 15. 2) 4

16. 2) 12 17. 3) 24 18. 3) 3

19. 4) 8 20. 4) 32 21. 5) 35

22. 4) 28 23. 2) 14 24. 5) 15

25. 3) 18 26. 5) 30 27. 4) 12

28. 4) 28 29. 4) 36 30. 3) 27

Challenge!

Complete each table.

Multiply by 4.

31.	3	
32.	2	
33.	5	
34.	4	
35.	1	

Divide by 4.

36.	12	
37.	8	
38.	20	
39.	16	
40.	4	

KEEPING SKILLS SHARP

Give the value of the red digit.

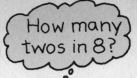

1. 63 _____
2. 821 _____
3. 45 _____
4. 759 _____
5. 983 _____
6. 2906 _____
7. 9421 _____
8. 7083 _____
9. 7777 _____
10. 7777 _____
11. 7777 _____
12. 7777 _____
13. 9086 _____
14. 3140 _____
15. 3104 _____

Name ____________________

Multiplication and division

Work in groups.
Get 24 beans.
Make cards.
Record your answers on a separate sheet of paper.

×2 ×3 ×4 ×5 ×6 ×7 ×8 ×9 ×10

÷2 ÷3 ÷4 ÷5 ÷6 ÷7 ÷8 ÷9 ÷10

Make a chart like the one shown below.

PART A

1. Put 3 beans in a pile. Write the number in the first column of the chart.
2. Pick a × card. Write it in the second column.
3. Change the numbers of beans. Write how many in the third column.
4. What card will change the beans back? Try it.
5. How many beans do you have now? Write that number in the chart. Did you change it back?

I'll pick ×4.

I'll put them into four equal groups and count the number in one group.

Before	Card	After	Card to change it back	How many now?
3	× 4	12		3

6. Try this activity with other numbers. Choose another number to start with. Repeat exercises 2 through 5.
7. Make up a rule that tells how to choose the right card. Have someone follow the rule. Does it work?
8. Use a calculator to try the activity with larger numbers. Does the rule work with larger numbers?

PART B

9. Start with 24 beans in a pile.
   Write the number in the first column of the chart.
10. Pick one of these division cards:

   ÷2 ÷3 ÷4 ÷6 ÷8

   Write the number in the second column.
11. Change the number of beans.
   Write how many beans are in each group in the third column.

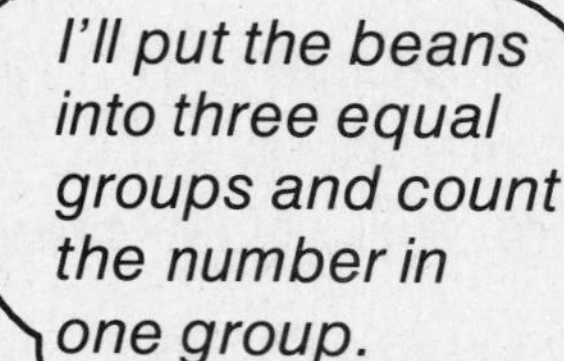

I'll pick
÷3.
÷3
I'll put the beans into three equal groups and count the number in one group.

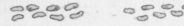

12. What card will change the beans back?
    Try it.
13. How many beans are there now?
    Write that number in the chart.
    Did you change it back?
14. Try this with other numbers.
15. Make up a rule that tells how to choose the right card. Have someone follow the rule. Does it work?
16. Use a calculator to try this with larger numbers. Does the rule work with larger numbers?

PART C

17. Pretend you used these cards: ×1 ÷1
    a. Talk about what would happen.
    b. Try it. What happened? Why?

Name ______________________

Multiplication and division

Multiplication and division are related.

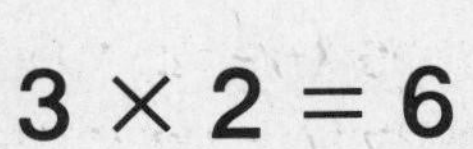

$3 \times 2 = 6$

$6 \div 2 = 3$

$2 \times 3 = 6$

$6 \div 3 = 2$

EXERCISES

Complete.

1. 

$3 \times 2 =$ 6

$6 \div 2 =$ 3

2. 

$4 \times 3 =$ 12

$12 \div 3 =$ 4

3. 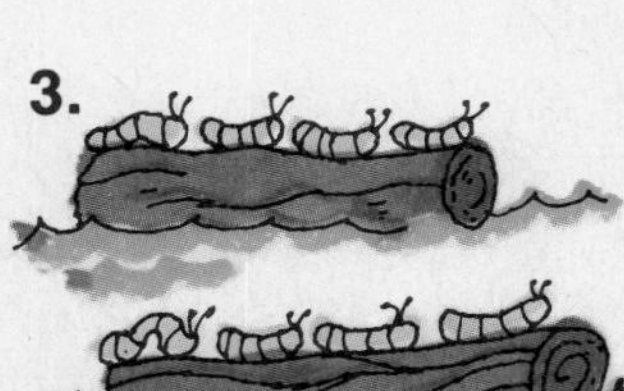

$3 \times 4 =$ 12

$12 \div 4 =$ 3

4. 

$5 \times 4 =$ 20

$20 \div 4 =$ 5

Use the numbers. Write two multiplication equations and two division equations.

5.

6.

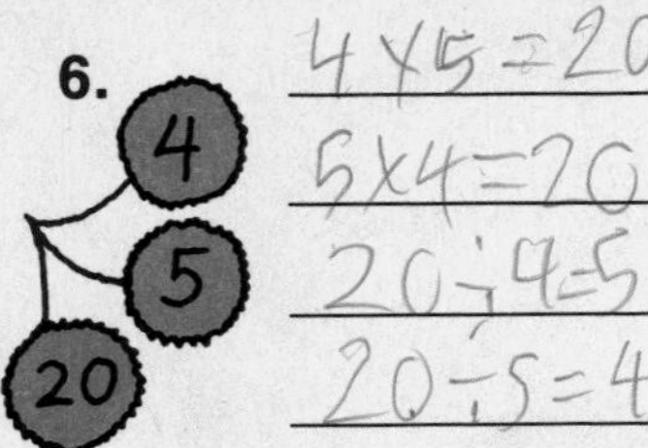

7.

8.

9.

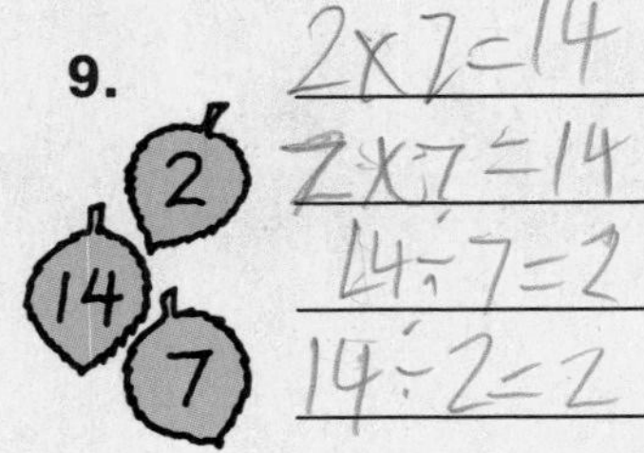

10.

11.

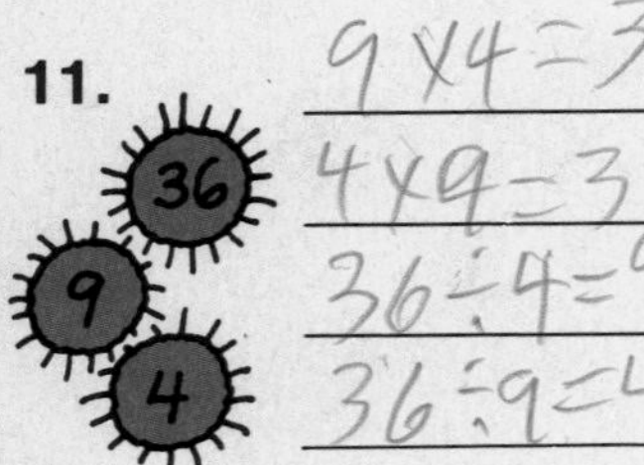

12.

13.

14.

15.

16.

Challenge!

Find the missing input or output.

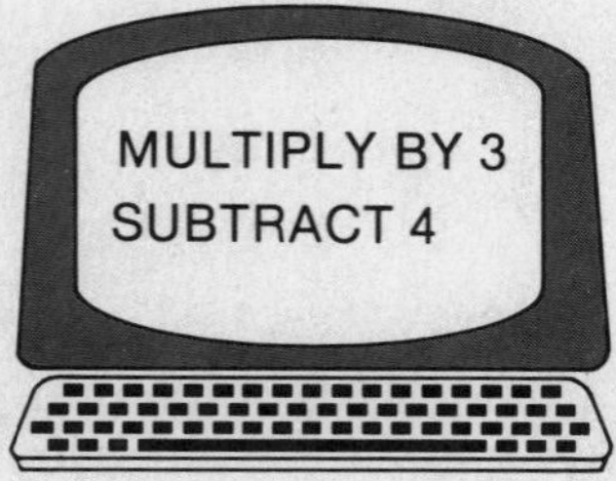

	Input	Output
	5	11
17.	8	
18.	7	
19.		23

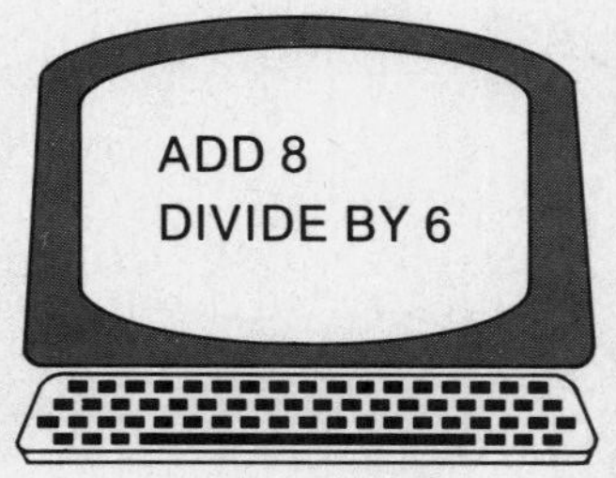

	Input	Output
	4	2
20.	16	
21.	28	
22.		3

Name ____________________

More about division

Division is finding a missing factor.

$$3\overline{)24}\quad\text{quotient } 8$$

$$1\overline{)5}\quad\text{quotient } 5$$

$$5\overline{)0}\quad\text{quotient } 0$$

?x0=4 We don't divide by 0.

There is no number times 0 that equals 4.

$0\overline{)4}$ (crossed out)

EXERCISES

Divide.

1. $4\overline{)4}$	**2.** $1\overline{)6}$	**3.** $5\overline{)0}$	**4.** $2\overline{)12}$	**5.** $5\overline{)30}$
6. $1\overline{)9}$	**7.** $4\overline{)16}$	**8.** $3\overline{)18}$	**9.** $3\overline{)21}$	**10.** $1\overline{)8}$
11. $5\overline{)45}$	**12.** $3\overline{)0}$	**13.** $4\overline{)28}$	**14.** $4\overline{)0}$	**15.** $5\overline{)5}$
16. $2\overline{)16}$	**17.** $4\overline{)24}$	**18.** $3\overline{)15}$	**19.** $2\overline{)14}$	**20.** $5\overline{)15}$
21. $4\overline{)20}$	**22.** $5\overline{)20}$	**23.** $2\overline{)18}$	**24.** $5\overline{)35}$	**25.** $3\overline{)12}$
26. $5\overline{)40}$	**27.** $4\overline{)32}$	**28.** $3\overline{)27}$	**29.** $4\overline{)36}$	**30.** $5\overline{)25}$

Problem Solving Choosing the operation

The numbers have been covered. Tell what you would do (+, −, ×, ÷) to solve the problem.

1. ● apples in one bag
   ● apples in another bag
   How many apples in all? _______

2. ● people in each car
   ● cars
   How many people in all? _______

3. ●¢ for a pear
   ●¢ for a banana
   How much more for the pear?
   ____

4. ●¢ in all
   ●¢ for each orange
   How many oranges? _______

5. $● for each record
   ● records
   What is the total cost? _______

6. ● marbles in a bag
   ● marbles lost
   How many marbles were left? _______

7. ● dogs in one ring
   ● dogs in another ring
   How many dogs in all? _______

8. ● books in all
   ● books in each package
   How many packages? _______

Mental Math

You can find these differences faster by using mental math than by using a calculator.

Think about subtracting 100 and adding.

Shortcut

9. 184 − 99 = _____

10. 276 − 99 = _____

11. 263 − 98 = _____

12. 391 − 97 = _____

Name ____________________

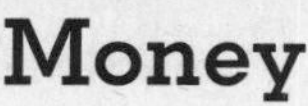

Postal workers pick up and deliver our mail. We buy stamps to help pay for this.

EXERCISES

Give the total cost of the stamps.

1. 3 

____

2. 7 

____

3. 5 

____

4. 4 

____

5. 8 

____

6. 6 

____

7. 5 

and 3 

____

8. 6 

and 4 

____

Solve.

9. How many  can you buy for  ? ______

10. How many  can you buy with   ? ______

11. You have 
You buy 8 
How much is left? ______

12. You have  
You buy 9 
How much is left? ______

13. You have 
You buy $1.39
How much is left? ______

14. You have 
You buy 

How much is left? ______

Mental Math

Here's how I add 99 in my head. I add 100. Then I subtract 1.

75+100=175
175−1=174

$$\begin{array}{r} 75 \\ +99 \\ \hline 174 \end{array}$$

SHORTCUT

Try the shortcut with these exercises.

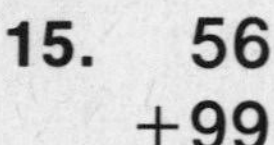

15. $\begin{array}{r} 56 \\ +99 \\ \hline \end{array}$ **16.** $\begin{array}{r} 38 \\ +99 \\ \hline \end{array}$ **17.** $\begin{array}{r} 143 \\ +99 \\ \hline \end{array}$ **18.** $\begin{array}{r} 267 \\ +99 \\ \hline \end{array}$ **19.** $\begin{array}{r} 483 \\ +99 \\ \hline \end{array}$ **20.** $\begin{array}{r} 638 \\ +99 \\ \hline \end{array}$

Name ____________________

Division with remainder

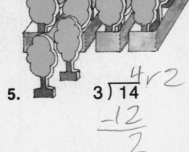

Make sets of 4.

There are 2 left over.

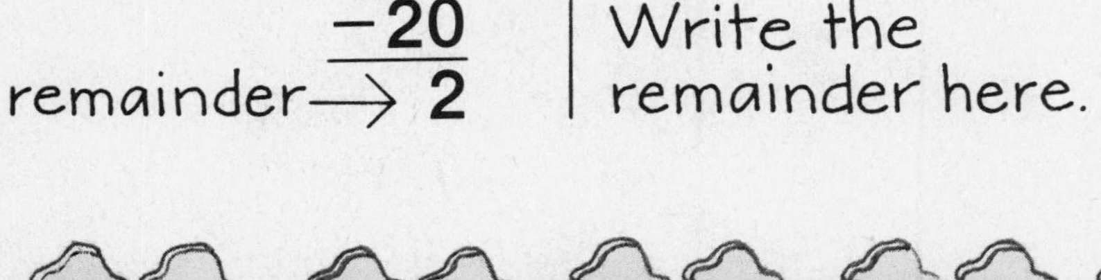

EXERCISES

Divide.

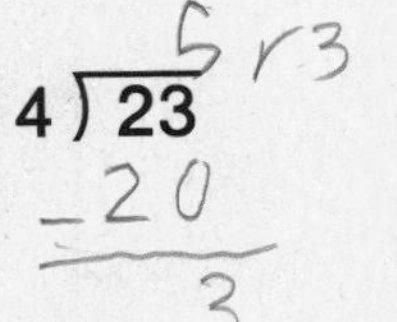

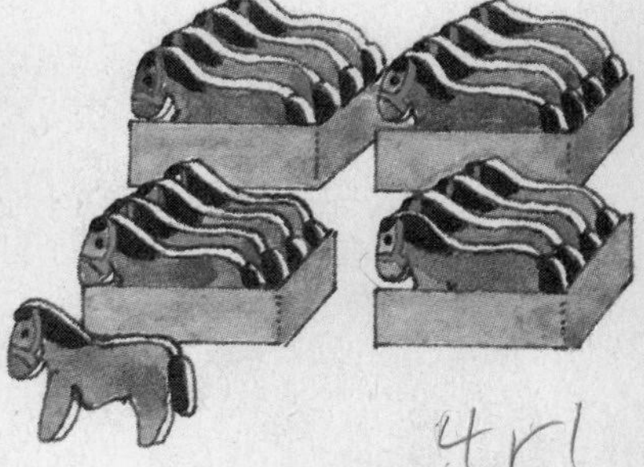

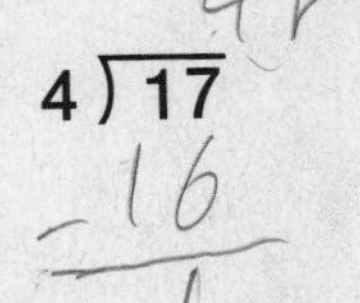

1. 3) 11

2. 4) 23

3. 4) 17

4. 5) 19

5. 3) 14

6. 4) 14

Divide.

7. $3\overline{)7}$	**8.** $5\overline{)12}$	**9.** $3\overline{)8}$	**10.** $4\overline{)18}$	**11.** $2\overline{)7}$
12. $5\overline{)31}$	**13.** $4\overline{)29}$	**14.** $5\overline{)18}$	**15.** $3\overline{)10}$	**16.** $4\overline{)21}$
17. $5\overline{)27}$	**18.** $4\overline{)35}$	**19.** $2\overline{)9}$	**20.** $3\overline{)20}$	**21.** $5\overline{)29}$
22. $5\overline{)48}$	**23.** $2\overline{)11}$	**24.** $4\overline{)34}$	**25.** $5\overline{)42}$	**26.** $3\overline{)22}$
27. $3\overline{)25}$	**28.** $5\overline{)37}$	**29.** $2\overline{)13}$	**30.** $4\overline{)33}$	**31.** $2\overline{)19}$
32. $5\overline{)36}$	**33.** $3\overline{)28}$	**34.** $3\overline{)26}$	**35.** $4\overline{)38}$	**36.** $2\overline{)15}$

Challenge!

Guess my number.

37. Divide mine by 4 and you get 7.

38. If you divide mine by 5, you get a quotient of 4 and a remainder of 2.

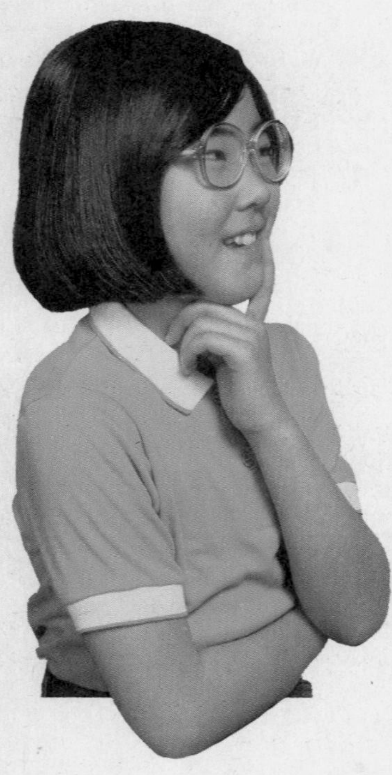

39. Divide my number by 2, add 3, and you get 11.

40. Divide mine by 3, subtract 4, and you get 1.

Name ____________________

Chapter Checkup

Give each quotient. [pages 190–195, 202–203]

1. 8 ÷ 2 = ____
2. 20 ÷ 5 = ____
3. 18 ÷ 3 = ____
4. 10 ÷ 5 = ____
5. 16 ÷ 2 = ____
6. 35 ÷ 5 = ____
7. 12 ÷ 4 = ____
8. 8 ÷ 4 = ____
9. 20 ÷ 4 = ____
10. 15 ÷ 3 = ____
11. 32 ÷ 4 = ____
12. 14 ÷ 2 = ____

Divide. [pages 198–200, 204]

13. 2) 6
14. 3) 3
15. 3) 9
16. 5) 25
17. 3) 24
18. 5) 15
19. 5) 30
20. 2) 18
21. 4) 36
22. 4) 24
23. 3) 12
24. 4) 28
25. 5) 0
26. 5) 45
27. 3) 21

Solve. [pages 196–197, 201, 205–207]

28. There were 15 turtles. 3 turtles were in each box. How many boxes were there? ____

29. There were 24 ladybugs. 4 ladybugs were in each bag. How many bags were there? ____

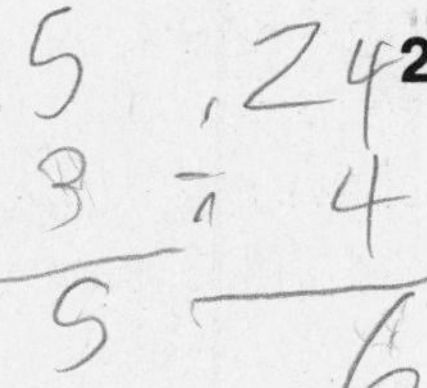

30. There were 9 plates. There were 3 eggs on each plate. How many eggs were there? ____

31. There were 8 straws. There were 2 straws in each glass. How many glasses were there? ____

Chapter Project

COLLECTING DATA

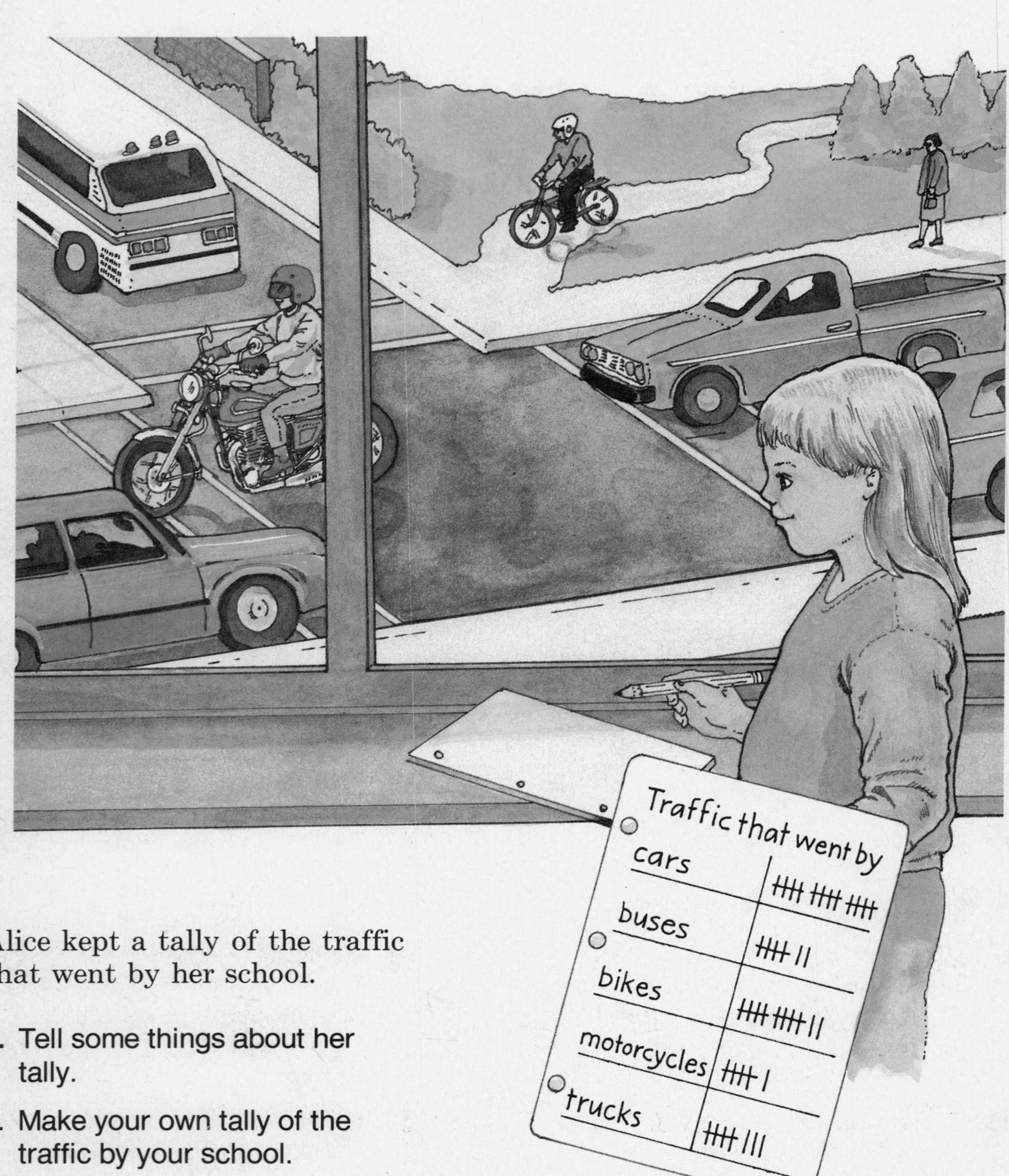

Alice kept a tally of the traffic that went by her school.

1. Tell some things about her tally.
2. Make your own tally of the traffic by your school.
3. Make a bar graph.
4. Tell what your graph shows.

Name ____________________

Chapter Review

Divide.

1. $2\overline{)4}$ 2. $2\overline{)6}$ 3. $2\overline{)10}$ 4. $2\overline{)8}$

5. $2\overline{)12}$ 6. $2\overline{)16}$ 7. $2\overline{)18}$ 8. $2\overline{)14}$

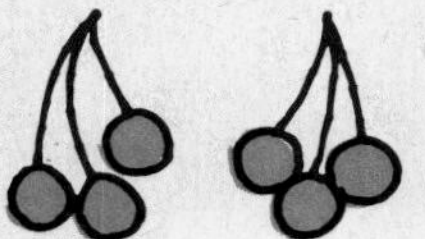

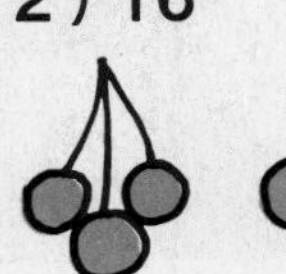

9. $3\overline{)6}$ 10. $3\overline{)9}$ 11. $3\overline{)15}$ 12. $3\overline{)12}$

13. $3\overline{)18}$ 14. $3\overline{)27}$ 15. $3\overline{)21}$ 16. $3\overline{)24}$

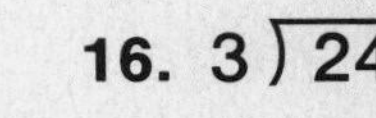

17. $4\overline{)8}$ 18. $4\overline{)16}$ 19. $4\overline{)12}$ 20. $4\overline{)20}$

21. $4\overline{)28}$ 22. $4\overline{)36}$ 23. $4\overline{)32}$ 24. $4\overline{)24}$

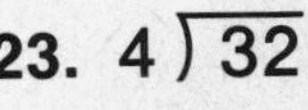

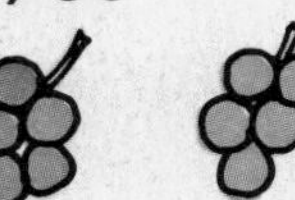

25. $5\overline{)15}$ 26. $5\overline{)10}$ 27. $5\overline{)25}$ 28. $5\overline{)20}$

29. $5\overline{)40}$ 30. $5\overline{)30}$ 31. $5\overline{)45}$ 32. $5\overline{)35}$

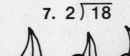

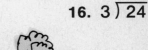

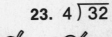

Chapter Challenge

GUESS AND CHECK

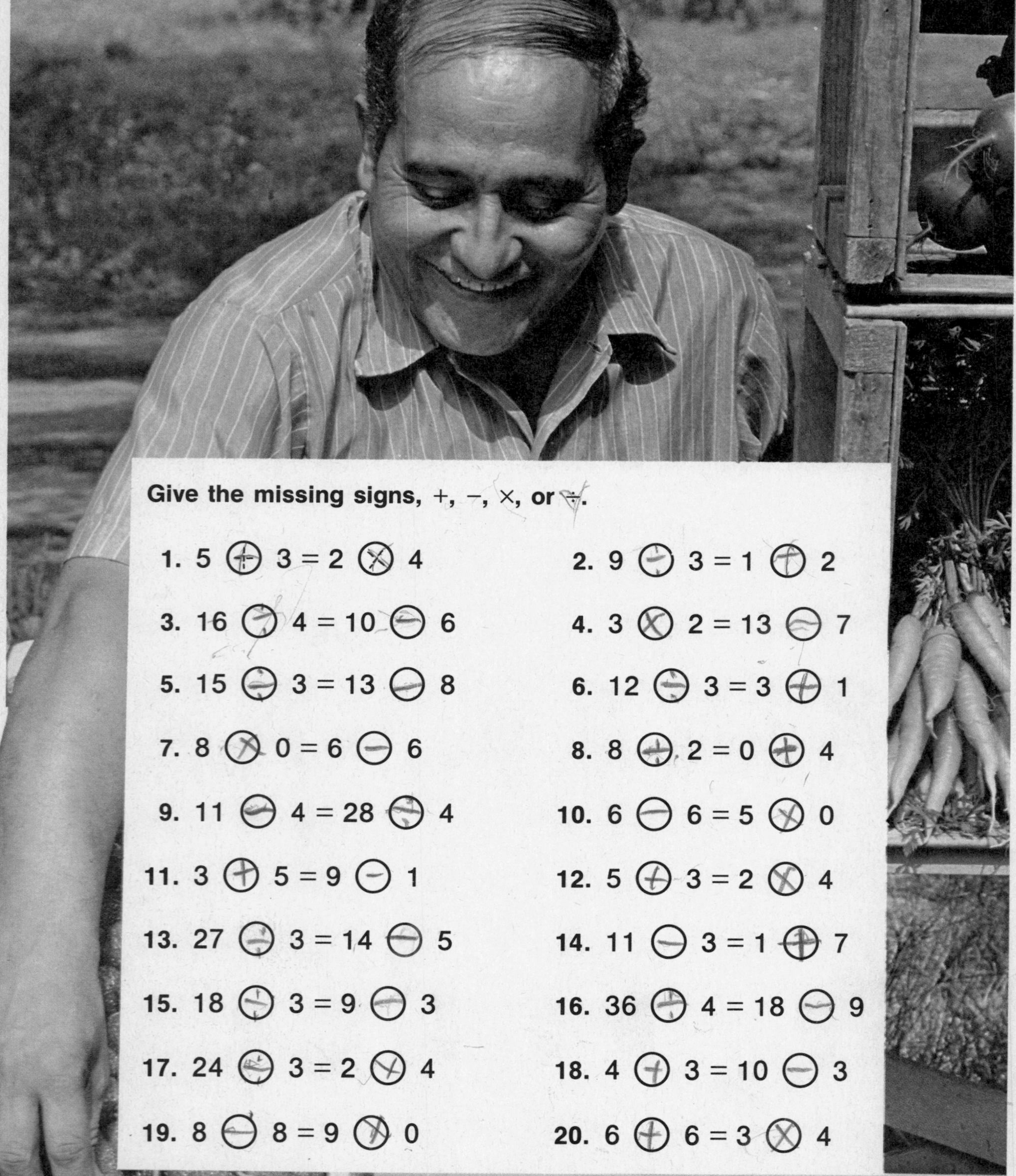

Give the missing signs, +, −, ×, or ÷.

1. 5 ○ 3 = 2 ○ 4
2. 9 ○ 3 = 1 ○ 2
3. 16 ○ 4 = 10 ○ 6
4. 3 ○ 2 = 13 ○ 7
5. 15 ○ 3 = 13 ○ 8
6. 12 ○ 3 = 3 ○ 1
7. 8 ○ 0 = 6 ○ 6
8. 8 ○ 2 = 0 ○ 4
9. 11 ○ 4 = 28 ○ 4
10. 6 ○ 6 = 5 ○ 0
11. 3 ○ 5 = 9 ○ 1
12. 5 ○ 3 = 2 ○ 4
13. 27 ○ 3 = 14 ○ 5
14. 11 ○ 3 = 1 ○ 7
15. 18 ○ 3 = 9 ○ 3
16. 36 ○ 4 = 18 ○ 9
17. 24 ○ 3 = 2 ○ 4
18. 4 ○ 3 = 10 ○ 3
19. 8 ○ 8 = 9 ○ 0
20. 6 ○ 6 = 3 ○ 4

Name ____________________

Cumulative Checkup

STANDARDIZED FORMAT

Give the correct letter.

1. Complete.
$6 + \underline{?} = 9$

a. 15
b. 6
c. 3
d. none of these

2. The 6 in 368 stands for what number?

a. 6
b. 600
c. 60
d. none of these

3. Which number is the smallest?

a. 794
b. 749
c. 947
d. 479

4. Six hundred six is

a. 6660
b. 6606
c. 6066
d. none of these

5. 274 rounded to the nearest hundred is

a. 270
b. 200
c. 300
d. none of these

6. How much money?
1 dollar
2 dimes
3 pennies

a. $1.50
b. $1.05
c. $1.23
d. none of these

7. Add.
$\begin{array}{r} 729 \\ +386 \\ \hline \end{array}$

a. 1115
b. 1005
c. 1015
d. none of these

8. What time is it?

a. 10:30
b. 6:50
c. 11:30
d. none of these

9. Which is the most money?

a. 2 quarters and 2 dimes
b. 6 dimes
c. 3 quarters
d. 7 dimes and 2 nickels

10. In $4 \times 3 = 12$, 12 is called the

a. addend
b. sum
c. product
d. none of these

11. 6 teams
4 boys on each team
3 girls on each team
How many boys in all?

a. 24 **b.** 10
c. 13 **d.** 42

12. 8 pens
2 pens in a package
How many packages?

a. 4 **b.** 6
c. 10 **d.** 16

8

Fractions and Decimals

Find the square that has a yellow triangle and a blue triangle. What part of that square is blue?

Name ____________________

Fractions and regions

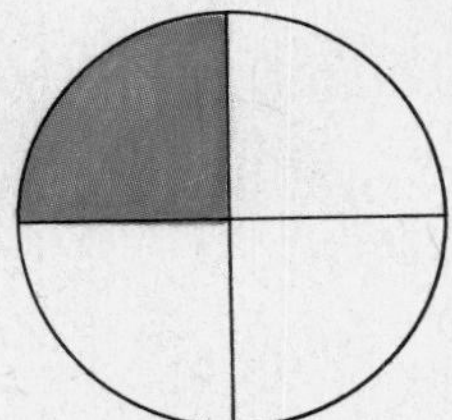

1 part is blue.
4 equal parts

$\frac{1}{4}$ is blue.
One fourth is blue.

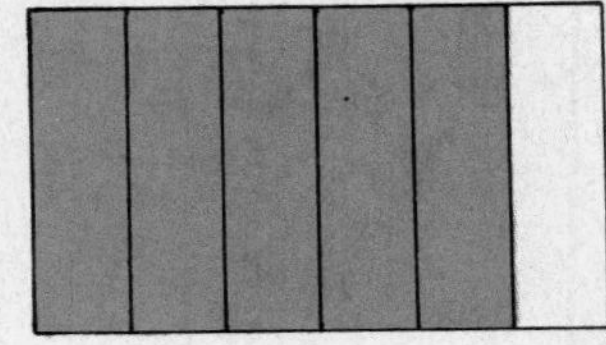

5 parts are red.
6 equal parts

$\frac{5}{6}$ is red.
Five sixths is red.

EXERCISES

What fraction is colored?

1. 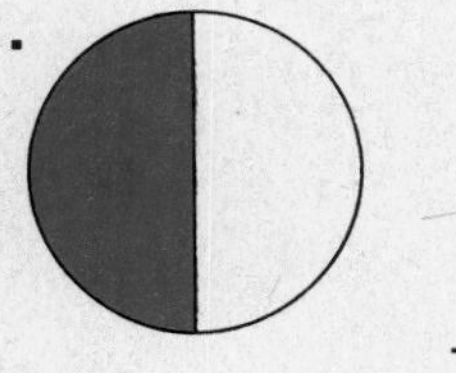 $\frac{1}{2}$

2. 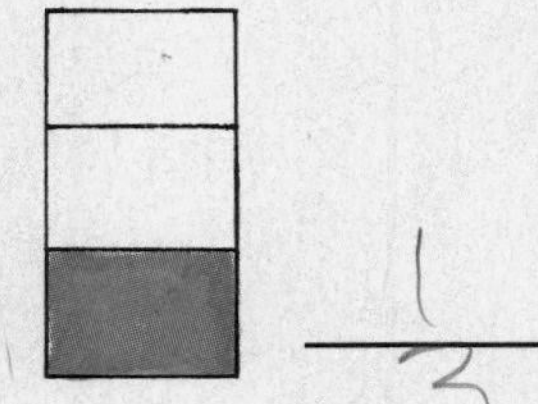 $\frac{1}{3}$

3.  $\frac{3}{4}$

4. 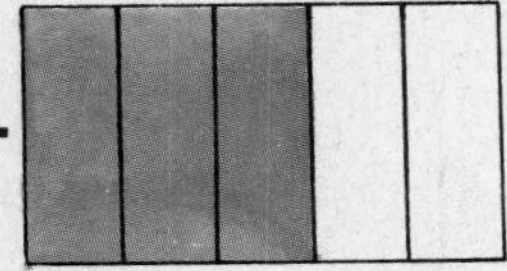 $\frac{3}{5}$

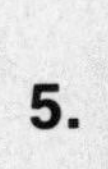

5.  $\frac{4}{6}$

6. 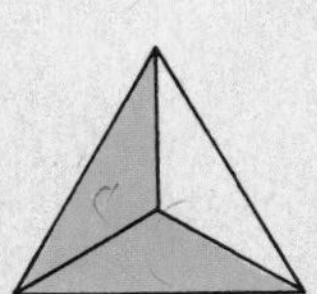 $\frac{2}{3}$

7. 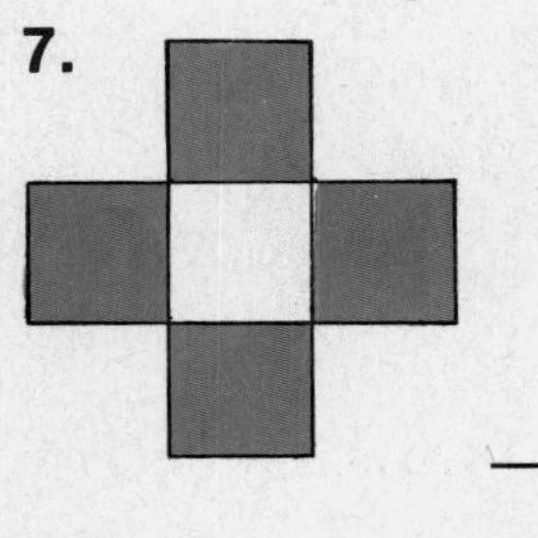 $\frac{4}{5}$

8. 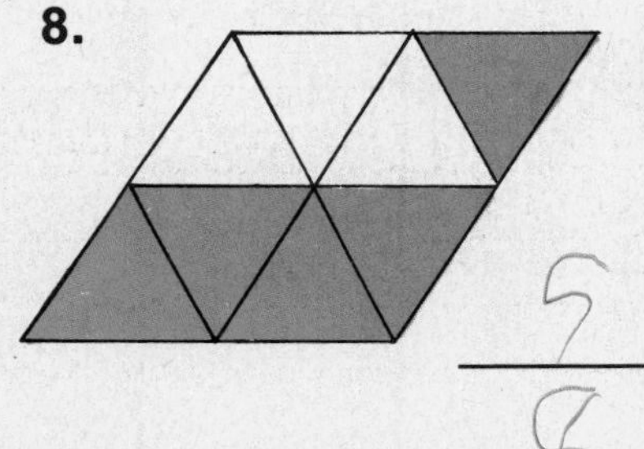 $\frac{5}{8}$

9. 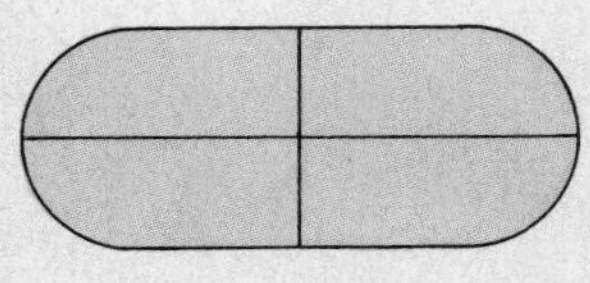 $\frac{4}{4}$

What fraction is red?

10. 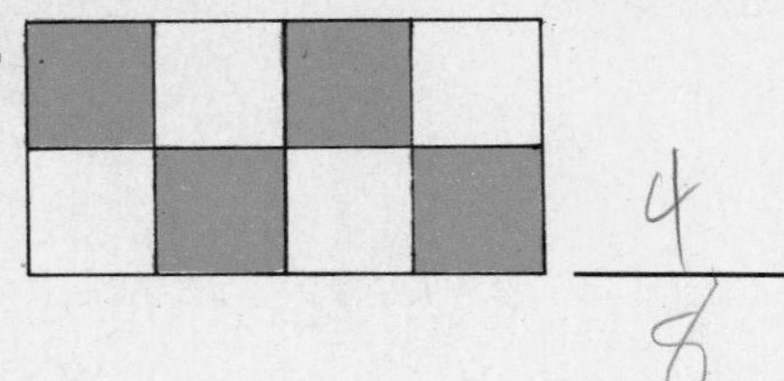 4/8

11. 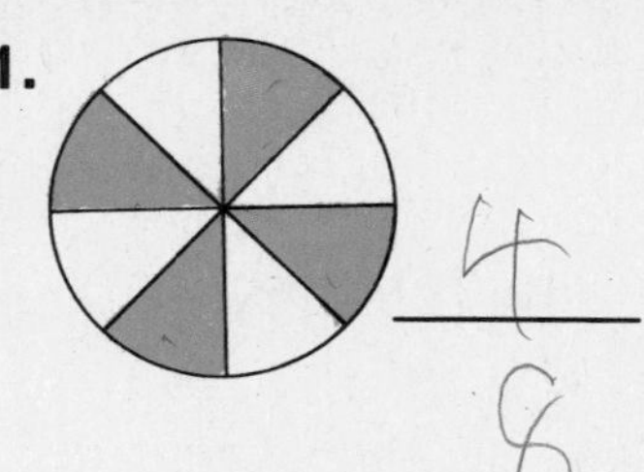 4/8

12. 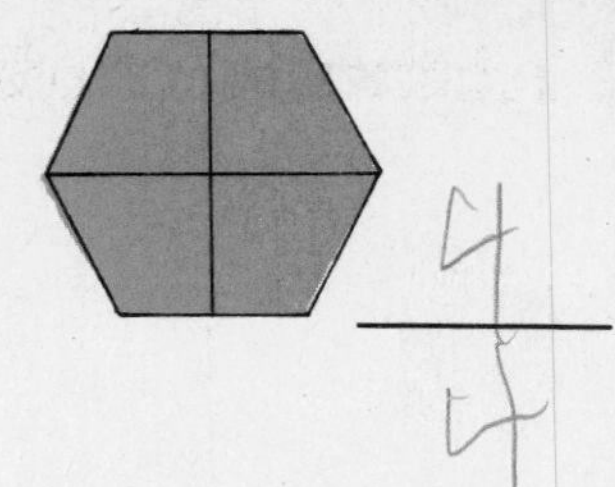 4/4

What fraction of the fence is

13. blue? 1/8

14. not blue? 7/8

15. green? 3/8

16. not green? 5/8

17. yellow? 4/8

18. not yellow? 4/8

19. painted? 8/8

20. not painted? 0/8

21. yellow or green? 7/8

22. blue or green? 4/8

23. blue or yellow? 5/8

Name ________________________________

Fractions and sets

2 shoes are blue.
5 shoes in all

$\frac{2}{5}$ of the shoes are blue.

EXERCISES

What fraction of the toys are blue?

1. 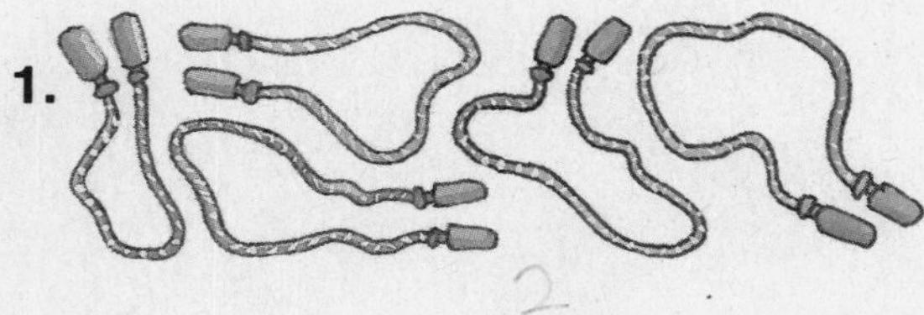

$\frac{2}{4}$

2. 

$\frac{3}{4}$

3. 

$\frac{1}{6}$

4. 

______

5. 

$\frac{5}{6}$

6. 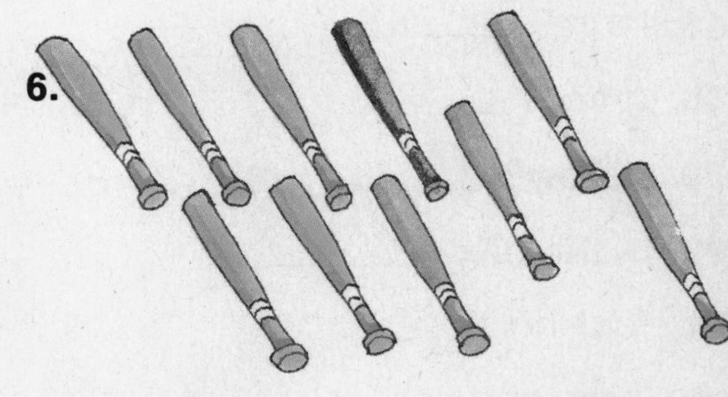

______

What fraction of the shirts are

7. yellow? _______
8. green? _______
9. red? _______
10. blue? _______

What fraction of the balls are

11. outside the box? _______
12. inside the box? _______
13. blue? _______
14. green? _______
15. red? _______

What fraction of the buttons are

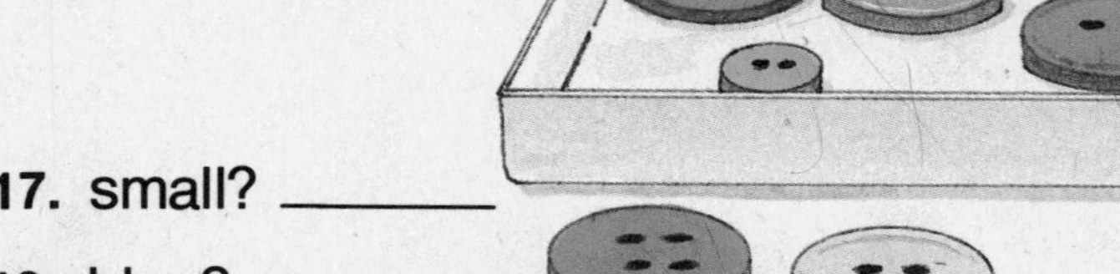

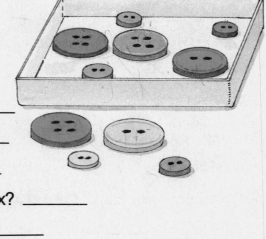

16. large? _______
17. small? _______
18. green? _______
19. blue? _______
20. yellow? _______
21. red? _______
22. in the box? _______
23. out of the box? _______
24. four-hole? _______
25. two-hole? _______
26. large and yellow? _______
27. small and green? _______

Name ________________________________

Problem Solving

Using a bar graph

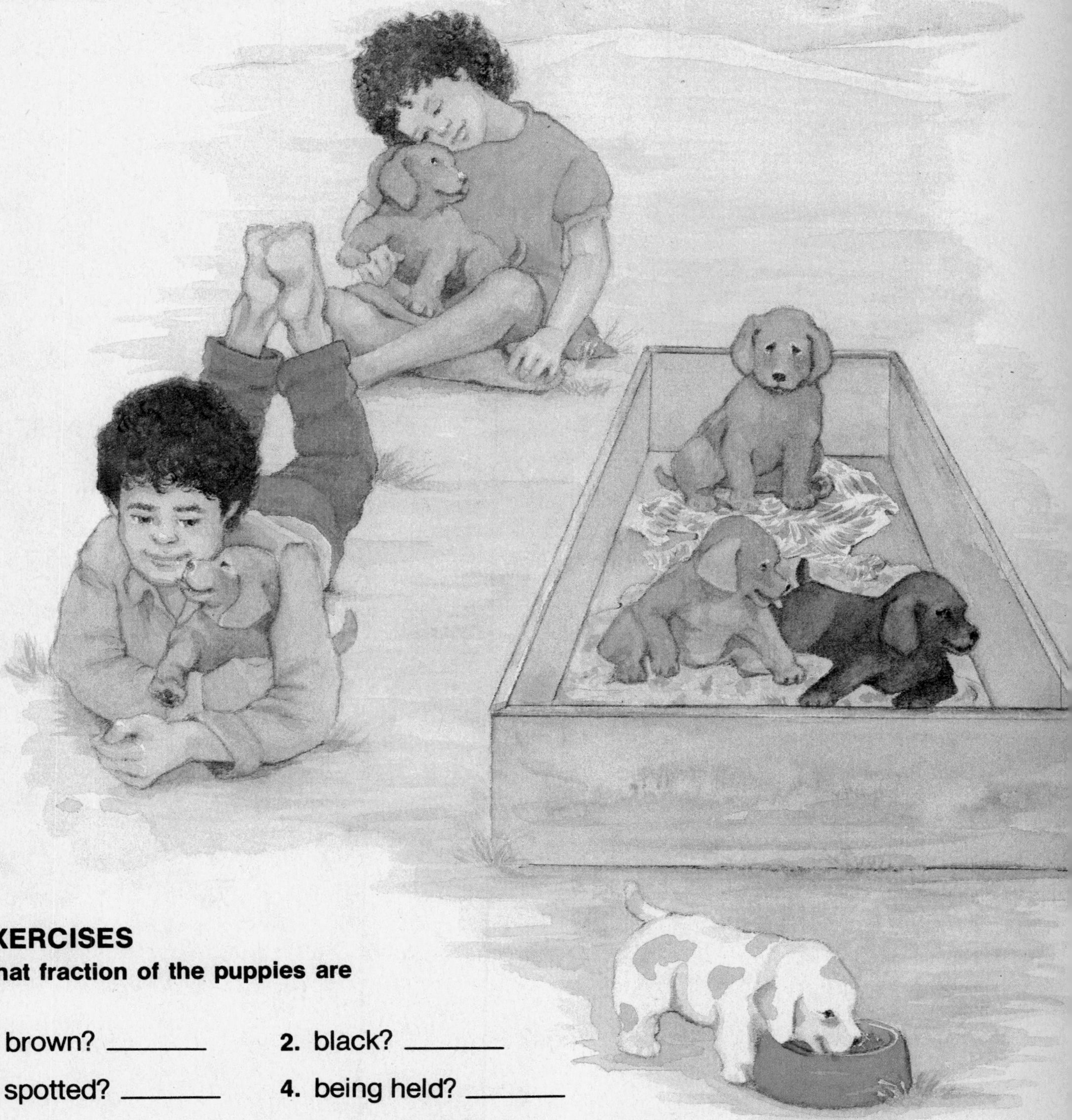

EXERCISES

What fraction of the puppies are

1. brown? ________ **2.** black? ________

3. spotted? ________ **4.** being held? ________

5. in the box? ________ **6.** out of the box? ________

7. eating? ________ **8.** not eating? ________

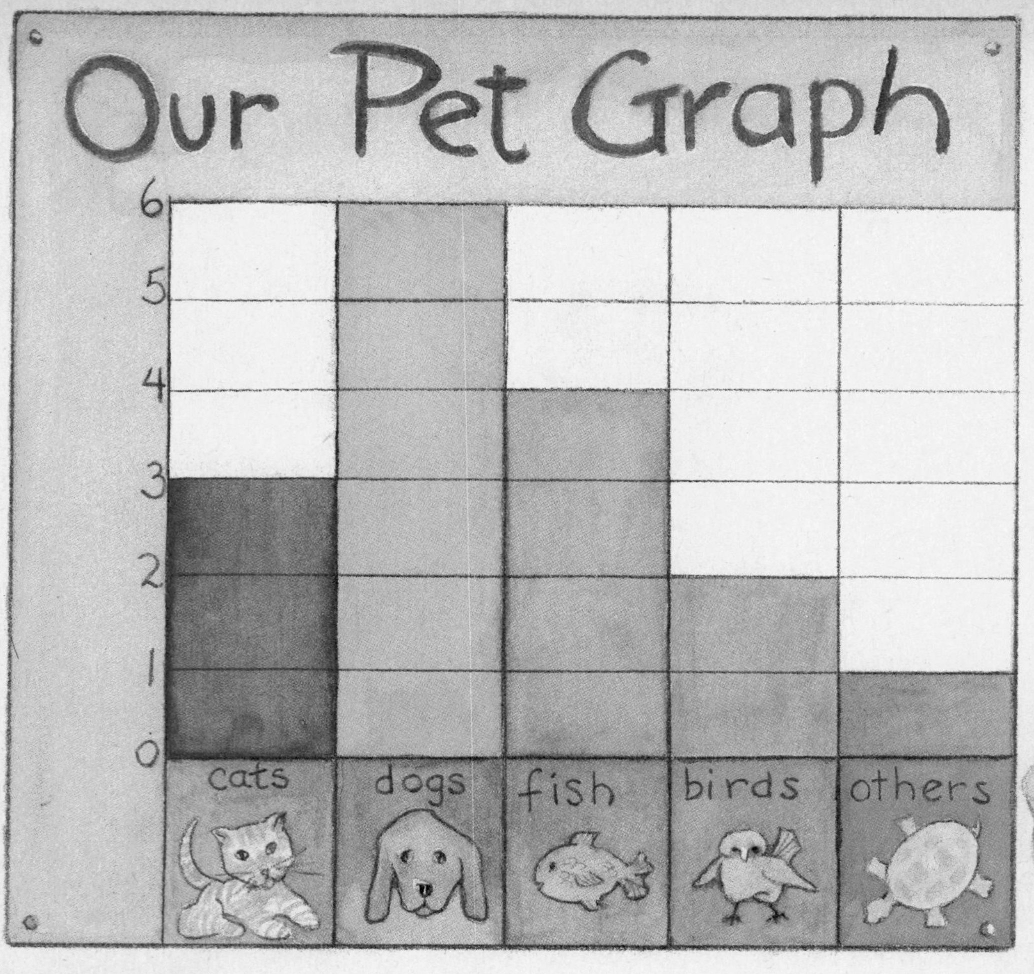

Look at the graph.
How many

9. cats? _______ **10.** dogs? _______ **11.** fish? _______

12. birds? _______ **13.** pets in all? _______

14. How many more dogs than cats? _______

15. How many fewer birds than dogs? _______

What fraction of the pets are

16. cats? _______ **17.** dogs? _______

18. fish? _______ **19.** birds? _______

20. not dogs? _______ **21.** not cats? _______

Name ____________________

Fraction of a number

To find $\frac{1}{2}$, divide by 2.

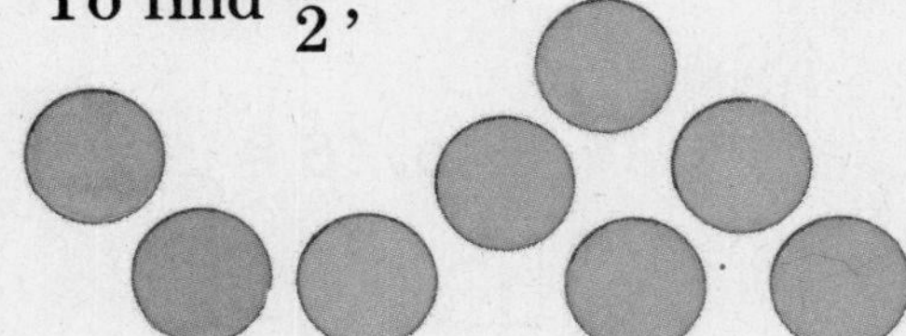

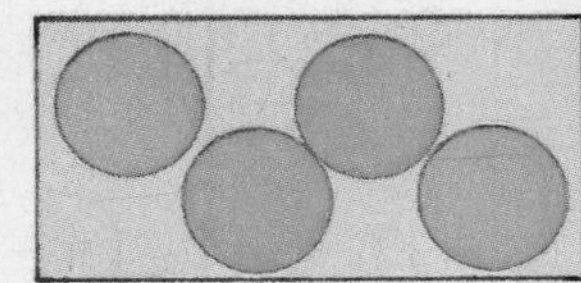

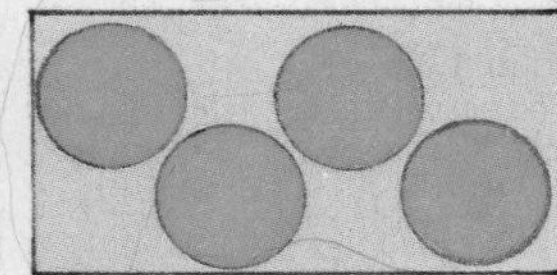

$\frac{1}{2}$ of 8 = 4

To find $\frac{1}{3}$, divide by 3.

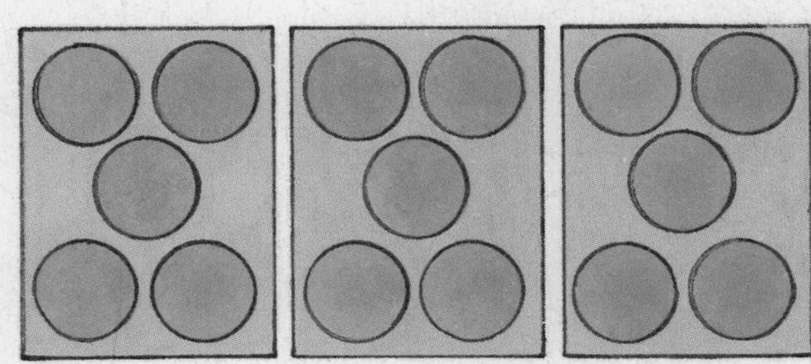

$\frac{1}{3}$ of 15 = 5

EXERCISES

Complete.

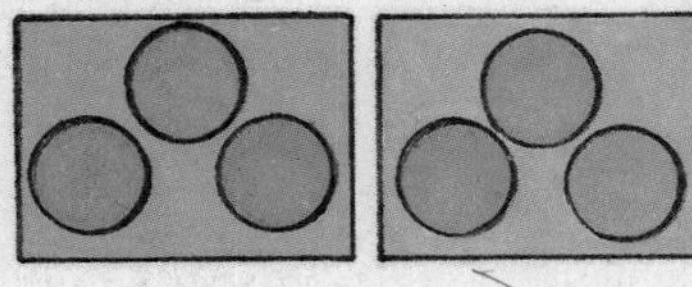

1. $\frac{1}{2}$ of 6 = 3

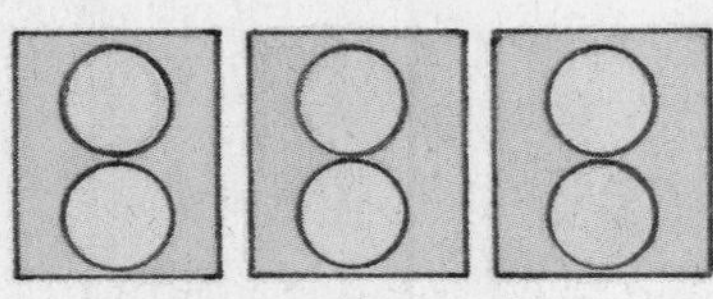

2. $\frac{1}{3}$ of 6 = 2

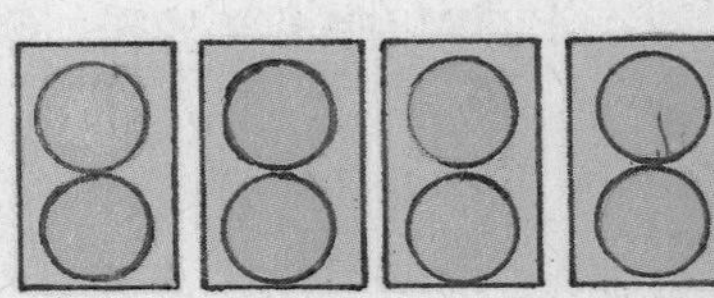

3. $\frac{1}{4}$ of 8 = 2

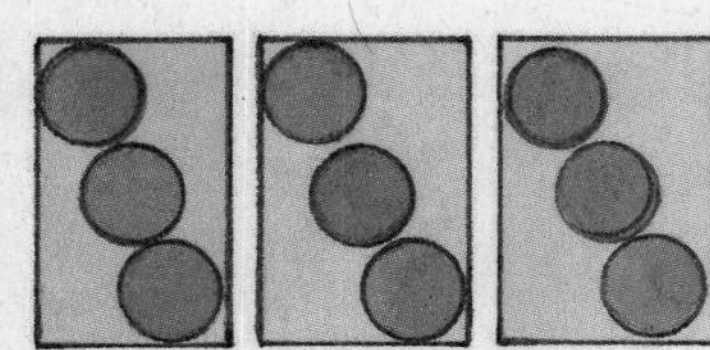

4. $\frac{1}{3}$ of 9 = 3

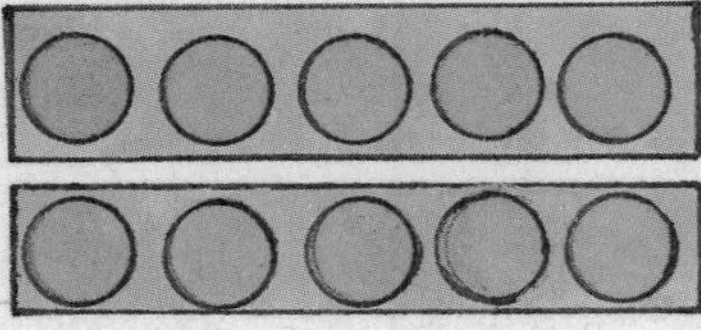

5. $\frac{1}{2}$ of 10 = 5

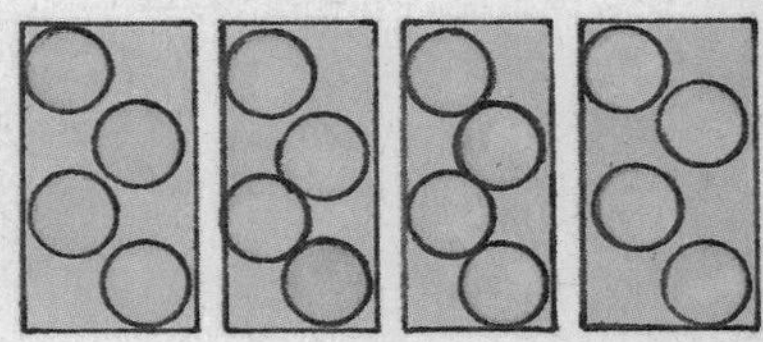

6. $\frac{1}{4}$ of 16 = 4

Complete.

7. $\frac{1}{2}$ of 8 = ____
8. $\frac{1}{5}$ of 5 = ____
9. $\frac{1}{3}$ of 18 = ____
10. $\frac{1}{2}$ of 12 = ____
11. $\frac{1}{4}$ of 8 = ____
12. $\frac{1}{4}$ of 24 = ____
13. $\frac{1}{3}$ of 21 = ____
14. $\frac{1}{4}$ of 16 = ____
15. $\frac{1}{2}$ of 16 = ____
16. $\frac{1}{5}$ of 10 = ____
17. $\frac{1}{2}$ of 14 = ____
18. $\frac{1}{5}$ of 35 = ____
19. $\frac{1}{5}$ of 40 = ____
20. $\frac{1}{5}$ of 15 = ____
21. $\frac{1}{3}$ of 24 = ____
22. $\frac{1}{5}$ of 30 = ____
23. $\frac{1}{3}$ of 12 = ____
24. $\frac{1}{2}$ of 18 = ____
25. $\frac{1}{4}$ of 24 = ____
26. $\frac{1}{4}$ of 32 = ____
27. $\frac{1}{3}$ of 27 = ____
28. $\frac{1}{4}$ of 28 = ____
29. $\frac{1}{4}$ of 12 = ____
30. $\frac{1}{3}$ of 15 = ____

Problem Solving

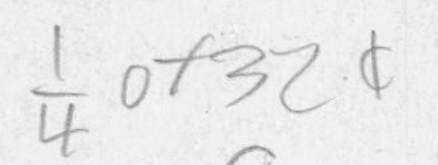

31. Had 24¢.
Spent $\frac{1}{3}$ of it.
How much was spent? ____

32. Had 36¢.
Gave $\frac{1}{4}$ of it away.
How much was given away? ____

★ 33. Had 32¢.
Spent $\frac{1}{4}$ of it.
How much was left? ____

★ 34. Had 21¢.
Spent $\frac{1}{3}$ of it.
How much was left? ____

Challenge!

Guess my number.

35. If you take $\frac{1}{2}$ of my number and then add 2, you get 6.

36. If you take $\frac{1}{3}$ of my number and then subtract 1, you get 7.

Name ____________________

Sale price

EXERCISES

Complete.

	Regular price	Amount off	Sale price
1.	24¢	$\frac{1}{4}$ of 24¢ = 6 ¢	24 − 6 = 18 18 ¢
2.	36¢	$\frac{1}{4}$ of 36¢ = ____¢	____¢
3.	8¢	$\frac{1}{2}$ of 8¢ = ____¢	____¢
4.	16¢	$\frac{1}{2}$ of 16¢ = ____¢	____¢
5.	18¢	$\frac{1}{3}$ of 18¢ = ____¢	____¢
6.	27¢	$\frac{1}{3}$ of 27¢ = ____¢	____¢

Complete.

	Regular price	Amount off	Sale price
7.	12¢	$\frac{1}{4}$ of 12¢ = ____ ¢	____ ¢
8.	25¢	$\frac{1}{5}$ of 25¢ = ____ ¢	____ ¢
9.	20¢	$\frac{1}{4}$ of 20¢ = ____ ¢	____ ¢
10.	15¢	$\frac{1}{3}$ of 15¢ = ____ ¢	____ ¢
11.	21¢	$\frac{1}{3}$ of 21¢ = ____ ¢	____ ¢
12.	32¢	$\frac{1}{4}$ of 32¢ = ____ ¢	____ ¢
13.	14¢	$\frac{1}{2}$ of 14¢ = ____ ¢	____ ¢
14.	35¢	$\frac{1}{5}$ of 35¢ = ____ ¢	____ ¢
15.	45¢	$\frac{1}{5}$ of 45¢ = ____ ¢	____ ¢

Give each sale price.

★ 16. Regular price:
Sale: $\frac{1}{4}$ off 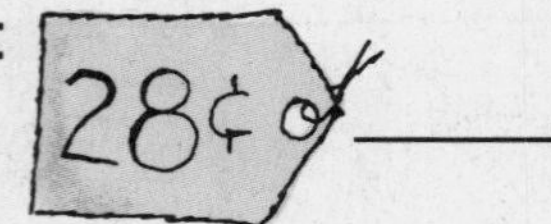

______

★ 17. Regular price:
Sale: $\frac{1}{3}$ off 

______

★ 18. Regular price:
Sale: $\frac{1}{5}$ off 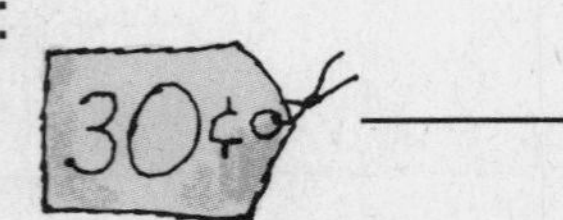

______

★ 19. Regular price:
Sale: $\frac{1}{5}$ off 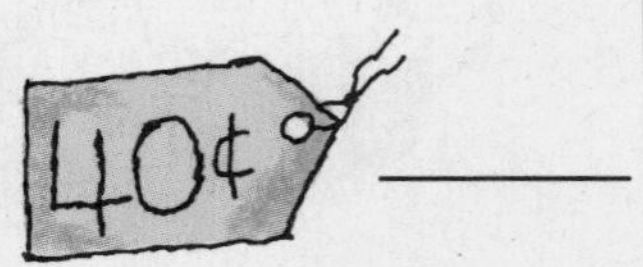

______

226-227 ALL

Name ______________________________

Equivalent fractions

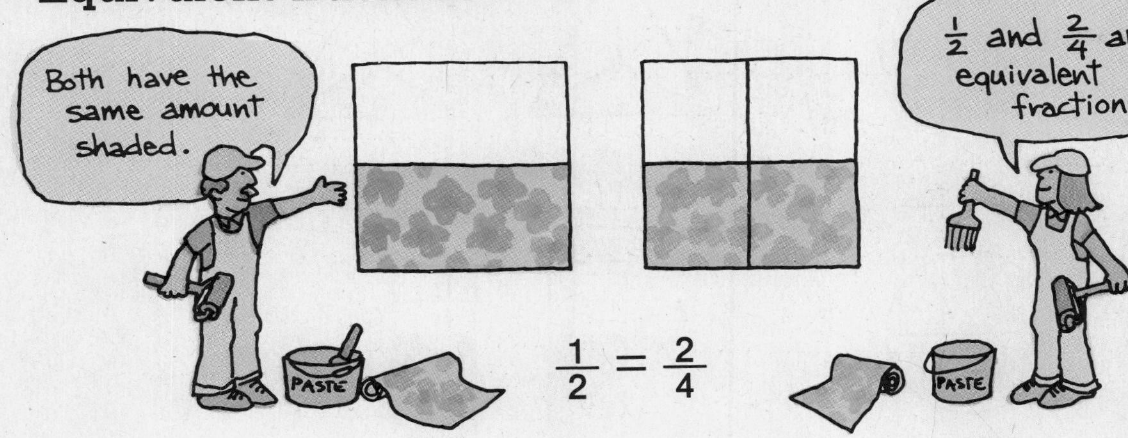

$$\frac{1}{2} = \frac{2}{4}$$

EXERCISES

Complete.

1. 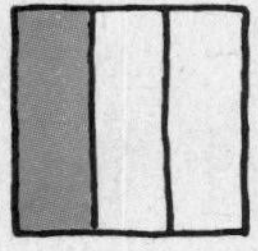 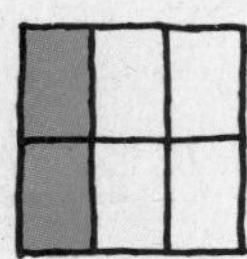

$\frac{1}{3} = \frac{2}{6}$

2. 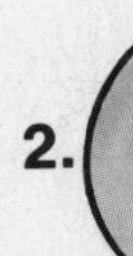 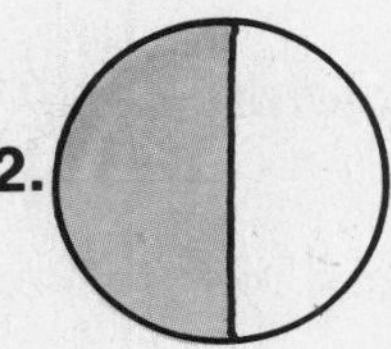 

$\frac{1}{2} = \frac{2}{4}$

3. 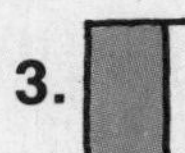 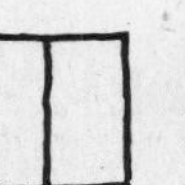 

$\frac{1}{4} = \frac{2}{8}$

4.  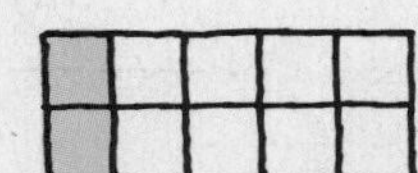

$\frac{1}{5} = \frac{2}{10}$

5.  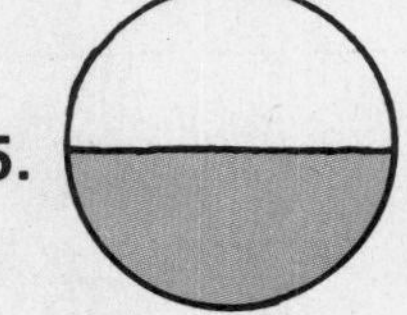 

$\frac{1}{2} = \frac{4}{8}$

6. 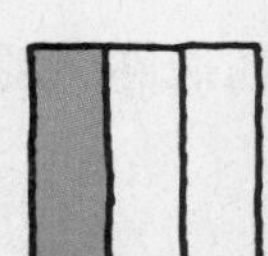 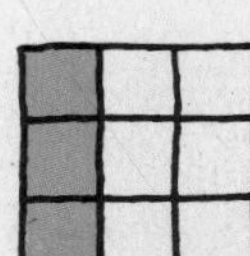

$\frac{1}{3} = \frac{3}{9}$

7. 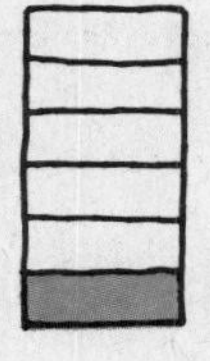 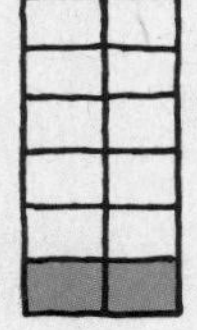

$\frac{1}{6} = \frac{2}{12}$

8. 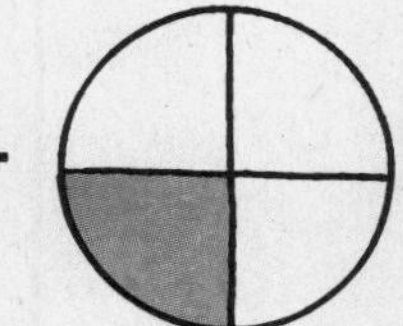 

$\frac{1}{4} = \frac{3}{12}$

Give two equivalent fractions.

9.  

$\frac{2}{4}$ $\frac{4}{8}$

10. 

$\frac{1}{3}$ $\frac{2}{6}$

11. 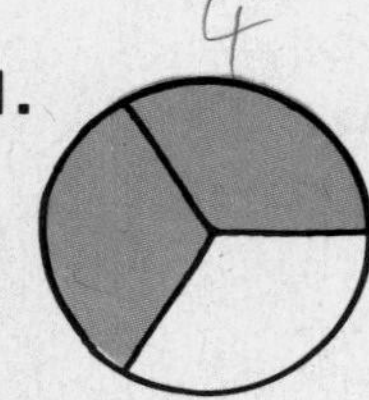 

$\frac{2}{3}$ $\frac{4}{6}$

12. 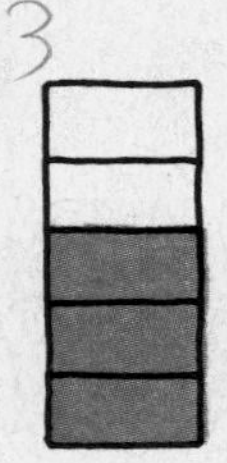 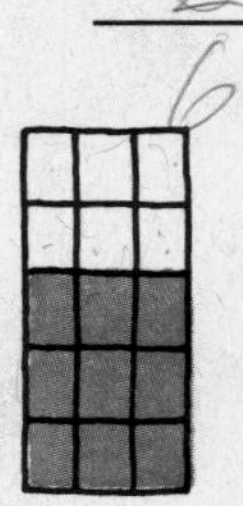

$\frac{3}{5}$ $\frac{9}{15}$

Complete. If you need to, draw pictures.

13. $\frac{1}{2} = \frac{2}{4}$	14. $\frac{1}{2} = \frac{3}{6}$	15. $\frac{1}{2} = \frac{4}{8}$	16. $\frac{1}{2} = \frac{5}{10}$
17. $\frac{1}{3} = \frac{2}{6}$	18. $\frac{1}{3} = \frac{3}{9}$	19. $\frac{1}{3} = \frac{4}{12}$	20. $\frac{1}{3} = \frac{5}{15}$
21. $\frac{1}{4} = \frac{2}{8}$	22. $\frac{1}{4} = \frac{3}{12}$	23. $\frac{1}{4} = \frac{4}{16}$	24. $\frac{1}{4} = \frac{5}{20}$
25. $\frac{2}{3} = \frac{4}{6}$	26. $\frac{2}{3} = \frac{6}{9}$	27. $\frac{2}{3} = \frac{8}{12}$	28. $\frac{2}{3} = \frac{10}{15}$

KEEPING SKILLS SHARP

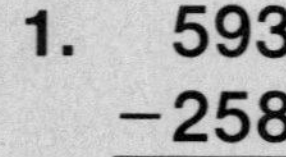

1. 593 − 258	2. 745 − 329	3. 852 − 171	4. 819 − 420	5. 635 − 254
6. 621 − 435	7. 830 − 666	8. 523 − 155	9. 742 − 374	10. 945 − 259
11. 302 − 154	12. 506 − 378	13. 708 − 249	14. 300 − 126	15. 900 − 358

Name Matin #2

Comparing fractions

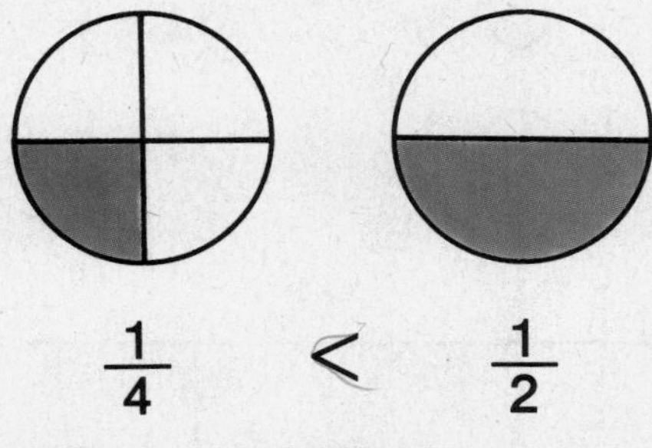

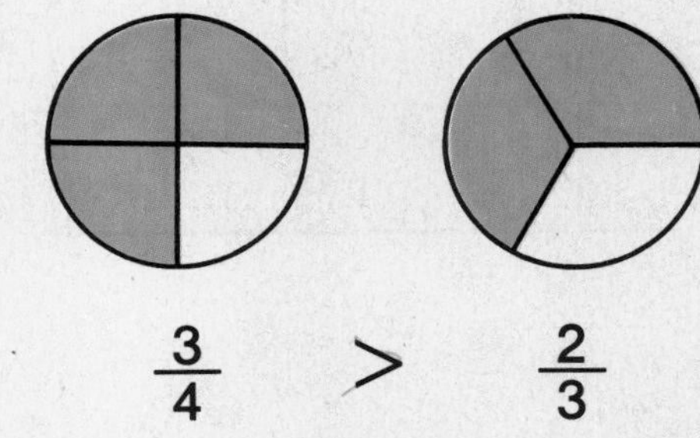

$\frac{1}{4} < \frac{1}{2}$ $\qquad$ $\frac{3}{4} > \frac{2}{3}$

is less than $\qquad$ is greater than

EXERCISES

<, =, or > ?

1. 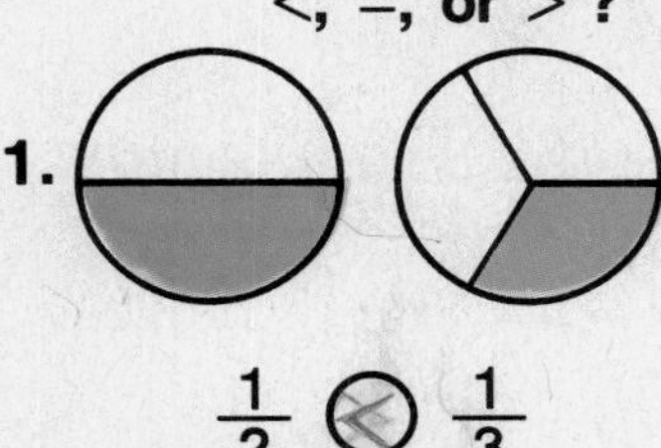

$\frac{1}{2}$ ○ $\frac{1}{3}$

2. 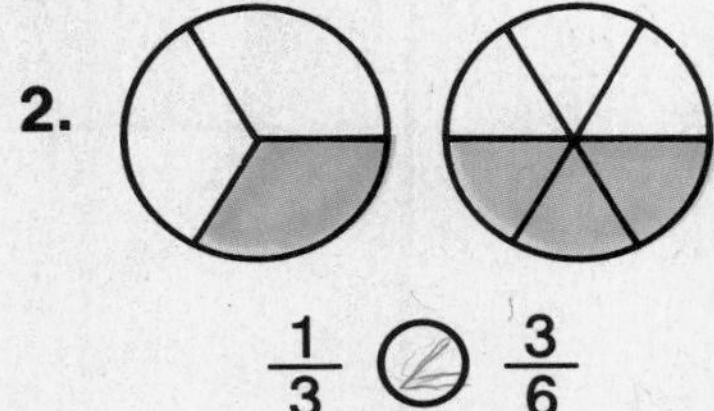

$\frac{1}{3}$ ○ $\frac{3}{6}$

3. 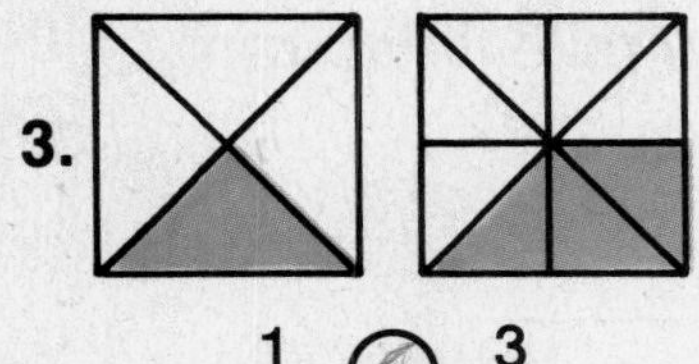

$\frac{1}{4}$ ○ $\frac{3}{8}$

4. 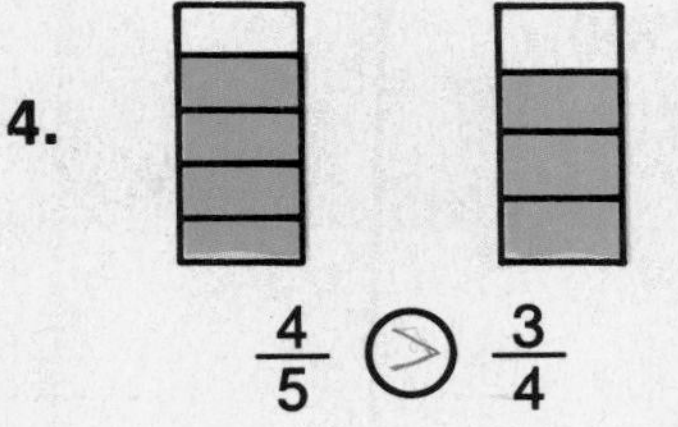

$\frac{4}{5}$ ○ $\frac{3}{4}$

5. 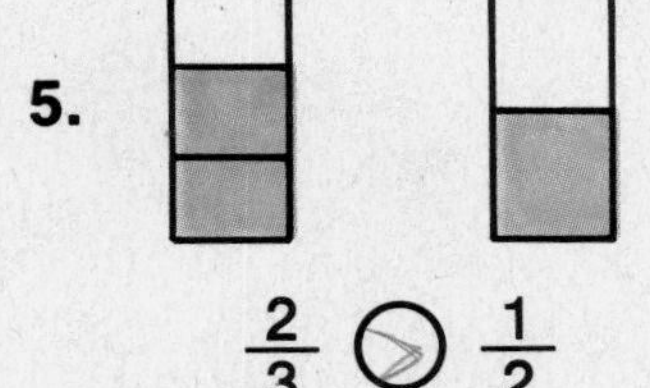

$\frac{2}{3}$ ○ $\frac{1}{2}$

6. 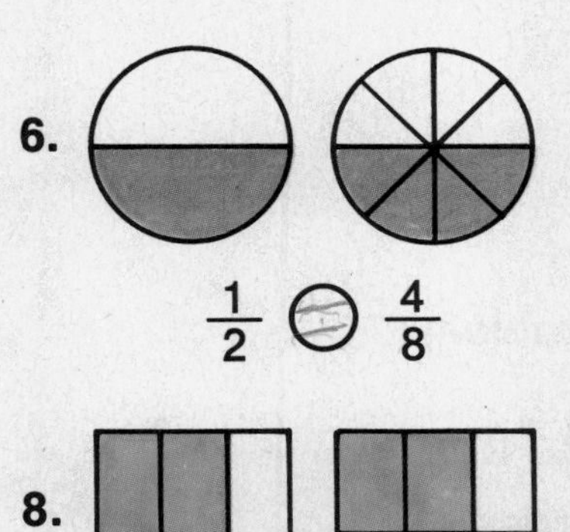

$\frac{1}{2}$ ○ $\frac{4}{8}$

7. 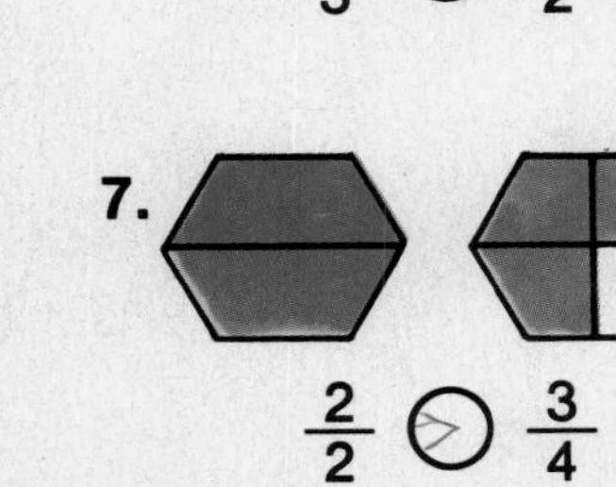

$\frac{2}{2}$ ○ $\frac{3}{4}$

8. 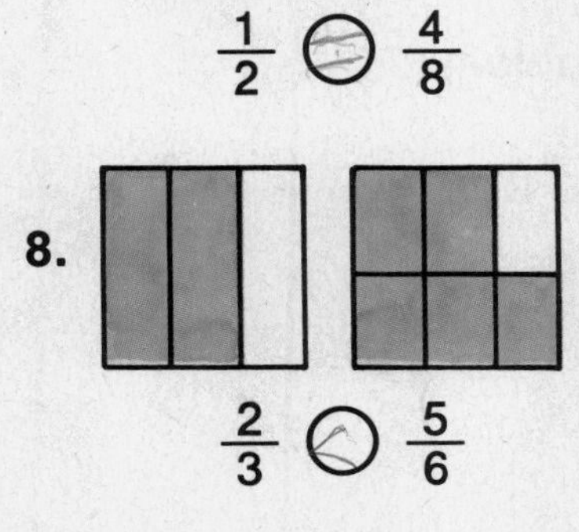

$\frac{2}{3}$ ○ $\frac{5}{6}$

<, =, or >? (*Hint:* Use the picture.)

$\frac{1}{2}$			$\frac{1}{2}$		
$\frac{1}{3}$		$\frac{1}{3}$		$\frac{1}{3}$	
$\frac{1}{4}$	$\frac{1}{4}$		$\frac{1}{4}$		$\frac{1}{4}$

9. $\frac{1}{2}$ ○ $\frac{1}{3}$
10. $\frac{1}{2}$ ○ $\frac{1}{4}$
11. $\frac{1}{3}$ ○ $\frac{1}{2}$
12. $\frac{1}{3}$ ○ $\frac{1}{4}$
13. $\frac{1}{4}$ ○ $\frac{1}{2}$
14. $\frac{1}{4}$ ○ $\frac{1}{3}$

15. $\frac{1}{3}$ ○ $\frac{1}{6}$
16. $\frac{1}{3}$ ○ $\frac{1}{8}$
17. $\frac{1}{6}$ ○ $\frac{1}{3}$
18. $\frac{1}{6}$ ○ $\frac{1}{8}$
19. $\frac{1}{8}$ ○ $\frac{1}{3}$
20. $\frac{1}{8}$ ○ $\frac{1}{6}$
21. $\frac{1}{3}$ ○ $\frac{3}{8}$
22. $\frac{1}{6}$ ○ $\frac{2}{8}$
23. $\frac{2}{3}$ ○ $\frac{5}{8}$
24. $\frac{7}{8}$ ○ $\frac{5}{6}$

$\frac{1}{3}$		$\frac{1}{3}$		$\frac{1}{3}$			
$\frac{1}{6}$	$\frac{1}{6}$	$\frac{1}{6}$	$\frac{1}{6}$	$\frac{1}{6}$	$\frac{1}{6}$		
$\frac{1}{8}$	$\frac{1}{8}$	$\frac{1}{8}$	$\frac{1}{8}$	$\frac{1}{8}$	$\frac{1}{8}$	$\frac{1}{8}$	$\frac{1}{8}$

Problem Solving

25. Tony and Jill each had 24¢. Tony spent $\frac{1}{4}$ of his. Jill spent $\frac{1}{3}$ of hers. Who spent less money? ______

26. Kelly ran $\frac{1}{4}$ of a mile. George ran $\frac{1}{8}$ of a mile. Who ran farther? ______

Draw a picture to solve the problem.

27. $\frac{1}{3}$ of the birds are outside the birdhouse. How many birds are there in all? ______

Name ________________________________

Problem Solving Consumer applications

The school store orders pencils, pens, erasers, and notepads by the dozen.

1 dozen = 12

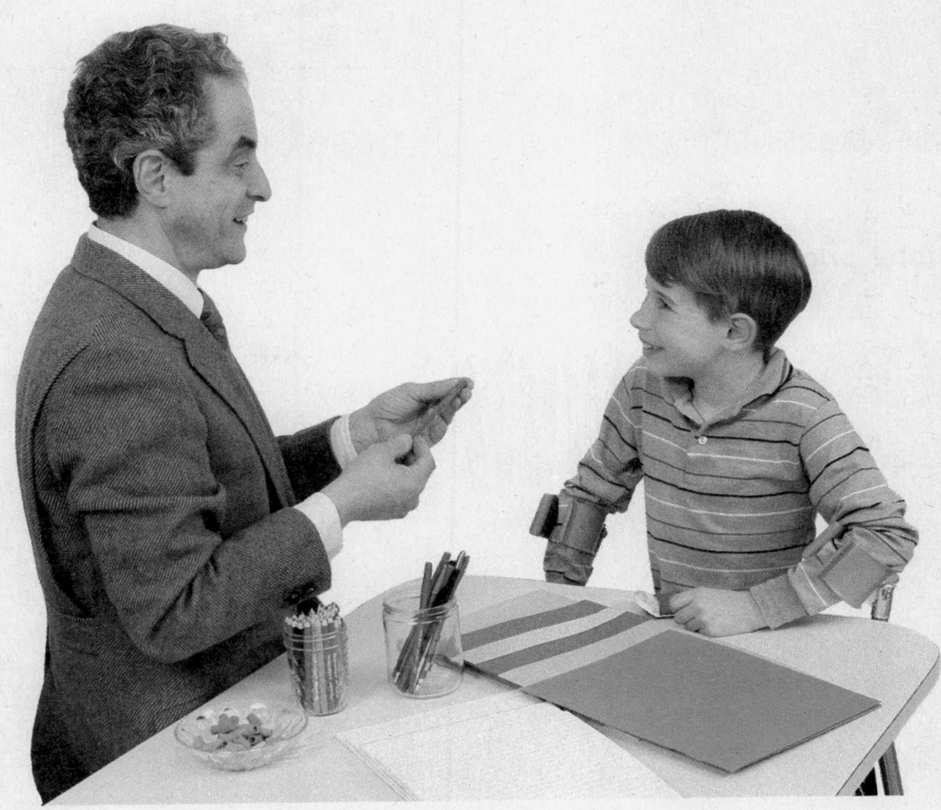

EXERCISES

Solve.

1. How many pencils in $\frac{1}{2}$ dozen? 6

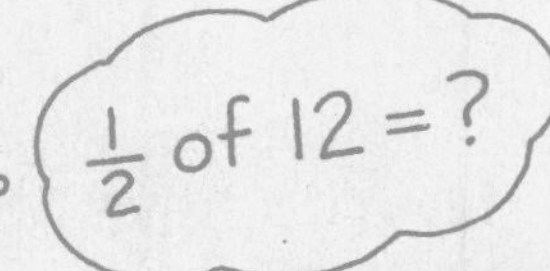

2. How many pens in $\frac{1}{3}$ dozen? 4

3. How many erasers in $\frac{1}{4}$ dozen? 3

4. Which would cost less, $\frac{1}{3}$ dozen pencils or $\frac{1}{2}$ dozen pencils? $\frac{1}{3}$

5. Which would you rather have, $\frac{1}{2}$ dozen pens or $\frac{1}{4}$ dozen pens? 4 dozen

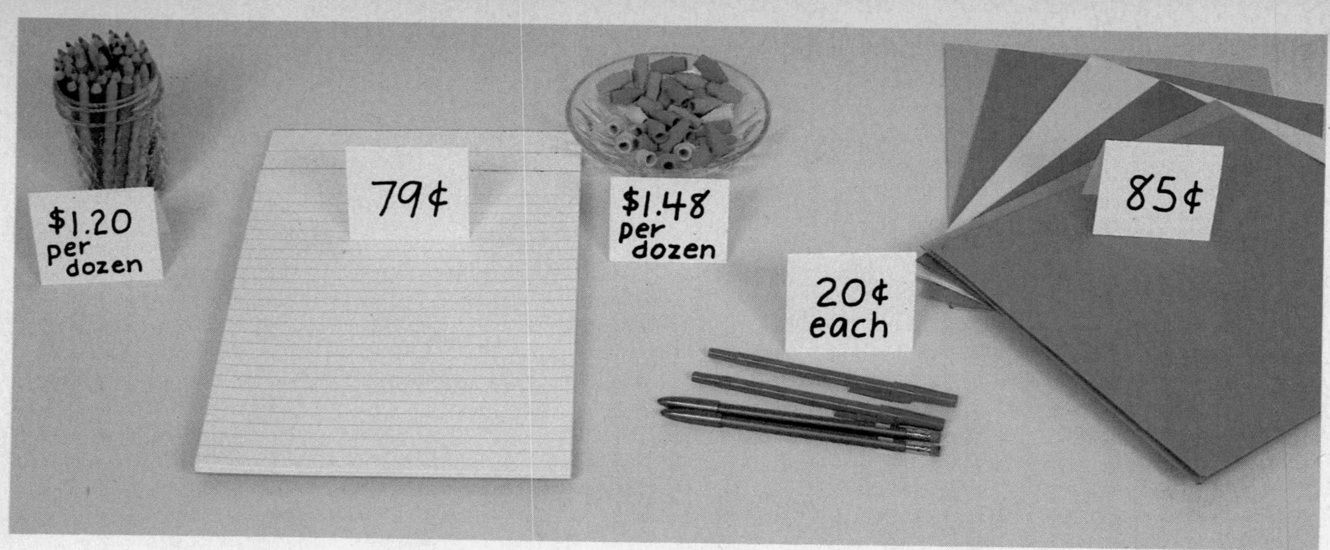

Give the total price.

6. **7.**

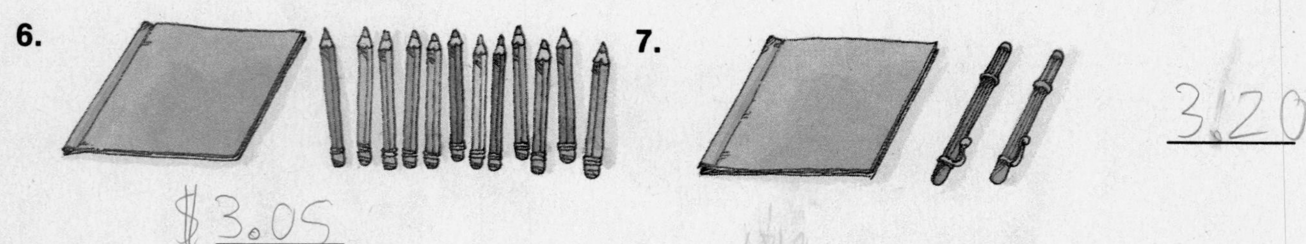

8. **9.**

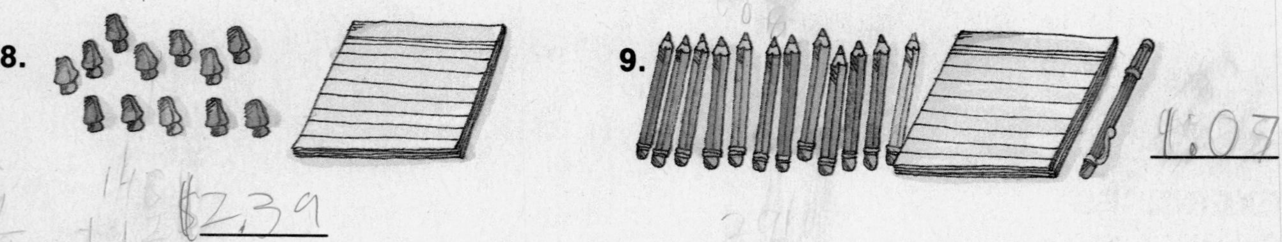

How much money will be left?

10. You have $1.00.

You buy

11. You have $3.00.

You buy

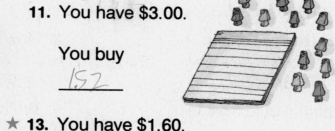

12. You have $1.32.

You buy

★ **13.** You have $1.60.

You buy

Name ____________________

Decimals

Work in groups. Get plain paper.

You can use decimals to write about tenths.

One tenth of
this circle
is red.

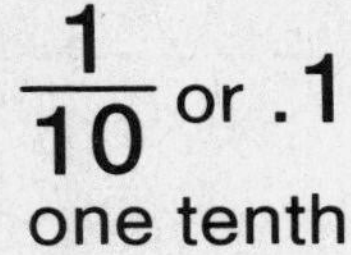

$\frac{1}{10}$ or .1
one tenth

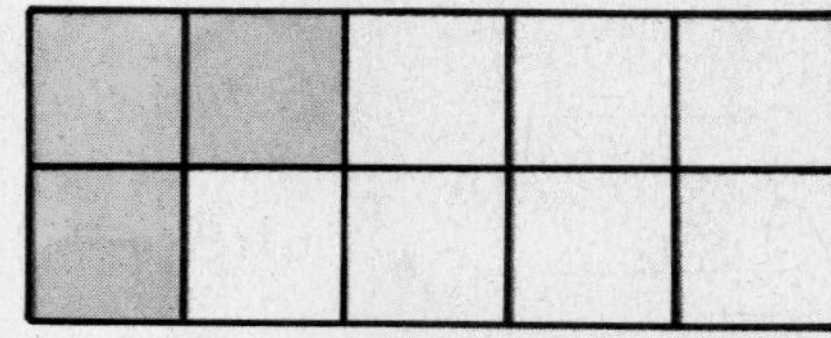

$\frac{3}{10}$ or .3
three tenths

$\frac{6}{10}$ or .6
six tenths

1. Estimate what part of this circle is blue. Write your answer as a decimal.

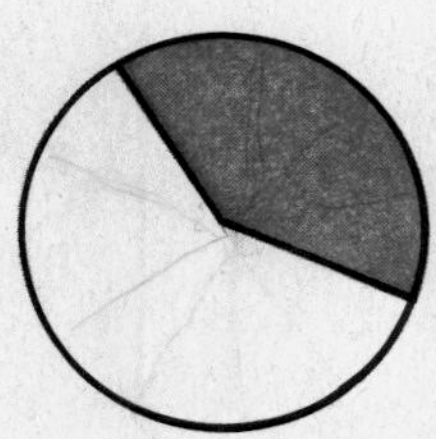

____

2. Check your estimate.
   a. Trace the circle at the top of the page. Trace the sections too.
   b. Put your traced circle over the circle you want to check. Is your estimate right?

____

What part of each figure is colored?
Estimate. Then use the tracing method to check.

3.

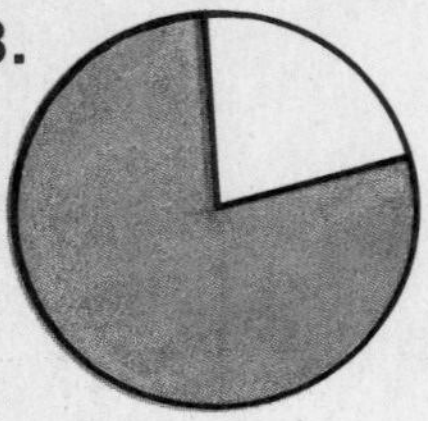

Estimate: _______

Answer: _______

4.

Estimate: _______

Answer: _______

5.

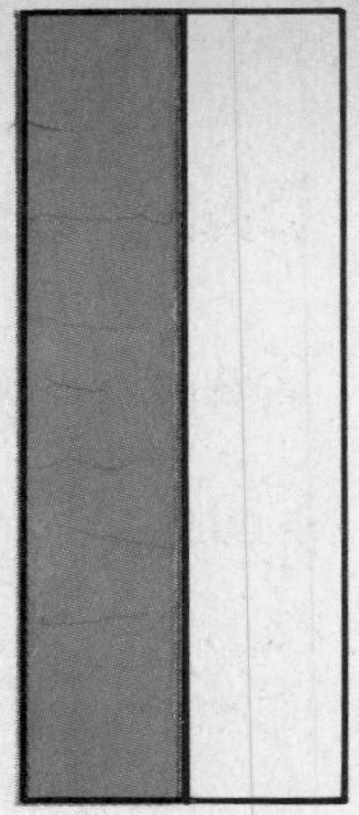

Estimate: _______

Answer: _______

6.

Estimate: _______ Answer: _______

7.

Estimate: _______ Answer: _______

8. Talk about how you estimated and checked figures **6** and **7**.

Now look at these figures. Estimate what parts are colored.
Think and talk about how you will check your estimates.

9.

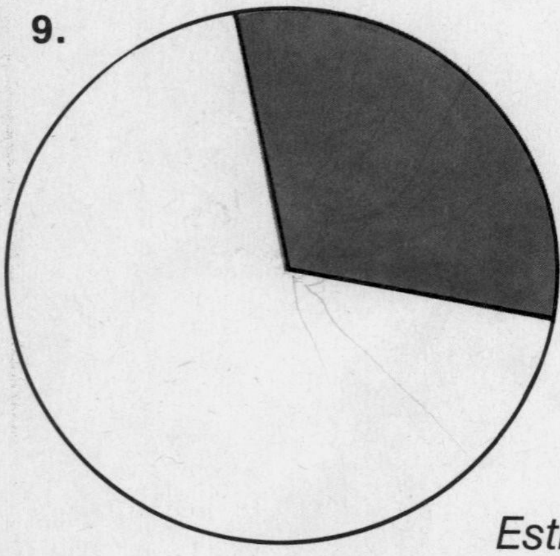

Estimate: _______ Answer: _______

10.

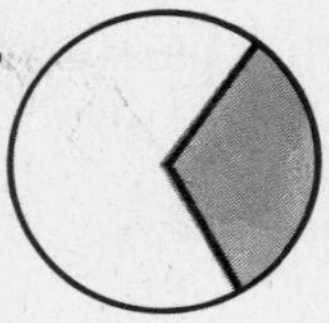

Estimate: _______

Answer: _______

11.

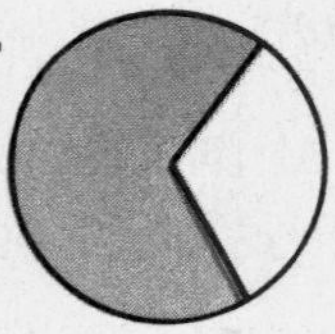

Estimate: _______

Answer: _______

12.

Estimate: _______ Answer: _______

13. What ways did you use to check your estimates?
Compare your ways with the ways used by one other group.

Name ________________________________

Estimating decimals

Work in groups.
Get plain paper.
Record your answers on a separate sheet of paper if you need more space.

Ones

1	2	3

Tenths

.1	.2	.3	.4	.5	.6	.7	.8	.9

PART A

1. Make cards like those shown above. Place them face down in two piles.

2. Pick two teams.

a. Ask each team to pick a card from the Ones pile and a card from the Tenths pile to form a decimal greater than 1. This is your team's secret number.

b. Draw a picture of your secret number, using the circles below as patterns. Use the circle on the left to trace the whole number. Use the circle on the right to trace the tenths.

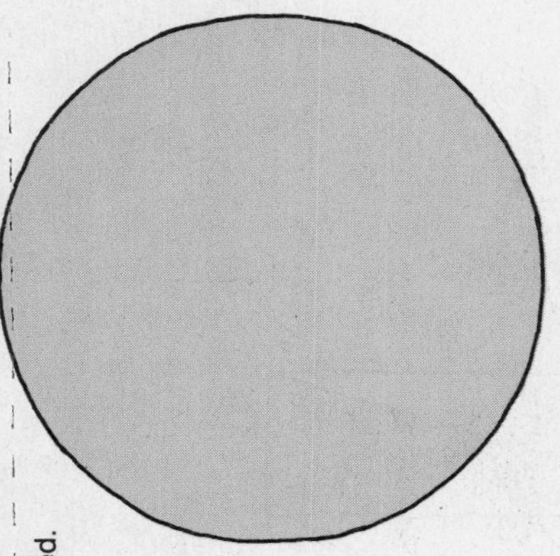

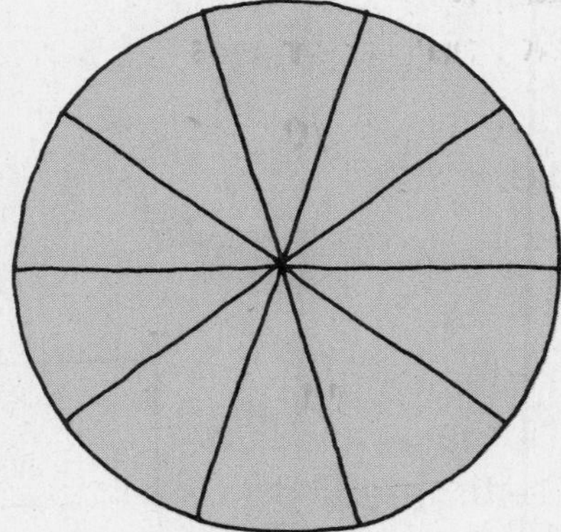

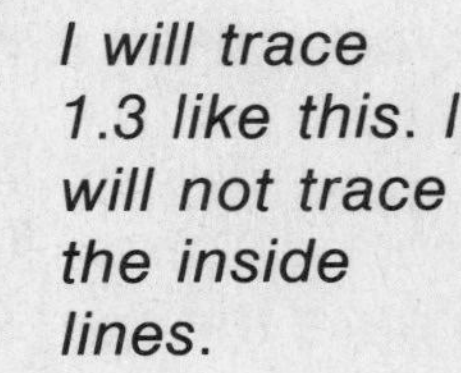
I will trace
1.3 like this. I
will not trace
the inside
lines.

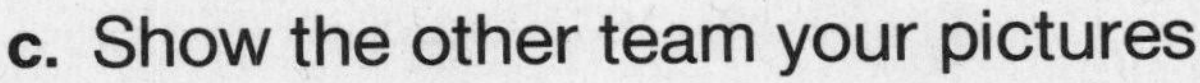

c. Show the other team your pictures.

d. Guess the other team's secret number and write it on a piece of paper.

e. Check your guess by placing the other team's picture over the circles on this page.

3. Try a few more rounds of exercise 2. After each round, put the Ones card back but keep the Tenths card.

4. a. How did you make your guesses?

   b. Did your guesses get better with each round?

   c. Which part was easier, estimating ones or tenths? Why?

PART B

5. Take all your pictures of parts of circles. Make new parts if you need to. Which pairs of parts make a whole? Less than a whole? More than a whole?

.7 and .3 make one whole.

6. Make a chart to keep a record.

Parts that make a whole	Parts that make less than a whole	Parts that make more than a whole
.7 and .3		

7. Without looking at the pictures, can you tell whether two decimals make a whole? How?

8. Find groups of three or more parts that make a whole, less than a whole, and more than a whole.

PART C

9. Estimate the part of the rectangle that is blue. Write a decimal to show your estimate.

   Figure out one or more ways to check your estimates. Compare your ways to the ways used by one other group.

a.

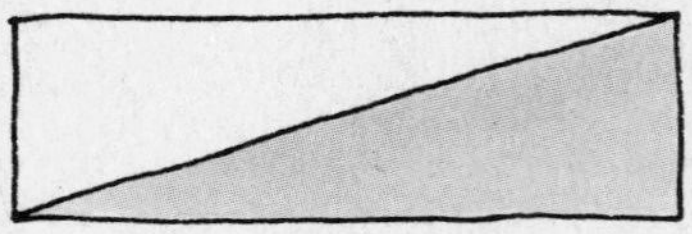

Estimate: ______

Answer: ______

b.

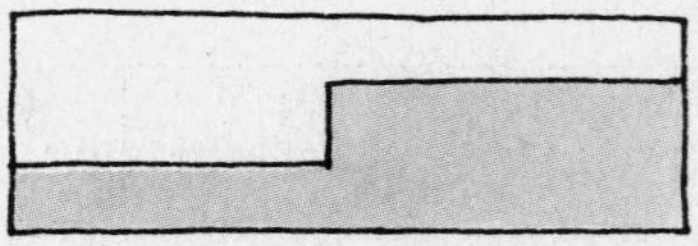

Estimate: ______

Answer: ______

Name Matin #2

Chapter Checkup

What fraction is colored? [pages 216–217]

1. 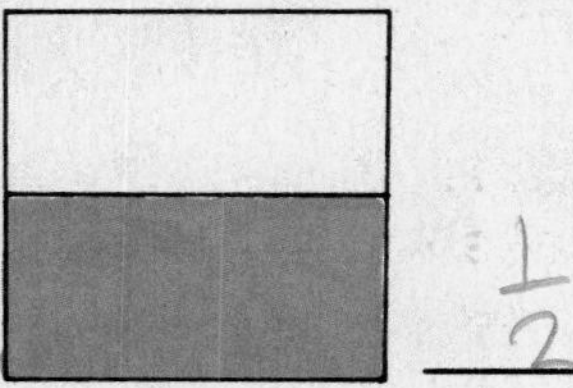 $\frac{1}{2}$

2. 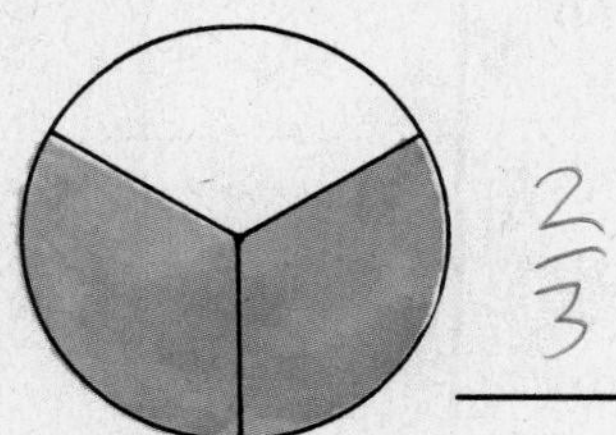 $\frac{2}{3}$

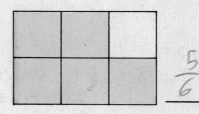

3.  $\frac{5}{6}$

What fraction are red? [pages 218–221]

4. 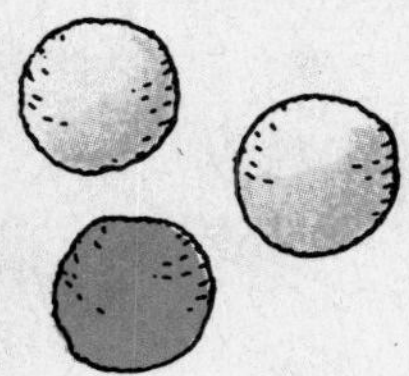 $\frac{1}{3}$

5.  $\frac{3}{4}$

6. 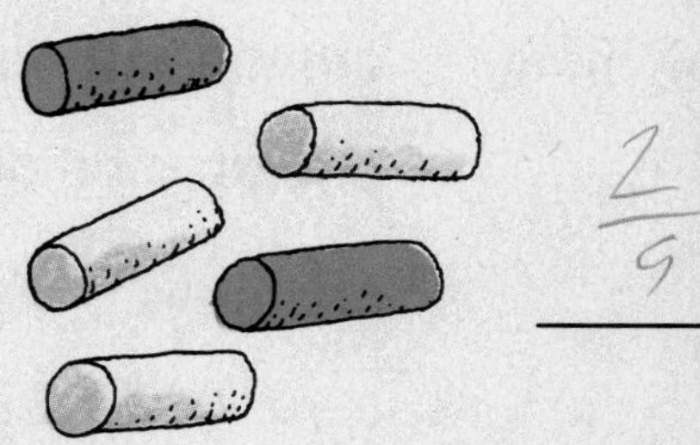 $\frac{2}{5}$

Complete. [pages 222–225, 230–231]

7. $\frac{1}{2}$ of 6 = 3

8. $\frac{1}{4}$ of 12 = 3

9. $\frac{1}{3}$ of 18 = 6

$<$, $=$, or $>$? [pages 226–229]

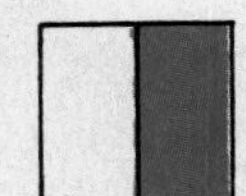 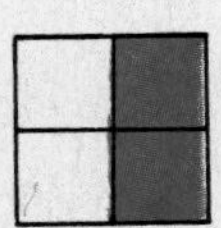

10. $\frac{1}{2}$ ○ $\frac{2}{4}$

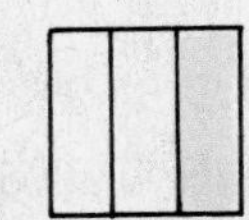

11. $\frac{1}{3}$ ○ $\frac{1}{4}$

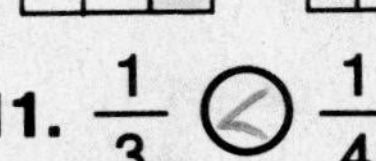

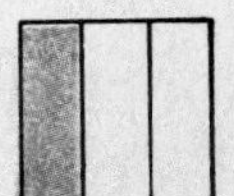 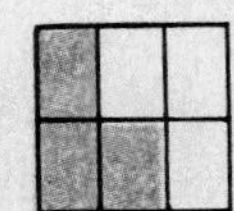

12. $\frac{1}{3}$ ○ $\frac{3}{6}$

How much is colored?
Write as a decimal. [pages 232–235]

13. 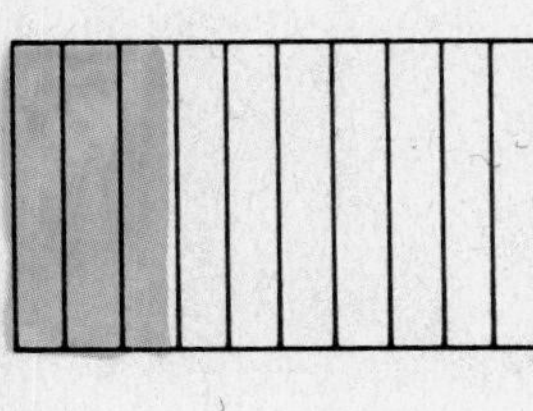 .3

14. 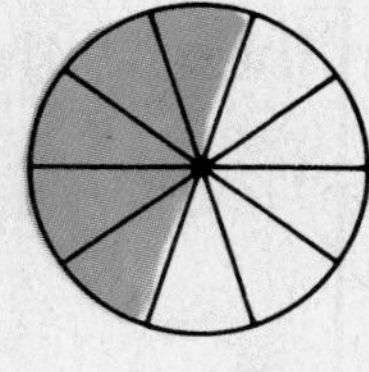 .5

15. 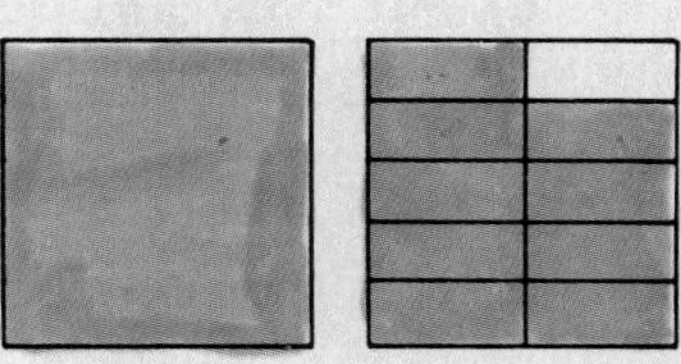 .10

Chapter Project

PROBABILITY

The chance of picking a red crayon is 3 out of 10, or $\frac{3}{10}$.

Copy and complete.

1. The chance of picking a yellow crayon is 2 out of 10, or _____.
2. The chance of picking a blue crayon is 5 out of 10, or _____.
3. If you picked a crayon without looking, the color of the crayon would most likely be _____.

Follow these directions.

4. a. Your teacher will put some red, blue, and yellow crayons into a box.
   b. Without looking, someone in your class will pick a crayon and show it to the class.
   c. Then your teacher will put the crayon back into the box, mix up the crayons, and let someone else pick a crayon.
   d. Keep a record of the colors that were picked.
   e. After everyone has picked a crayon, guess which color crayon there is the most of in the box.
   f. Check your guess.

Name Matin #2

Chapter Review

What fraction is blue?

1. 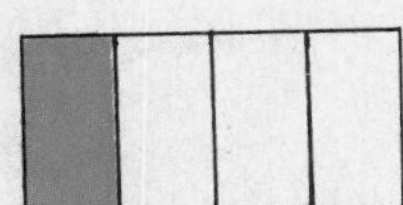

(1) parts blue
[4] parts in all

2. 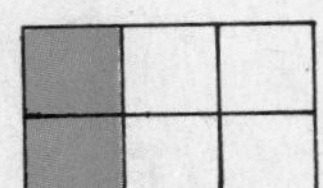

(2) parts blue
[6] parts in all

3. 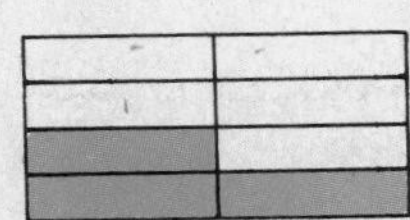

(3) parts blue
[8] parts in all

What fraction are green?

4. 

(2) green cars
[5] cars in all

5. 

(1) green apples
[3] apples in all

6. 

(5) green pencils
[6] pencils in all

<, =, or > ?

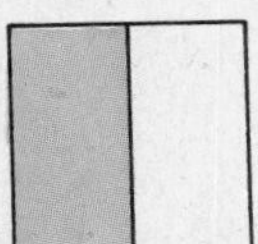

7. $\frac{1}{2}$ (>) $\frac{1}{3}$

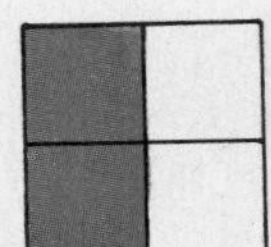

8. $\frac{2}{4}$ (>) $\frac{1}{2}$

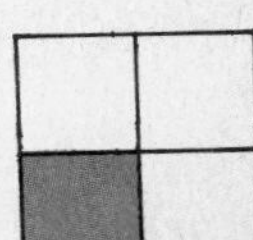

9. $\frac{1}{4}$ (<) $\frac{4}{8}$

How much is colored?
Write as a decimal.

10. 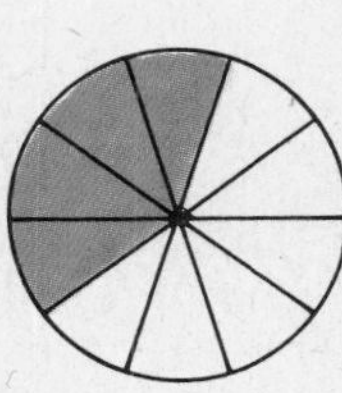

.4

11. 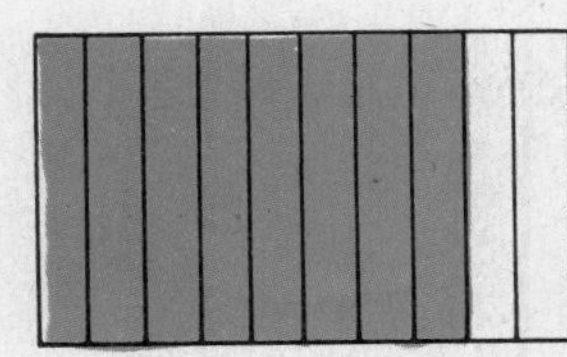

.8

12. 

.8

Chapter Challenge

USING A CIRCLE GRAPH

Tell what fraction of the garden is

 **1.** ______

 **2.** ______

 **3.** ______

 **4.** ______

 **5.** ______

 **6.** or ______

 **7.** or ______

 **8.** or ______

 **9.** or ______

 **10.**  or  or ______

Name ______________________

Cumulative Checkup

STANDARDIZED FORMAT

Give the correct letter.

1. Add.

$$\begin{array}{r} 7 \\ 2 \\ +8 \\ \hline \end{array}$$

a. 16
b. 17
c. 18
d. none of these

2. Which letter is the fifth letter?

ARITHMETIC

a. T
b. M
c. E
d. H

3. Which number is the greatest?

a. 756
b. 576
c. 765
d. 675

4. Three thousand forty-four is

a. 3044
b. 3404
c. 3440
d. none of these

5. Add.

$$\begin{array}{r} 75 \\ 29 \\ +68 \\ \hline \end{array}$$

a. 152
b. 172
c. 162
d. none of these

6. Subtract.

$$\begin{array}{r} 624 \\ -358 \\ \hline \end{array}$$

a. 334
b. 376
c. 366
d. 266

7. What time is it?

a. 4:30
b. 3:30
c. 6:20
d. none of these

8. How much money?
2 quarters
1 dime
2 nickels
1 penny

a. 71¢
b. 67¢
c. 91¢
d. 80¢

9. Multiply.

$$\begin{array}{r} 4 \\ \times 7 \\ \hline \end{array}$$

a. 24
b. 28
c. 32
d. none of these

10. Divide.

$3\overline{)24}$

a. 6
b. 9
c. 7
d. none of these

11. Divide.

$4\overline{)27}$

a. 3 R6
b. 8 R3
c. 6 R3
d. none of these

12. Tom had 3 balls. Anne gave him 18 more. How many did he have then?

a. 15 **b.** 6
c. 21 **d.** none of these

9

Measurement

How many containers can you see in the picture? Which container holds the most? How can you tell?

Name ______________________________

Centimeter

The **centimeter** is used for measuring length in the metric system.
Here is a centimeter ruler.

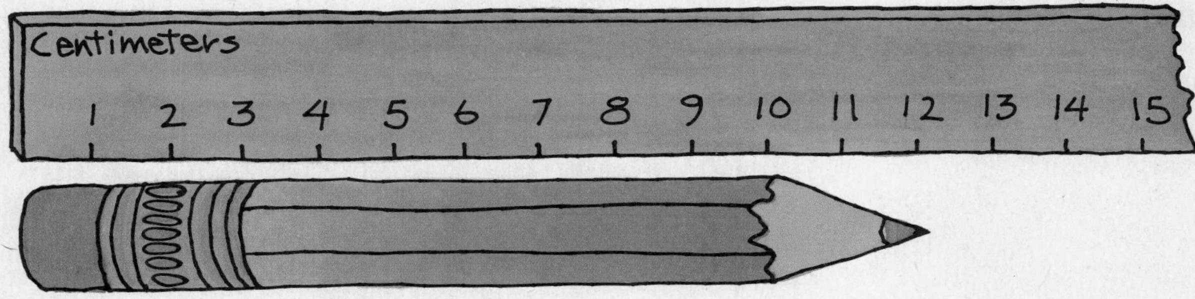

The pencil is between 12 and 13 centimeters (cm) long.
It is nearer 12 cm.
It is about 12 cm long.

EXERCISES

About how long is each pencil?
Measure with a centimeter ruler.

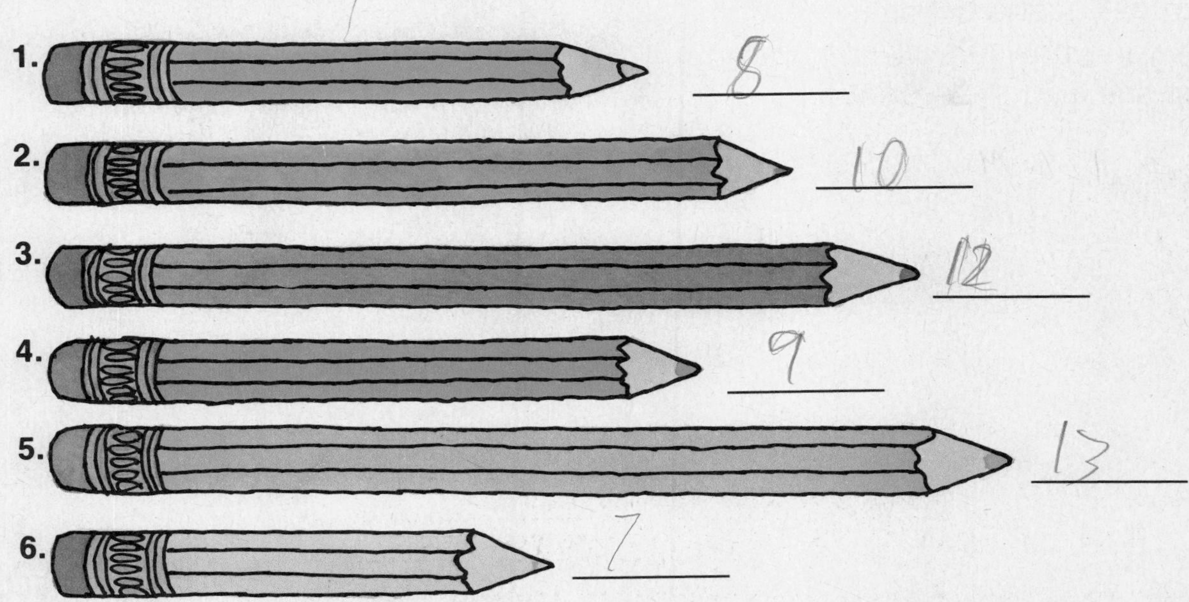

Measure each stick with a centimeter ruler.

7. 6 cm

8. 5 cm

9. 4 cm

10. 8 cm

Draw sticks with these lengths.

11. 3 cm
12. 8 cm
13. 11 cm
14. 16 cm
15. 10 cm
16. 13 cm
17. 18 cm
18. 21 cm

Measure with a centimeter ruler

19. the width of your math book. 27

20. the length of your shoe. 23

21. the thickness of your desk top. $2\frac{1}{2}$

22. the height of your desk. 58

Problem Solving—making a table

23. Mia is in the third grade. She is 98 cm tall. If she grows 5 cm each year, how tall will she be when she is in the seventh grade? 128cm

Name ____________________

Centimeters and meters

The **meter** is used to measure longer lengths.

1 meter (m) = 100 centimeters (cm)

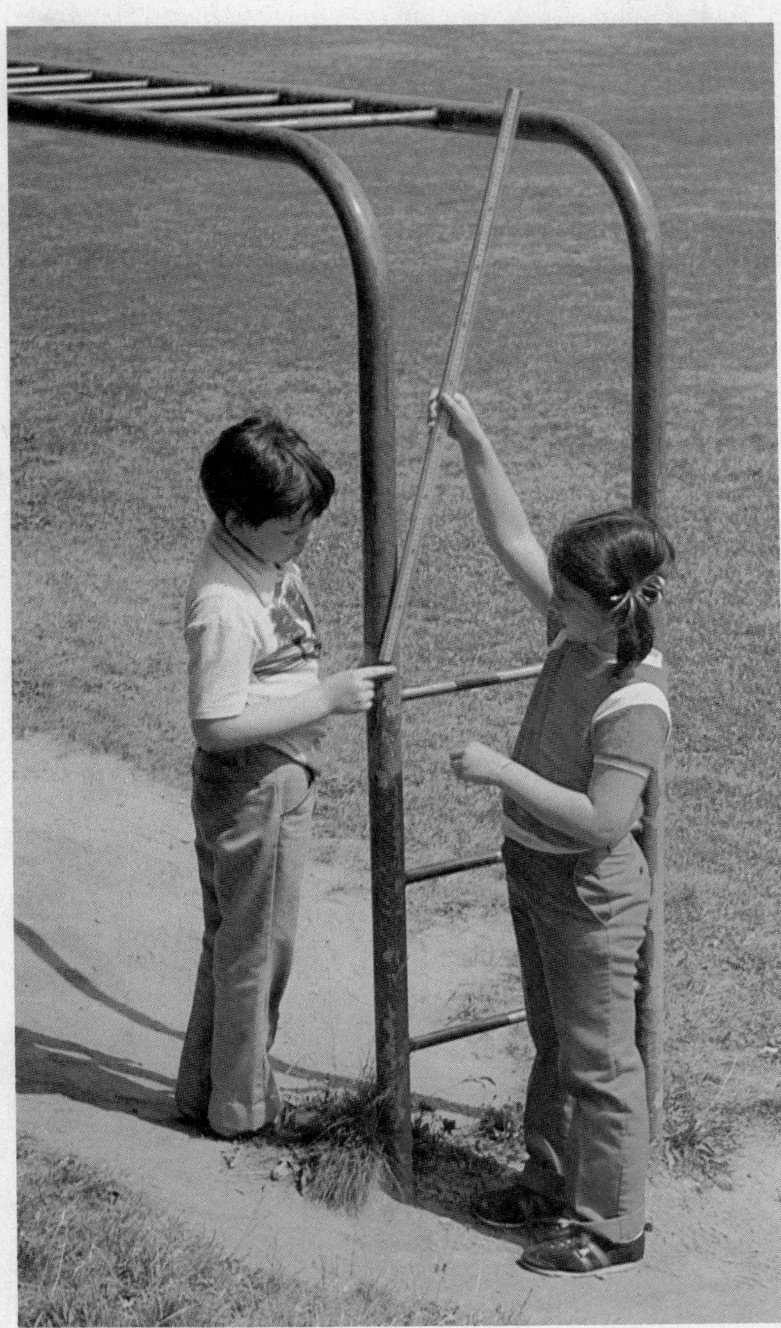

EXERCISES
Complete. If you need to, look at a meterstick.

1. 1 m = _____ cm
2. 2 m = _____ cm
3. 3 m = _____ cm
4. 6 m = _____ cm
5. 8 m = _____ cm
6. 9 m = _____ cm
7. 7 m = _____ cm
8. 100 cm = _____ m
9. 400 cm = _____ m
10. 700 cm = _____ m
11. 800 cm = _____ m
12. 500 cm = _____ m
13. 200 cm = _____ m
14. 600 cm = _____ m
15. ★ 1000 cm = _____ m

Measure with a meter stick

16. the width of the door. ______

17. the length of the chalkboard. ______

18. the height of the chalkboard. ______

19. the length of the room. ______

20. the width of the room. ______

21. the height of the ceiling. ______

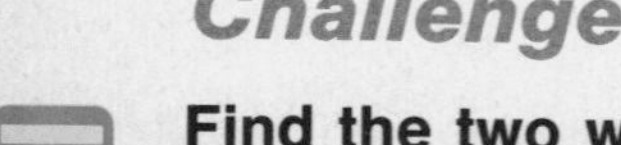

Challenge!

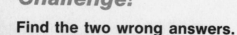

Find the two wrong answers.
Correct them.

22. Eleven plus sixty-nine plus two hundred five equals

330

______

23. Five hundred six plus one thousand seven plus thirty-six equals

1549

______

24. Seventy-seven plus three thousand ninety plus eight thousand two equals

11579

______

Name ____________________

Perimeter

The distance around a figure is called the **perimeter** of the figure.

The perimeter of this rectangle is 18 cm. To find a perimeter, you can add the lengths of the sides.

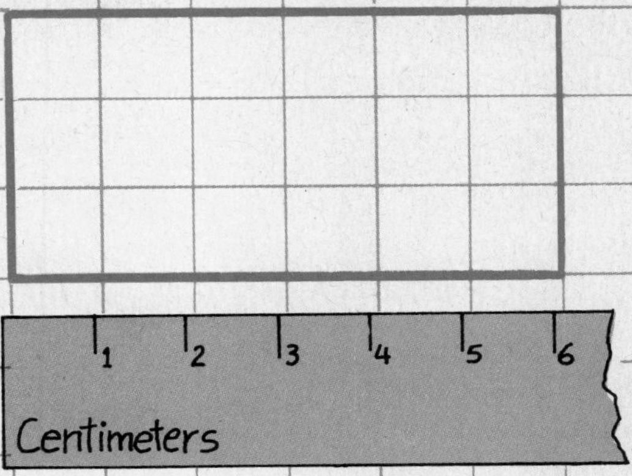

1 2 3 4 5 6

Centimeters

EXERCISES

Give the perimeter.

1.

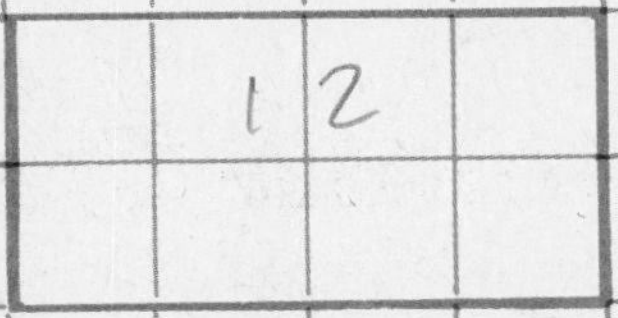

2.

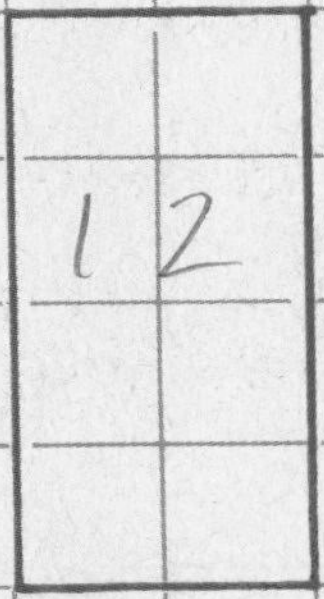

3.

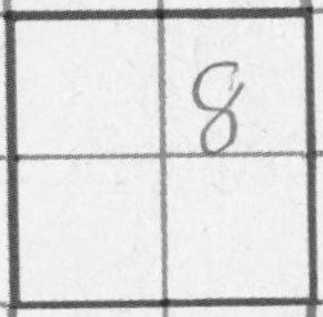

4.

5.

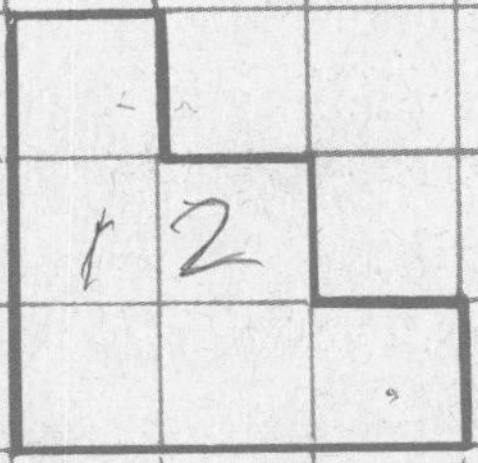

6.

7.

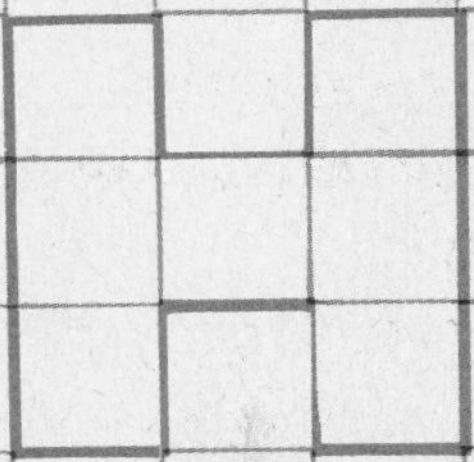

The length of each side is given. Find the perimeter.

8. 5 cm, 5 cm, 5 cm, 5 cm ______

9. 3 cm, 5 cm, 4 cm ______

10. 3 cm, 10 cm, 10 cm, 3 cm ______

11. 6 cm, 6 cm, 6 cm ______

12. 4 cm, 4 cm, 4 cm, 4 cm, 4 cm, 4 cm ______

13. 5 cm, 5 cm, 5 cm, 5 cm, 5 cm ______

14. 6 cm, 7 cm, 11 cm ______

15. 8 cm, 7 cm, 7 cm, 8 cm ______

16. 7 cm, 8 cm, 8 cm, 13 cm ______

Find the perimeter of

17. your math-book cover. ______

18. your desk top. ______

★ **19.** the top of a wastebasket. ______

Name ____________________

Area

To find the **area** of the blue rectangle, we can count the **square centimeter** tiles that it takes to cover it.

square centimeter

The area is 15 square centimeters.

EXERCISES

Give each area.

1. 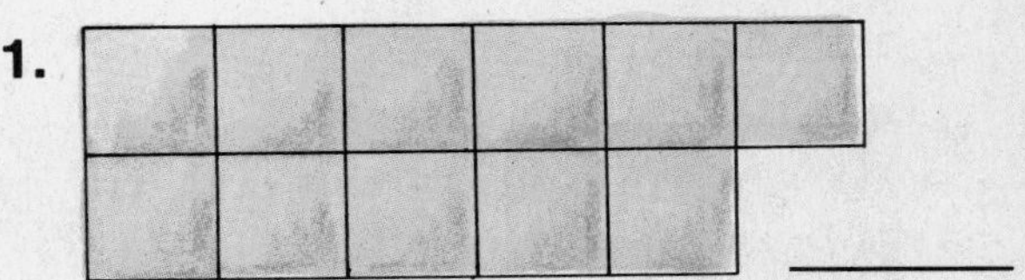 ________

2. 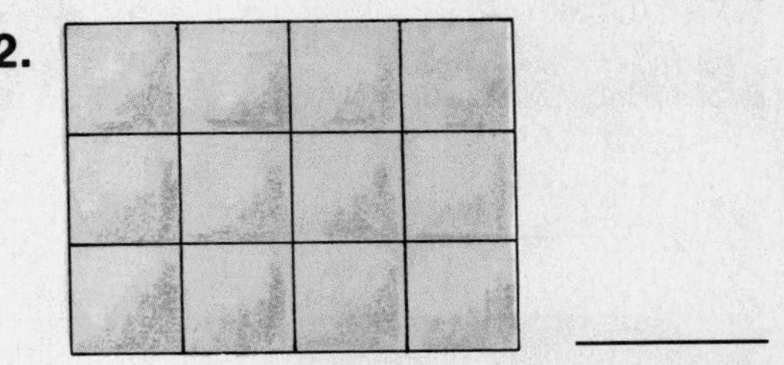 ________

3. 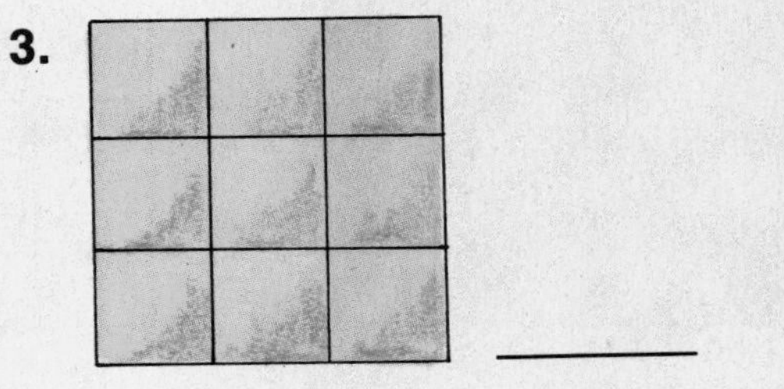 ________

4. 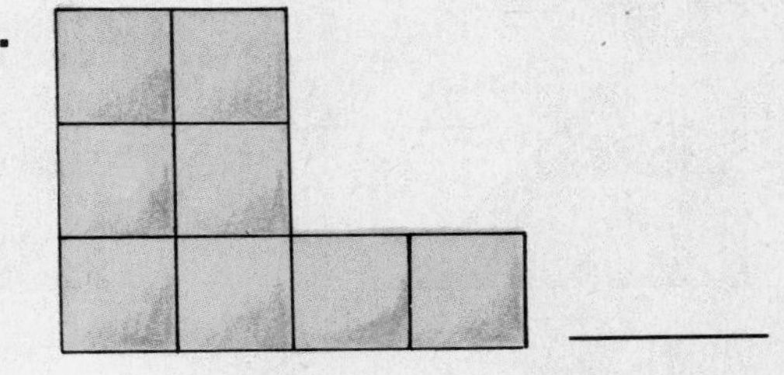 ________

These pieces were cut from graph paper. Each square is one square centimeter. Give each area.

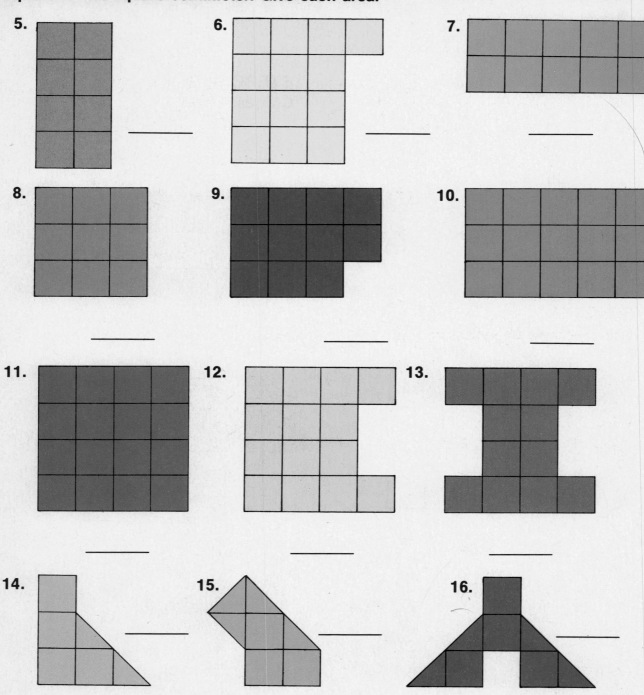

5. ______

6. 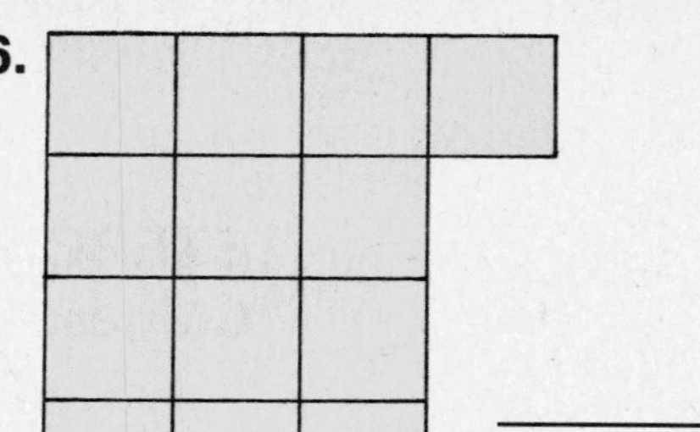 ______

7. 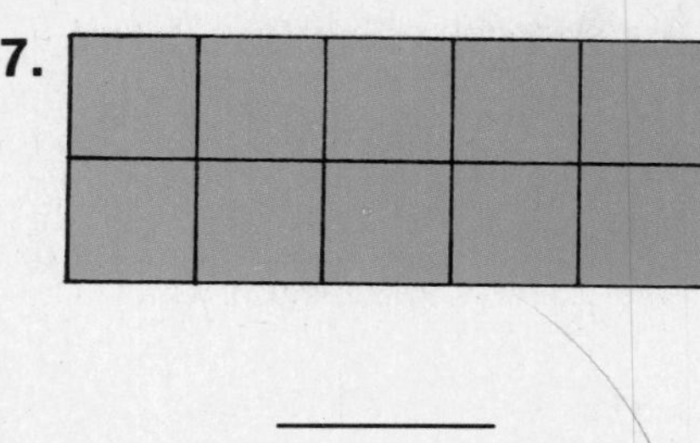 ______

8. ______

9. 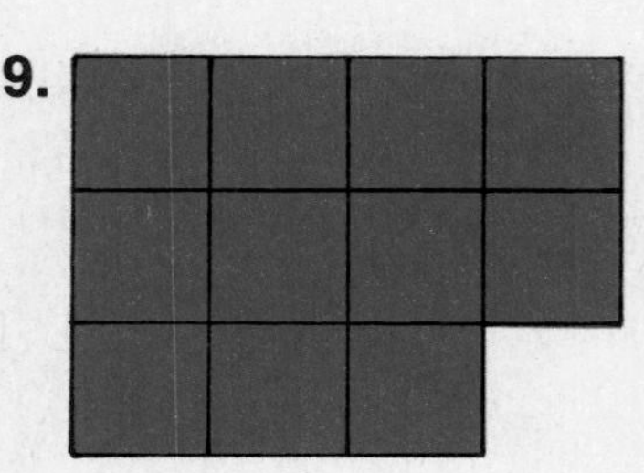 ______

10. 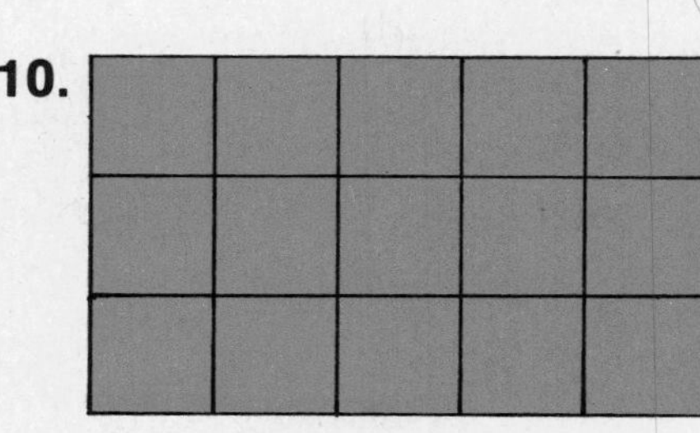 ______

11. ______

12. 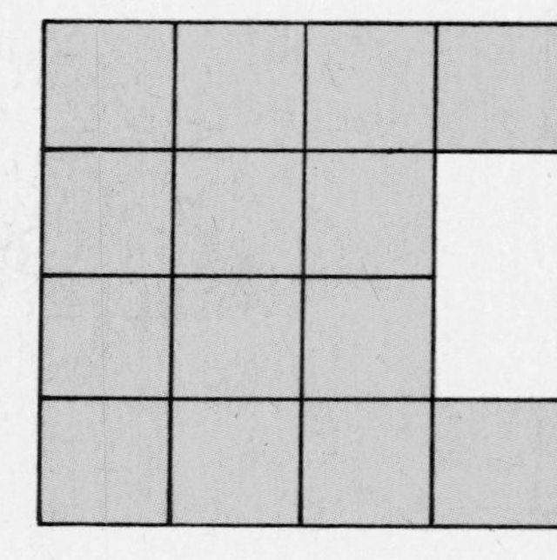 ______

13. 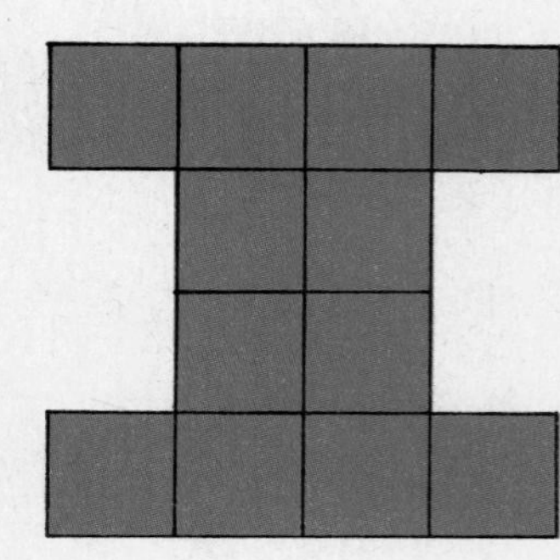 ______

14. ______

15. 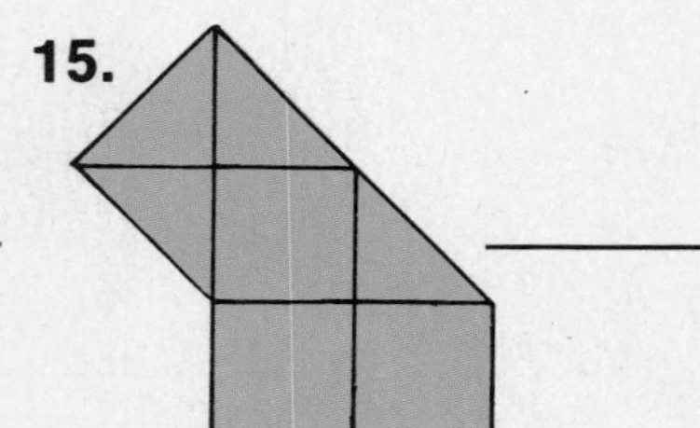 ______

16. 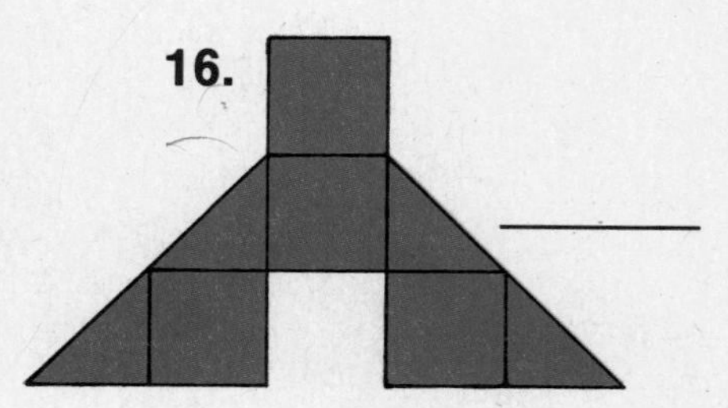 ______

Challenge!

17. a. Get a piece of graph paper with the lines one centimeter apart.
    b. Draw around your hand.
    c. Find the area of your handprint. ______

18. Find the area of your footprint. ______

Name ____________________

Volume

cubic centimeter

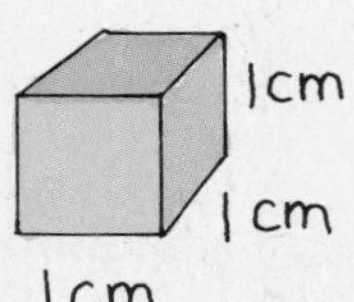

To find the **volume** of this box, we can count the **cubic centimeter** blocks that it takes to fill the box.

The volume is 8 cubic centimeters.

EXERCISES

Give the volume of each box.

1.

______

2.

______

3.

______

4.

______

5.

______

★ **6.**

______

Liquid measure

The **liter** is used for measuring liquids.

1 liter = 1000 cubic centimeters

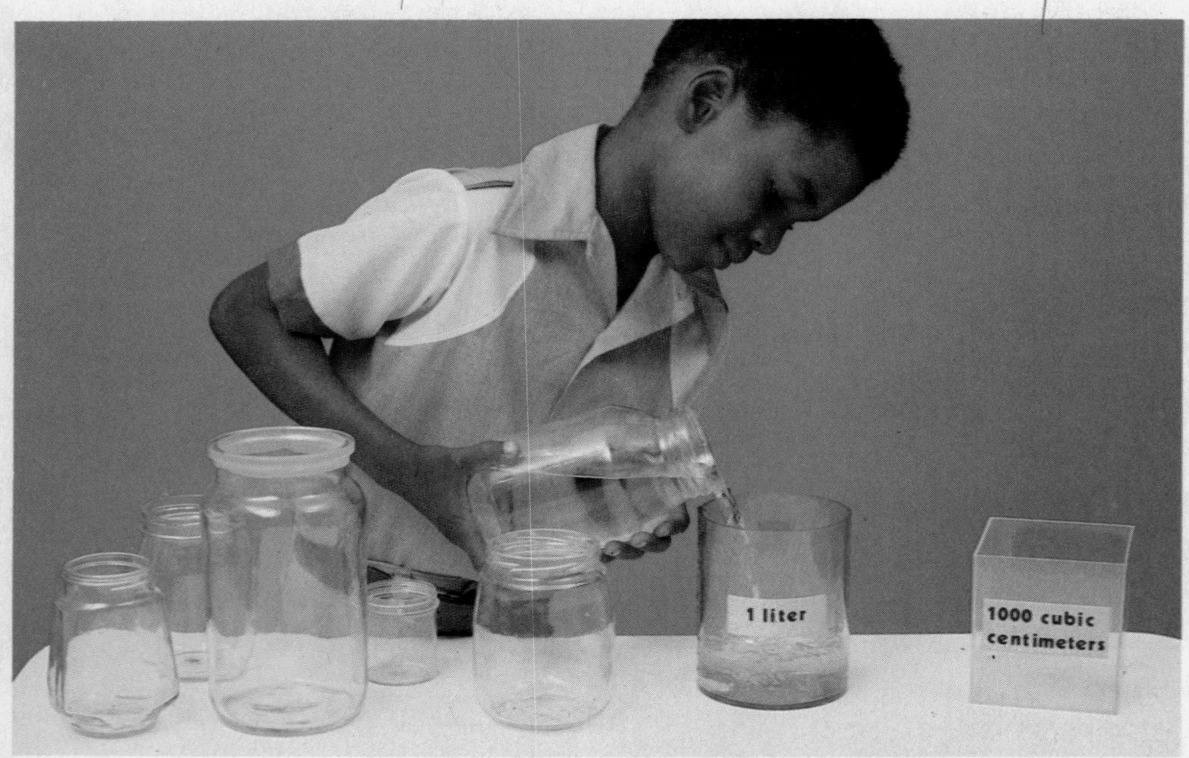

1. a. Get some jars and a liter measure.
   b. Estimate whether each jar holds less than a liter, more than a liter, or just a liter.
   c. Check your estimates.
   d. Put your jars in order from smallest to largest.

2. a. Get a paper cup. How many paper cups of water do you drink in a day?
   b. Do you drink more or less than a liter of water in a day?

Name Matin 2

Grams and kilograms

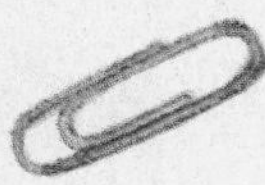

paper clip
about one **gram (g)**
1 g

math book
about one **kilogram (kg)**

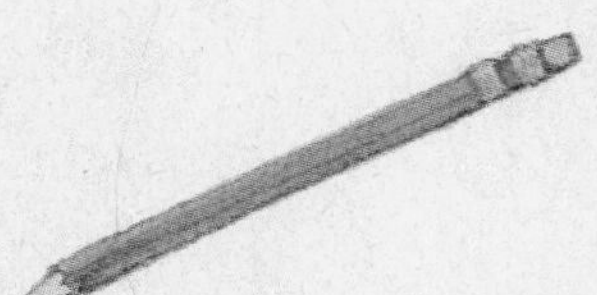

new pencil
about 4 g

large football player
about 130 kg

EXERCISES

Choose the better estimate.

1.

a. 35 g **b.** 35 kg

2.

a. 105 g **b.** 105 kg

3.

a. 2 g **b.** 2 kg

4.

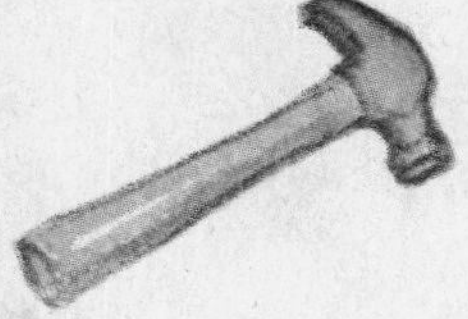

a. 1 g **b.** 1 kg

5.

a. 12 g **b.** 12 kg

6.

a. 3 g **b.** 3 kg

Measuring temperature

The **degree Celsius** (°C) is used for measuring **temperature.**

This thermometer shows a temperature reading of 24°C.

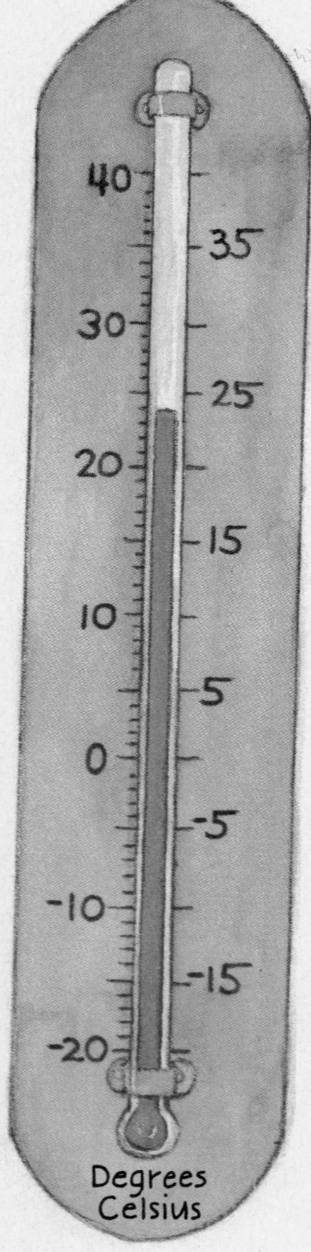

EXERCISES

Give each temperature.

Get a Celsius thermometer. What is the temperature

4. inside your classroom? _______

5. outdoors? _______

Name ______________________

Inch

In the customary system, the **inch** is used to measure length.

The straw is between 4 and 5 inches (in.) long.
It is nearer 5 in.
It is about 5 in. long.

EXERCISES

About how long is each straw?
Measure with an inch ruler

1.  

2.  3

3. 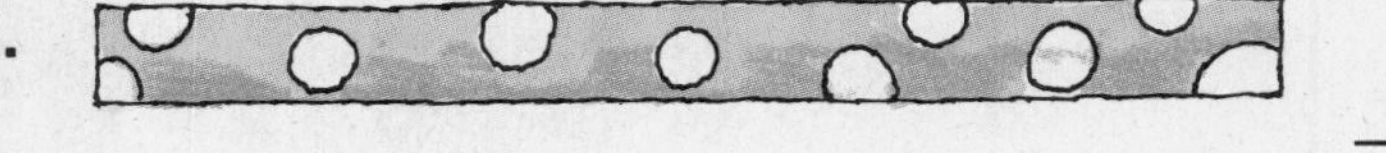 5

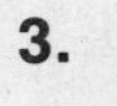

4. 3

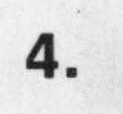

5. 1

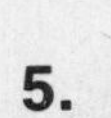

6. 6

Measure each stick in inches.

7.

8.

9.

10.

Draw sticks with these lengths.

11. 2 in.
12. 3 in.
13. 6 in.
14. 1 in.
15. 5 in.
16. 7 in.
17. 4 in.
18. 8 in.

Measure with an inch ruler

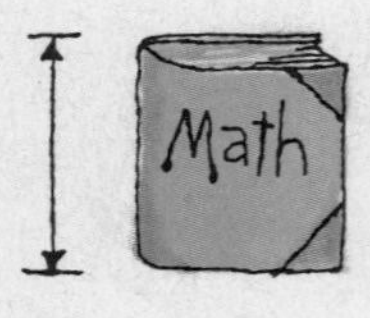

19. the height of your math book.

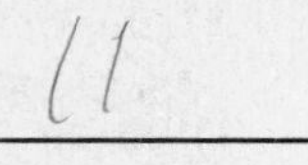

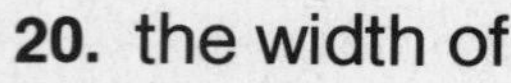

20. the width of your desk top.

21. the length of your desk top.

22. the height of your desk top.

23. your height.

Name Marti is #2

Half-inch

This ruler is marked in half-inches.

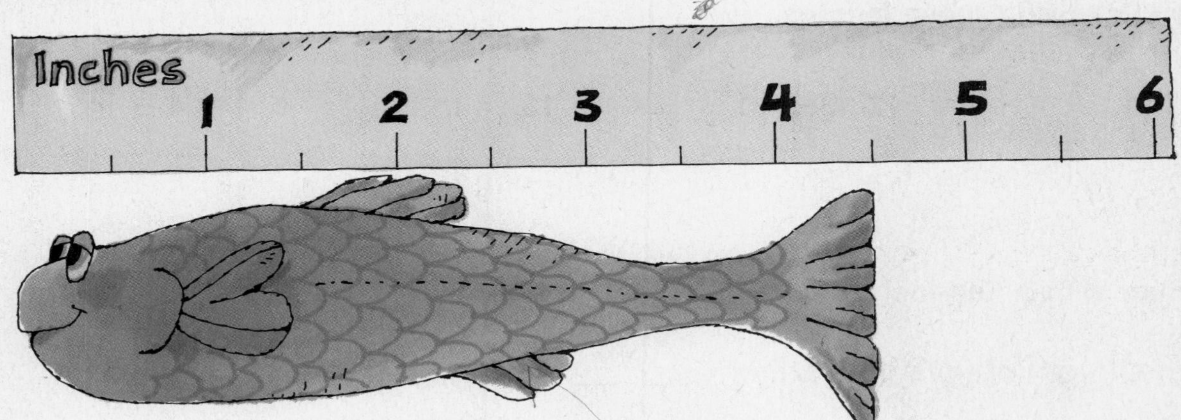

The fish is between 4 and 5 inches long.
It is nearer $4\frac{1}{2}$ (4 and $\frac{1}{2}$) inches long.
The fish is about $4\frac{1}{2}$ in. long.

EXERCISES
About how long is each?
Measure with a half-inch ruler.

1.

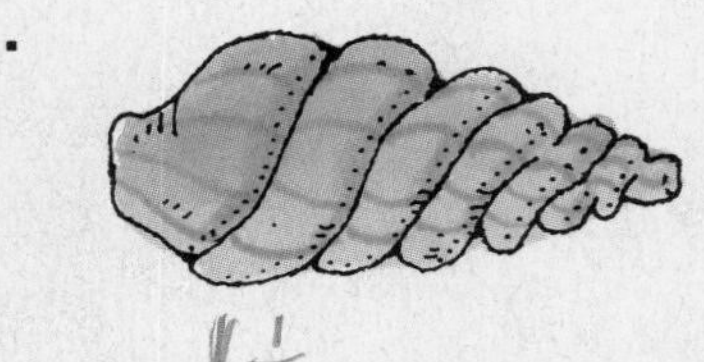

$1\frac{1}{2}$

2. 3

3. $3\frac{1}{2}$

4.

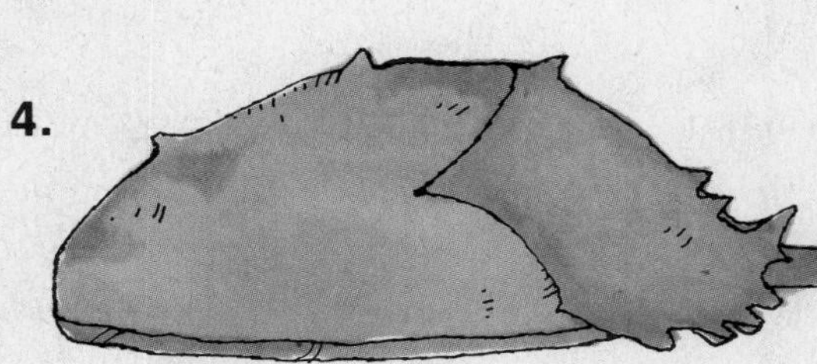

$4\frac{1}{2}$

5. 2

6.

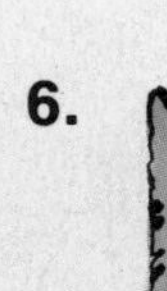

$5\frac{1}{2}$

Measure each stick with a half-inch ruler.

7.

8.

9.

10.

Draw sticks with these lengths.

11. 3 in.

12. $3\frac{1}{2}$ in.

13. 4 in.

14. $4\frac{1}{2}$ in.

15. $7\frac{1}{2}$ in.

16. 5 in.

17. 6 in.

18. $5\frac{1}{2}$ in.

Measure with a half-inch ruler

19. the length of your little finger. ______

20. the width of your hand. ______

21. the length of your arm reach. ______

22. your height. ______

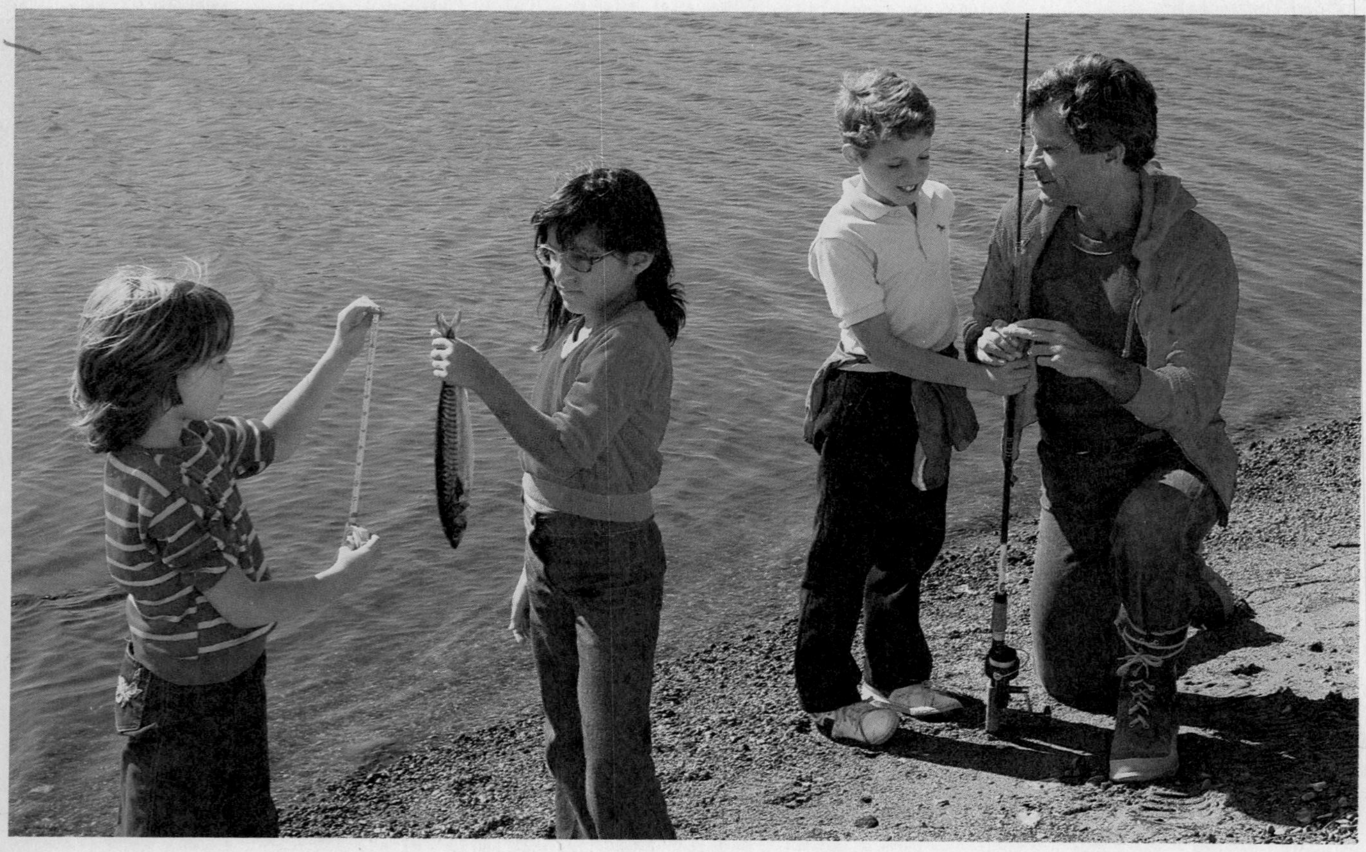

Name Martin

Inches, feet, and yards

inches 1 2 3 4 5 6 7 8 9 10 11 12

1 foot (ft) = 12 inches (in.)

inches 1 2 3 4 5 6 7 8 9 10 11 12 | inches 1 2 3 4 5 6 7 8 9 10 11 12 | inches 1 2 3 4 5 6 7 8 9 10 11 12

1 yard (yd) = 3 feet (ft)

inches 1 2 3 4 5 6 7 8 9 10 11 12 13 14 15 16 17 18 19 20 21 22 23 24 25 26 27 28 29 30 31 32 33 34 35 36

1 yard (yd) = 36 inches (in.)

EXERCISES

Complete. (*Hint:* Use the picture.)

1. 1 ft = 12 in.

2. 2 ft = 24 in.

3. 3 ft = 36 in.

4. 1 yd = 3 ft

5. 2 yd = 6 ft

6. 3 yd = 1 ft

7. 4 yd = 12 ft

8. 5 yd = 15 ft

9. 6 yd = 18 ft

10. 14 in. = 1 ft and 2 in.

11. 17 in. = 1 ft and 5 in.

12. 21 in. = 1 ft and 9 in.

13. 27 in. = 2 ft and 3 in.

14. 1 ft and 1 in. = 13 in.

15. 1 ft and 4 in. = 16 in.

16. 1 ft and 10 in. = 22 in.

17. 2 ft and 5 in. = 29 in.

Measure in feet

18. the width of the door. ________

19. the height of the door. ________

Measure in yards

20. the length of the room.

____

21. the width of the room.

____

Measure and complete.

22.

width of room	____ ft and ____ in.
length of hall	____ ft and ____ in.
length of chalkboard	____ ft and ____ in.
length of bulletin board	____ ft and ____ in.
length of sidewalk	____ yd and ____ ft
length of playground	____ yd and ____ ft

Find an object to measure. Complete this sentence.

23. The length of the ________________________

is ______ ft and ______ in.

KEEPING SKILLS SHARP

1. 4×6
2. 3×5
3. 5×4
4. 4×7
5. 3×7
6. 5×5
7. 5×3
8. 5×0
9. 3×8
10. 5×6
11. 4×8
12. 4×5
13. 3×9
14. 3×4
15. 5×9
16. 3×6
17. 4×4
18. 5×8

Name ____________________

Perimeter and area

The perimeter was measured in inches. The area was measured in **square inches.**

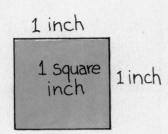

1 inch

1 square inch

1 inch

The perimeter is 8 inches.
Inches
1
2
The area is 4 square inches.

EXERCISES

Give the perimeter and area of each figure.

1.

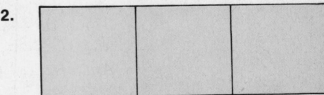

P: __________ A: __________

2.

P: __________ A: __________

3.

P: __________ A: __________

4.

P: __________ A: __________

Problem Solving Finding a pattern

1. Study and understand. 2. Plan and do. 3. Answer and check.	*You can solve the problem by finding a pattern.*

Robert has 12 1-inch tiles. If he lays them side by side, what is the perimeter?

Find a pattern. Copy and complete the table.

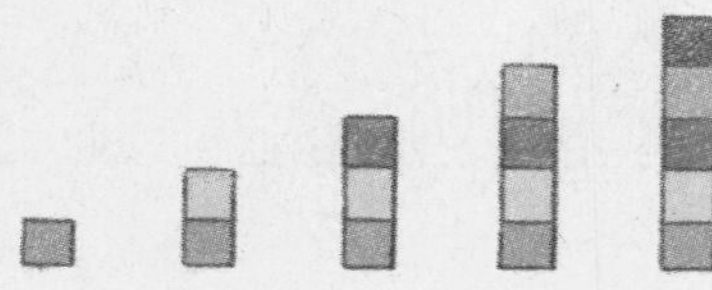

Tiles	1	2	3	4	5	6	7	8	9	10	11	12
Perimeter	4	6	8	10	12							

Use your pattern to find the perimeter of 12 1-inch tiles laid side by side.

Answer: The perimeter is 26 inches.

Solve by finding a pattern.

1. Laura had 12 1-inch tiles. She laid out the tiles in the pattern shown below. What will the perimeter be when she has laid out all

   12 tiles? _______

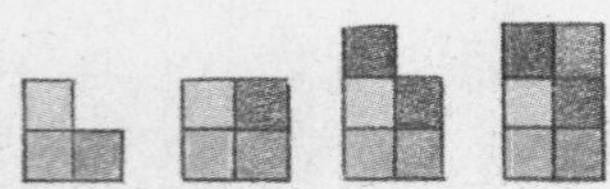

Tiles	3	4	5	6	7	8	9	10	11	12
Perimeter	8	8	10	10						

Name Martin #2

Volume

The **cubic inch** is used for measuring volume.

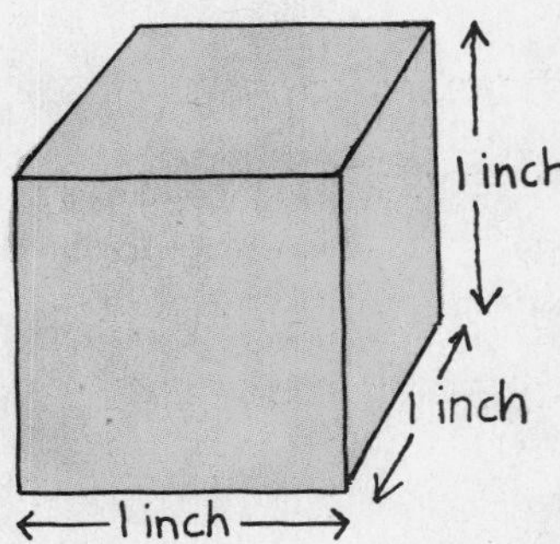

We can find the volume of the box by counting the number of cubic-inch blocks it holds.

EXERCISES

These boxes have been filled with cubic-inch blocks. Give each volume.

1.

8

2. 10

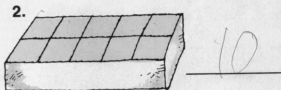

3. 16

★ **4.** 24

Liquid measure

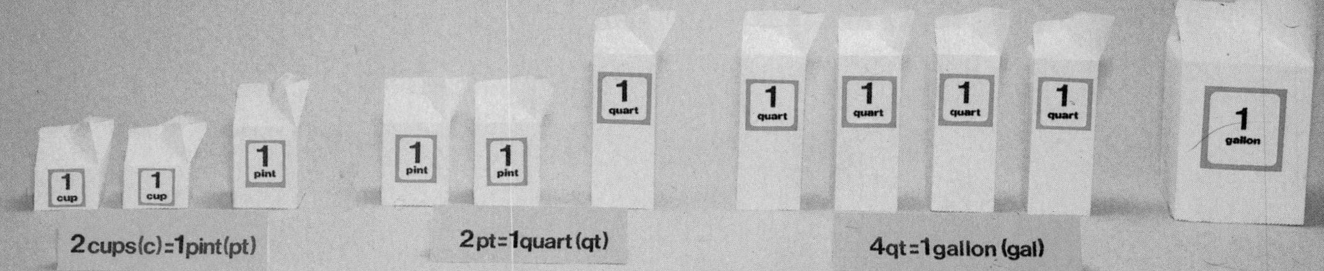

EXERCISES

Complete.

5. 2 pints = ______ quart
6. 2 c = ______ pt
7. 4 qt = ______ gal
8. 1 qt = ______ pt
9. 8 qt = ______ gal
10. 3 qt = ______ pt
11. 2 qt = ______ pt
12. 3 pt = ______ c
13. 2 gal = ______ qt

Which is more

14. 3 pt or 1 qt?
15. 3 qt or 1 gal?
16. 3 c or 1 pt?
17. 3 pt or 2 qt?
18. 5 c or 2 pt?
19. 5 qt or 1 gal?

Complete.

20. 8 c = ______ qt
21. 8 pt = ______ gal
22. $\frac{1}{2}$ gal = ______ pt
23. $\frac{1}{2}$ gal = ______ qt
24. 12 pt = 1 gal and ______ qt

Name ______________________________

Ounces and pounds

The **ounce (oz)** and the **pound (lb)** are used to measure weight.

slice of bread
about 1 ounce

loaf of bread
about 1 pound

EXERCISES

Choose the better estimate.

1.

a. 25 oz **b.** 25 lb

2.

a. 4 oz **b.** 4 lb

3.

a. 8 oz **b.** 8 lb

4.

a. 50 oz **b.** 50 lb

5.

a. 6 oz **b.** 6 lb

6.

a. 2 oz **b.** 2 lb

Measuring temperature

The degree **Fahrenheit** (°F) is used to measure temperature. This thermometer shows a temperature of 62°F.

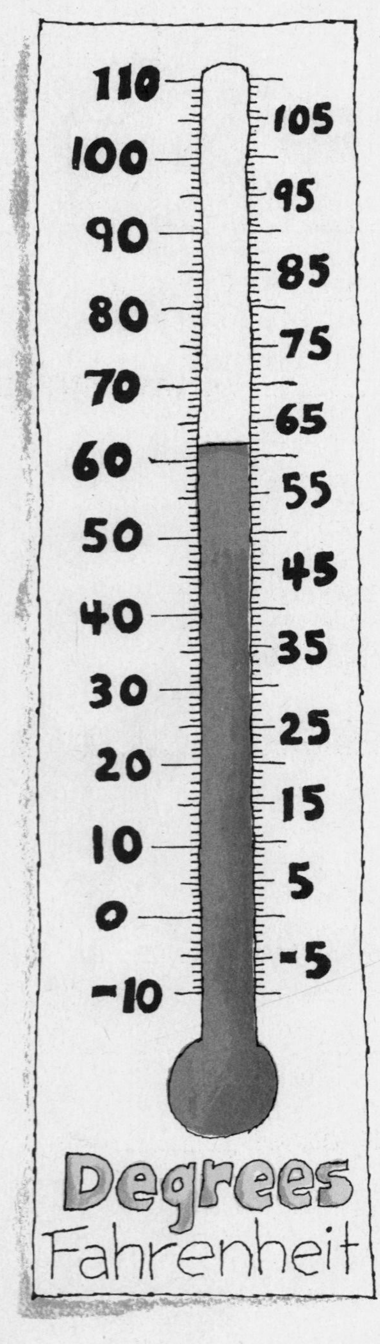

EXERCISES

Give each temperature.

Get a Fahrenheit thermometer.
What is the temperature

4. inside your classroom? _______

5. outdoors? _______

Name ____________________

Chapter Checkup

Complete. [pages 242–250, 253–257, 260–262]

1.

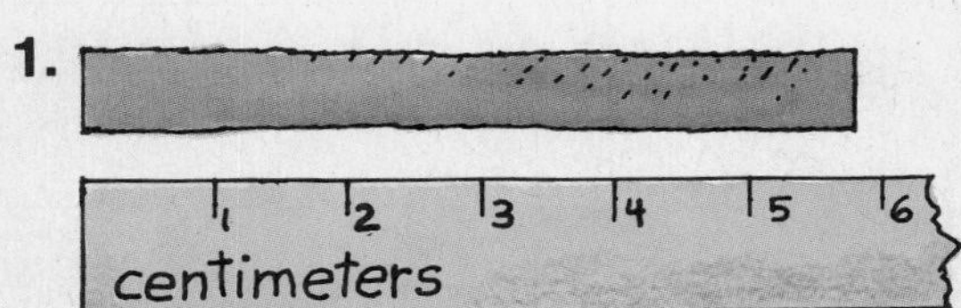

Length: about ______ cm

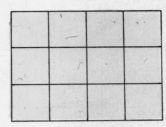

2. Each ☐ is a square centimeter.

Perimeter: __14__ cm

Area: __12__ square centimeters

3. Each ▣ is a cubic centimeter.

Volume: __6__ cubic centimeters

4.

25
20
°C

Temperature: __23__ °C

5.

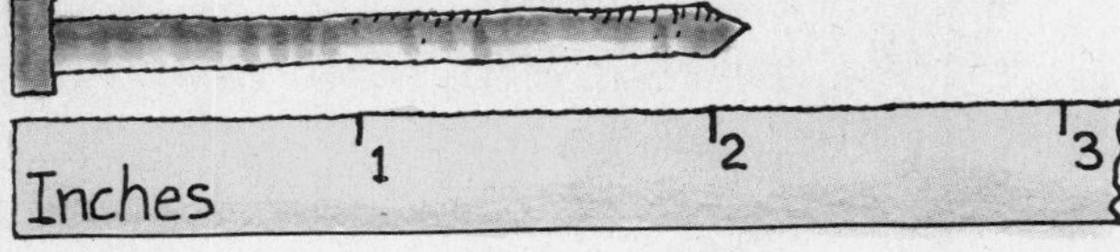

Length: about __2__ in.

6.

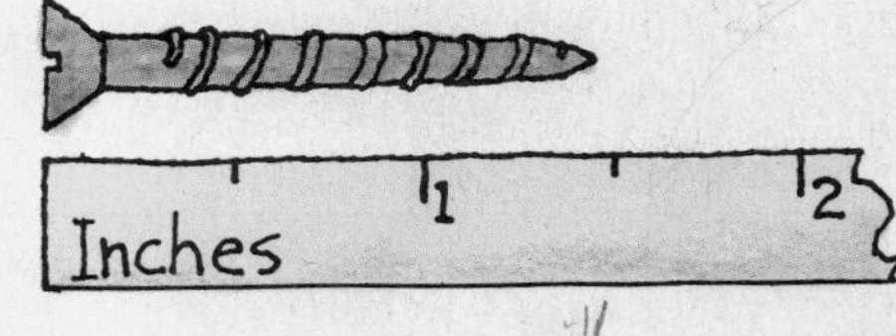

Length: about __1/2__ in.

Complete. [pages 258–259, 263]

7. 1 ft = ______ in.

8. 1 yd = __3__ ft

9. 1 yd = ______ in.

10. 2 pt = ______ qt

11. 1 gal = ______ qt

12. 1 pt = ______ c

Chapter Project

PERIMETER AND AREA

P:10
A:5

P:14
A:8

P:8
A:4

P:16
A:10

1. Get a piece of graph paper.
2. Color some shapes.
3. Give the perimeter and area of each shape.

Name math #2

Chapter Review

Complete.

1.

Length: about 6 cm

2.

Length: about 6 cm

3.

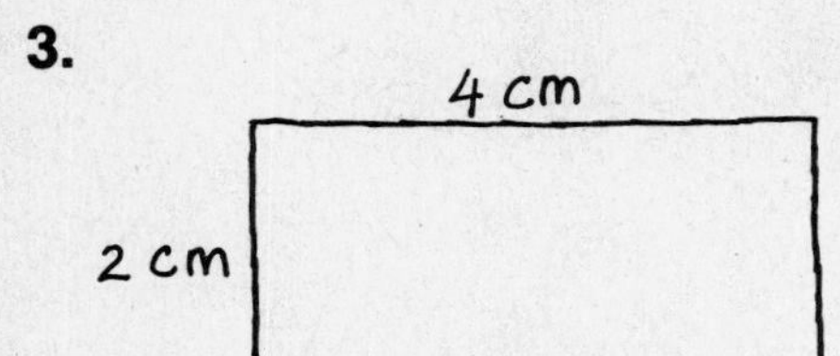

Perimeter: 12 cm

4.

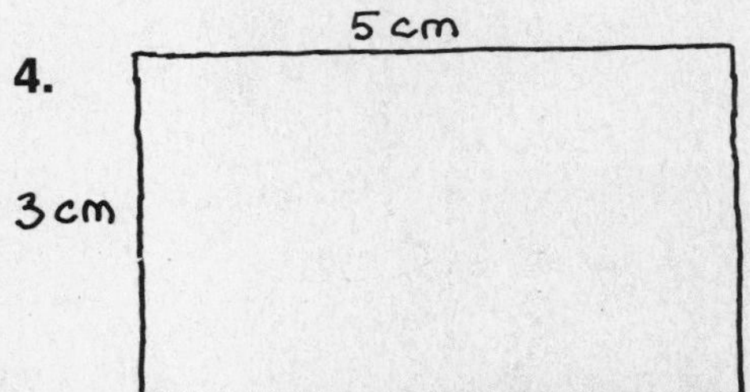

Perimeter: 16 cm

5.

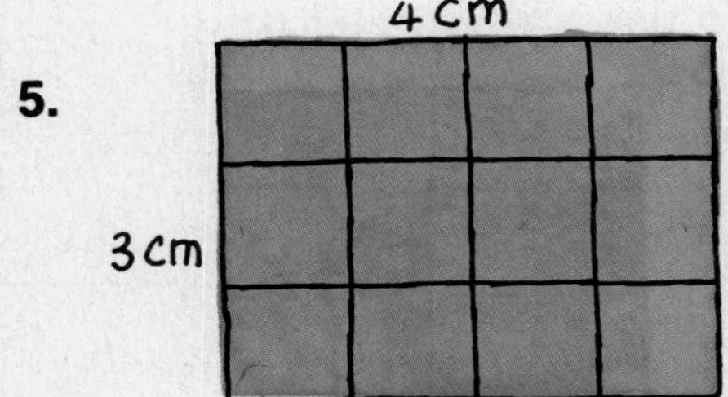

Area: 12 square centimeters

6.

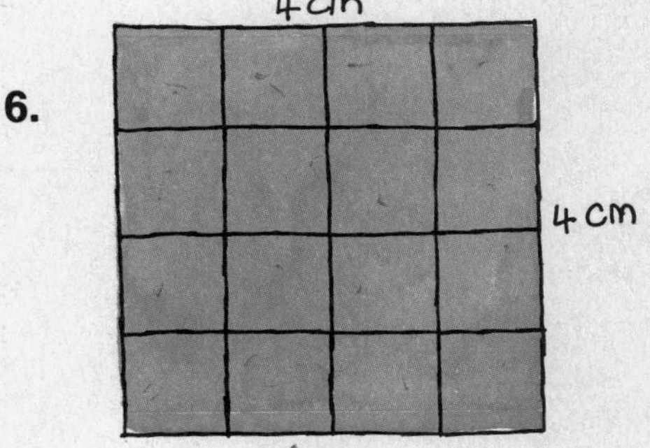

Area: 16 square centimeters

7.

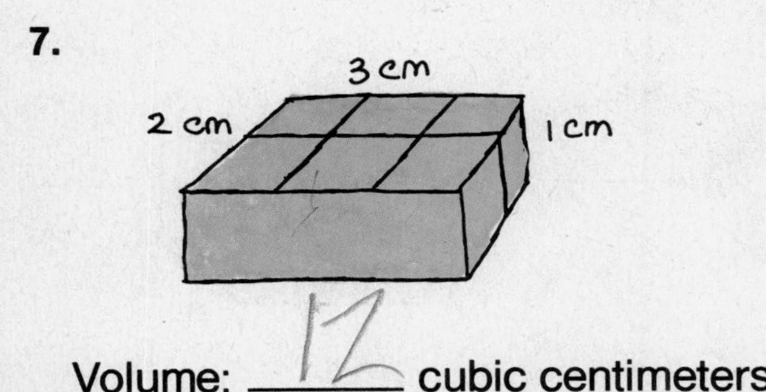

Volume: 12 cubic centimeters

8.

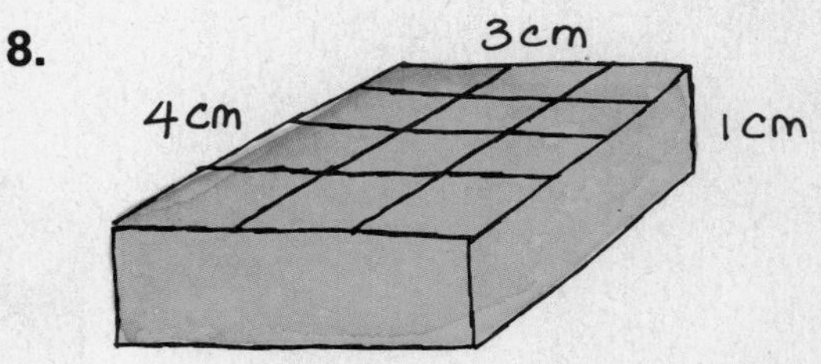

Volume: 20 cubic centimeters

Chapter Challenge

SURFACE AREA

It took six stamps to cover all the sides of this block.

How many stamps will you need to cover the outside?

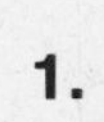 **1.** 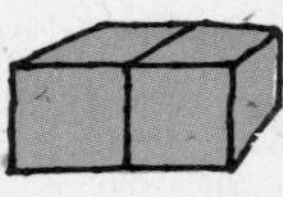 4

 **2.** 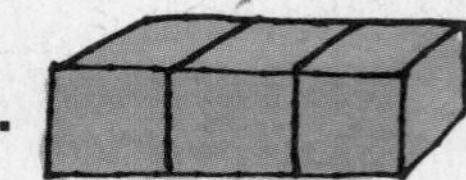 6

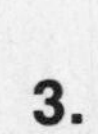 **3.**  8

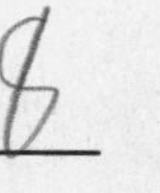 **4.**  10

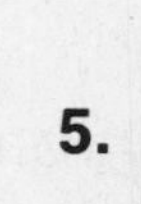 **5.** 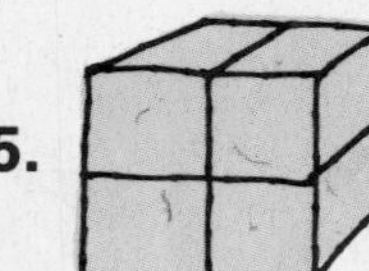 10

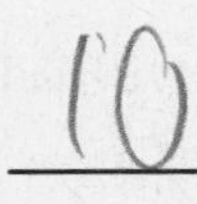 **6.**  20

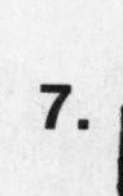 **7.**  30

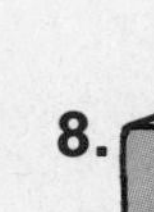 **8.**  56

Name ____________________

Cumulative Checkup

STANDARDIZED FORMAT

Give the correct letter.

1. Six hundred twenty-eight is

a. 682
b. 608
c. 628
d. none of these

2. Which numeral has a 4 in the tens place?

a. 7934
b. 9473
c. 3749
d. 4793

3. Add.

$$\begin{array}{r} 59 \\ 38 \\ +17 \\ \hline \end{array}$$

a. 114
b. 104
c. 94
d. none of these

4. Add.

$$\begin{array}{r} 759 \\ +386 \\ \hline \end{array}$$

a. 1035
b. 1045
c. 1145
d. none of these

5. Subtract.

$$\begin{array}{r} 535 \\ -276 \\ \hline \end{array}$$

a. 261
b. 259
c. 347
d. 359

6. Time now: 6:40
Next train: 7:15
How many minutes waiting time?

a. 25 **b.** 75
c. 55 **d.** 35

7. How much money?
1 dollar
1 half-dollar
1 quarter
1 dime
1 nickel

a. $1.65
b. $1.76
c. $1.81
d. $1.90

8. Multiply.

$$\begin{array}{r} 4 \\ \times 7 \\ \hline \end{array}$$

a. 24
b. 21
c. 29
d. 28

9. Divide.

$4\overline{)18}$

a. 3 R2
b. 4 R2
c. 5 R2
d. 2 R4

10. Complete.

$\frac{1}{3}$ of 12 = ?

a. 9
b. 4
c. 6
d. 3

11. Complete.

$\frac{1}{2}$ = ?

a. $\frac{1}{3}$
b. $\frac{2}{3}$
c. $\frac{1}{4}$
d. $\frac{2}{4}$

12. 5 teams
3 boys on each team
4 girls on each team
How many children in all?

a. 15 **b.** 12
c. 20 **d.** 35

10

Multiplication and Division through 9 × 9

How many cards are there with brushes? How many brushes are there in all?

Name ________________________________

Multiplication review

1. 1 × 0 = ____
2. 2 × 0 = ____
3. 3 × 0 = ____
4. 4 × 0 = ____
5. 5 × 0 = ____
6. 6 × 0 = ____
7. 7 × 0 = ____
8. 8 × 0 = ____
9. 9 × 0 = ____
10. 1 × 1 = ____
11. 2 × 1 = ____
12. 3 × 1 = ____
13. 4 × 1 = ____
14. 5 × 1 = ____
15. 6 × 1 = ____
16. 7 × 1 = ____
17. 8 × 1 = ____
18. 9 × 1 = ____
19. 1 × 2 = ____
20. 2 × 2 = ____
21. 3 × 2 = ____
22. 4 × 2 = ____
23. 5 × 2 = ____
24. 6 × 2 = ____
25. 7 × 2 = ____
26. 8 × 2 = ____
27. 9 × 2 = ____
28. 1 × 3 = ____
29. 2 × 3 = ____
30. 3 × 3 = ____
31. 4 × 3 = ____
32. 5 × 3 = ____
33. 6 × 3 = ____
34. 7 × 3 = ____
35. 8 × 3 = ____
36. 9 × 3 = ____
37. 1 × 4 = ____
38. 2 × 4 = ____
39. 3 × 4 = ____
40. 4 × 4 = ____
41. 5 × 4 = ____
42. 6 × 4 = ____
43. 7 × 4 = ____
44. 8 × 4 = ____
45. 9 × 4 = ____
46. 1 × 5 = ____
47. 2 × 5 = ____
48. 3 × 5 = ____
49. 4 × 5 = ____
50. 5 × 5 = ____
51. 6 × 5 = ____
52. 7 × 5 = ____
53. 8 × 5 = ____
54. 9 × 5 = ____

Division review

Division is finding a missing factor.

55. 1 ÷ 1 = 1
56. 2 ÷ 1 = 2
57. 3 ÷ 1 = ____
58. 4 ÷ 1 = 4
59. 5 ÷ 1 = ____
60. 6 ÷ 1 = 6
61. 7 ÷ 1 = ____
62. 8 ÷ 1 = 8
63. 9 ÷ 1 = ____

64. 2 ÷ 2 = 1
65. 4 ÷ 2 = 2
66. 6 ÷ 2 = 3
67. 8 ÷ 2 = ____
68. 10 ÷ 2 = 5
69. 12 ÷ 2 = ____
70. 14 ÷ 2 = 7
71. 16 ÷ 2 = ____
72. 18 ÷ 2 = 9

73. 3 ÷ 3 = 1
74. 6 ÷ 3 = 2
75. 9 ÷ 3 = ____
76. 12 ÷ 3 = 4
77. 15 ÷ 3 = ____
78. 18 ÷ 3 = 6
79. 21 ÷ 3 = ____
80. 24 ÷ 3 = 8
81. 27 ÷ 3 = ____

82. 4 ÷ 4 = 1
83. 8 ÷ 4 = ____
84. 12 ÷ 4 = 3
85. 16 ÷ 4 = ____
86. 20 ÷ 4 = 5
87. 24 ÷ 4 = ____
88. 28 ÷ 4 = 7
89. 32 ÷ 4 = ____
90. 36 ÷ 4 = 9

91. 5 ÷ 5 = ____
92. 10 ÷ 5 = 2
93. 15 ÷ 5 = ____
94. 20 ÷ 5 = 4
95. 25 ÷ 5 = ____
96. 30 ÷ 5 = 6
97. 35 ÷ 5 = ____
98. 40 ÷ 5 = 8
99. 45 ÷ 5 = ____

Name ____________________

6 as a factor

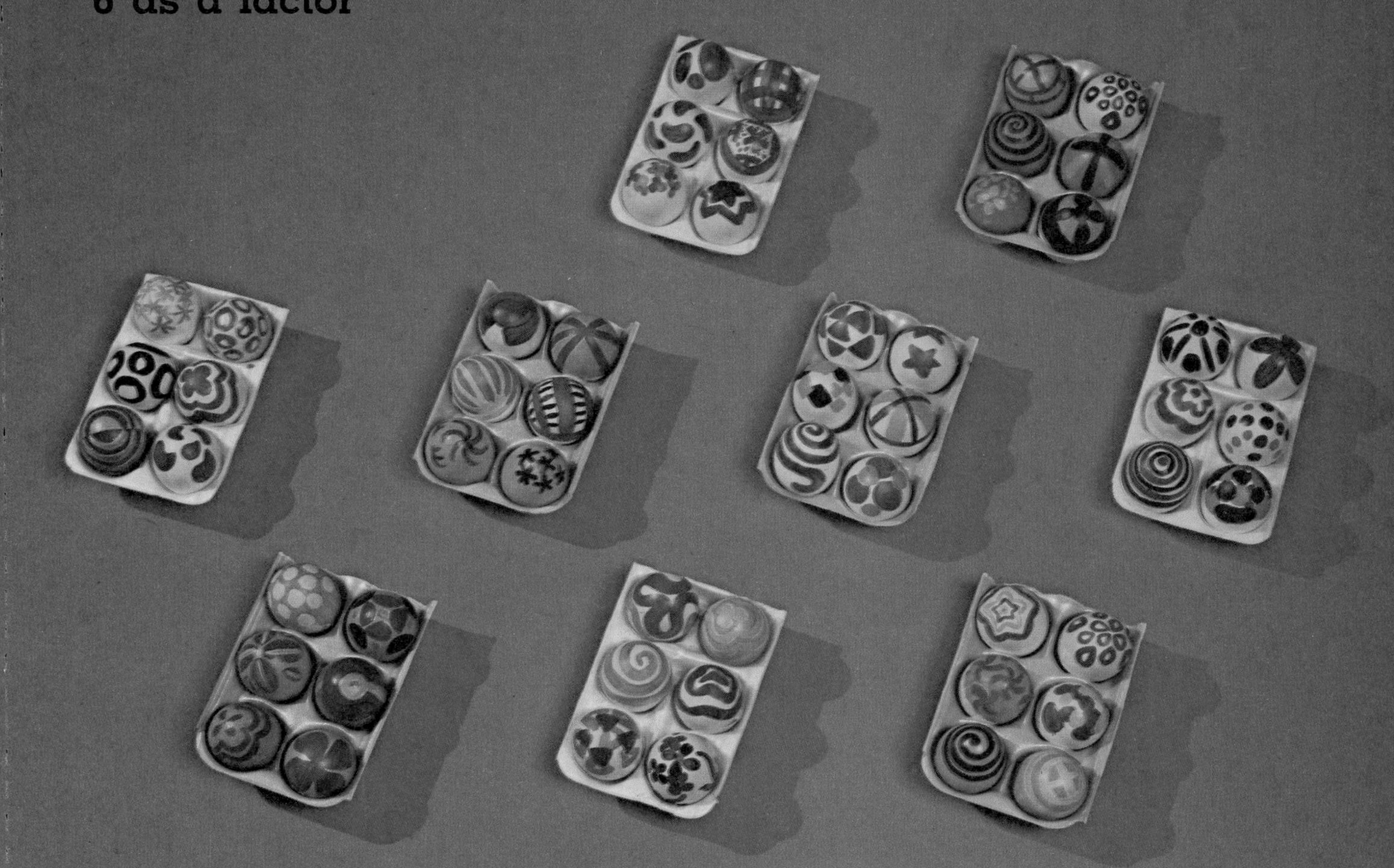

EXERCISES

Give each product.

1. 1 × 6 = 6
2. 2 × 6 = 12
3. 3 × 6 = 18
4. 4 × 6 = 24
5. 5 × 6 = 30
6. 6 × 6 = 42
7. 7 × 6 = 48
8. 8 × 6 = ______
9. 9 × 6 = 54
10. 2 × 6 = 12
11. 4 × 6 = 24
12. 1 × 6 = 6
13. 6 × 6 = 42
14. 3 × 6 = 18
15. 8 × 6 = 44
16. 5 × 6 = 30
17. 9 × 6 = 54
18. 7 × 6 = 48

Multiply.

19. 3×5	20. 2×7	21. 4×5	22. 6×5	23. 5×3	24. 2×6
25. 4×6	26. 6×4	27. 5×4	28. 3×9	29. 5×7	30. 6×2
31. 6×9	32. 4×7	33. 5×8	34. 6×1	35. 2×9	36. 3×7
37. 5×5	38. 6×8	39. 2×8	40. 4×9	41. 6×7	42. 5×6
43. 3×8	44. 4×8	45. 6×3	46. 5×9	47. 3×6	48. 6×6

Problem Solving

49. How many  in 7 ? ________

50. How many  in 6  ? ________

51. How many  in 9  ? ________

52. How many  in 8  ? ________

Name ______________________________

Dividing by 6

Remember that division is finding a missing factor.

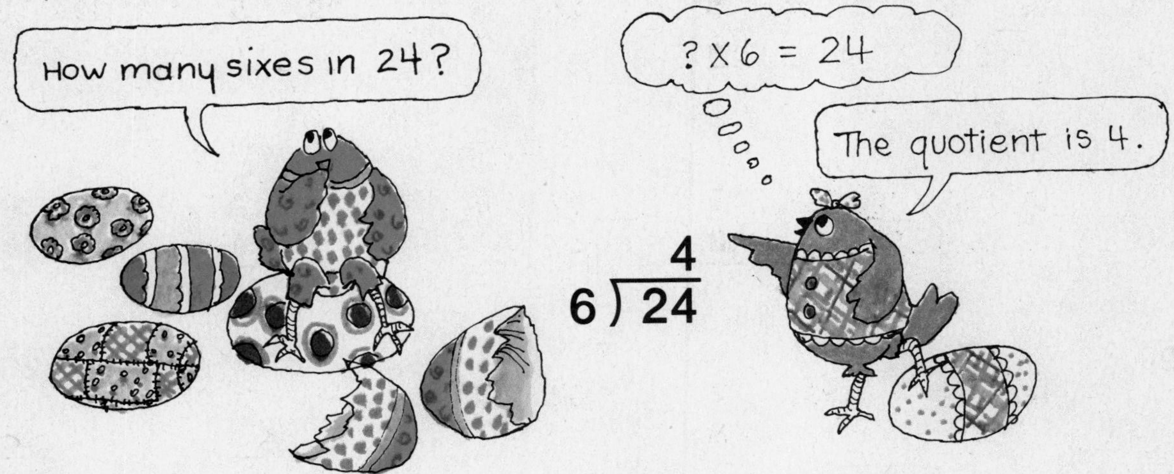

To divide by 6, think of the multiplication facts for 6.

EXERCISES

Divide.

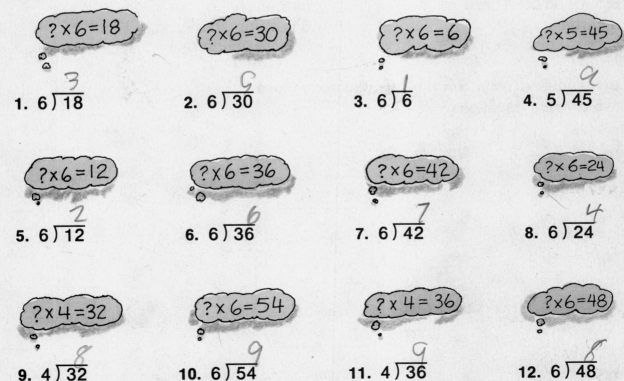

?x6=18	?x6=30	?x6=6	?x5=45
1. $6\overline{)18}$	2. $6\overline{)30}$	3. $6\overline{)6}$	4. $5\overline{)45}$
?x6=12	?x6=36	?x6=42	?x6=24
5. $6\overline{)12}$	6. $6\overline{)36}$	7. $6\overline{)42}$	8. $6\overline{)24}$
?x4=32	?x6=54	?x4=36	?x6=48
9. $4\overline{)32}$	10. $6\overline{)54}$	11. $4\overline{)36}$	12. $6\overline{)48}$

Give each quotient.

13. 6) 18 14. 6) 12 15. 6) 24 16. 6) 6 17. 6) 30

18. 6) 42 19. 6) 36 20. 6) 54 21. 6) 48 22. 3) 18

23. 4) 36 24. 3) 24 25. 4) 12 26. 3) 21 27. 6) 12

28. 6) 36 29. 6) 54 30. 4) 32 31. 4) 16 32. 6) 18

33. 4) 20 34. 6) 24 35. 3) 15 36. 6) 48 37. 4) 28

38. 3) 27 39. 6) 42 40. 4) 24 41. 6) 6 42. 6) 30

Problem Solving

43. 

6 buttons on a card
5 cards
How many buttons? ______

44. 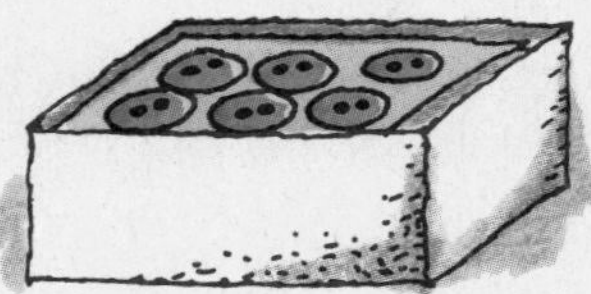

54 buttons in all
6 buttons on a card
How many cards? ______

Use the numbers. Write two multiplication equations and two division equations.

45. 

46. 

47. 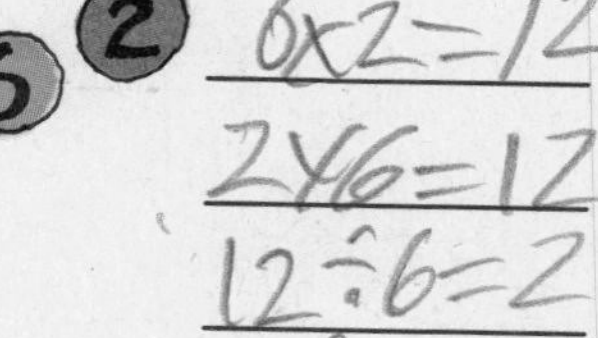

48. 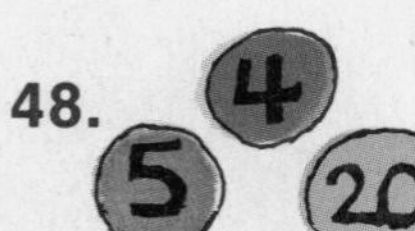

49.

Name ______________________________

7 as a factor

How many ⬡s in each Hexaflower?

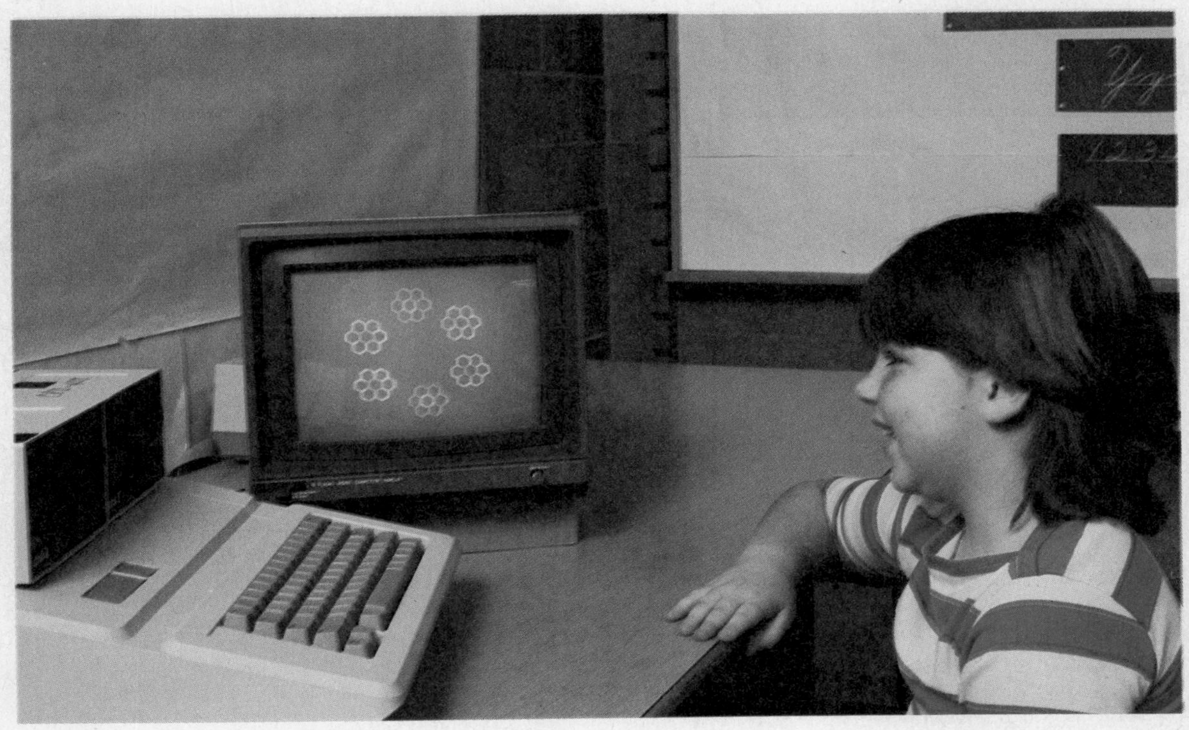

EXERCISES

Give each product.

1. 1 × 7 = ______
2. 2 × 7 = ______
3. 3 × 7 = ______
4. 4 × 7 = ______
5. 5 × 7 = ______
6. 6 × 7 = ______
7. 7 × 7 = ______
8. 8 × 7 = ______
9. 9 × 7 = ______
10. 3 × 7 = ______
11. 5 × 7 = ______
12. 2 × 7 = ______
13. 4 × 7 = ______
14. 1 × 7 = ______
15. 8 × 7 = ______
16. 7 × 7 = ______
17. 9 × 7 = ______
18. 6 × 7 = ______

Multiply.

19. 7×5	20. 6×5	21. 7×2	22. 7×3	23. 4×8	24. 7×4
25. 3×9	26. 7×8	27. 7×9	28. 7×7	29. 5×9	30. 7×9
31. 6×5	32. 9×2	33. 4×9	34. 8×5	35. 6×9	36. 7×6
37. 8×4	38. 6×6	39. 6×4	40. 6×8	41. 8×7	42. 6×7
43. 3×6	44. 9×6	45. 4×5	46. 5×7	47. 8×6	48. 9×5

Problem Solving

49. How many wheels are there on 8 skates? _______

50. How many wheels are there on 6 tricycles? _______

51. How many cents are there in 7 nickels? _______

52. How many pints are there in 5 quarts? _______

53. José has 21 red marbles and 19 blue ones. He wants to put 5 marbles in each box. How many boxes does he need?

____

54. Lee has 40¢. He wants to buy 8 pencils that cost 6¢ each. How much more money does he need? _______

55. Steve bought a boat that cost $1.28. Then he bought a race car that cost $.52 more than the boat. How much did he pay for both? _______

★ **56.** Sue bought 9 candles for 6¢ each. She also bought a holder. The total price of the candles was 14¢ less than the price of the holder. How much did she spend in all? _______

Name ________________________________

Dividing by 7

EXERCISES

Divide.

? × 6 = 42

1. $7\overline{)14}$ **2.** $7\overline{)7}$ **3.** $6\overline{)48}$ **4.** $6\overline{)42}$

5. $6\overline{)54}$ **6.** $7\overline{)35}$ **7.** $7\overline{)21}$ **8.** $7\overline{)63}$

9. $7\overline{)56}$ **10.** $7\overline{)42}$ **11.** $7\overline{)49}$ **12.** $7\overline{)28}$

13. $2\overline{)16}$ **14.** $3\overline{)27}$ **15.** $4\overline{)24}$ **16.** $5\overline{)35}$

17. $5\overline{)40}$ **18.** $4\overline{)36}$ **19.** $3\overline{)18}$ **20.** $5\overline{)45}$

Give each quotient.

21. 7) 35
22. 4) 36
23. 7) 21
24. 4) 28
25. 7) 49
26. 7) 42
27. 6) 42
28. 5) 30
29. 6) 24
30. 6) 48
31. 6) 18
32. 7) 56
33. 6) 36
34. 6) 54
35. 7) 63

There are seven days in a week.

36. How many days in 2 weeks? _______

37. How many days in 4 weeks? _______

38. How many weeks in 21 days? _______

39. How many weeks in 35 days? _______

Challenge!

Give the missing number.

40.

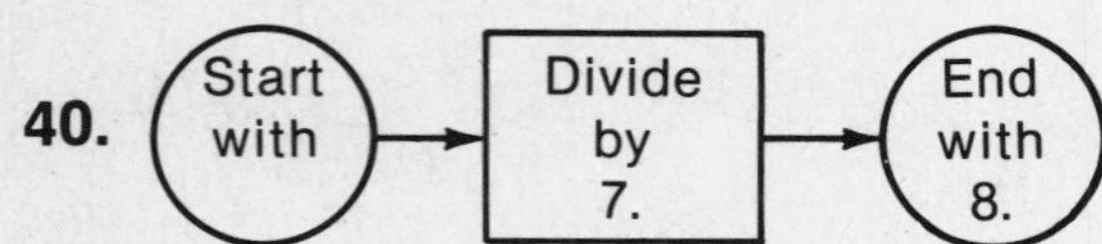

41. Start with → Multiply by 6. → End with 42.

42. Start with → Multiply by 5. → Add 7. → End with 37.

KEEPING SKILLS SHARP

1. 53 + 21
2. 58 + 34
3. 29 + 83
4. 75 + 75
5. 98 + 56
6. 352 + 741
7. 529 + 138
8. 652 + 278
9. 946 + 387
10. 274 + 888
11. 56 34 + 75
12. 58 39 + 3
13. 76 5 + 48
14. 64 27 + 89

Name ________________________________

Problem Solving Finding the cost

Carpenters build and fix the homes we live in. They work with many tools.

EXERCISES

Give the total cost.

1. 

2. 

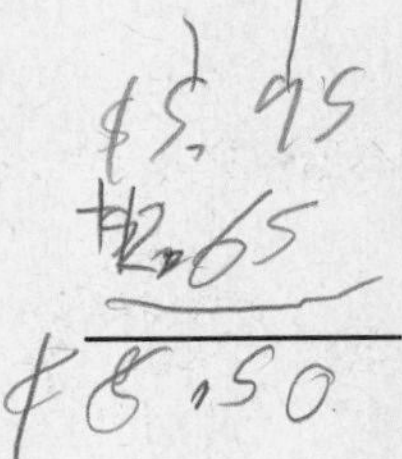

3. 

4. 

Which costs more?
How much more?

5.

6.

7.

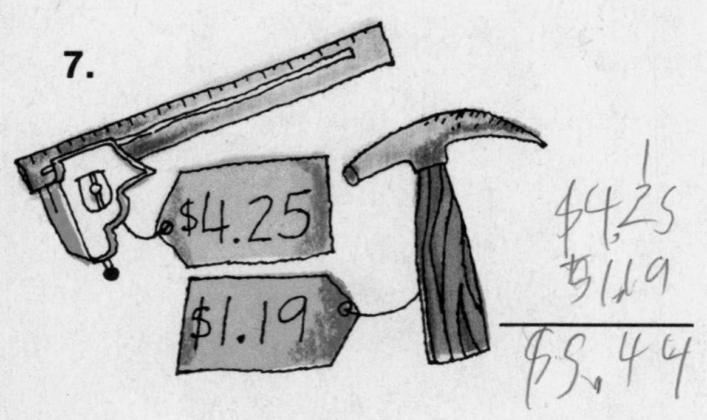

8.

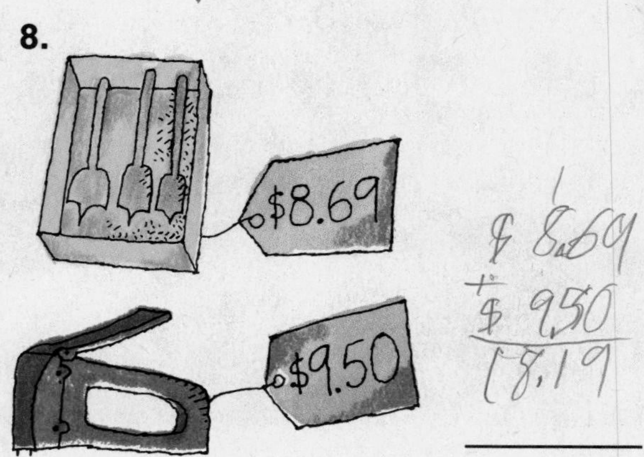

Solve.

9. How many nails will be needed for 8 [hinge] ? ______

10. How many nails will be needed for 7 [hinge] ? ______

11. One board needs 6 nails.

How many boards can be put up with these nails? ______

★ 12. One shelf needs 7 nails.

60 NAILS

How many shelves can be put up with these nails? ______
How many nails will be left over? ______

Name ______________________________

8 as a factor

EXERCISES

Give each product.

1. 1 × 8 = 8
2. 2 × 8 = ______
3. 3 × 8 = 24
4. 4 × 8 = ______
5. 5 × 8 = 40
6. 6 × 8 = ______
7. 7 × 8 = 56
8. 8 × 8 = ______
9. 9 × 8 = 72
10. 4 × 8 = ______
11. 1 × 8 = 8
12. 3 × 8 = ______
13. 2 × 8 = 16
14. 5 × 8 = ______
15. 7 × 8 = 63
16. 9 × 8 = ______
17. 6 × 8 = 48
18. 8 × 8 = ______

Multiply.

19. 8×2	20. 6×4	21. 7×2	22. 8×3	23. 6×3	24. 7×6
25. 8×8	26. 7×5	27. 8×6	28. 6×5	29. 8×4	30. 7×7
31. 6×9	32. 8×1	33. 6×7	34. 7×8	35. 6×8	36. 8×9
37. 7×4	38. 6×6	39. 8×7	40. 7×3	41. 8×5	42. 7×9

Complete.

43. 

8 cost ______ ¢.

44. 

9 cost ______ ¢.

45. 

5 cost 35¢.

46. 

6 cost 48¢.

47. 

7 cost ______ ¢.

48. 

9 cost 72¢.

Give the missing digits.

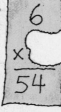

49. $\square \times 7 = 56$

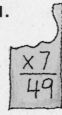

50. $6 \times \square = 54$

51. $\square \times 7 = 49$

52. $8 \times \square = 48$

Name ____________________

Dividing by 8

Remember that you can divide by finding a missing factor.

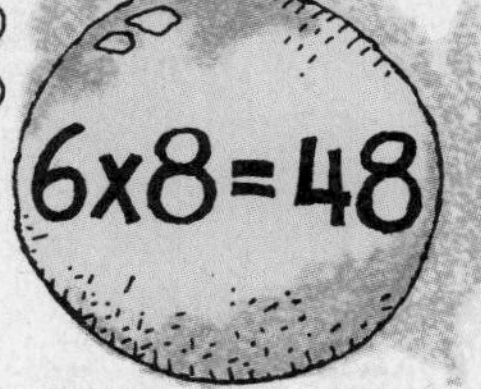

4x8=32

5x8=40

7x8=56

8x8=64

9x8=72

EXERCISES

Divide.

1. 8) 16	**2.** 8) 40	**3.** 8) 8
4. 8) 32	**5.** 8) 24	**6.** 8) 48
7. 8) 56	**8.** 8) 72	**9.** 8) 64
10. 7) 49	**11.** 6) 54	**12.** 7) 56
13. 7) 63	**14.** 6) 42	**15.** 7) 42

Divide.

16. $8\overline{)16}$	**17.** $6\overline{)18}$	**18.** $7\overline{)28}$	**19.** $6\overline{)12}$	**20.** $8\overline{)56}$
21. $7\overline{)35}$	**22.** $6\overline{)24}$	**23.** $8\overline{)8}$	**24.** $7\overline{)14}$	**25.** $8\overline{)72}$
26. $8\overline{)48}$	**27.** $7\overline{)21}$	**28.** $6\overline{)30}$	**29.** $8\overline{)24}$	**30.** $7\overline{)49}$
31. $6\overline{)36}$	**32.** $8\overline{)32}$	**33.** $6\overline{)42}$	**34.** $7\overline{)42}$	**35.** $8\overline{)64}$
36. $7\overline{)56}$	**37.** $6\overline{)48}$	**38.** $7\overline{)63}$	**39.** $6\overline{)54}$	**40.** $8\overline{)40}$

Problem Solving

41. 6 pencils in a box
7 boxes
How many pencils? ______

42. 48 pencils in all
6 pencils in a box
How many boxes? ______

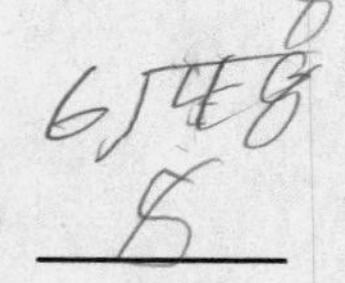

43. 9 balls
3 balls in a package
How many packages? ______

44. 8 bells in a package
4 packages
How many bells? ______

45. 4 blocks in a package
9 packages
How many blocks? ______

46. 35 buttons on one card
7 buttons on another card
How many buttons? ______

Name ______________________________

9 as a factor

EXERCISES

Give each product.

1. 1 × 9 = 9	**2.** 2 × 9 = 18	**3.** 3 × 9 = ______
4. 4 × 9 = 36	**5.** 5 × 9 = ______	**6.** 6 × 9 = 104
7. 7 × 9 = ______	**8.** 8 × 9 = 72	**9.** 9 × 9 = ______
10. 3 × 9 = 27	**11.** 1 × 9 = ______	**12.** 4 × 9 = 36
13. 2 × 9 = ______	**14.** 5 × 9 = 45	**15.** 7 × 9 = ______
16. 9 × 9 = 81	**17.** 6 × 9 = ______	**18.** 8 × 9 = 72

Multiply.

19. $\begin{array}{r}9\\ \times 1\\ \hline\end{array}$	20. $\begin{array}{r}9\\ \times 3\\ \hline\end{array}$	21. $\begin{array}{r}7\\ \times 8\\ \hline\end{array}$	22. $\begin{array}{r}9\\ \times 2\\ \hline\end{array}$	23. $\begin{array}{r}8\\ \times 5\\ \hline\end{array}$	24. $\begin{array}{r}9\\ \times 8\\ \hline\end{array}$
25. $\begin{array}{r}7\\ \times 9\\ \hline\end{array}$	26. $\begin{array}{r}7\\ \times 5\\ \hline\end{array}$	27. $\begin{array}{r}8\\ \times 3\\ \hline\end{array}$	28. $\begin{array}{r}7\\ \times 6\\ \hline\end{array}$	29. $\begin{array}{r}8\\ \times 9\\ \hline\end{array}$	30. $\begin{array}{r}9\\ \times 7\\ \hline\end{array}$
31. $\begin{array}{r}7\\ \times 4\\ \hline\end{array}$	32. $\begin{array}{r}9\\ \times 5\\ \hline\end{array}$	33. $\begin{array}{r}8\\ \times 8\\ \hline\end{array}$	34. $\begin{array}{r}9\\ \times 4\\ \hline\end{array}$	35. $\begin{array}{r}8\\ \times 6\\ \hline\end{array}$	36. $\begin{array}{r}8\\ \times 2\\ \hline\end{array}$
37. $\begin{array}{r}8\\ \times 4\\ \hline\end{array}$	38. $\begin{array}{r}7\\ \times 7\\ \hline\end{array}$	39. $\begin{array}{r}9\\ \times 9\\ \hline\end{array}$	40. $\begin{array}{r}8\\ \times 7\\ \hline\end{array}$	41. $\begin{array}{r}8\\ \times 1\\ \hline\end{array}$	42. $\begin{array}{r}9\\ \times 6\\ \hline\end{array}$

Problem Solving

43.

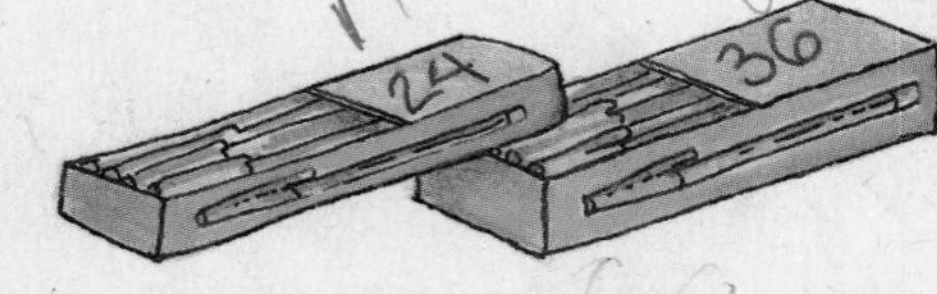

How many pens? ______

44.

How much more for the red shirt? ______

45.

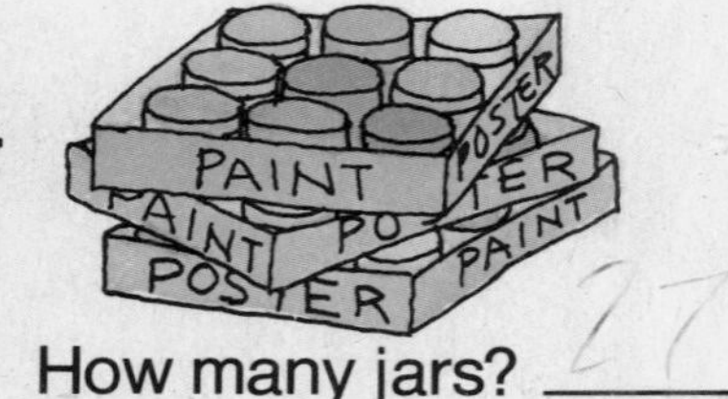

How many jars? ______

46.

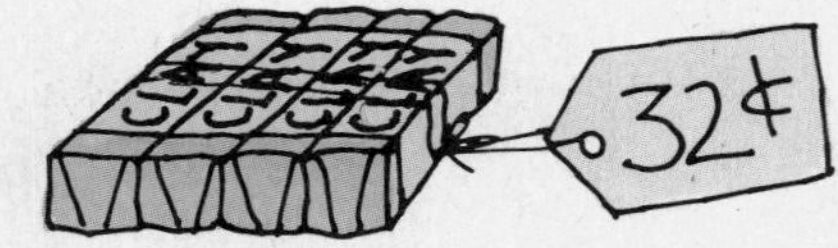

How much for 1 package? ______

Challenge!

Find the missing input or output.

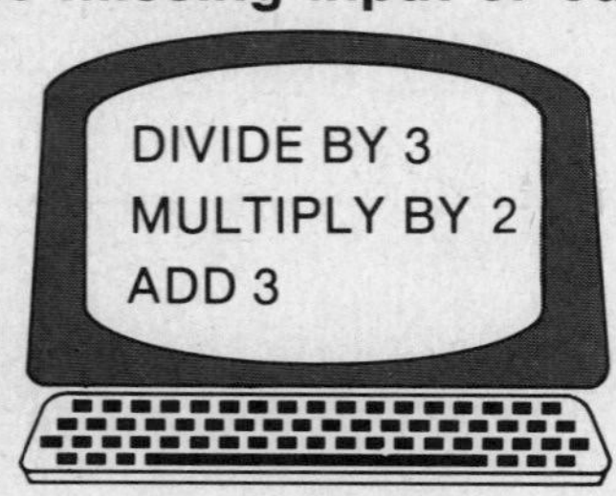

	Input	Output
	24	19
47.	18	
48.	9	
49.		7

Name ____________________

Dividing by 9

EXERCISES

Divide.

1. 9) 27	**2.** 9) 36	**3.** 9) 9	**4.** 9) 45	**5.** 9) 18
6. 9) 63	**7.** 9) 54	**8.** 9) 81	**9.** 9) 72	**10.** 7) 28
11. 8) 40	**12.** 7) 49	**13.** 8) 64	**14.** 7) 63	**15.** 8) 48
16. 8) 32	**17.** 8) 56	**18.** 7) 42	**19.** 7) 35	**20.** 8) 72
21. 6) 48	**22.** 9) 9	**23.** 6) 36	**24.** 6) 54	**25.** 9) 27
26. 8) 24	**27.** 9) 18	**28.** 9) 81	**29.** 6) 30	**30.** 6) 24
31. 7) 21	**32.** 6) 42	**33.** 8) 16	**34.** 9) 63	**35.** 9) 72
36. 9) 45	**37.** 7) 56	**38.** 9) 36	**39.** 6) 18	**40.** 9) 54

41. There are 63 candles. There are 9 candles on each cake.
How many cakes are there? ______

42. There are 48 red hats. There are 6 blue hats. How many more red hats are there? ______

43. There are 8 balloons. Each clown has 4 balloons. How many clowns are there? ______

44. There are 9 clowns. Each clown has 3 balls. How many balls are there? ______

Challenge!

Complete.

45.

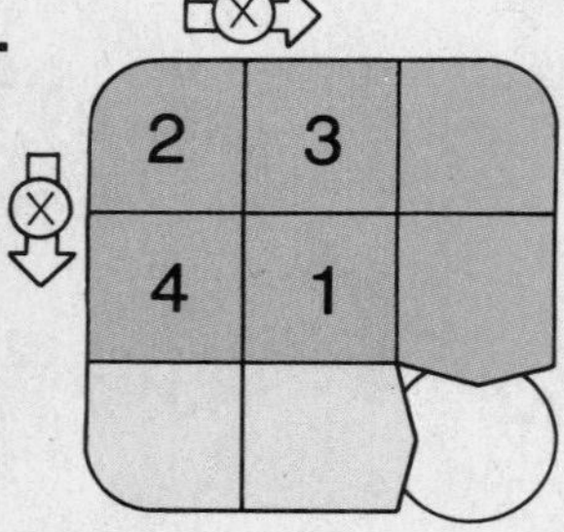

★ 46.

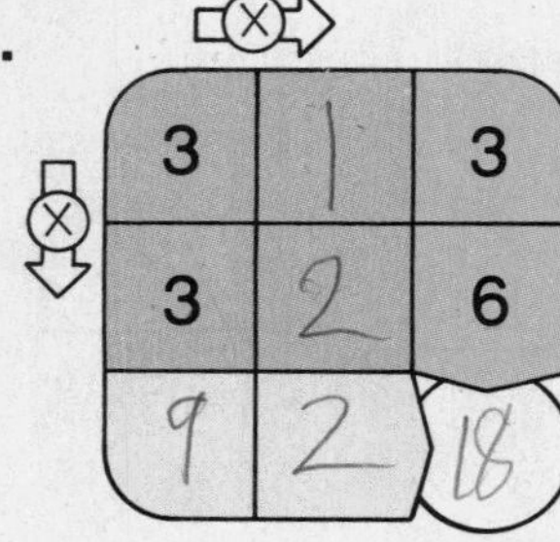

★ 47.

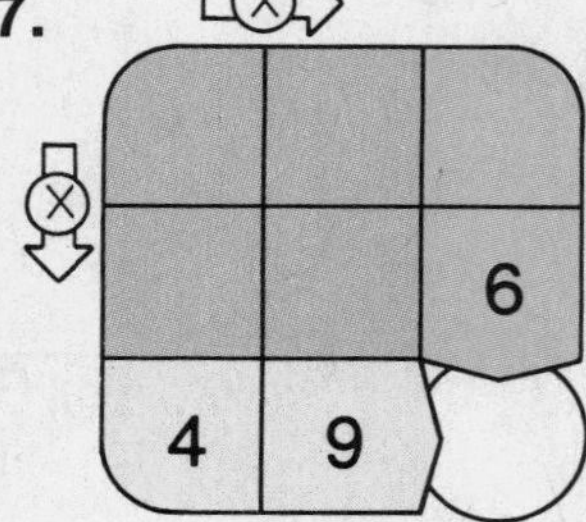

KEEPING SKILLS SHARP

1. 523 − 109	2. 462 − 446	3. 842 − 538	4. 629 − 448	5. 728 − 658
6. 743 − 259	7. 516 − 348	8. 832 − 176	9. 924 − 455	10. 635 − 199
11. 506 − 278	12. 307 − 159	13. 402 − 148	14. 600 − 267	15. 500 − 345

Name ____________________

Division with remainder

Kim had 43¢.

She spent it for some 8¢ Ticket.

How many  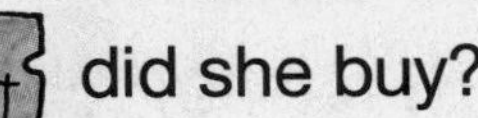 did she buy?

```
    5 R3
8 ) 43
   -40
     3
```

She got 5 8¢ Ticket and had 3¢ left over.

EXERCISES

Divide.

1. 6) 13	2. 6) 14	3. 8) 25	4. 6) 29	5. 8) 11
6. 8) 29	7. 8) 23	8. 9) 85	9. 6) 50	10. 6) 38
11. 6) 19	12. 9) 43	13. 7) 46	14. 9) 36	15. 8) 47
16. 8) 19	17. 9) 58	18. 6) 55	19. 7) 29	20. 7) 38
21. 7) 45	22. 8) 53	23. 6) 49	24. 9) 50	25. 8) 50

Solve.

26. How many 8¢ Ticket can you buy with

  ? ________

27. How many 7¢ Ticket can you buy with

  ? ________

28. How many 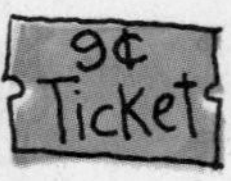

can you buy with

   ? ________

How much money will be left? ________

29. How many 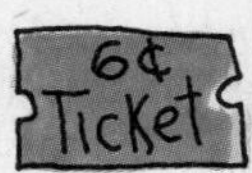

can you buy with

 ? ________

How much money will be left? ________

30. You have:  

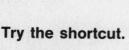

You buy: 5 9¢ Ticket and 2 8¢ Ticket

How much money do you have left? ________

31. You have: 

You buy: 4 7¢ Ticket and 6 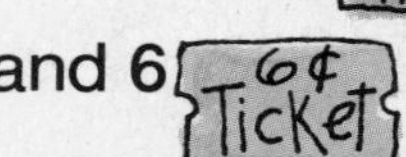

How much money do you have left? ________

Mental Math

Here's how I subtract 99 in my head.
I subtract 100. Then I add back 1.
SHORT CUT
238
− 99
139
238 − 100 = 138
138 + 1 = 139

Try the shortcut.

32.	**33.**	**34.**	**35.**	**36.**
463	284	500	607	320
−99	−99	−99	−99	−99

Name Math 2

Grouping symbols

The marks ( ) tell us what to do first.

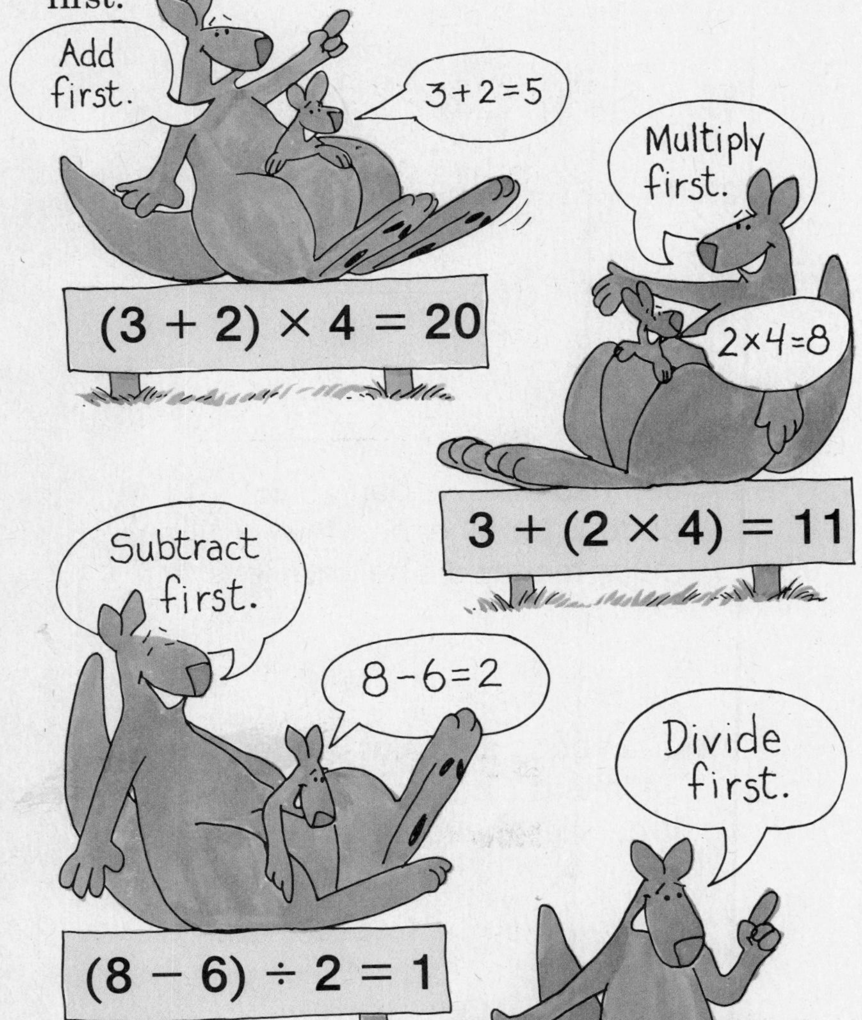

Add first.
3+2=5
(3 + 2) × 4 = 20
Multiply first.
2×4=8
3 + (2 × 4) = 11
Subtract first.
8-6=2
Divide first.
8 − (6 ÷ 2) = 5

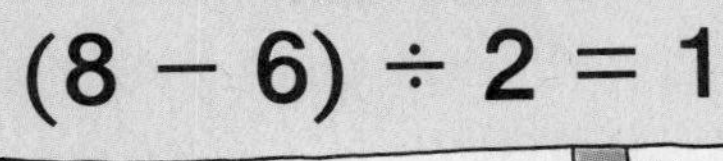

EXERCISES

Complete.

12

1. (8 + 4) ÷ 2 = 6

2

2. 8 + (4 ÷ 2) = 10

3

3. (6 − 3) ÷ 3 = 1

1

4. 6 − (3 ÷ 3) = 5

6

5. (4 + 2) + 3 = 9

5

6. 4 + (2 + 3) = 9

7. (3 × 2) × 2 = 12

8. 4 × (2 × 2) = 16

9. (8 − 3) − 1 = 4

10. 8 − (3 − 1) = 6

11. (8 ÷ 4) ÷ 2 = 1

12. 8 ÷ (4 ÷ 2) = 6

13. 8 × (4 ÷ 2) = 16

Complete.

14. $(5 - 2) \times 4 =$ ______

15. $(8 \div 2) - 4 =$ ______

16. $3 \times (0 \div 5) =$ ______

17. $(3 + 6) \times 5 =$ ______

18. $17 - (4 \times 2) =$ ______

19. $18 \div (2 + 4) =$ ______

20. $24 \div (1 + 7) =$ ______

21. $(18 \div 3) - 2 =$ ______

22. $(6 \times 4) \div 8 =$ ______

23. $(4 + 8) \div 3 =$ ______

24. $9 + (36 \div 4) =$ ______

25. $7 \times (9 - 3) =$ ______

Problem Solving

26. Sally bought 3 pencils for 8¢ each and 1 eraser for 6¢. What was the total cost?

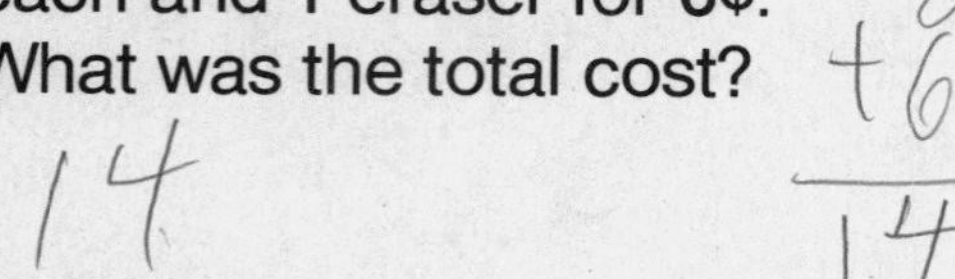

______

27. Jeff had 53¢. He bought 6 buttons for 4¢ each. How much money did he have left?

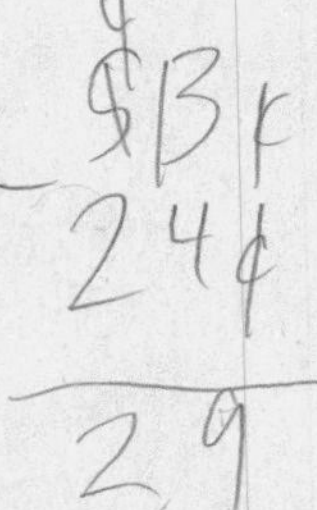

______

28. Brian had 75¢. He bought 5 crayons for 6¢ each. How much money does he have left? ______

29. Joan bought 4 paint jars for 8¢ each and 1 paintbrush for 10¢. What was the total cost?

______

Challenge!

Give the key (+, −, ×, or ÷) you would push to get the answer.

30. (8 ☐ 2) ☐ 5 = 2

31. (8 ☐ 2) ☐ 5 = 9

32. (8 ☐ 2) ☐ 5 = 20

33. (8 ☐ 2) ☐ 5 = 30

34. (8 ☐ 2) ☐ 5 = 50

Name ______________________________

Another meaning of division

Division tells how many in each set.

4 in each set
3 sets) 12 in all

EXERCISES

How many apples would be on each plate?

1.  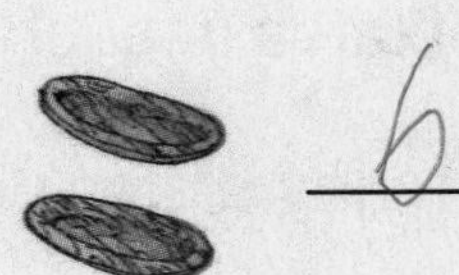 6

2.   3

3.   6

4.  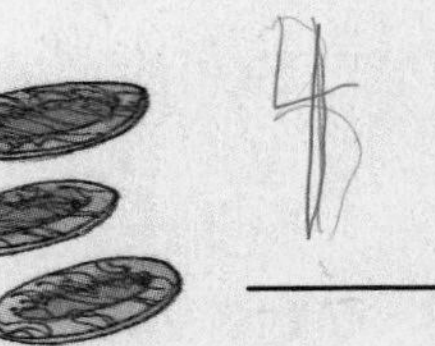 4

5.  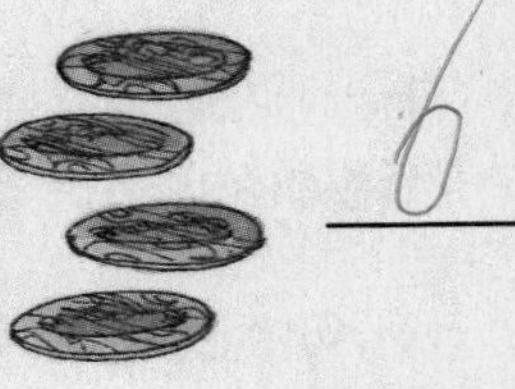 6

6.  7

Solve.

7. The class went to the picnic in 8 cars. There were 5 people in each car. How many people went to the picnic? ______

8. Twenty-four people were picked for 4 teams. Each team had the same number of people. How many people were on each team? ______

9. There were 8 packages of paper plates. There were 6 plates in each package. How many plates were there? ______

10. There were 24 blue paper cups and 36 red paper cups. How many more red cups were there? ______

11. There were 6 pickles in each jar. There were 4 jars. How many pickles were there? ______

12. There were 18 cartons of chocolate milk and 36 cartons of white milk. How many cartons of milk were there? ______

13. There are 12 hot dogs.
    a. If you put 3 hot dogs on a plate, how many plates would you use? ______
    b. Suppose you had 2 plates and put the same number of hot dogs on each plate. How many hot dogs would you put on each plate? ______

14. There were 72 hot dogs in all. The class ate 59 of them. How many hot dogs were left? ______

15. There were 40 people at the picnic. Fourteen had chocolate milk. How many did not have chocolate milk? ______

★ 16. Each of 4 people carried away 2 bags of trash, and each of 3 people carried away 3 bags of trash. How many bags of trash were carried away? ______

★ 17. There were 40 people at the picnic. They returned home in 7 cars (one of the 8 cars broke down). Each of 6 cars carried 6 people. How many people were in the seventh car? ______

Name ____________________

Problem Solving Choosing the operation

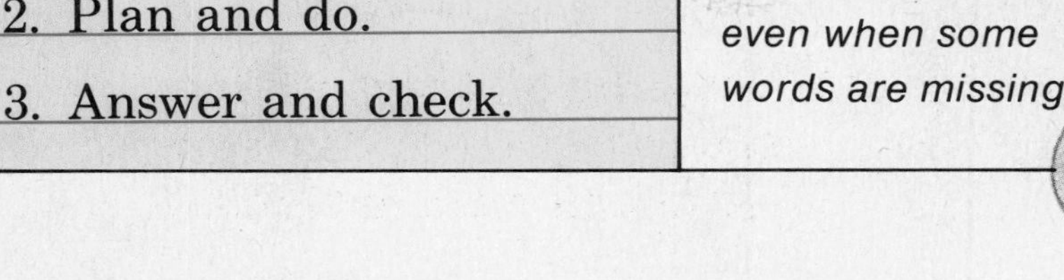

1. Study and understand. 2. Plan and do. 3. Answer and check.	*Sometimes you can decide what to do even when some words are missing.*

George put 8 in each .
He has 2 .
How many in all?

$2 \times 8 = 16$

Answer: 16 in all.

Sarah had 8 .
She put 2 in each .
How many ?

$8 \div 2 = 4$

Answer: 4 .

EXERCISES

Solve.

1. Bill bought 8 and 4 . How many and did he buy in all?

   ______

2. Jill bought 8 and 4 . How many more did she buy?

   ______

3. There were 6 with 3 in each . How many in all?

   ______

4. Mary bought 8 . There were 4 in each . How many did she buy?

   ______

5. Harry bought 8 ▬.
He put 4 of them in each ▬. How many ▬ did he use?

______

6. ● bought 10 ▬.
● bought 4 ▬.
How many more did ● buy?

______

7. ■ had 10 ●.
■ had 4 ●.
How many ● did they have together?

______

8. ▲ had 10 ●.
▲ gave 4 ● to ●.
How many ● did ▲ have left?

______

★ 9. ● had $1.50.
● bought ▲ for $.73 and ■ for $.56.
How much did ● have left?

______

★ 10. ● had 75¢.
● bought 5 ▲ for 6¢ each and 4 ■ for 7¢ each.
How much did ● have then?

______

Name ______________________________

Problem Solving Mixed practice

1. Some students left Day Elementary School at 9:30. They got to the airport at 10:13. How long did the ride take? 

2. There were 34 students on one bus and 29 on another. How many students in all? 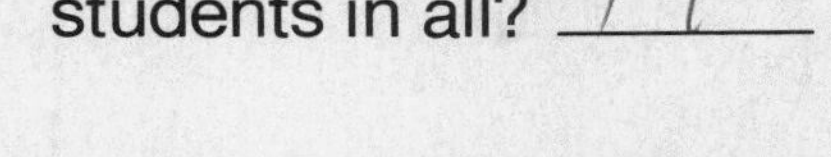

3. Each group leader took 9 students. How many students would 6 group leaders take? ______

4. If each group leader took 9 students, how many leaders were needed for all 63 students? ______

5. One kind of airplane needed a crew of 7 people. How many people would 8 of these airplanes need? ______

6. One airplane had 6 seats in each row. How many seats were in 8 rows? ______

7. If there were 6 seats in each row, how many rows were needed to seat 54 people? ______

8. One airplane had 186 seats. 137 people got on. How many more people could the airplane hold? ______

9. There were 148 people on another airplane but only 119 meals. How many more meals were needed? ______

10. A pilot said that he flew 2083 miles one day and 1957 the next. How many miles did he fly in all? ______

11. There are 25 takeoffs and 25 landings each hour. How many takeoffs are there in 3 hours? ______

12. When the students went back to school, 27 rode on one bus. How many rode on the other? (See exercise 2.) ______

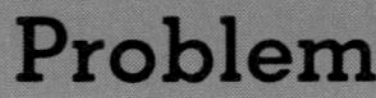

Problem Solving Using guess and check

You can solve the problem by guessing and checking.

Jan bought 2 things. She spent $1.78.
What did she buy?

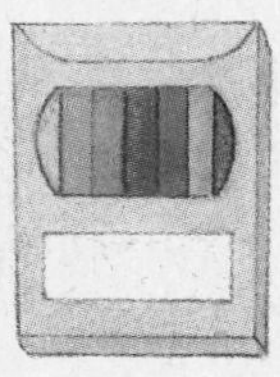

First guess:	Could Jan have bought colored pencils and a ruler?	**Check:**	$1.69 +.59 $2.28	No, the total is too high.
Second guess:	Could Jan have bought scissors and a ruler?	**Check:**	$ .89 +.59 $1.48	The total is too low.
Third guess:	Could Jan have bought notebook paper and a ruler?	**Check:**	$1.19 +.59 $1.78	Just right!

Answer: Jan bought notebook paper and a ruler.

EXERCISES

Solve by guessing and checking.

1. David bought 2 things. He spent $1.48. What did he buy?

____

____

★ **2.** Robert bought 3 things. He spent $3.17. What did he buy?

____

____

Name ____________________

Chapter Checkup

Multiply. [pages 272, 274–275, 278–279, 284–285, 288–289]

1. 8×4	**2.** 8×6	**3.** 7×5	**4.** 6×6	**5.** 8×7	**6.** 7×4
7. 8×8	**8.** 8×9	**9.** 9×6	**10.** 7×7	**11.** 7×6	**12.** 9×7
13. 7×8	**14.** 9×5	**15.** 8×5	**16.** 9×9	**17.** 6×8	**18.** 8×9

Divide. [pages 273, 276–277, 280–281, 286–287, 290–291]

19. $8\overline{)32}$	**20.** $6\overline{)42}$	**21.** $9\overline{)36}$	**22.** $6\overline{)30}$	**23.** $9\overline{)45}$
24. $8\overline{)40}$	**25.** $6\overline{)48}$	**26.** $9\overline{)27}$	**27.** $6\overline{)54}$	**28.** $7\overline{)49}$
29. $7\overline{)35}$	**30.** $7\overline{)63}$	**31.** $8\overline{)24}$	**32.** $7\overline{)28}$	**33.** $8\overline{)72}$
34. $7\overline{)56}$	**35.** $7\overline{)21}$	**36.** $9\overline{)81}$	**37.** $6\overline{)36}$	**38.** $8\overline{)64}$

Solve. [pages 282–283, 296–301]

39. 

How much will 7  cost? ________

40. 

How many [9¢] can you buy with 63¢? ________

41. 48 people went on a field trip. There were 6 people in each car. How many cars were there? ________

42. 36 people went to the zoo in a bus. 6 people went to the zoo in a car. How many people went to the zoo? ________

Chapter Project

FINDING A PATTERN

1. Complete this multiplication table.

x	0	1	2	3	4	5	6	7	8	9
0	0	0	0	0	0	0	0	0	0	0
1	0	1	2	3	4	5	6	7	8	9
2	0	2	4	6	8					
3	0	3								
4	0									
5	0									
6	0									
7	0									
8	0									
9	0									

2. Look at your table.
3. What patterns can you find?
   Hint:
   Look at the rows. (⟷)
   Look at the columns. (↕)
   Look at the diagonals. (⤡⤢)

Name ______________________________

Chapter Review

Multiply or divide.

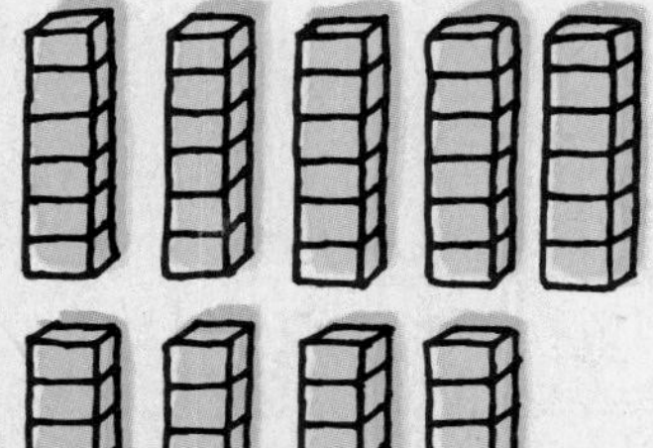

1. $\begin{array}{r} 6 \\ \times 2 \\ \hline \end{array}$
2. $\begin{array}{r} 6 \\ \times 7 \\ \hline \end{array}$
3. $\begin{array}{r} 6 \\ \times 4 \\ \hline \end{array}$
4. $\begin{array}{r} 6 \\ \times 9 \\ \hline \end{array}$

5. $6\overline{)18}$
6. $6\overline{)36}$
7. $6\overline{)48}$
8. $6\overline{)30}$

9. $\begin{array}{r} 7 \\ \times 7 \\ \hline \end{array}$
10. $\begin{array}{r} 7 \\ \times 2 \\ \hline \end{array}$
11. $\begin{array}{r} 7 \\ \times 9 \\ \hline \end{array}$
12. $\begin{array}{r} 7 \\ \times 5 \\ \hline \end{array}$

13. $7\overline{)21}$
14. $7\overline{)42}$
15. $7\overline{)28}$
16. $7\overline{)56}$

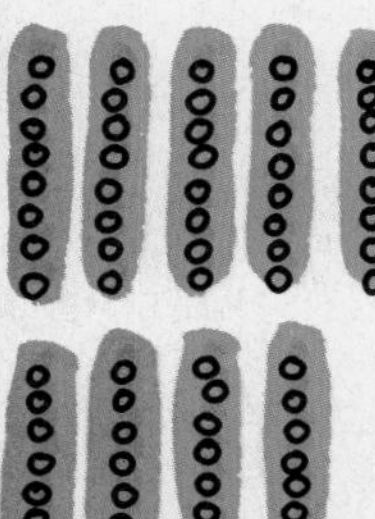

17. $\begin{array}{r} 8 \\ \times 3 \\ \hline \end{array}$
18. $\begin{array}{r} 8 \\ \times 8 \\ \hline \end{array}$
19. $\begin{array}{r} 8 \\ \times 4 \\ \hline \end{array}$
20. $\begin{array}{r} 8 \\ \times 6 \\ \hline \end{array}$

21. $8\overline{)16}$
22. $8\overline{)40}$
23. $8\overline{)72}$
24. $8\overline{)56}$

25. $\begin{array}{r} 9 \\ \times 5 \\ \hline \end{array}$
26. $\begin{array}{r} 9 \\ \times 2 \\ \hline \end{array}$
27. $\begin{array}{r} 9 \\ \times 9 \\ \hline \end{array}$
28. $\begin{array}{r} 9 \\ \times 6 \\ \hline \end{array}$

29. $9\overline{)27}$
30. $9\overline{)63}$
31. $9\overline{)36}$
32. $9\overline{)72}$

Chapter Challenge

FACTORING

When you multiply, the product of the numbers in each row is 24.

24			
3	8		
3	2	4	
3	2	2	2

Sharon's way

24			
4	6		
4	2	3	
2	2	2	3

Arthur's way

Copy and complete.
Do not use the number 1.
(There is more than one way to fill in each row.)

1.

12		
2	6	

2.

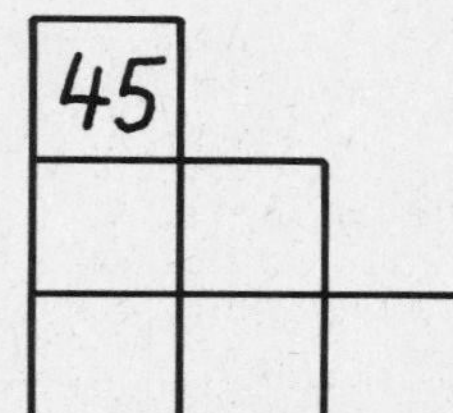
45

3.

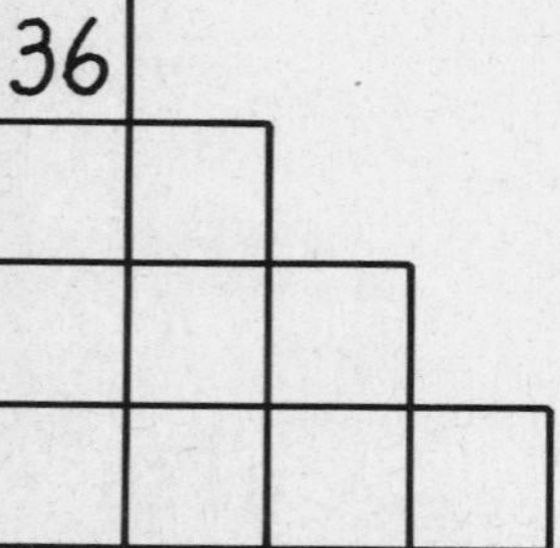
36

4.

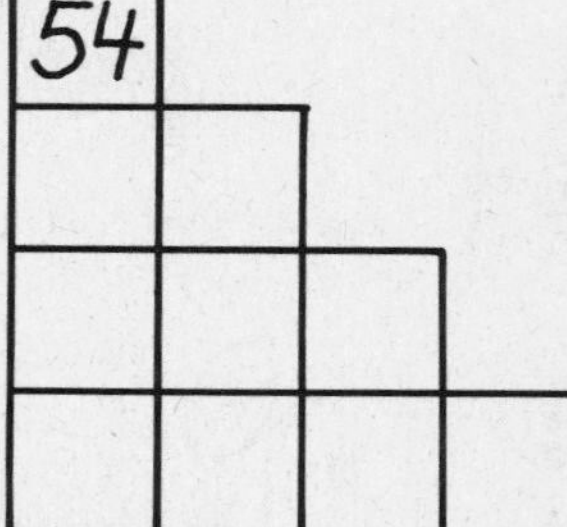
54

5.

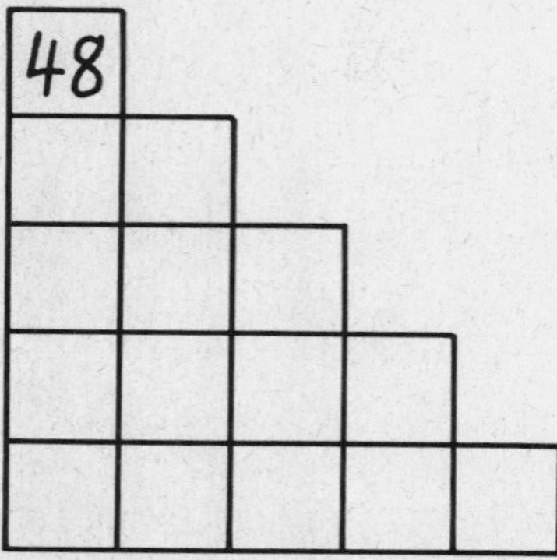
48

6.

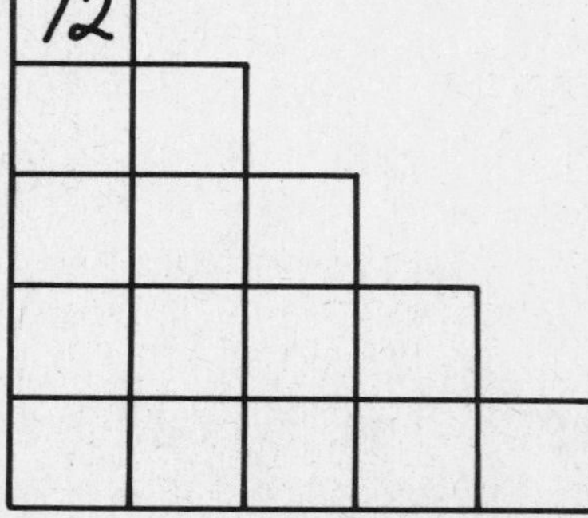
72

Name Martin #2

Cumulative Checkup

STANDARDIZED FORMAT

Give the correct letter.

1. Which letter is seventh?

QUOTIENT

a. I
b. N
c. E
d. T

2. Round 74 to the nearest ten.

a. 70
b. 50
c. 80
d. none of these

3. Add.

$$\begin{array}{r} 538 \\ +296 \\ \hline \end{array}$$

a. 724
b. 834
c. 824
d. none of these

4. Subtract.

$$\begin{array}{r} 600 \\ -238 \\ \hline \end{array}$$

a. 462
b. 372
c. 472
d. 362

5. What time is it?

a. 2:35
b. 7:13
c. 3:35
d. none of these

6. Multiply.

$$\begin{array}{r} 3 \\ \times 8 \\ \hline \end{array}$$

a. 18
b. 16
c. 21
d. none of these

7. Divide.

$24 \div 4$

a. 4
b. 6
c. 8
d. 9

8. Divide.

$5\overline{)28}$

a. 5 R3
b. 3 R5
c. 4 R3
d. 6 R3

9. What fraction is yellow?

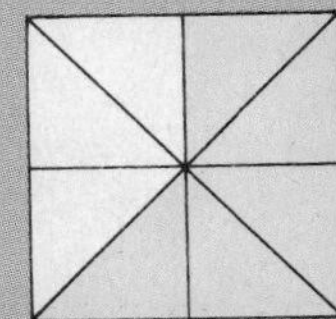

a. $\frac{3}{8}$
b. $\frac{3}{5}$
c. $\frac{5}{8}$
d. none of these

10. How long?

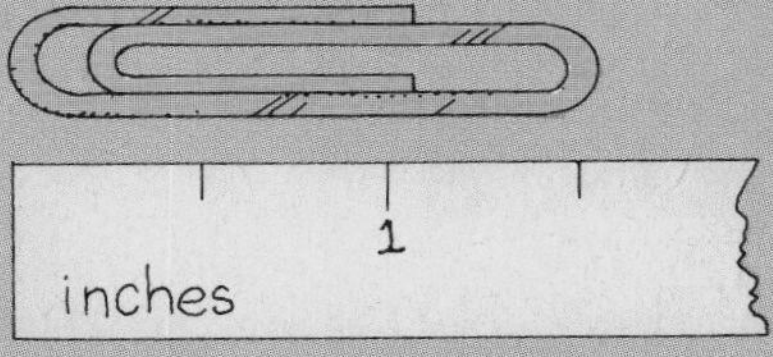

a. about 1 in.
b. about 3 in.
c. about $1\frac{1}{2}$ in.
d. none of these

11. 6 jars in a box
2 boxes
How many jars?

a. 12
b. 8
c. 4
d. 3

12. 28 books on a shelf
4 books on a table
How many books?

a. 7
b. 32
c. 24
d. none of these

11

Geometry

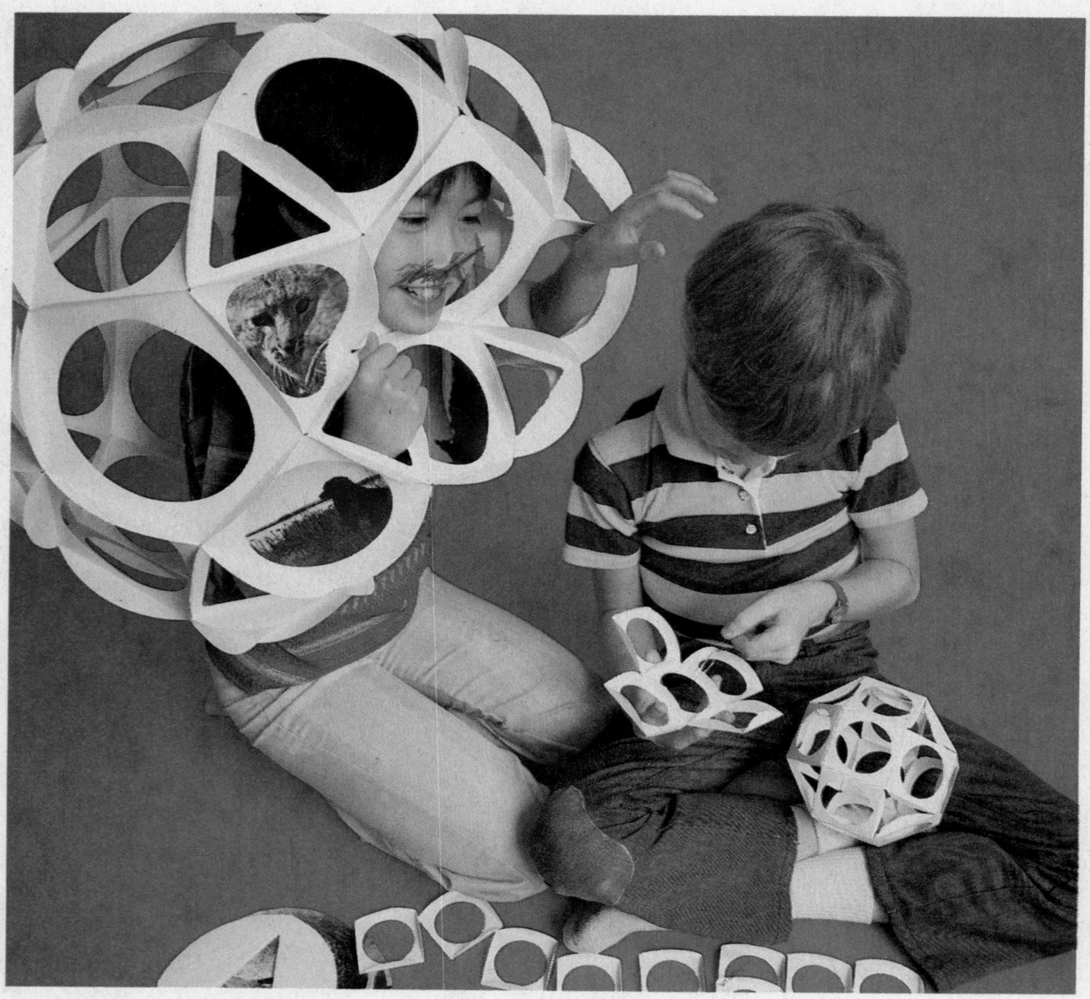

What shapes can you see in the picture? How many cutout circles are there in the model on Lee's lap?

Name ____________________

Solids

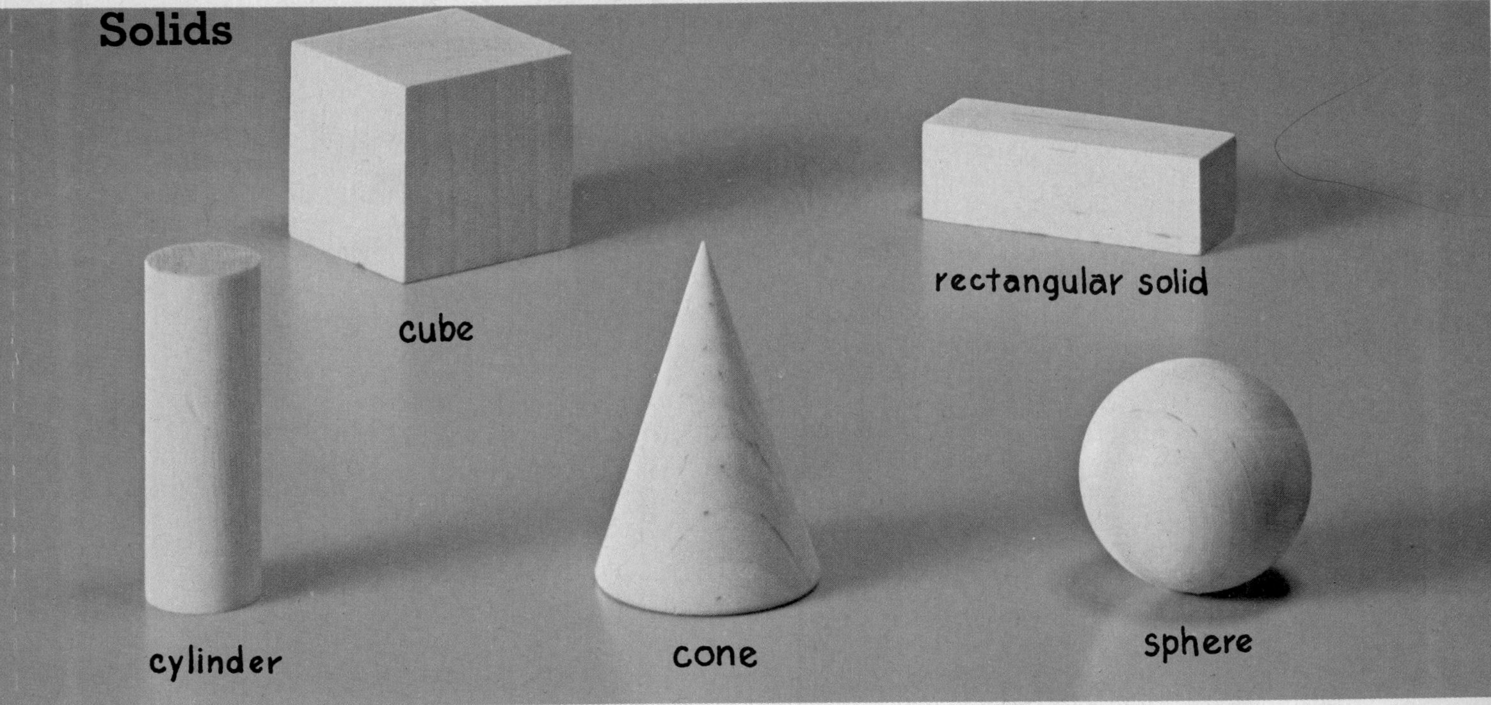

EXERCISES

Name each shape.

1.  cylinder

2. sphere

3.  cube

4.  rectangulersolid

5. cone

6.  cylinder

7.  sphere

8. 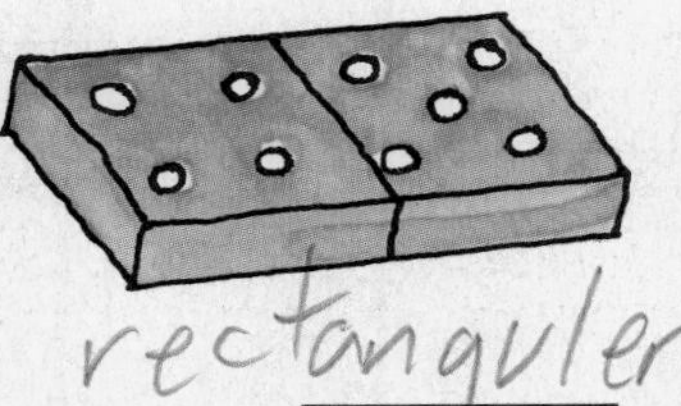 rectanguler soild

9.  cube

Name each shape.

10. ______

11. ______

12. ______

13. ______

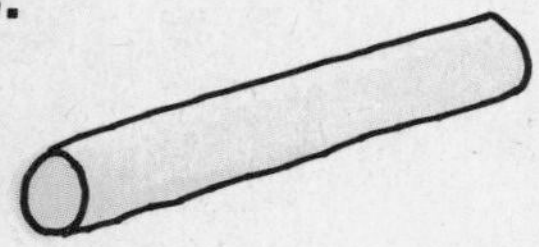

14. ______

15. ______

Look for these shapes in your classroom.
List what you find.

16. cube ______

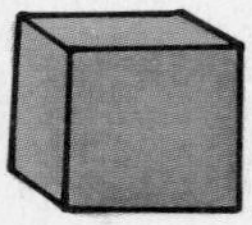

______

17. rectangular solid ______

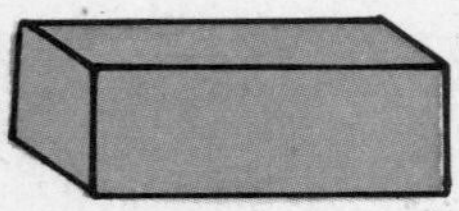

______

18. sphere ______

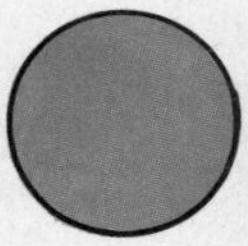

______

19. cylinder ______

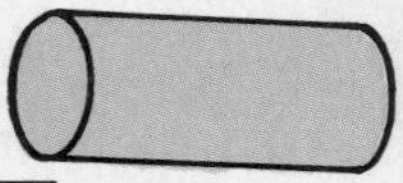

______

20. cone ______

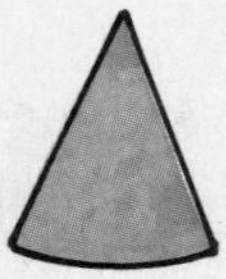

______

Name ______________________

More about solids

A sphere has one curved surface.

A cube has six flat surfaces.

EXERCISES

How many?

1.

a. flat surfaces 6

b. curved surfaces 0

2.

a. flat surfaces 0

b. curved surfaces 1

3.

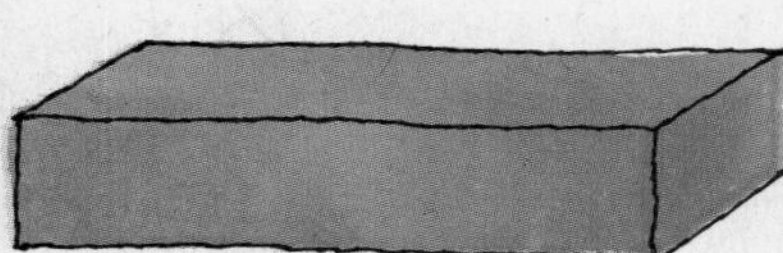

a. flat surfaces 6

b. curved surfaces 0

4.

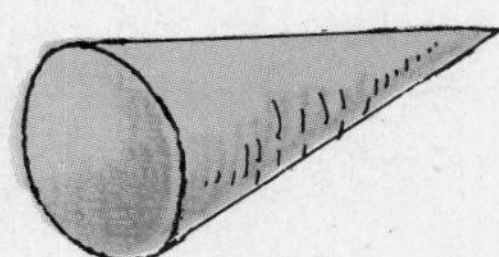

a. flat surfaces 1

b. curved surfaces 1

5.

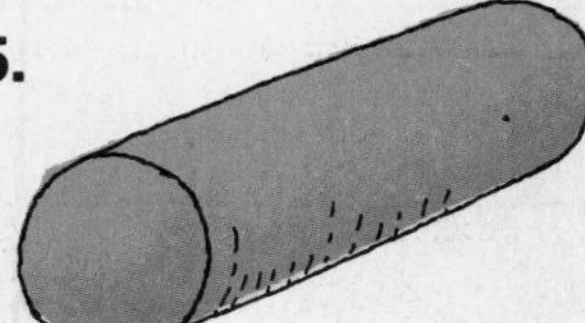

a. flat surfaces 2

b. curved surfaces 1

This is a corner.
EXCELLENT
This is an edge.

Copy and complete the table.

Solid	6.	7.	8.	9.	10.
Number of flat surfaces	6	6	6	5	8
Number of curved surfaces	0	0	0	0	0
Number of corners	8	8	8	5	6
Number of edges	12	12	12	8	12

Name ____________________

Plane figures

The plane figures we see most often are square, rectangle, circle, and triangle.

square

rectangle

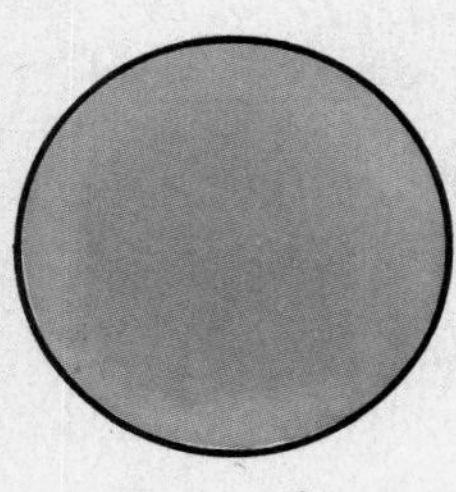

circle

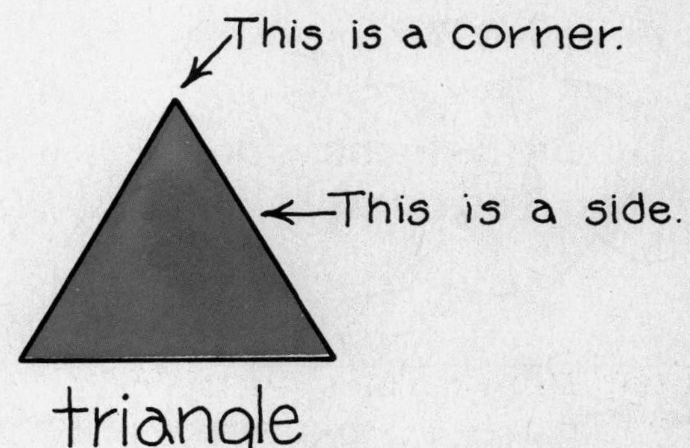

triangle

EXERCISES

Name each shape.

1.

____

2.

____

3.

____

4.

____

5.

____

6.

____

Look for these shapes in your classroom.
List what you find.

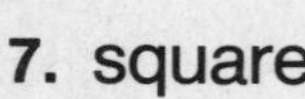

7. square  ____________

8. rectangle ____________

9. triangle ____________

10. circle ____________

Square, rectangle, triangle, or circle?
What shape am I?

11. 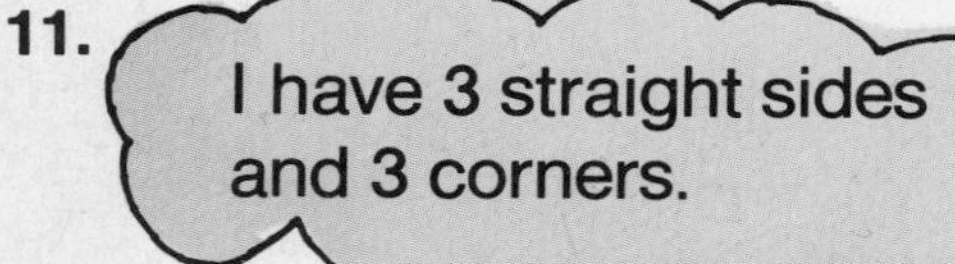
I have 3 straight sides and 3 corners.

____

12. I have 4 straight sides and 4 corners. All my sides are the same length.

____

13. 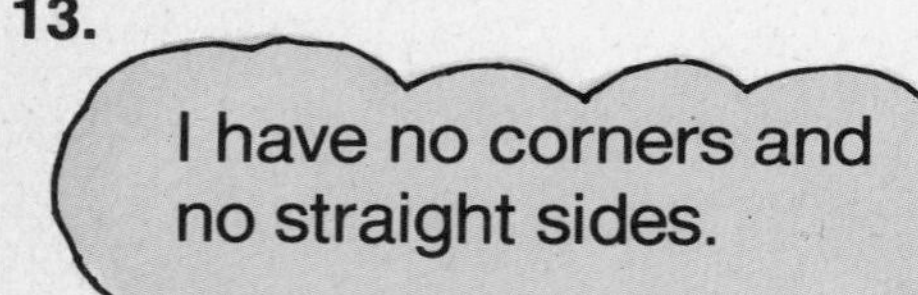
I have no corners and no straight sides.

____

14. I have 4 straight sides and 4 corners. I am longer than I am wide.

____

KEEPING SKILLS SHARP

1. 514 + 368	**2.** 259 + 464	**3.** 382 + 715	**4.** 259 + 376	**5.** 309 + 176
6. 785 + 294	**7.** 642 + 198	**8.** 392 + 176	**9.** 894 + 513	**10.** 281 + 736
11. 298 + 364	**12.** 281 + 364	**13.** 576 + 139	**14.** 278 + 142	**15.** 398 + 176

Name ______________________________

More about plane figures

The sides of these figures are **segments.**

The edges of these figures are **segments.**

Segments

Point A and point B are the **endpoints** of the red segment.

We call it segment AB or segment BA.

EXERCISES

Which are segments?

1.

2.

3.

4.

Which segment is the

5. longest? ______

6. shortest? ______

How many corners?
How many sides?

7. 

______
______

8. 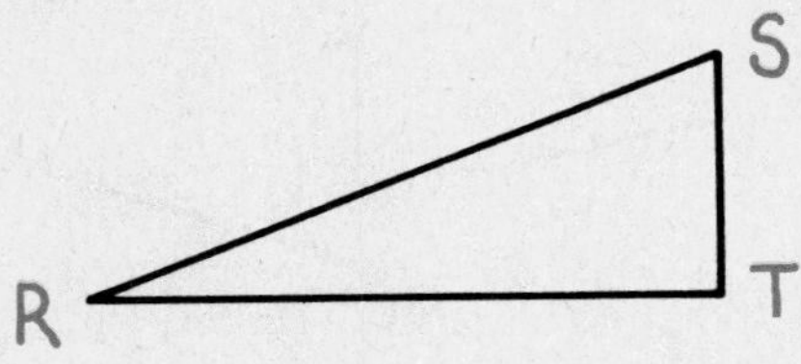

______
______

9. 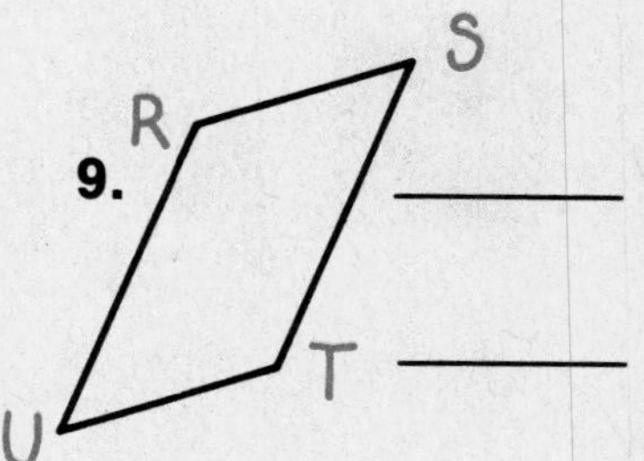

______
______

10. The sides of this triangle are segments. List them.

______

______

______

Complete.

11. Segment AB crosses segment CD at point ______.

12. Segment MN crosses ______ at point O.

Challenge!

How many sides?
How many diagonals?

13. 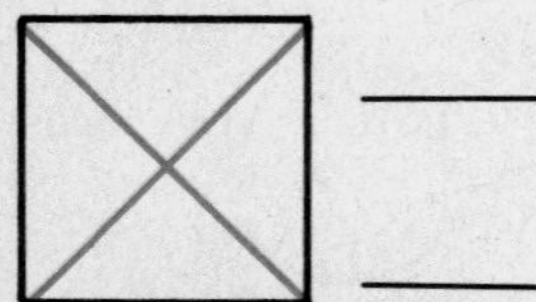
______
______

14. 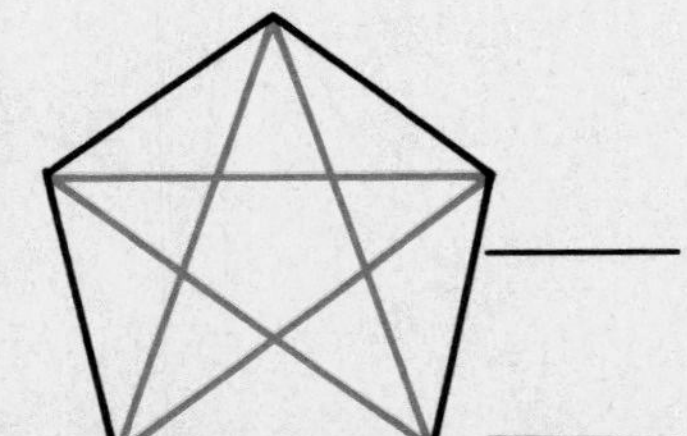
______
______

15. 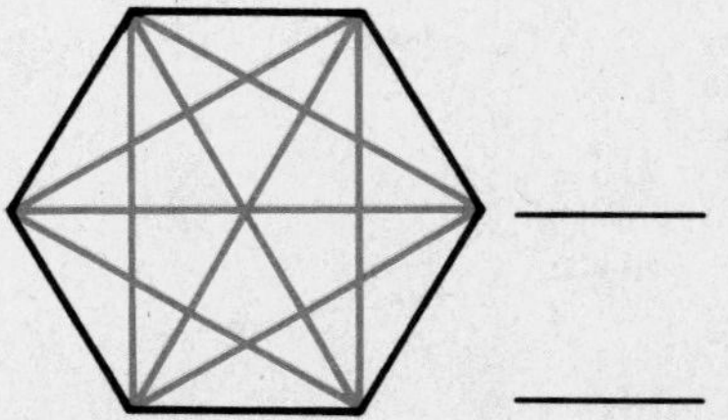
______
______

Name ______________________________

Congruent figures

Figures that are the same size and shape are **congruent figures.**

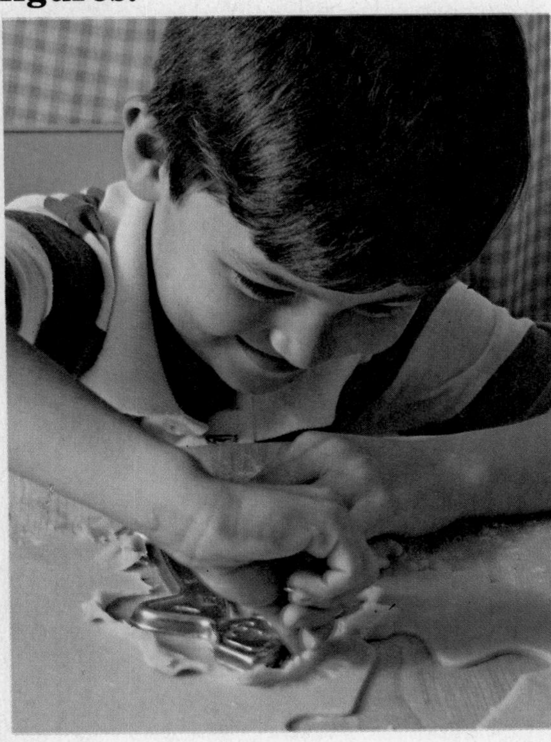

Andrew cut out some cookies with a cookie cutter. Here is one of his cookies.

EXERCISES

Which of these cookies could have been made with Andrew's cookie cutter?

1. 

2. 

3. 

4. 

5. 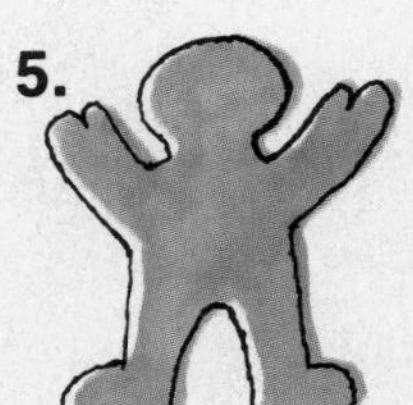

6. 

Mark each pair of congruent figures.

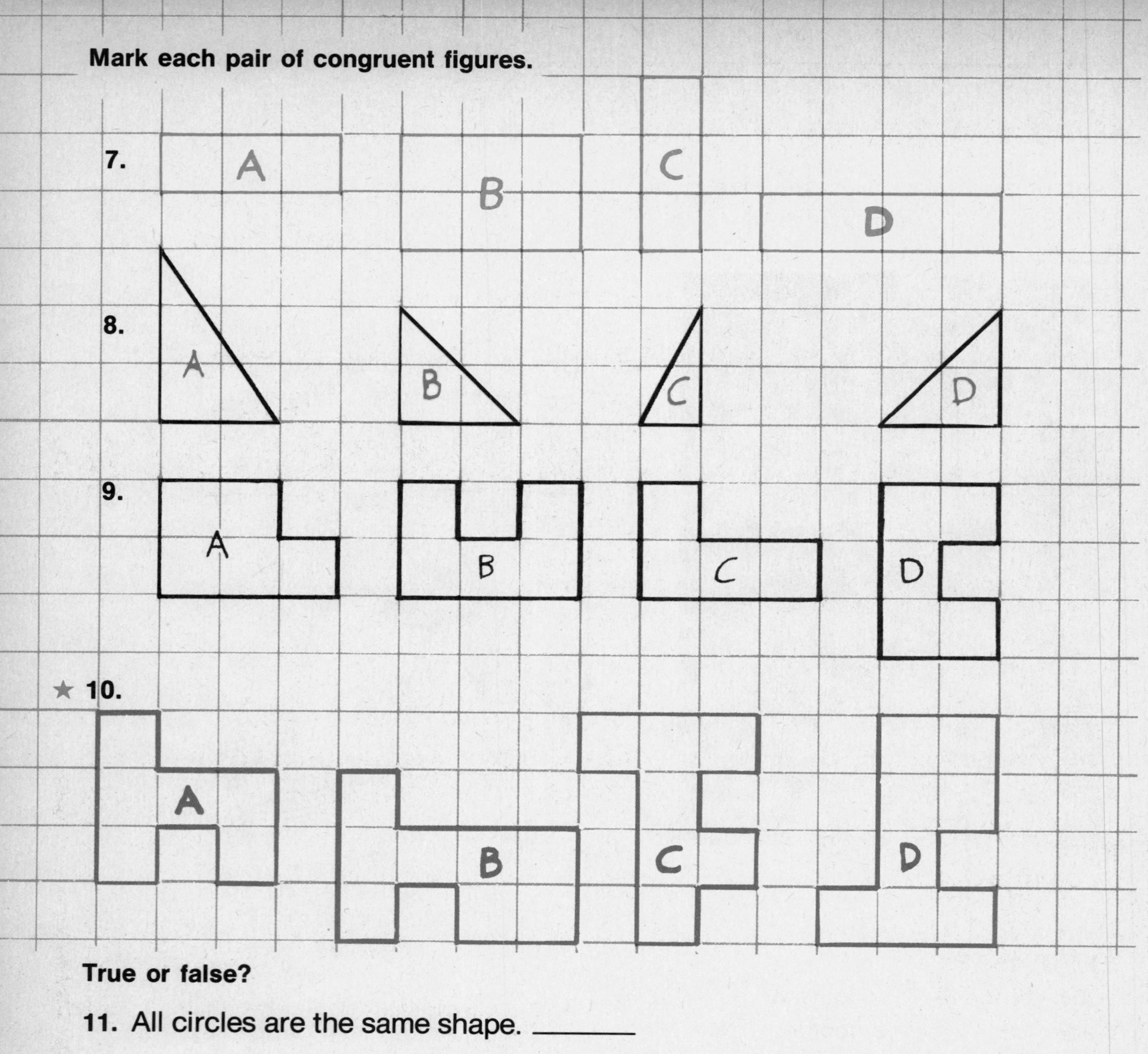

True or false?

11. All circles are the same shape. _______

12. All circles are the same size. _______

13. All circles are congruent. _______

14. All squares are the same shape. _______

15. All squares are the same size. _______

16. All triangles are congruent. _______

Name ______________________________

More about congruent figures

We can use a tracing to find congruent figures.

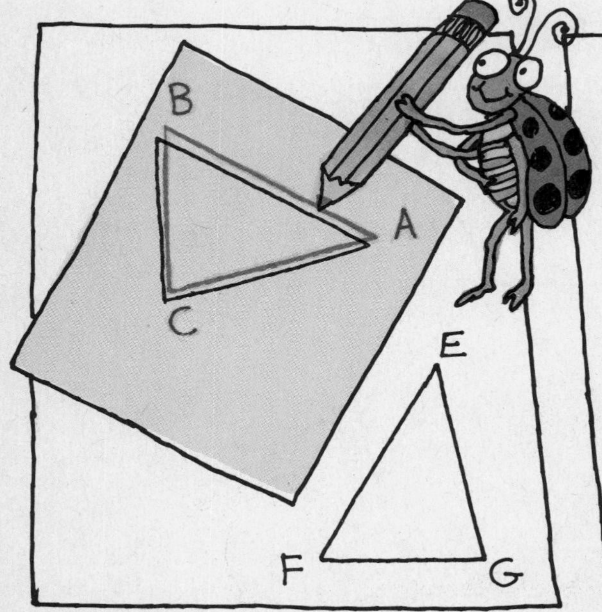

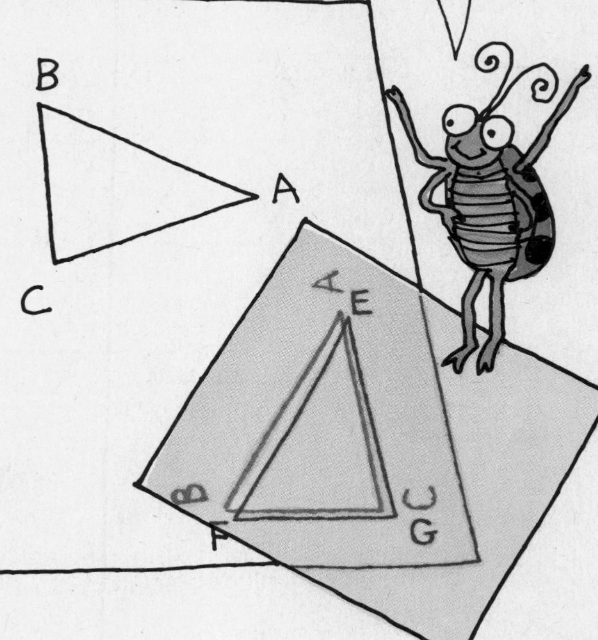

EXERCISES

Trace this triangle:

Mark the triangles that are congruent to the red triangle.

1. 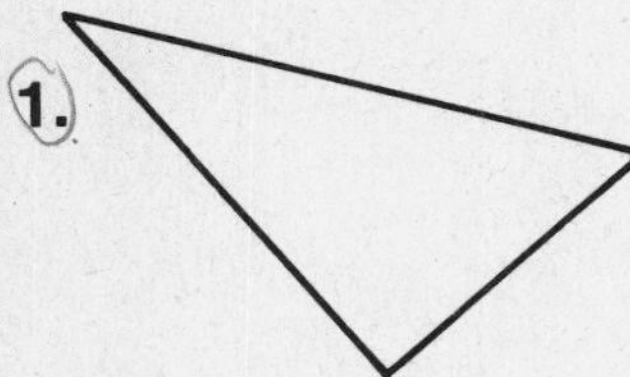

2. 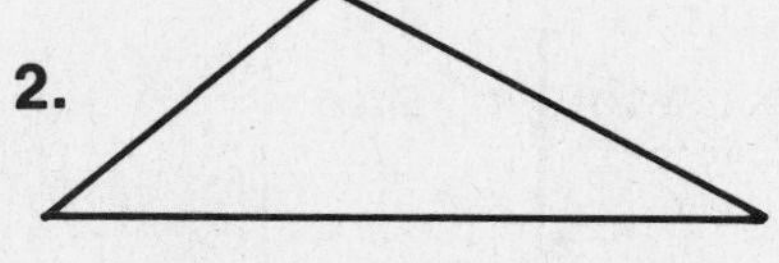

3. 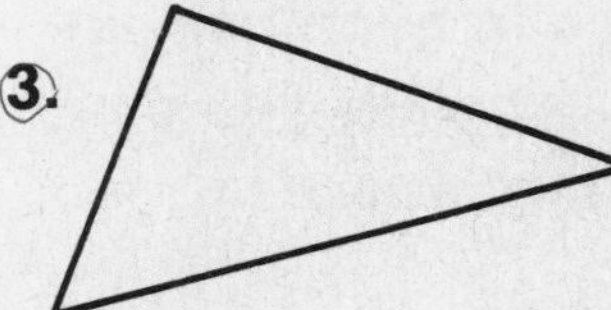

4. 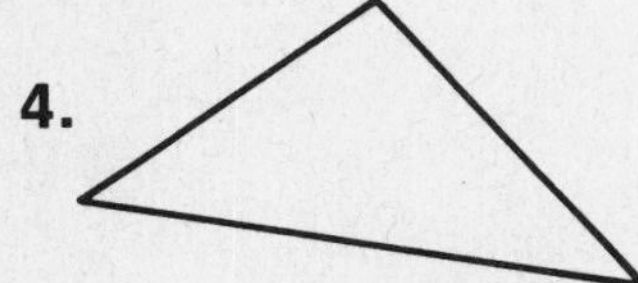

5. 

6. 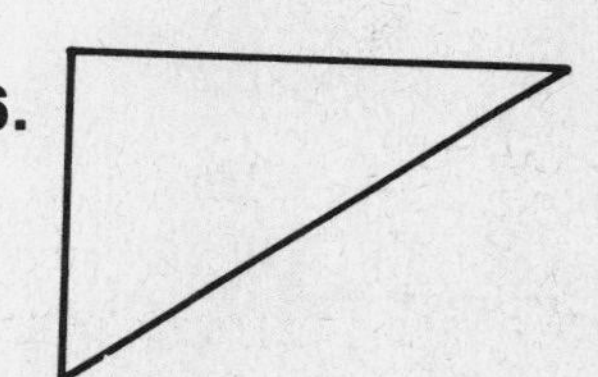

Mark the figure that is congruent to the red figure.

7. A B C

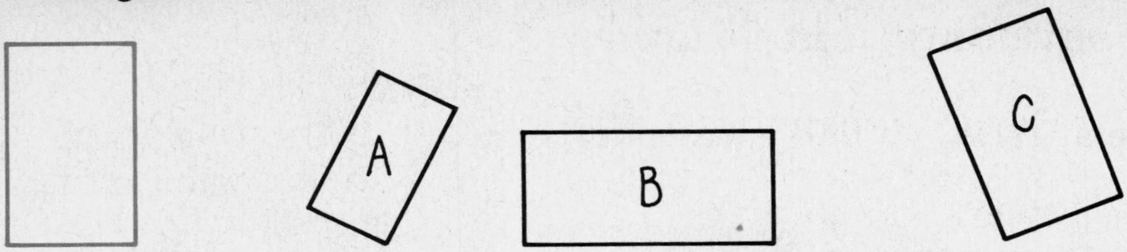

8. A B C

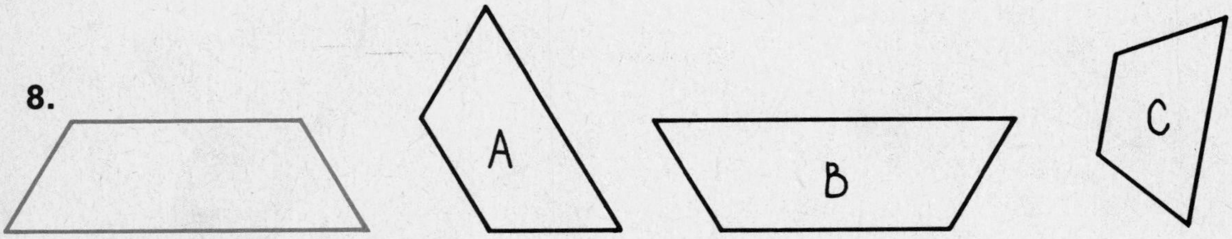

9. A B C

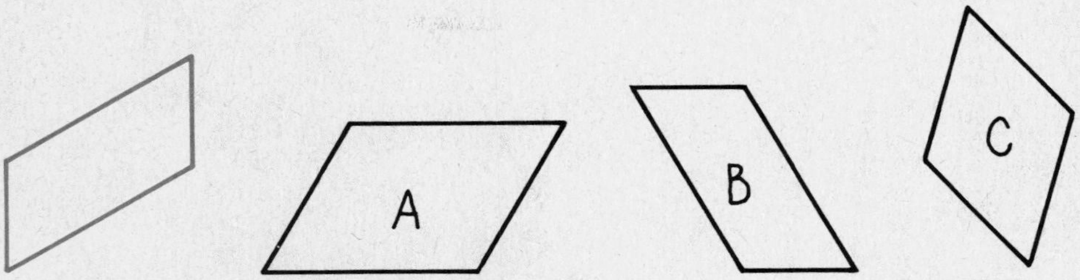

10. A B C

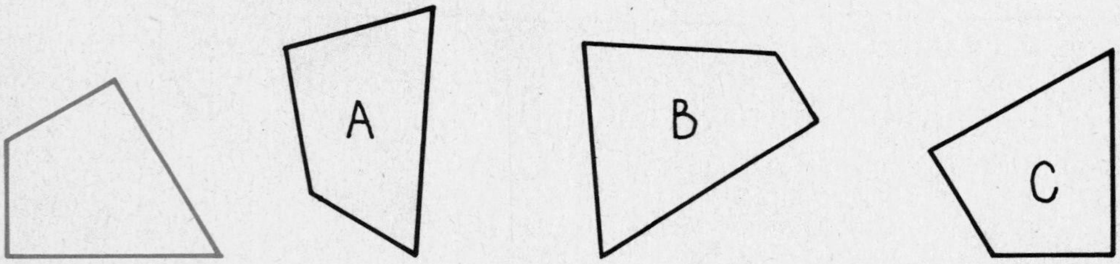

Challenge!

The triangles in each pair are congruent. Tell how many ways you can fit a tracing of one triangle on the other.

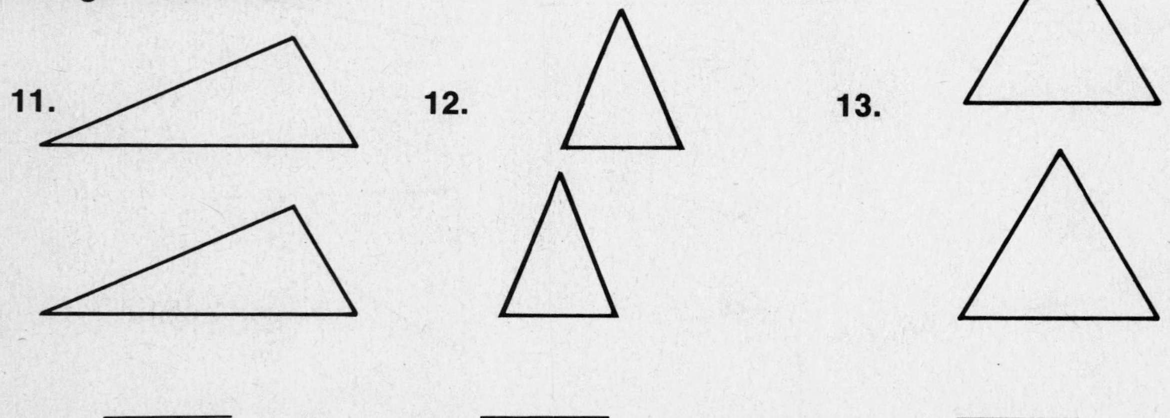

Name ______________________________

Lines of symmetry

If you fold this shape on the dashed line, the two parts fit. The dashed line is a **line of symmetry.**

EXERCISES

Is the dashed line a line of symmetry?

1.

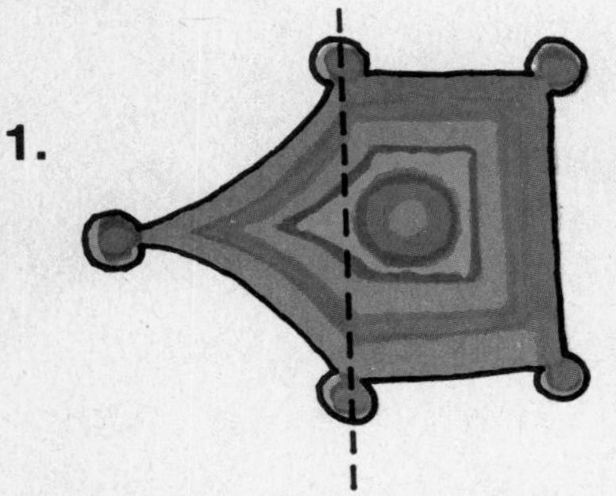

______

2.

______

3.

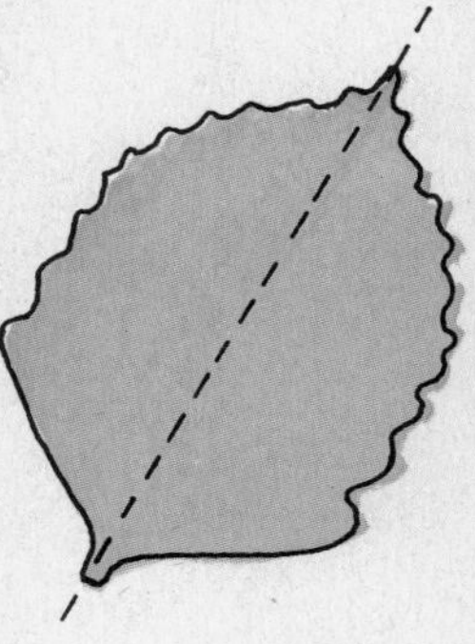

______

4.

______

5.

______

6.

______

1. Fold a piece of paper in half.
2. Cut out a shape from the folded edge.
3. Open your cutout. Does your cutout have a line of symmetry?
4. Cut out another shape that has a line of symmetry.

KEEPING SKILLS SHARP

1. 746 −214	2. 829 −153	3. 742 −378	4. 706 −355	5. 436 −395
6. 624 −583	7. 801 −459	8. 318 −106	9. 900 −253	10. 943 −300
11. 749 −582	12. 800 −465	13. 607 −558	14. 866 −794	15. 742 −231

Name ____________________

More about lines of symmetry

0 lines of symmetry

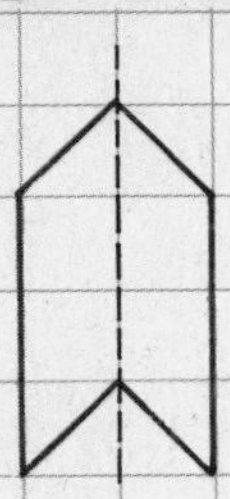

1 line of symmetry

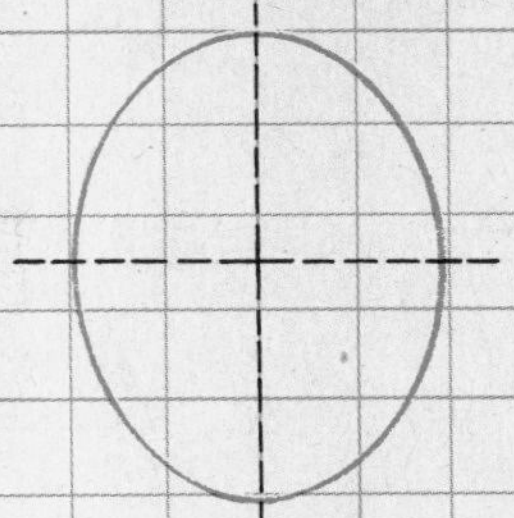

2 lines of symmetry

EXERCISES

How many lines of symmetry?

1.

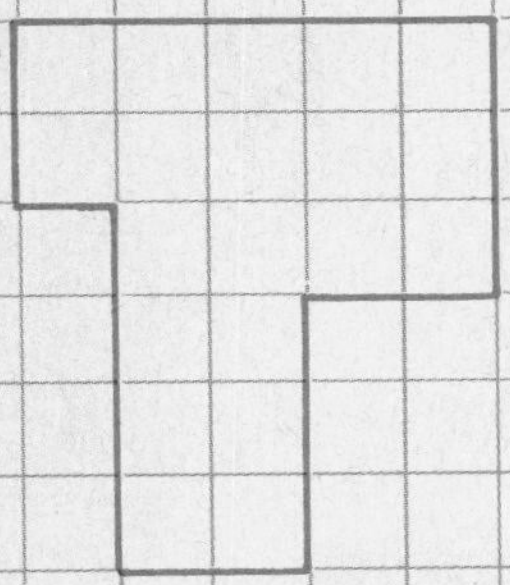

2.

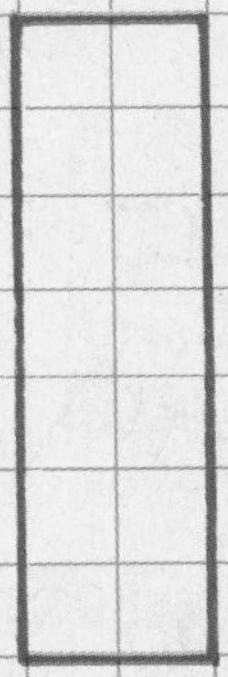

3.

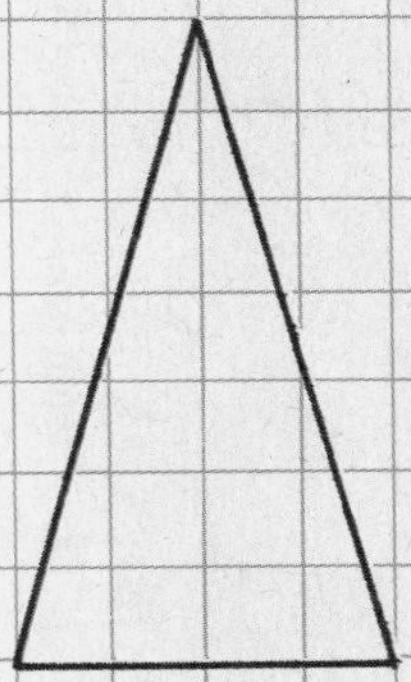

4.

5.

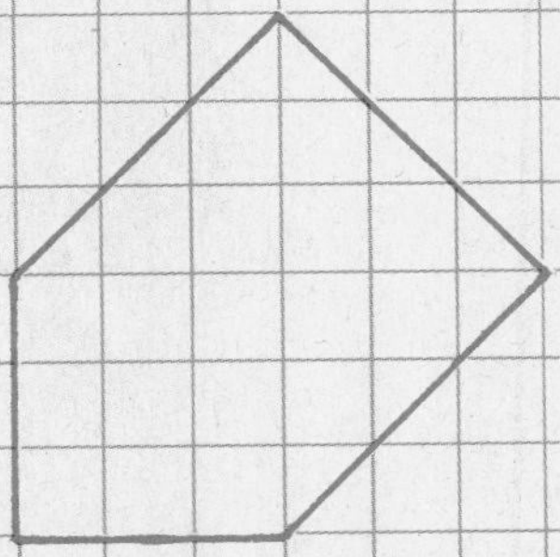

6.

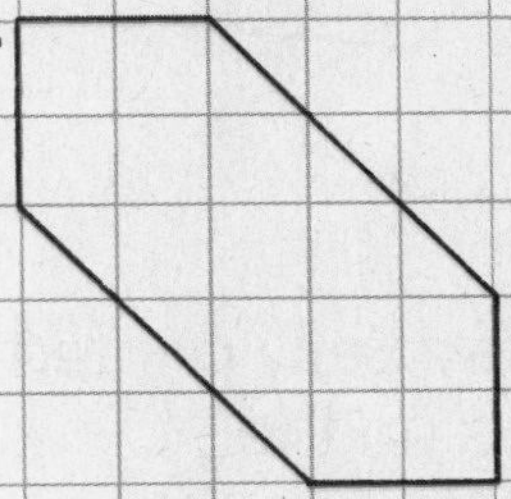

How many lines of symmetry?

7. 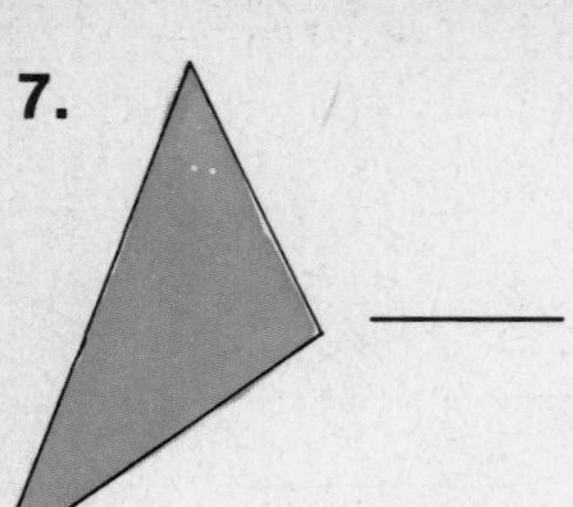 ____

8. 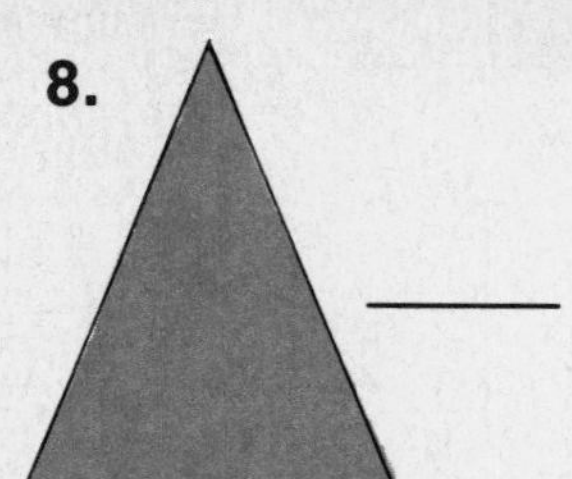 ____

9.  ____

10. 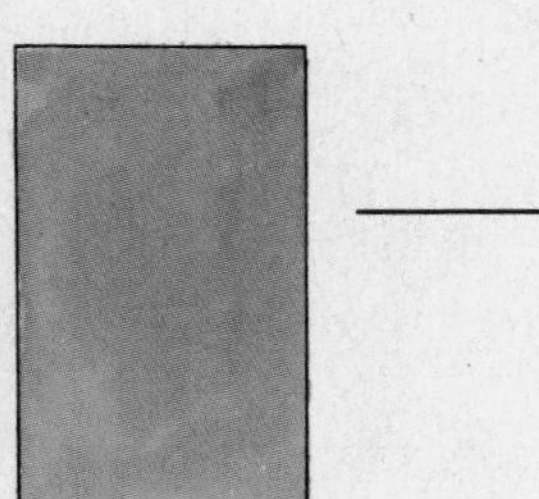 ____

11.  ____

★ 12. 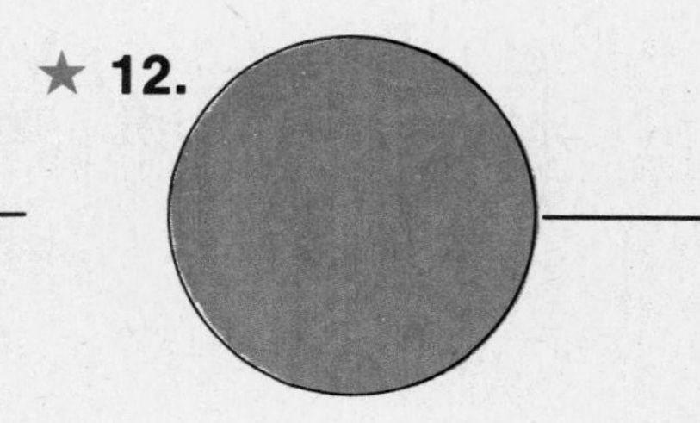 ____

13. Which of these digits have lines of symmetry? ________

Challenge!

14. One cold day Sally printed these letters on the inside of a frosty window. Which looked the same on the outside? ________

Name ______________________________

Chapter Checkup

Match. [pages 308–309]

1. 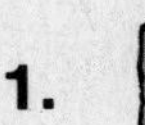 ______

2.  ______

3. 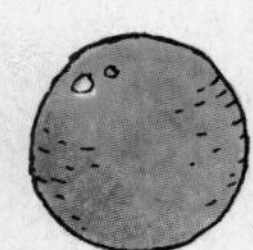 ______

4. 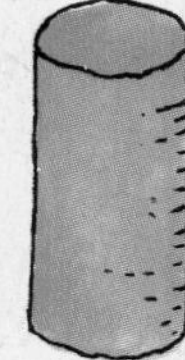 ______

5. 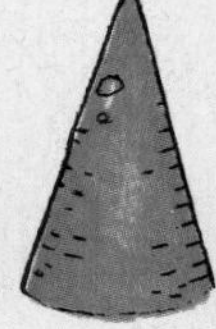 ______

a. sphere **b.** cylinder **c.** cube **d.** cone **e.** rectangular solid

True or false? [pages 310–315]

6. A cube has one curved surface. ______

7. A cylinder has two flat surfaces. ______

8. One end of a cone is a circle. ______

9. The sides of a triangle are segments. ______

10. A circle has no corners. ______

Are the two figures congruent? [pages 316–319]
(*Hint:* You may need to use a tracing.)

11.  ______

12.  ______

How many lines of symmetry? [pages 320–323]

13.  ______

14. 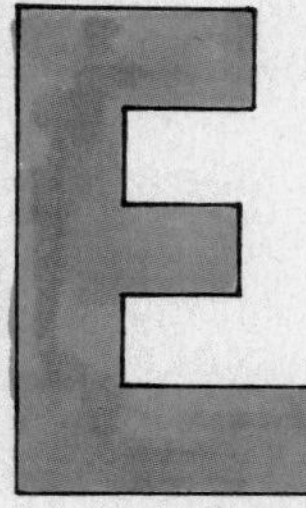 ______

15.  ______

Chapter Project

SYMMETRY

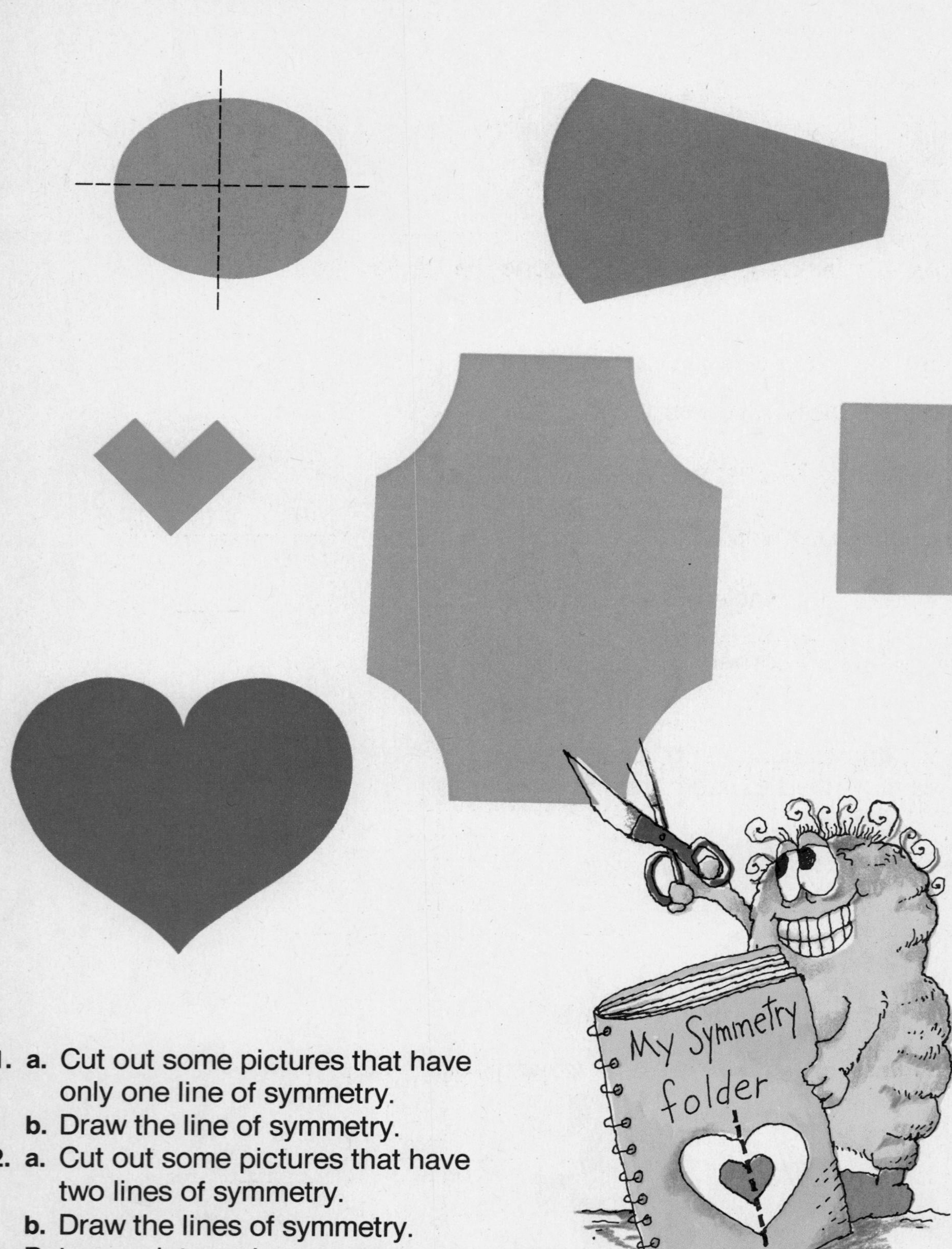

1. **a.** Cut out some pictures that have only one line of symmetry.
   b. Draw the line of symmetry.
2. **a.** Cut out some pictures that have two lines of symmetry.
   b. Draw the lines of symmetry.
3. Put your pictures in a symmetry folder.

Name ______________________________

Chapter Review

Match.

1.  ____

2.  ____

3. 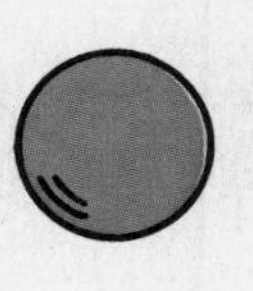 ____

4. 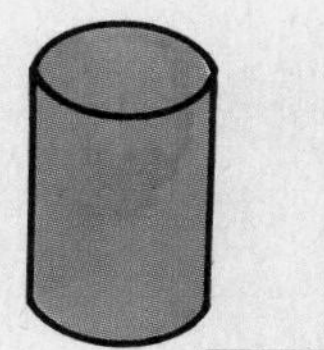 ____

5. 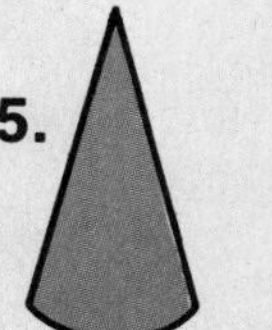 ____

a. rectangular solid **b.** cylinder **c.** cube **d.** cone **e.** sphere

Match.

6. 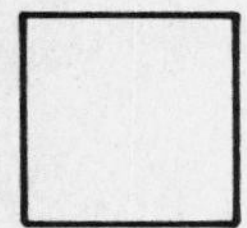 ____

7.  ____

8.  ____

9.  ____

a. rectangle **b.** circle **c.** triangle **d.** square

10. Are the two triangles congruent?

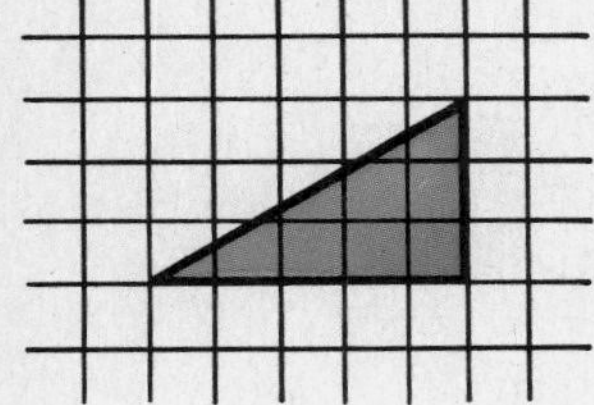 ____

Is the dashed line a line of symmetry?

11. 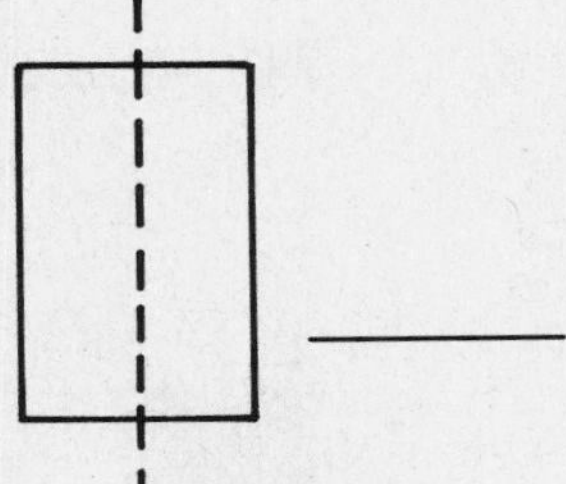 ____

12. 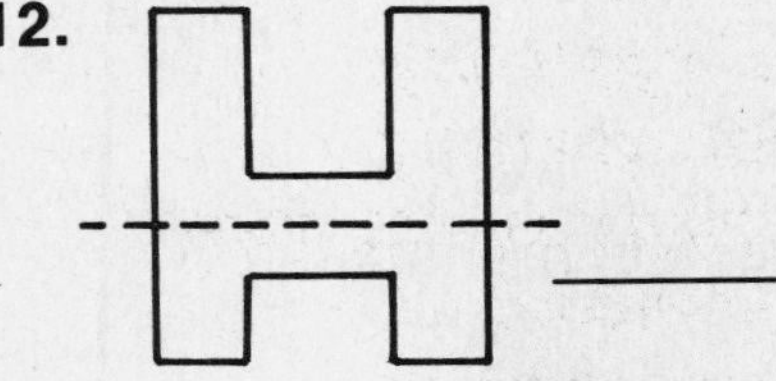 ____

Chapter Challenge

NUMBER PAIRS

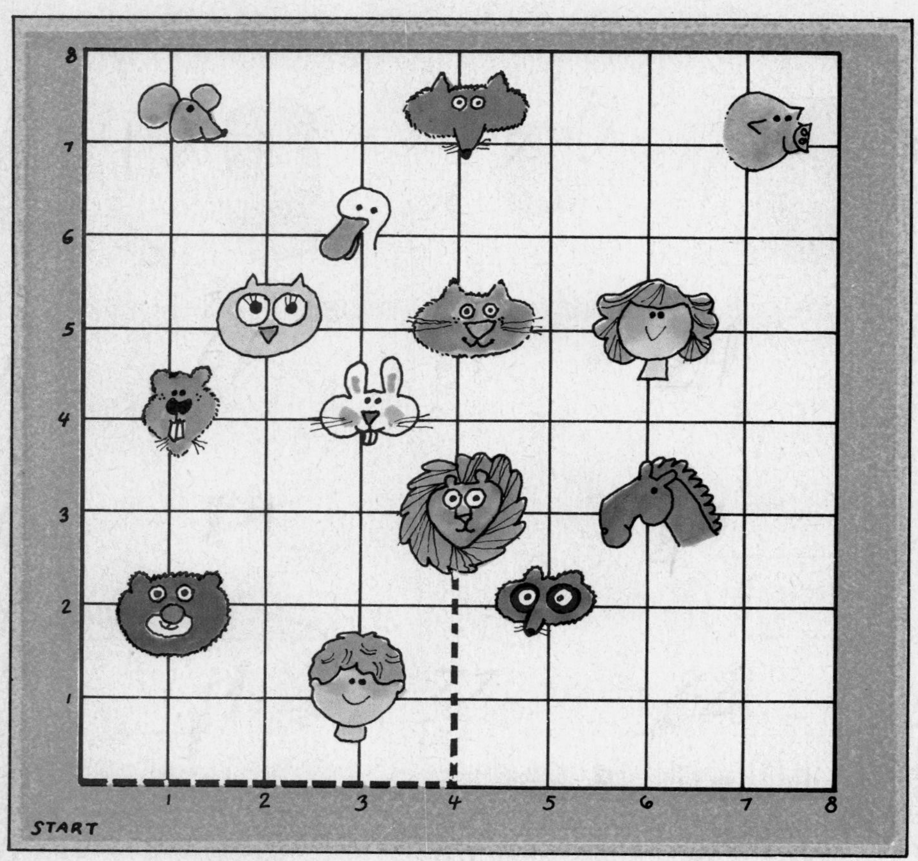

A **number pair** is used to find points on a grid. The number pair (4, 3) tells you how to find the . Begin at START. Go to the right 4 spaces and then up 3 spaces.

What do you find at these number pairs?

1. (3, 1)__________ **2.** (6, 5)__________ **3.** (5, 2)__________

4. (4, 3)__________ **5.** (7, 7)__________ **6.** (1, 7)__________

Give a number pair for each animal.

7.  ________ **8.** ________ **9.**  ________ **10.**  ________

11. ________ **12.** ________ **13.**  ________ **14.** ________

Name ______________________________

Cumulative Checkup

STANDARDIZED FORMAT

Give the correct letter.

1. What is 275 rounded to the nearest hundred?

a. 270
b. 300
c. 280
d. 200

2. Which numeral has a 6 in the hundreds place?

a. 6483
b. 4836
c. 4368
d. 8634

3. Add.

$$\begin{array}{r} 78 \\ 29 \\ +65 \\ \hline \end{array}$$

a. 152
b. 172
c. 162
d. none of these

4. Subtract.

$$\begin{array}{r} 503 \\ -257 \\ \hline \end{array}$$

a. 256
b. 254
c. 244
d. 246

5. How much money?

1 dollar
1 half-dollar
1 quarter
1 dime
1 nickel
2 pennies

a. \$.92
b. \$1.83
c. \$1.92
d. \$1.97

6. Multiply.

$$\begin{array}{r} 5 \\ \times 7 \\ \hline \end{array}$$

a. 25
b. 30
c. 45
d. none of these

7. Divide.

$4 \overline{)36}$

a. 7
b. 9
c. 8
d. none of these

8. Divide.

$3 \overline{)29}$

a. 9 R1
b. 8 R1
c. 7 R2
d. 9 R2

9. What fraction of the balls are red?

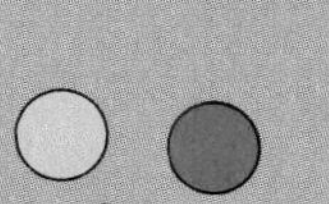

a. $\frac{2}{5}$
b. $\frac{3}{5}$
c. $\frac{3}{3}$
d. $\frac{2}{3}$

10. What is the perimeter?

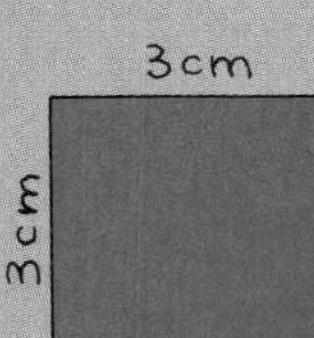

a. 3 cm
b. 6 cm
c. 9 cm
d. 12 cm

11. 27 apples
15 lemons
32 oranges
How many more oranges than lemons?

a. 17
b. 12
c. 5
d. none of these

12. 20 people in a bus
4 people in a car
How many more people in the bus?

a. 16
b. 5
c. 24
d. none of these

12

Multiplication and Division

Roberta keeps her marble collection in 4 jars. There are 96 marbles in each jar. How many marbles are there altogether?

Name ____________________

Multiplying a 2- or 3-digit number

3 sets of 12

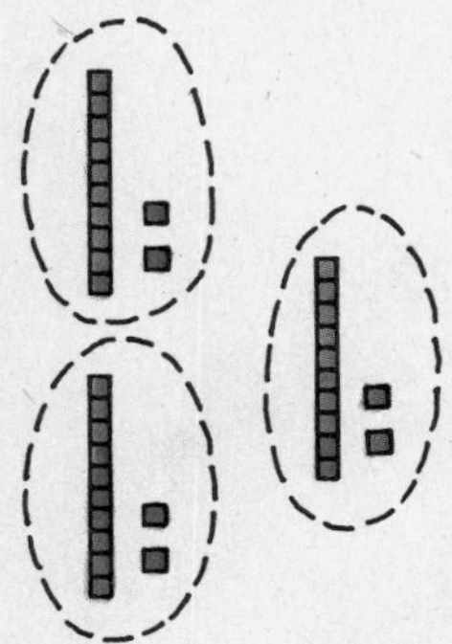

Tens	Ones
1	2
	× 3

Step 1. Multiply the ones.

Tens	Ones
	2
	× 3
	6

Step 2. Multiply the tens.

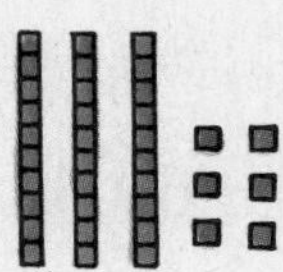

Tens	Ones
1	2
	× 3
3	6

There is a total of 36 blocks.

READY OR NOT?

Multiply.

1. 6 ×7 = 42	2. 5 ×5 = 25	3. 9 ×5 = 45
4. 6 ×5 = 30	5. 3 ×7 = 21	6. 4 ×4 = 16
7. 3 ×8 = 24	8. 8 ×9 = 72	9. 6 ×4 = 24
10. 4 ×7 = 28	11. 6 ×8 = 48	12. 3 ×9 = 27

Divide.

13. 3) 27 = 9	14. 5) 35 = 7
15. 5) 40 = 8	16. 4) 32 = 8
17. 4) 36 = 9	18. 6) 36 = 6
19. 8) 64 = 7	20. 6) 54 = 8
21. 6) 24 = 4	22. 7) 63 = 9
23. 7) 56 = 8	24. 6) 48 = 8

EXERCISES

Multiply.

1. 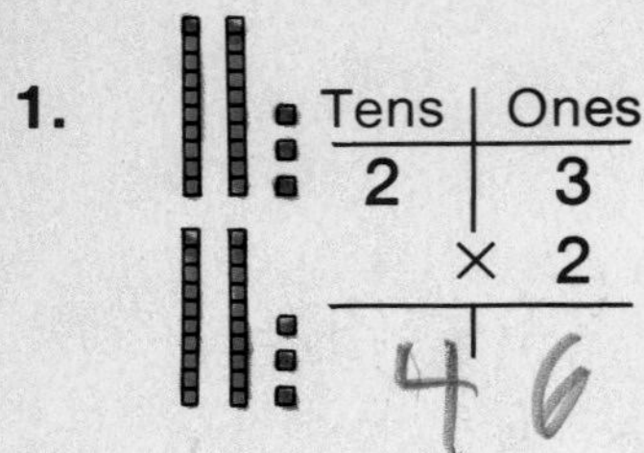

Tens	Ones
2	3
	× 2

2.

Tens	Ones
1	0
	× 3

3.

Tens	Ones
2	1
	× 3

4. 32×3	**5.** 22×3	**6.** 10×6	**7.** 20×3	**8.** 22×2	**9.** 21×4
10. 11×4	**11.** 12×2	**12.** 42×2	**13.** 22×4	**14.** 14×2	**15.** 13×3
16. 23×3	**17.** 21×3	**18.** 11×7	**19.** 41×2	**20.** 12×3	**21.** 11×9
22. 18×0	**23.** 34×2	**24.** 12×4	**25.** 10×8	**26.** 43×1	**27.** 40×2

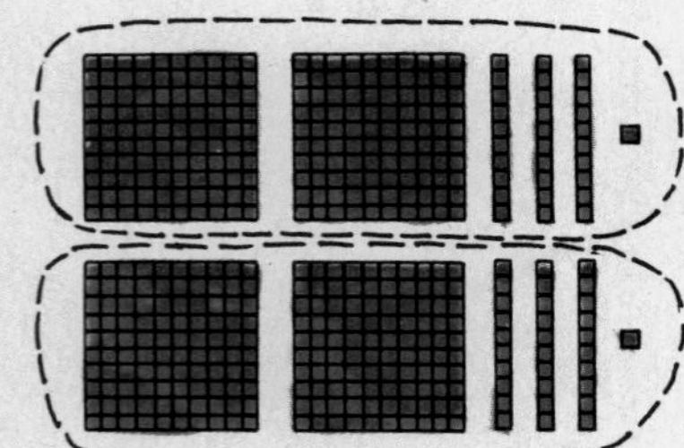

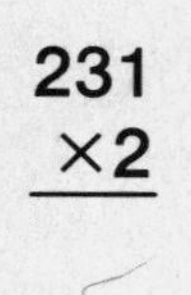

$$\begin{array}{r} 231 \\ \times 2 \\ \hline \end{array}$$

Follow these steps to multiply 231 by 2.

Multiply the ones.	Multiply the tens.	Multiply the hundreds.
$\begin{array}{r} 231 \\ \times 2 \\ \hline 2 \end{array}$	$\begin{array}{r} 231 \\ \times 2 \\ \hline 62 \end{array}$	$\begin{array}{r} 231 \\ \times 2 \\ \hline 462 \end{array}$

Multiply.

28. 181×0	**29.** 234×2	**30.** 112×4	**31.** 100×8	**32.** 432×1	**33.** 403×2

Name ____

Multiplying with regrouping

Sometimes you will need to regroup when you multiply.

Step 1. Multiply in the ones column.

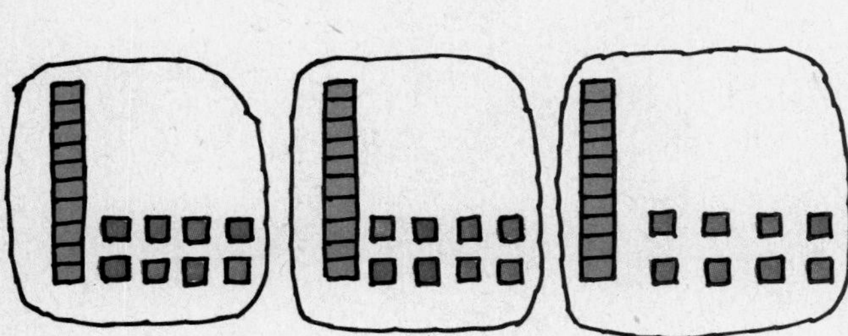

$$\begin{array}{r} 18 \\ \times 3 \\ \hline \end{array}$$

Step 2. Regroup 24 ones.

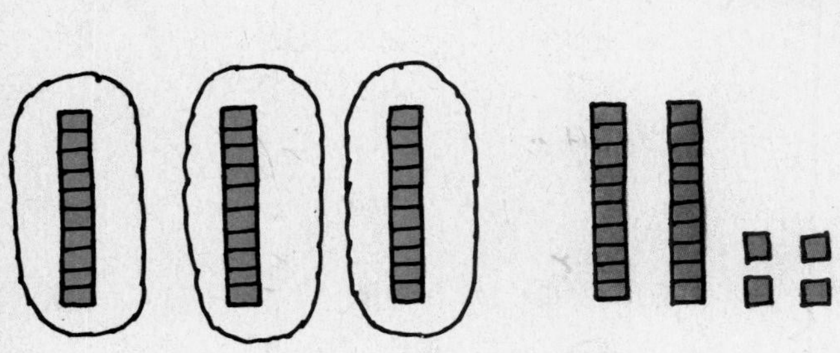

$$\begin{array}{r} {\scriptstyle 2} \\ 18 \\ \times 3 \\ \hline 4 \end{array}$$

Step 3. Multiply the tens. Then add the two tens that were regrouped.

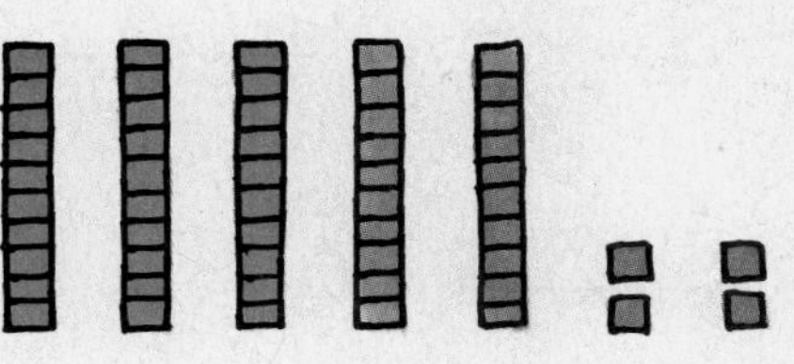

$$\begin{array}{r} {\scriptstyle 2} \\ 18 \\ \times 3 \\ \hline 54 \end{array}$$

EXERCISES

Complete.

1. $\overset{1}{24} \times 4 = \square 6$	**2.** $\overset{2}{19} \times 3 = \square 7$	**3.** $\overset{1}{25} \times 2 = \square 0$	**4.** $\overset{3}{19} \times 4 = \square 6$	**5.** $\overset{1}{37} \times 2 = \square 4$	**6.** $\overset{1}{26} \times 3 = \square 8$

Multiply.

7. 14 ×4	**8.** 35 ×2	**9.** 27 ×3	**10.** 18 ×4	**11.** 25 ×3	**12.** 14 ×7
13. 36 ×2	**14.** 39 ×2	**15.** 17 ×3	**16.** 16 ×3	**17.** 17 ×5	**18.** 16 ×6
19. 16¢ ×4	**20.** 12¢ ×7	**21.** 24¢ ×3	**22.** 28¢ ×3	**23.** 38¢ ×2	**24.** 18¢ ×5
25. 13¢ ×6	**26.** 27¢ ×2	**27.** 48¢ ×2	**28.** 19¢ ×5	**29.** 17¢ ×4	**30.** 29¢ ×3

Complete.

31. If 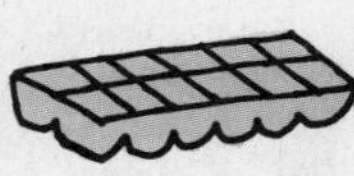 holds 12 eggs, then 8  hold ______ eggs.

32. If  costs 15¢, then 5  cost ______ ¢.

33. If  has 25 m of string, then 3  have ______ m of string.

34. If  fills 4 glasses, then 15 fill ______ glasses.

Name ____________________

Multiplication with two regroupings

Sometimes we get hundreds when we multiply the tens.

Here is another example.

Step 1.

$$\begin{array}{r} \overset{1}{5}4 \\ \times\ 4 \\ \hline 6 \end{array}$$

Step 2.

$$\begin{array}{r} \overset{1}{5}4 \\ \times\ 4 \\ \hline 216 \end{array}$$

EXERCISES

Multiply.

1. 20 ×8	**2.** 30 ×4	**3.** 40 ×5	**4.** 32 ×4	**5.** 51 ×6	**6.** 43 ×3
7. 84 ×2	**8.** 70 ×7	**9.** 74 ×2	**10.** 40 ×9	**11.** 83 ×3	**12.** 31 ×8
13. 50 ×4	**14.** 67 ×6	**15.** 74 ×7	**16.** 66 ×5	**17.** 78 ×5	**18.** 36 ×3

Multiply.

19. 73 × 8
20. 89 × 6
21. 45 × 3
22. 85 × 4
23. 37 × 5
24. 55 × 4

25. 79 × 6
26. 54 × 6
27. 88 × 6
28. 70 × 3
29. 87 × 7
30. 76 × 9

Here's how to multiply with money.

Multiply.	Write a $ and . in the answer.
$.93 × 5 = 465	$.93 × 5 = $4.65

31. $.36 × 2
32. $.12 × 7
33. $.25 × 3
34. $.43 × 2
35. $.15 × 6
36. $.29 × 3

37. $.58 × 8
38. $.46 × 3
39. $.86 × 7
40. $.69 × 8
41. $.46 × 5
42. $.77 × 8

Challenge!

Find a way to get the answer by pushing each marked key once.

43. _ × 4 =

44. ______________

45. ______________

387 | 9 | 4 | × | 3 | =

Name ____________________

Problem Solving Application

$0.50 $2 $7 $8 $24

Kate wants an aquarium and some fish. She has to decide whether she can pay for them. The facts are listed below.

- The aquarium costs $24.
- The fish cost $8.
- The fish food will cost $0.50 a month.
- Kate's parents will pay $\frac{1}{2}$ the cost of the aquarium and fish.
- Kate's parents will lend her the other $\frac{1}{2}$ for 4 months.
- Kate's allowance is $7 per month.
- Each month she saves $2 of her allowance.

Could Kate buy the aquarium and fish? The answers to these questions will help you decide.

1. How much would the aquarium and fish cost? ______
2. How much would Kate owe her parents? ______
3. How much would she have to pay her parents each month? ______
4. How much would the fish food cost each month? ______
5. What is the total that Kate should pay each month? ______

Computers help us shop

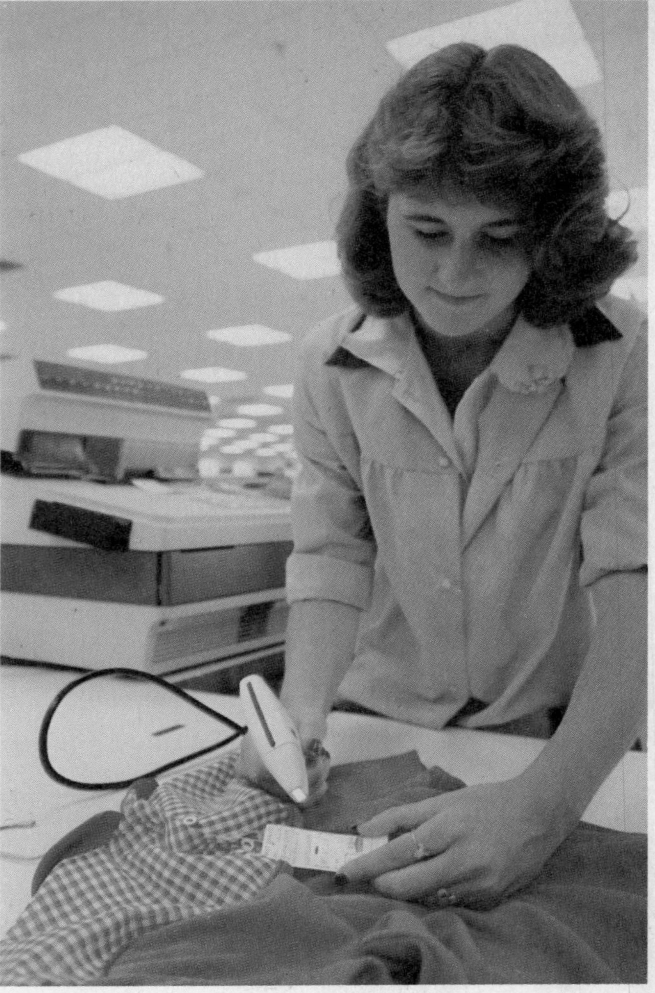

The clerk told Brad that a computer found the cost of the things that he bought. When Brad bought

the clerk told the computer to find the price of 2 jars of paste at $.39 a jar. The computer found the total price and printed it on a paper tape.

2 jars at $.39 each total

EXERCISES

Complete these tapes.

1. 

2. 

3. 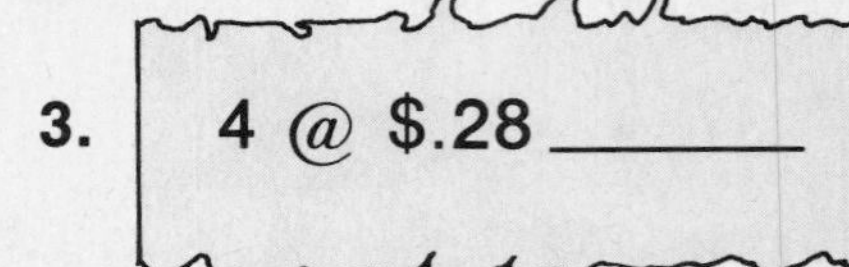

4. 6 @ $.72 ______

5. 

6. 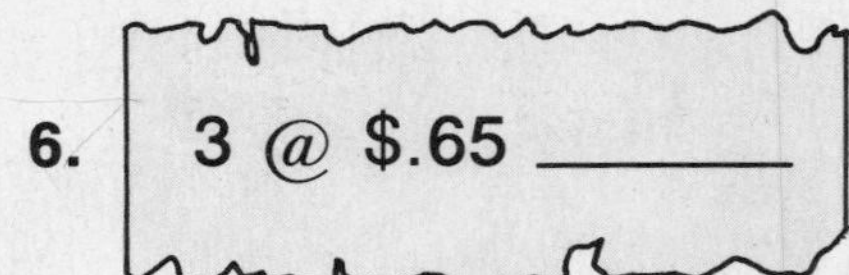

7. 8 @ $.24 ______

8. 9 @ $.18 ______

9. 7 @ $.49 ______

Name ______________________________

Division

The example shows how to divide larger numbers.

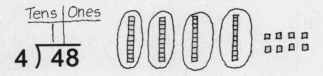

$4\overline{)48}$

Step 1. Divide the tens. Put 1 ten in each set.

Tens | Ones

1

$4\overline{)48}$

Step 2. Divide the ones. Put 2 ones in each set.

Tens | Ones

1 | 2

$4\overline{)48}$

EXERCISES

Divide.

Tens | Ones

1. $2\overline{)24}$

Tens | Ones

2. $2\overline{)42}$

Tens | Ones

3. $3\overline{)36}$

Tens | Ones

4. $3\overline{)60}$

Divide.

5. 2) 62 6. 2) 44 7. 4) 88 8. 4) 84 9. 2) 42

10. 2) 46 11. 3) 39 12. 3) 63 13. 2) 22 14. 3) 90

15. 3) 93 16. 2) 24 17. 4) 80 18. 3) 33 19. 3) 36

20. 2) 26 21. 3) 60 22. 3) 66 23. 4) 40 24. 2) 48

25. 3) 30 26. 2) 40 27. 4) 44 28. 2) 20 29. 2) 28

30. 6) 66 31. 8) 80 32. 5) 55 33. 7) 77 34. 5) 50

Problem Solving

35. 48¢
4 children
How much money for
each child? _______

36. 24 pennies
2 children
How many pennies for
each child? _______

37. 36¢ for 3 balloons
How much for 1 balloon? _______

38. 36¢ for 1 balloon
How much for 3 balloons? _______

39. 69 balloons
3 balloons in each bag
How many bags?
____

40. 69 balloons in two bags
3 balloons in one of the bags
How many balloons in the
other bag? _______

Challenge!

Give the missing number.

41.

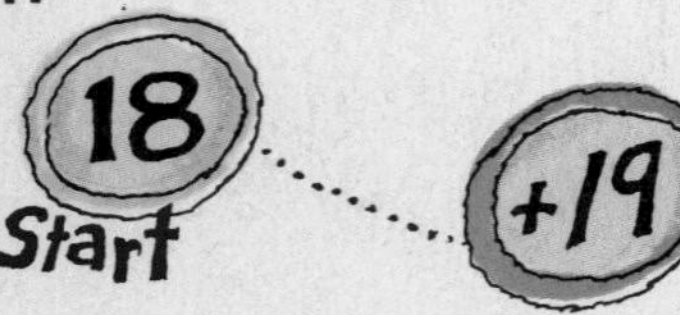

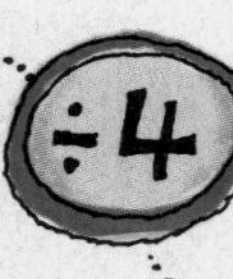

×7

÷4

End

Name ____________________

More about division

Divide.

$3\overline{)51}$

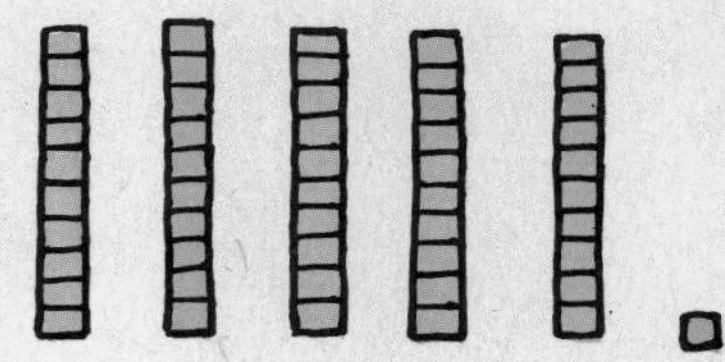

Step 1. Divide the tens. Subtract.

	Tens	Ones
1 ten in each set ➡	1	
	$3\overline{)5}$	1
used 3 tens ➡	−3	
2 tens left over ➡	2	

Step 2. Regroup the left-over tens.

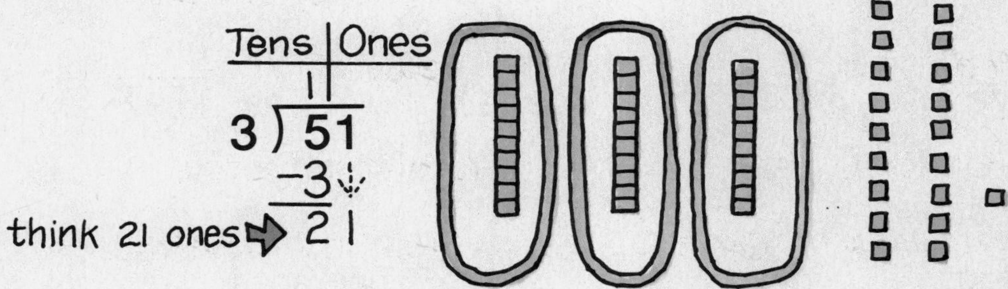

Step 3. Divide the ones. Subtract.

	Tens	Ones
	1	7
	$3\overline{)5}$	1
	−3	
	2	1
used 21 ones ➡	−2	1
0 ones left over ➡		0

EXERCISES

Complete each division.

1. $3\overline{)45}$
2. $4\overline{)56}$
3. $5\overline{)85}$
4. $3\overline{)81}$
5. $4\overline{)72}$
6. $6\overline{)84}$
7. $2\overline{)94}$
8. $3\overline{)87}$
9. $6\overline{)78}$
10. $4\overline{)68}$

Divide.

11. $3\overline{)45}$
12. $5\overline{)65}$
13. $2\overline{)58}$
14. $5\overline{)70}$
15. $4\overline{)52}$
16. $6\overline{)96}$
17. $3\overline{)84}$
18. $4\overline{)76}$
19. $3\overline{)57}$
20. $6\overline{)72}$
21. $2\overline{)38}$
22. $5\overline{)95}$
23. $2\overline{)74}$
24. $5\overline{)60}$
25. $6\overline{)90}$
26. $3\overline{)78}$
27. $4\overline{)96}$
28. $3\overline{)75}$
29. $4\overline{)92}$
30. $2\overline{)56}$

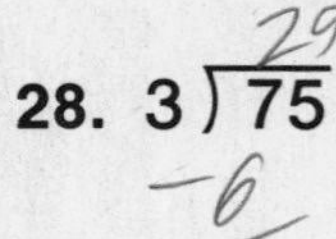

Problem Solving

31. 72 eggs
6 eggs in each package

How many packages? _______

32. 56 packages
4 sweet rolls per package

How many sweet rolls? _______

Challenge!

Guess my number.

33. If you divide my number by 6, you get 13.

____

34. If you multiply my number by 4, you get 92.

____

Name ________________________________

Practice

C	H	R	I	A	V	E	U	M	S	N
27	85	177	273	324	469	576	1135	1206	1240	1371

First give the number.
Then give the letter.

302 −217	36 ×9	173 +296	72 ×8
85			
H			

54 ×6

495 +876	700 −427	3) 81	277 +299

547 +693	389 +746	599 +607	783 +423	801 −225	926 −749

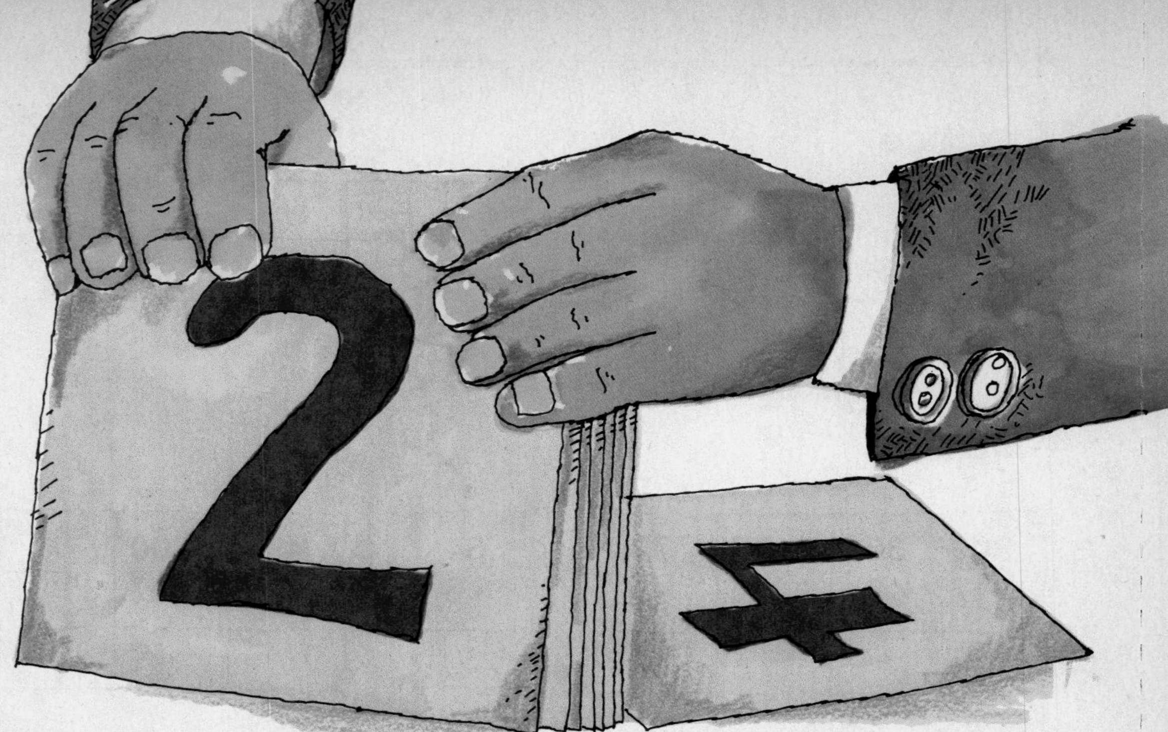

Which product is greater?

1.  

2.  

3. 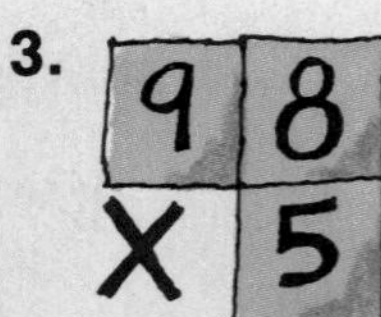 

4.  

5. **Play this game.**
   a. Draw a table like this:
   b. As your teacher picks a number card from 0 through 9, write the digit in any place in your table.
   c. After three digits have been picked, multiply.
   d. The player with the greatest product wins!

★ 6. Use your game table. How many different ways can you arrange these three digits? ________

 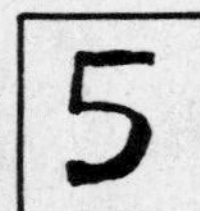 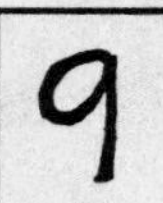

★ 7. Did you find an arrangement where the product was 245?

____

Name ______________________________

Chapter Checkup

Multiply. [pages 330–335, 342–343]

1. 24×2
2. 13×3
3. 21×4
4. 11×6
5. 43×2
6. 27×3
7. 48×2
8. 19×5
9. 37×2
10. 18×4
11. 65×5
12. 58×4
13. 76×8
14. 94×9
15. 87×7

Divide. [pages 338–342]

16. $2\overline{)42}$
17. $4\overline{)48}$
18. $3\overline{)93}$
19. $5\overline{)55}$
20. $3\overline{)69}$
21. $2\overline{)72}$
22. $2\overline{)54}$
23. $3\overline{)72}$
24. $5\overline{)85}$
25. $3\overline{)48}$
26. $4\overline{)52}$
27. $5\overline{)65}$
28. $3\overline{)51}$
29. $2\overline{)94}$
30. $4\overline{)68}$

Solve. [pages 336–337]

31. 

How much will 9 stamps cost?

______

32. 

How much will 4 boxes weigh?

______

33. 56 erasers in a box
7 erasers in another box

How many erasers? ______

34. 72 belts
3 belts in each box

How many boxes? ______

Chapter Project

COLLECTING DATA

1. **a.** How many minutes of the school day do you spend eating lunch? ______
   b. How many minutes do you spend eating lunch in a school week? ______
2. **a.** How many minutes do you spend on the playground during a school day? ______
   b. How many minutes do you spend on the playground during a school week? ______
3. How many minutes do you spend eating in a day? ______ In a week? ______
4. How many minutes do you spend sleeping in a week? ______ In 4 weeks? ______

Name ____________________

Chapter Review

Multiply.

1. 32 × 3
2. 42 × 2
3. 22 × 4

Example: 48 × 2 = 96 (regroup 1)

4. 37 × 2
5. 28 × 3
6. 19 × 4

Example: 76 × 4 = 304 (regroup 2)

7. 85 × 5
8. 74 × 7
9. 96 × 6

Divide.

Example: 3) 96 = 32

10. 4) 48
11. 2) 86
12. 3) 63

Example: 3) 57 = 19
-3
27
-27
0

13. 4) 96
14. 3) 84
15. 5) 95

Chapter Challenge

COMBINATIONS

Choose a party costume!
Here are your choices:

1. How many different costumes can you make? _____
2. Use 3 letters to name each costume. ________________

____
3. If there were 3 hats, how many different costumes could you make? _____

Hint:

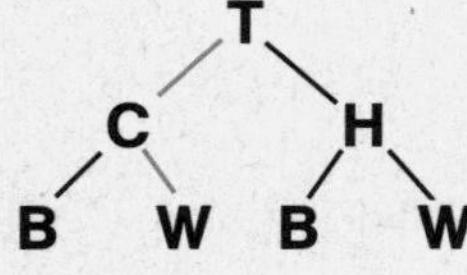

The red path is Dan's choice. (T, C, W)

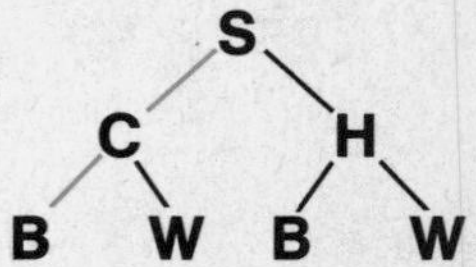

The blue path is Lisa's choice. (S, C, B)

Name ____________________

Cumulative Checkup

STANDARDIZED FORMAT

Give the correct letter.

1. Which number is greatest?
   a. 3826
   b. 3854
   c. 3796
   d. 2978

2. Subtract.
   624
   −278
   a. 356
   b. 456
   c. 454
   d. 346

3. What time is it?
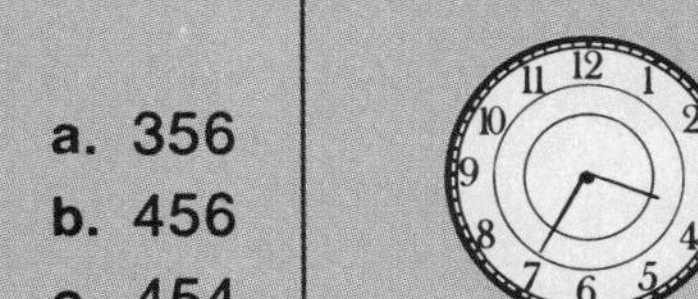
   a. 3:35
   b. 7:18
   c. 4:35
   d. none of these

4. Multiply.
   4
   ×9
   a. 32
   b. 28
   c. 24
   d. none of these

5. Divide.
   5) 38
   a. 3 R7
   b. 6 R3
   c. 8 R3
   d. 7 R3

6. Complete.
   $\frac{1}{4}$ of 12 = ?
   a. 6
   b. 8
   c. 3
   d. 2

7. How long is the pin?
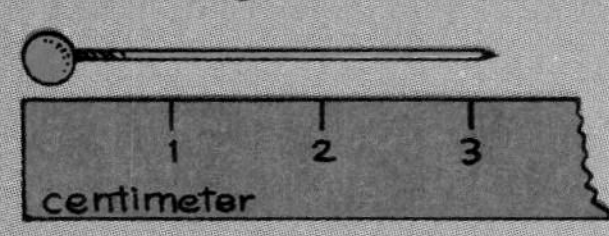

   a. about 2 cm
   b. about 4 cm
   c. about 3 cm
   d. none of these

8. What is the area?
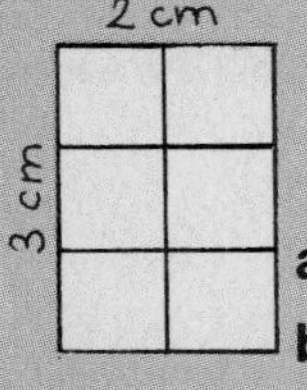

   a. 5 cm
   b. 5 square cm
   c. 6 square cm
   d. none of these

9. Which triangle is congruent to 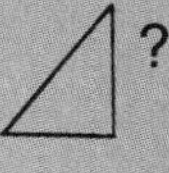 ?
   a. 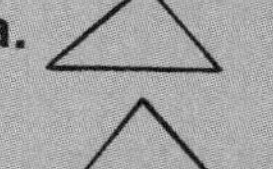 b.
   c. d. 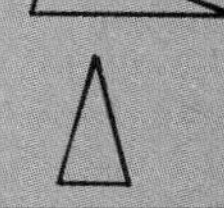

10. Which figure has no line of symmetry?
   a. 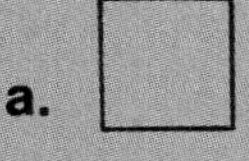 b. 
   c. d.

11. 32 bags
   4 pens in each bag
   How many pens in all?
   a. 8 b. 28
   c. 36 d. none of these

12. Ella had $5. She bought a book for $2.25. How much money did she have left?
   a. $2.25 b. $2.75
   c. $3.25 d. $3.75

RESOURCES

Name ______________________________

GETTING READY FOR COMPUTER PROGRAMMING

Using commands in programs

You write a **program** to tell the boat where to move. The directions you write in the program are called **commands.**

1. Use your finger to follow the path on the map.

PROGRAM CLIFF/TINY
BEGIN CLIFF BAY
E1
N3
W1
END TINY COVE

a. Where did you begin? Cliff Bay

b. Where did you end? Tiny Cove

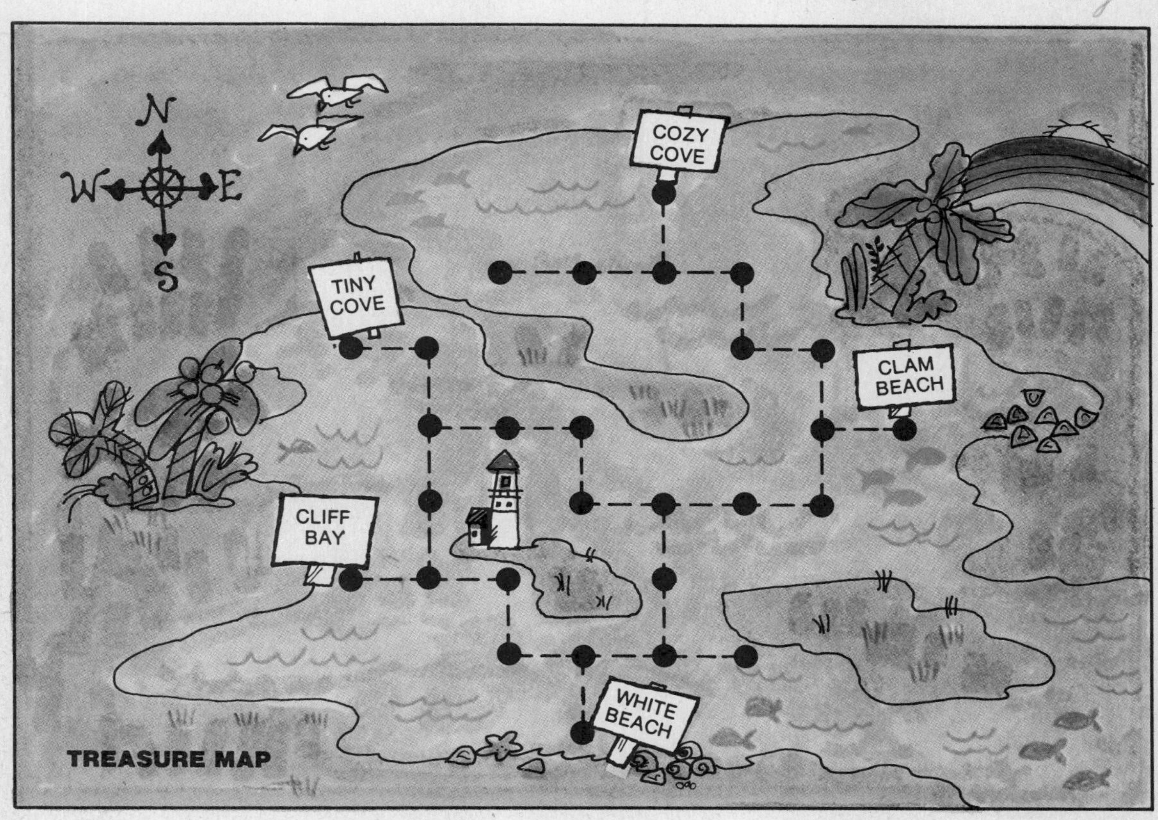

Use your finger to follow the path on the map.
Complete each program.

2. PROGRAM CLIFF/ ______
BEGIN CLIFF BAY
E2
S1
E1
S1
END White Beach

3. PROGRAM WHITE/ ______
BEGIN WHITE BEACH
N1
E1
N2
E2
N1
E1
END ______

4. PROGRAM CLAM/ ______
BEGIN CLAM BEACH
W1
S1
W3
N1
W2
S2
W1
END Cliff Bay

5. PROGRAM TINY/ ______
BEGIN TINY COVE
E1
S1
E2
S1
E1
S2
W1
S1
END ______

6. PROGRAM COZY/CLAM
BEGIN COZY COVE
S1
East 1
South 1
East 1
South 1
East 1
END CLAM BEACH

★7.

Write programs for two ways to go from Clam Beach to Cliff Bay.

Name____

New commands—take and leave

Tell the boat to pick up a treasure by using the command TAKE TREASURE. Tell the boat to leave the treasure with the command LEAVE TREASURE.

The treasure boat can carry only one treasure at a time!

1. Use your finger to follow the path on the map.

PROGRAM SLEEPY / ROCKY
BEGIN SLEEPY BAY
N2
E1
N1
TAKE TREASURE
N1
E1
LEAVE TREASURE
END ROCKY COVE

a. Where did you begin?____________

b. Where did you leave the treasure?____________

c. Where did you end?____________

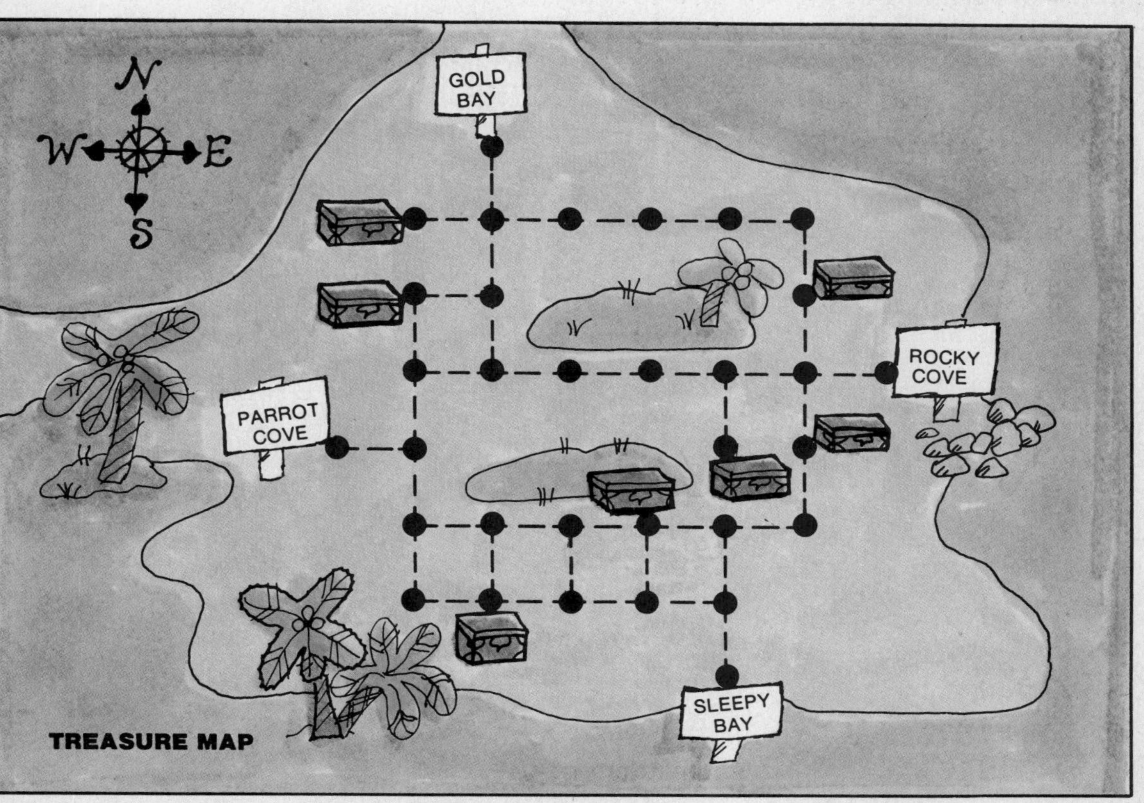

Name ____________________

Use your finger to follow the path on the map. Then answer the questions.

2. PROGRAM SLEEPY/GOLD
BEGIN SLEEPY BAY
N2
E1
N3
TAKE TREASURE
N1
W4
N1
LEAVE TREASURE
END GOLD BAY

a. Where did you begin? __________

b. Where did you leave the treasure? __________

c. Where did you end? __________

3. PROGRAM SLEEPY/ROCKY
BEGIN SLEEPY BAY
N2
W1
TAKE TREASURE
E2
N2
E1
LEAVE TREASURE
END ROCKY COVE

a. Where did you begin? __________

b. Where did you leave the treasure? __________

c. Where did you end? __________

Complete each program. Follow the shortest path.

4. PROGRAM PARROT/GOLD
BEGIN PARROT COVE
E1
N2
____
____
____
LEAVE TREASURE
END GOLD BAY

5. PROGRAM SLEEPY/PARROT
BEGIN SLEEPY BAY
N1
W3
____
W1
____
____
LEAVE TREASURE
END PARROT COVE

★**6.**

Write a program for a path from Sleepy Bay to Parrot Cove that does not go over any treasure.

Name ____

New command—jump

You can use the command JUMP to make the treasure boat jump over an island in its path.

1. Use your finger to follow the path on the map. Tell where the treasure boat is going.

PROGRAM SHELL/ __________
E1
JUMP N
N1
E1
N1
END ______________________________

The treasure boat can jump over any island in its path. Be sure you tell the boat which way to jump!

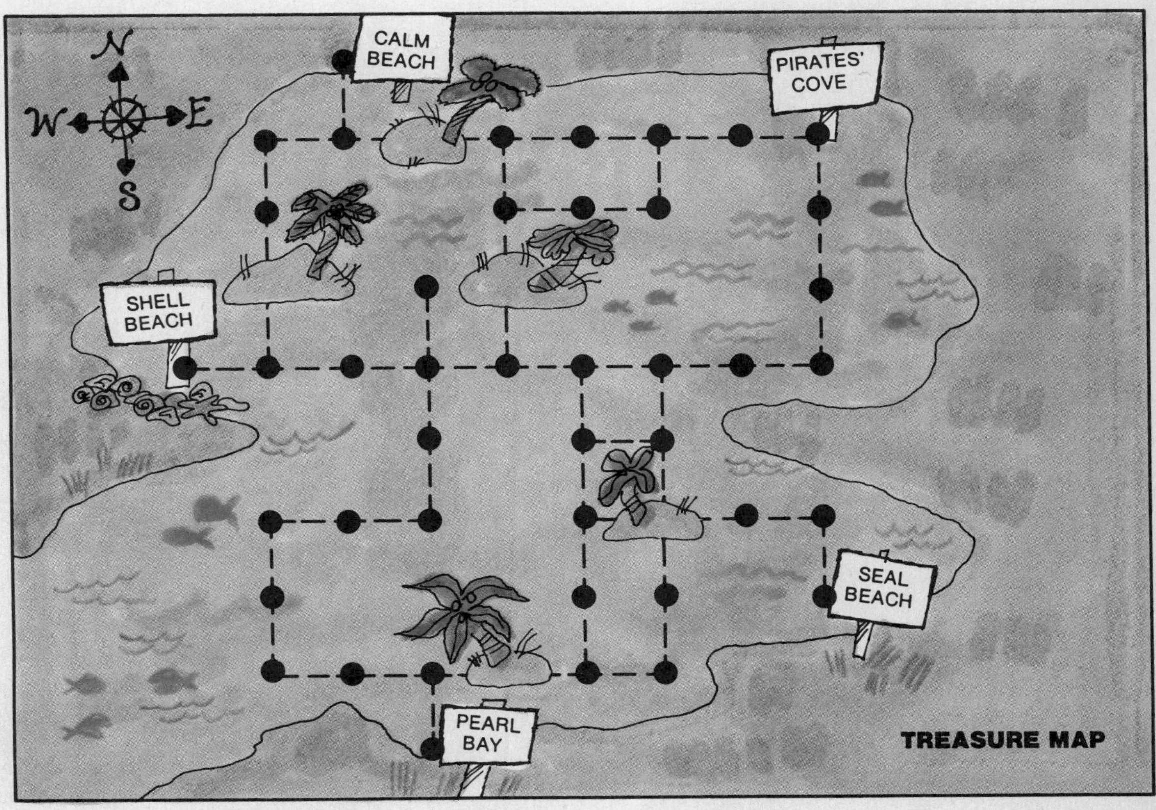

Name____________________

Use your finger to follow the path on the map.
Tell where the treasure boat is going.

2. PROGRAM PIRATES' / ________
BEGIN PIRATES' COVE
S3
W3
S2
JUMP E
E1
S1
END ________

3. PROGRAM CALM/ ________
BEGIN CALM BEACH
S1
JUMP E
S1
JUMP S
E1
S4
JUMP W
S1
END ________

Complete each program.

4. PROGRAM PIRATES' / CALM
BEGIN PIRATES' COVE
W4
____
____
END CALM BEACH

5. PROGRAM CALM / SHELL
BEGIN CALM BEACH
S1
W1
____
____
____
END SHELL BEACH

6. PROGRAM SEAL / CALM
BEGIN SEAL BEACH
N1
W1
____
____
E3
____
____
____
____
END CALM BEACH

★7.

Write programs for three ways to get from Calm Beach to Pearl Bay jumping two islands.

Name____

New command—go back

In this lesson the treasure boat will always begin at Home Port. You can use the command GO BACK to make the treasure boat return to Home Port along the same path.

The treasure boat can turn around and go back along its path to Home Port.

Use your finger to follow the path on the map.

1. PROGRAM TREASURE 1
   BEGIN HOME PORT
   N3
   JUMP E
   E1
   S2
   W1
   TAKE TREASURE
   GO BACK
   LEAVE TREASURE
   END HOME PORT

a. Which treasure did you pick up?______

b. Where did you leave it?______________

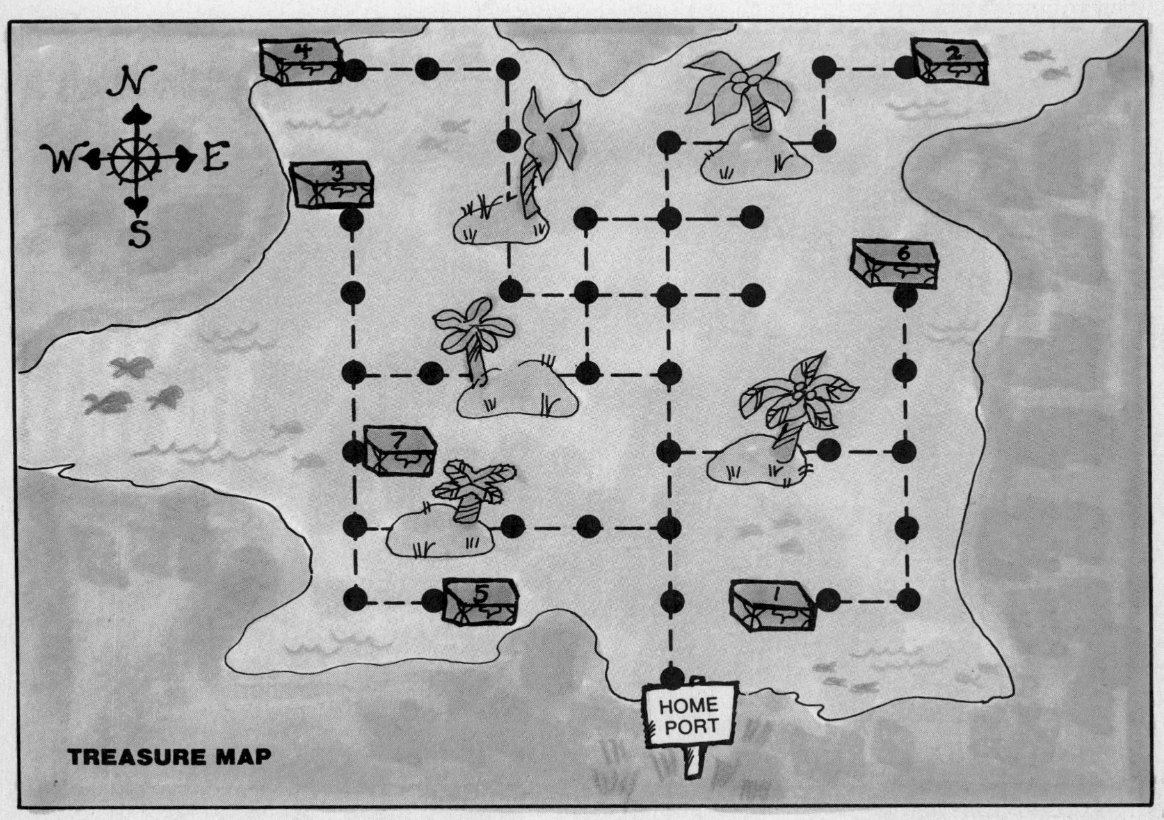

Complete each program.

2. PROGRAM TREASURE 2
BEGIN HOME PORT
N7
____
____
____
TAKE TREASURE
____
LEAVE TREASURE
END HOME PORT

3. PROGRAM TREASURE 3
BEGIN HOME PORT
N4
____
____
____
____
____
____
LEAVE TREASURE
END HOME PORT

4. PROGRAM TREASURE 4
BEGIN HOME PORT
N5
____
____
____
____
____
____
LEAVE TREASURE
END HOME PORT

5. PROGRAM TREASURE 5
____
____
____
____
____
____
____
____
LEAVE TREASURE
____

6. PROGRAM TREASURE 6
____
____
____
____
____
____
____
LEAVE TREASURE
____

★7. Write two different programs for finding Treasure 7 and bringing it to Home Port.

Name ______________________________

SKILL TEST

1	Basic addition facts, sums to 10	5 +4	3 +7	8 +2	2 +6	3 +4
2	Basic addition facts, sums to 18	9 +5	6 +7	9 +8	6 +6	8 +7
3	Basic subtraction facts, sums to 10	10 −9	8 −3	7 −4	10 −7	9 −5
4	Basic subtraction facts, sums to 18	16 −7	11 −9	14 −8	13 −5	15 −6
5	Addition, no regrouping	48 +21	165 +324	3841 +2044	2607 +5322	
6	Addition, regrouping ones to tens	57 +24	38 +52	268 +127	4825 +1138	
7	Addition, one regrouping	23 +95	52 +38	276 +183	3457 +3812	
8	Addition, more than one regrouping	27 +96	35 +68	243 +689	1521 +5899	
9	Subtraction, no regrouping	57 −23	246 −25	385 −163	5834 −2813	

10	Subtraction, regrouping tens to ones	$\begin{array}{r}83\\-57\\\hline\end{array}$	$\begin{array}{r}46\\-19\\\hline\end{array}$	$\begin{array}{r}324\\-106\\\hline\end{array}$	$\begin{array}{r}4832\\-1729\\\hline\end{array}$	
11	Subtraction, one regrouping	$\begin{array}{r}227\\-183\\\hline\end{array}$	$\begin{array}{r}542\\-81\\\hline\end{array}$	$\begin{array}{r}324\\-106\\\hline\end{array}$	$\begin{array}{r}4932\\-1929\\\hline\end{array}$	
12	Subtraction, more than one regrouping	$\begin{array}{r}163\\-87\\\hline\end{array}$	$\begin{array}{r}243\\-168\\\hline\end{array}$	$\begin{array}{r}3442\\-1651\\\hline\end{array}$	$\begin{array}{r}8324\\-685\\\hline\end{array}$	
13	Multiplication, basic facts through 5 × 9	$\begin{array}{r}4\\\times 3\\\hline\end{array}$	$\begin{array}{r}4\\\times 8\\\hline\end{array}$	$\begin{array}{r}5\\\times 6\\\hline\end{array}$	$\begin{array}{r}5\\\times 9\\\hline\end{array}$	$\begin{array}{r}3\\\times 7\\\hline\end{array}$
14	Division, basic facts through 45 ÷ 9	$3\overline{)21}$	$4\overline{)36}$	$5\overline{)30}$	$2\overline{)16}$	$4\overline{)16}$

15 Fraction of a region

What fraction is red?

____ ____ ____

____ ____

16 Decimals

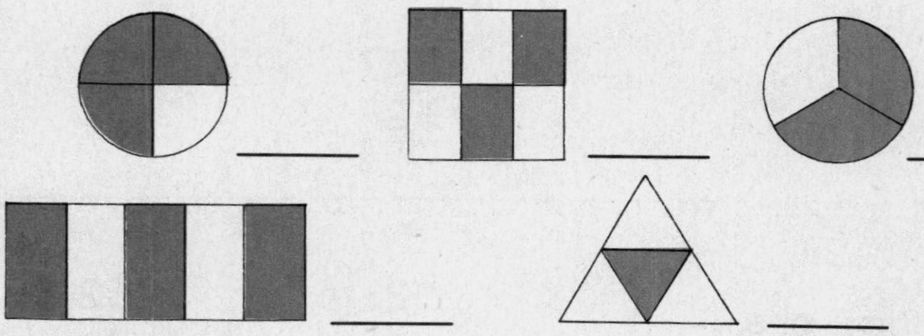

How much is blue? Write as a decimal.

____ ____

____ ____

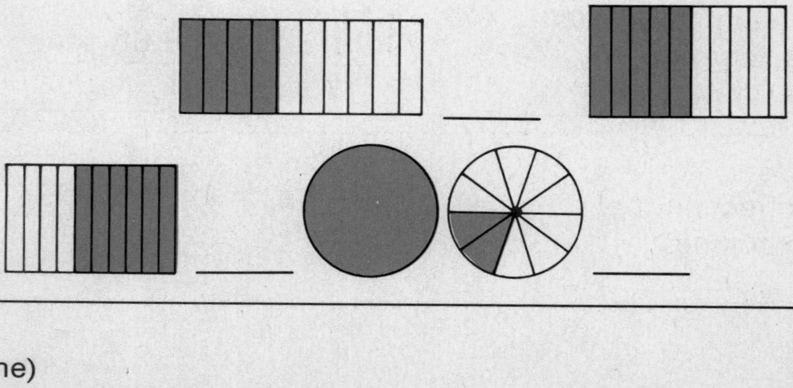

Name ____

	Skill					
17	Multiplication, basic facts through 9 × 9	$\begin{array}{r}8\\ \times 7\\ \hline\end{array}$	$\begin{array}{r}9\\ \times 9\\ \hline\end{array}$	$\begin{array}{r}6\\ \times 8\\ \hline\end{array}$	$\begin{array}{r}7\\ \times 7\\ \hline\end{array}$	$\begin{array}{r}9\\ \times 6\\ \hline\end{array}$
18	Division, basic facts to 81 ÷ 9	$9\overline{)63}$	$7\overline{)42}$	$6\overline{)36}$	$9\overline{)72}$	$8\overline{)64}$
19	Division with remainder	$2\overline{)13}$	$4\overline{)26}$	$5\overline{)24}$	$6\overline{)52}$	$3\overline{)19}$
20	Multiplication, no regrouping	$\begin{array}{r}20\\ \times 4\\ \hline\end{array}$	$\begin{array}{r}31\\ \times 3\\ \hline\end{array}$	$\begin{array}{r}203\\ \times 3\\ \hline\end{array}$	$\begin{array}{r}423\\ \times 2\\ \hline\end{array}$	
21	Multiplication, regrouping ones to tens	$\begin{array}{r}25\\ \times 2\\ \hline\end{array}$	$\begin{array}{r}13\\ \times 7\\ \hline\end{array}$	$\begin{array}{r}15\\ \times 5\\ \hline\end{array}$	$\begin{array}{r}36\\ \times 2\\ \hline\end{array}$	
22	Multiplication, regrouping tens to hundreds	$\begin{array}{r}31\\ \times 4\\ \hline\end{array}$	$\begin{array}{r}82\\ \times 3\\ \hline\end{array}$	$\begin{array}{r}42\\ \times 4\\ \hline\end{array}$	$\begin{array}{r}51\\ \times 4\\ \hline\end{array}$	
23	Multiplication, two regroupings	$\begin{array}{r}37\\ \times 3\\ \hline\end{array}$	$\begin{array}{r}44\\ \times 5\\ \hline\end{array}$	$\begin{array}{r}26\\ \times 5\\ \hline\end{array}$	$\begin{array}{r}57\\ \times 4\\ \hline\end{array}$	
24	Division, no regrouping	$3\overline{)63}$	$5\overline{)50}$	$2\overline{)48}$	$4\overline{)84}$	
25	Division, one regrouping	$2\overline{)52}$	$6\overline{)72}$	$4\overline{)76}$	$5\overline{)85}$	

EXTRA PRACTICE

Set 1 **Add.**

1. 4 +3 7	2. 2 +4	3. 4 +1	4. 1 +5	5. 5 +5	6. 3 +5	7. 5 +2
8. 7 +2	9. 0 +8	10. 6 +4	11. 2 +8	12. 6 +3	13. 5 +4	14. 7 +0
15. 0 +1	16. 1 +6	17. 6 +2	18. 3 +7	19. 4 +4	20. 2 +3	21. 1 +9
22. 4 +5	23. 5 +3	24. 2 +7	25. 8 +2	26. 3 +6	27. 2 +6	28. 7 +3

Set 2 **Give each sum.**

1. 6 + 8 = 14	2. 3 + 8 = ____	3. 6 + 6 = ____	4. 9 + 6 = ____
5. 5 + 6 = ____	6. 2 + 9 = ____	7. 7 + 9 = ____	8. 5 + 9 = ____
9. 8 + 8 = ____	10. 9 + 4 = ____	11. 5 + 8 = ____	12. 9 + 8 = ____
13. 9 + 3 = ____	14. 9 + 9 = ____	15. 7 + 7 = ____	16. 7 + 8 = ____
17. 8 + 7 = ____	18. 8 + 9 = ____	19. 6 + 9 = ____	20. 9 + 7 = ____

Set 3 **Give each missing addend.**

1. 7 + 9 = 16	2. 4 + ___ = 6	3. 5 + ___ = 8	4. 5 + ___ = 7
5. 3 + ___ = 12	6. 8 + ___ = 12	7. 3 + ___ = 4	8. 6 + ___ = 9
9. 9 + ___ = 13	10. 5 + ___ = 14	11. 9 + ___ = 17	12. 8 + ___ = 10
13. 5 + ___ = 13	14. 9 + ___ = 15	15. 6 + ___ = 12	16. 5 + ___ = 10
17. 7 + ___ = 16	18. 8 + ___ = 15	19. 9 + ___ = 18	20. 6 + ___ = 14

Name______________________________

Set 4 Add.

1. 5 4 +3 12	2. 3 6 +5	3. 1 4 +5	4. 3 3 +3	5. 2 4 +6	6. 6 2 +3	7. 4 4 +4
8. 7 1 +9	9. 2 3 +7	10. 6 3 +4	11. 2 5 +8	12. 3 6 +7	13. 2 5 +9	14. 1 2 +6
15. 4 5 +9	16. 3 3 +8	17. 8 0 +5	18. 4 3 +9	19. 1 6 +7	20. 4 4 +6	21. 3 5 +4

Set 5 Subtract.

1. 8 −3 5	2. 8 −5	3. 10 −2	4. 8 −8	5. 6 −3	6. 9 −4	7. 10 −3
8. 8 −6	9. 7 −5	10. 4 −2	11. 10 −5	12. 9 −6	13. 8 −2	14. 10 −7
15. 9 −5	16. 8 −0	17. 10 −6	18. 7 −4	19. 8 −4	20. 6 −0	21. 9 −9
22. 8 −7	23. 9 −3	24. 6 −5	25. 9 −7	26. 7 −3	27. 10 −4	28. 6 −4

Set 6 Subtract.

1. 11 − 2 = 9	2. 14 − 7 = ____	3. 16 − 8 = ____
4. 14 − 9 = ____	5. 13 − 6 = ____	6. 14 − 6 = ____
7. 12 − 8 = ____	8. 18 − 9 = ____	9. 16 − 9 = ____
10. 17 − 8 = ____	11. 11 − 8 = ____	12. 14 − 5 = ____
13. 13 − 4 = ____	14. 16 − 7 = ____	15. 17 − 9 = ____

Set 7 **Which letter in MATHEMATICS is**

1. first? M
2. fifth? ______
3. fourth? ______
4. tenth? ______
5. second? ______
6. seventh? ______
7. ninth? ______
8. third? ______

Which letter in ARITHMETIC is

9. third? ______
10. first? ______
11. fifth? ______
12. seventh? ______
13. ninth? ______
14. sixth? ______
15. tenth? ______
16. eighth? ______

Set 8 **How many?**

1. 

13

2. ______
3. ______
4. 

______

5. ______
6. ______
7. ______
8. ______
9. ______

Set 9 < or >?

1. 23 (<) 33
2. 18 ◯ 21
3. 29 ◯ 28
4. 32 ◯ 29
5. 30 ◯ 28
6. 29 ◯ 32
7. 41 ◯ 40
8. 43 ◯ 45
9. 52 ◯ 48
10. 45 ◯ 54
11. 86 ◯ 73
12. 65 ◯ 56
13. 171 ◯ 177
14. 193 ◯ 179
15. 184 ◯ 193
16. 168 ◯ 170
17. 190 ◯ 189
18. 194 ◯ 197
19. 180 ◯ 190
20. 178 ◯ 169
21. 183 ◯ 196

Name ______________________________

Set 10 **Round to the nearest ten.**

1. 37 40	2. 23	3. 19	4. 33	5. 89	6. 29
7. 53	8. 75	9. 48	10. 96	11. 83	12. 45
13. 11	14. 36	15. 81	16. 17	17. 65	18. 88
19. 73	20. 15	21. 55	22. 93	23. 25	24. 77
25. 38	26. 62	27. 94	28. 41	29. 68	30. 56

Set 11 **Round to the nearest hundred.**

1. 237 200	2. 465	3. 134	4. 350	5. 676	6. 590
7. 901	8. 880	9. 615	10. 875	11. 783	12. 219
13. 449	14. 650	15. 921	16. 150	17. 551	18. 821
19. 838	20. 178	21. 743	22. 936	23. 666	24. 364
25. 329	26. 632	27. 403	28. 536	29. 250	30. 795

Set 12 **How many?**

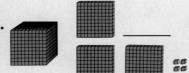

1. 1123

2. ______

3.  ______

4. 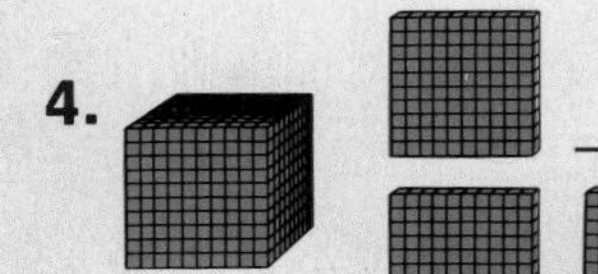 ______

5. 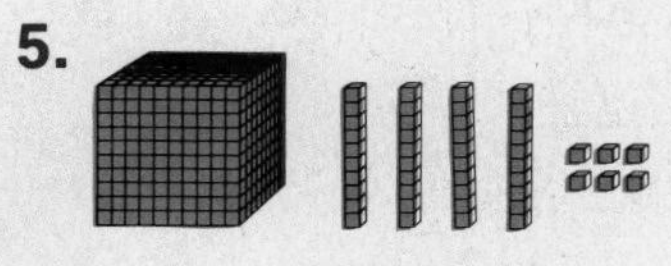 ______

6. 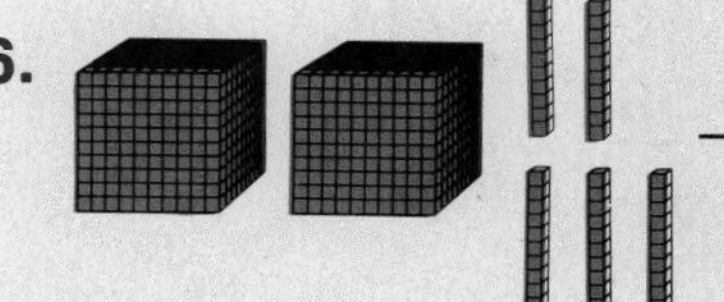 ______

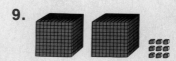

7.  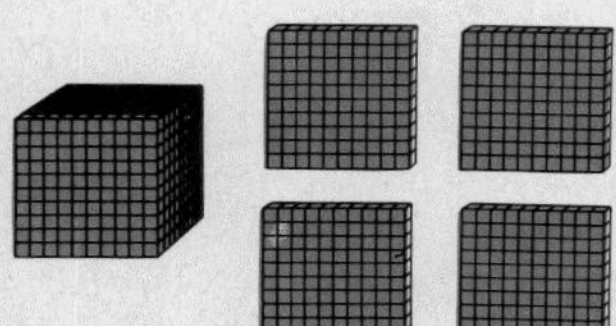 ______

8. 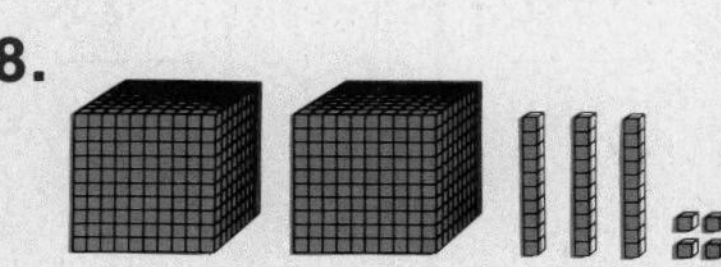 ______

9. ______

Set 13 < or >?

1. 57 ⊘ 58 (<)	2. 37 ◯ 47	3. 851 ◯ 723
4. 287 ◯ 290	5. 306 ◯ 320	6. 873 ◯ 598
7. 4326 ◯ 4321	8. 2806 ◯ 2811	9. 3954 ◯ 3754
10. 3000 ◯ 2999	11. 4573 ◯ 2188	12. 9999 ◯ 6103
13. 8035 ◯ 8053	14. 3872 ◯ 3794	15. 7389 ◯ 7398

Set 14 Add.

1. 65 + 29 = 94	2. 18 + 33	3. 46 + 28	4. 77 + 13	5. 74 + 16	6. 26 + 48
7. 28 + 37	8. 54 + 27	9. 36 + 36	10. 54 + 26	11. 39 + 46	12. 48 + 27
13. 53 + 29	14. 65 + 18	15. 39 + 26	16. 48 + 48	17. 75 + 17	18. 27 + 35

Set 15 Add.

1. 45 + 68 = 113	2. 57 + 74	3. 89 + 36	4. 43 + 57	5. 85 + 76	6. 87 + 45
7. 76 + 48	8. 73 + 48	9. 65 + 89	10. 55 + 85	11. 68 + 67	12. 58 + 75
13. 46 + 59	14. 78 + 49	15. 65 + 78	16. 75 + 97	17. 68 + 68	18. 85 + 29
19. 75 + 56	20. 68 + 39	21. 94 + 76	22. 39 + 88	23. 65 + 67	24. 83 + 98

Name ____________________

Set 16 **Add.**

1. 46 43 +62 151	2. 72 27 +92	3. 24 54 +83	4. 52 93 +66	5. 79 72 +71	6. 56 83 +65
7. 78 93 +41	8. 59 52 +56	9. 35 78 +48	10. 29 26 +97	11. 74 35 +89	12. 58 77 +46
13. 52 68 +29	14. 37 39 +18	15. 83 78 +35	16. 76 92 +48	17. 94 64 +57	18. 69 47 +85

Set 17 **Give each sum.**

1. 223 +158 381	2. 312 +179	3. 448 +325	4. 356 +437	5. 735 +149
6. 533 +227	7. 623 +48	8. 437 +316	9. 545 +225	10. 439 +238
11. 357 +429	12. 348 +548	13. 486 +405	14. 209 +369	15. 518 +239
16. 536 +249	17. 471 +119	18. 328 +328	19. 602 +158	20. 436 +436

Set 18 **Add.**

1. 356 +282 638	2. 567 +261	3. 143 +287	4. 354 +597	5. 443 +288
6. 563 +288	7. 137 +279	8. 479 +286	9. 351 +399	10. 567 +288
11. 438 +497	12. 356 +229	13. 374 +374	14. 627 +198	15. 463 +279
16. 507 +294	17. 355 +355	18. 756 +178	19. 464 +357	20. 693 +168

Set 19 **Add.**

1. 536 +877
2. 395 +866
3. 351 +871
4. 931 +486
5. 535 +778
6. 694 +844
7. 935 +826
8. 537 +867
9. 975 +846
10. 477 +888
11. 673 +857
12. 268 +732
13. 473 +867
14. 543 +295
15. 864 +939
16. 536 +728
17. 653 +653
18. 837 +695
19. 436 +987
20. 354 +859

Set 20 **Round each addend to the nearest ten. Estimate the sum.**

1. 27 +42
2. 42 +37
3. 53 +19
4. 34 +48
5. 19 +18
6. 48 +28
7. 62 +27
8. 59 +28
9. 38 +38
10. 65 +24
11. 50 +38
12. 28 +29
13. 45 +13
14. 31 +31
15. 48 +25
16. 61 +16
17. 22 +22
18. 29 +29

Set 21 **Add.**

1. 4647 +1984
2. 2753 +2654
3. 3543 +3987
4. 4873 +1544
5. 4357 +3463
6. 2743 +2541
7. 6325 +2144
8. 7385 +2194
9. 2358 +4577
10. 4803 +2877
11. 4293 +1689
12. 5280 +3286
13. 2578 +5967
14. 1926 +3487
15. 3746 +2975

Name____

Set 22 Give each difference.

1. 2 14 34 −18 16	**2.** 28 −19	**3.** 53 −28	**4.** 61 −44	**5.** 72 −36	**6.** 53 −47
7. 85 −46	**8.** 93 −59	**9.** 41 −16	**10.** 92 −18	**11.** 56 −18	**12.** 75 −36
13. 90 −35	**14.** 80 −56	**15.** 90 −72	**16.** 80 −42	**17.** 78 −29	**18.** 56 −19
19. 81 −18	**20.** 72 −36	**21.** 93 −27	**22.** 65 −48	**23.** 80 −37	**24.** 92 −65

Set 23 Subtract.

1. 4 14 543 −291 252	**2.** 628 −483	**3.** 383 −177	**4.** 423 −171	**5.** 570 −126
6. 381 −191	**7.** 653 −229	**8.** 674 −306	**9.** 403 −172	**10.** 503 −181
11. 826 −509	**12.** 938 −352	**13.** 504 −350	**14.** 782 −215	**15.** 611 −530
16. 747 −254	**17.** 629 −375	**18.** 853 −381	**19.** 571 −259	**20.** 983 −426

Set 24

1. 4 15 14 564 −298 266	**2.** 426 −197	**3.** 845 −396	**4.** 743 −645	**5.** 837 −238
6. 453 −177	**7.** 268 −199	**8.** 843 −586	**9.** 934 −655	**10.** 203 −97
11. 560 −281	**12.** 426 −129	**13.** 833 −427	**14.** 628 −199	**15.** 375 −199
16. 623 −246	**17.** 730 −453	**18.** 815 −167	**19.** 926 −359	**20.** 780 −297

Set 25

1. 704 −197	2. 603 −248	3. 601 −487	4. 805 −146	5. 203 −158
6. 402 −146	7. 302 −73	8. 604 −56	9. 908 −149	10. 603 −116
11. 304 −255	12. 800 −426	13. 700 −563	14. 800 −443	15. 803 −277
16. 502 −158	17. 600 −274	18. 904 −498	19. 701 −376	20. 500 −381

Set 26 Round each number to the nearest hundred. Estimate the difference.

1. 816 −295	2. 724 −119	3. 689 −293	4. 578 −369	5. 800 −413
6. 708 −394	7. 537 −329	8. 936 −247	9. 700 −579	10. 893 −415
11. 869 −580	12. 900 −309	13. 721 −319	14. 843 −197	15. 600 −487

Set 27 Subtract.

1. 8357 −2649	2. 5634 −2783	3. 4052 −2563	4. 4337 −2156	5. 5831 −2654
6. 8714 −1999	7. 6453 −2781	8. 6305 −1486	9. 5000 −4132	10. 8704 −3526
11. 7432 −3586	12. 6358 −2849	13. 8000 −3568	14. 9302 −4659	15. 5004 −3755

Name ____________________

Set 28 Give each time.

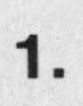

1.  5:42
2.  ______
3.  ______
4.  ______
5.  ______
6.  ______
7.  ______
8.  ______

Set 29 Give the total value in dollars.

1.   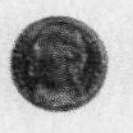 $1.55
2.   ______
3.   ______
4.  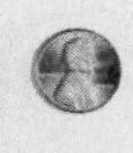 ______
5.  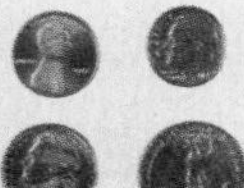 ______
6.    ______

Set 30 Multiply.

1. 2×1 = 2	2. 2×7	3. 2×8	4. 2×9	5. 2×3	6. 2×1	7. 2×6
8. 2×5	9. 2×4	10. 2×2	11. 2×9	12. 2×8	13. 2×3	14. 2×7
15. 2×9	16. 2×5	17. 2×7	18. 2×4	19. 2×2	20. 2×6	21. 2×8

Set 31 Multiply.

1. $\begin{array}{r}3\\ \times 1\\ \hline 3\end{array}$ 2. $\begin{array}{r}2\\ \times 1\\ \hline\end{array}$ 3. $\begin{array}{r}3\\ \times 9\\ \hline\end{array}$ 4. $\begin{array}{r}2\\ \times 7\\ \hline\end{array}$ 5. $\begin{array}{r}3\\ \times 7\\ \hline\end{array}$ 6. $\begin{array}{r}3\\ \times 3\\ \hline\end{array}$ 7. $\begin{array}{r}2\\ \times 5\\ \hline\end{array}$

8. $\begin{array}{r}2\\ \times 4\\ \hline\end{array}$ 9. $\begin{array}{r}2\\ \times 8\\ \hline\end{array}$ 10. $\begin{array}{r}3\\ \times 2\\ \hline\end{array}$ 11. $\begin{array}{r}2\\ \times 2\\ \hline\end{array}$ 12. $\begin{array}{r}3\\ \times 8\\ \hline\end{array}$ 13. $\begin{array}{r}2\\ \times 6\\ \hline\end{array}$ 14. $\begin{array}{r}3\\ \times 5\\ \hline\end{array}$

15. $\begin{array}{r}2\\ \times 9\\ \hline\end{array}$ 16. $\begin{array}{r}3\\ \times 6\\ \hline\end{array}$ 17. $\begin{array}{r}2\\ \times 3\\ \hline\end{array}$ 18. $\begin{array}{r}3\\ \times 8\\ \hline\end{array}$ 19. $\begin{array}{r}3\\ \times 4\\ \hline\end{array}$ 20. $\begin{array}{r}3\\ \times 9\\ \hline\end{array}$ 21. $\begin{array}{r}3\\ \times 7\\ \hline\end{array}$

22. $\begin{array}{r}3\\ \times 6\\ \hline\end{array}$ 23. $\begin{array}{r}2\\ \times 7\\ \hline\end{array}$ 24. $\begin{array}{r}3\\ \times 8\\ \hline\end{array}$ 25. $\begin{array}{r}2\\ \times 8\\ \hline\end{array}$ 26. $\begin{array}{r}3\\ \times 7\\ \hline\end{array}$ 27. $\begin{array}{r}2\\ \times 9\\ \hline\end{array}$ 28. $\begin{array}{r}3\\ \times 9\\ \hline\end{array}$

Set 32 Multiply.

1. $\begin{array}{r}3\\ \times 9\\ \hline 27\end{array}$ 2. $\begin{array}{r}4\\ \times 1\\ \hline\end{array}$ 3. $\begin{array}{r}2\\ \times 6\\ \hline\end{array}$ 4. $\begin{array}{r}3\\ \times 3\\ \hline\end{array}$ 5. $\begin{array}{r}2\\ \times 7\\ \hline\end{array}$ 6. $\begin{array}{r}4\\ \times 3\\ \hline\end{array}$ 7. $\begin{array}{r}4\\ \times 8\\ \hline\end{array}$

8. $\begin{array}{r}4\\ \times 7\\ \hline\end{array}$ 9. $\begin{array}{r}3\\ \times 5\\ \hline\end{array}$ 10. $\begin{array}{r}4\\ \times 9\\ \hline\end{array}$ 11. $\begin{array}{r}4\\ \times 2\\ \hline\end{array}$ 12. $\begin{array}{r}3\\ \times 8\\ \hline\end{array}$ 13. $\begin{array}{r}2\\ \times 5\\ \hline\end{array}$ 14. $\begin{array}{r}2\\ \times 8\\ \hline\end{array}$

15. $\begin{array}{r}3\\ \times 4\\ \hline\end{array}$ 16. $\begin{array}{r}4\\ \times 4\\ \hline\end{array}$ 17. $\begin{array}{r}3\\ \times 6\\ \hline\end{array}$ 18. $\begin{array}{r}4\\ \times 6\\ \hline\end{array}$ 19. $\begin{array}{r}2\\ \times 9\\ \hline\end{array}$ 20. $\begin{array}{r}4\\ \times 5\\ \hline\end{array}$ 21. $\begin{array}{r}3\\ \times 7\\ \hline\end{array}$

22. $\begin{array}{r}4\\ \times 7\\ \hline\end{array}$ 23. $\begin{array}{r}2\\ \times 8\\ \hline\end{array}$ 24. $\begin{array}{r}3\\ \times 8\\ \hline\end{array}$ 25. $\begin{array}{r}3\\ \times 9\\ \hline\end{array}$ 26. $\begin{array}{r}4\\ \times 9\\ \hline\end{array}$ 27. $\begin{array}{r}2\\ \times 9\\ \hline\end{array}$ 28. $\begin{array}{r}4\\ \times 8\\ \hline\end{array}$

Set 33 Give each product.

1. $3 \times 5 =$ 15 2. $8 \times 3 =$ ____ 3. $3 \times 3 =$ ____ 4. $6 \times 5 =$ ____

5. $4 \times 4 =$ ____ 6. $4 \times 5 =$ ____ 7. $2 \times 5 =$ ____ 8. $3 \times 4 =$ ____

9. $8 \times 4 =$ ____ 10. $9 \times 5 =$ ____ 11. $6 \times 4 =$ ____ 12. $5 \times 3 =$ ____

13. $5 \times 5 =$ ____ 14. $6 \times 3 =$ ____ 15. $9 \times 3 =$ ____ 16. $8 \times 5 =$ ____

17. $7 \times 3 =$ ____ 18. $1 \times 5 =$ ____ 19. $2 \times 4 =$ ____ 20. $5 \times 4 =$ ____

21. $4 \times 3 =$ ____ 22. $7 \times 4 =$ ____ 23. $7 \times 5 =$ ____ 24. $9 \times 4 =$ ____

Name________________________________

Set 34 **Give each product.**

1. 8 × 0 = 0
2. 5 × 3 = ___
3. 6 × 4 = ___
4. 3 × 1 = ___
5. 8 × 3 = ___
6. 6 × 1 = ___
7. 5 × 5 = ___
8. 4 × 0 = ___
9. 7 × 4 = ___
10. 7 × 1 = ___
11. 5 × 0 = ___
12. 5 × 4 = ___
13. 3 × 0 = ___
14. 6 × 3 = ___
15. 3 × 4 = ___
16. 9 × 1 = ___
17. 4 × 3 = ___
18. 9 × 3 = ___
19. 4 × 5 = ___
20. 6 × 5 = ___
21. 8 × 5 = ___
22. 8 × 4 = ___
23. 9 × 0 = ___
24. 4 × 1 = ___
25. 7 × 0 = ___
26. 5 × 1 = ___
27. 7 × 3 = ___
28. 9 × 4 = ___
29. 7 × 5 = ___
30. 8 × 1 = ___
31. 9 × 5 = ___
32. 6 × 0 = ___

Set 35 **Divide.**

1. 6 ÷ 2 = 3
2. 12 ÷ 3 = ___
3. 4 ÷ 2 = ___
4. 9 ÷ 3 = ___
5. 15 ÷ 3 = ___
6. 2 ÷ 2 = ___
7. 6 ÷ 3 = ___
8. 18 ÷ 2 = ___
9. 12 ÷ 2 = ___
10. 21 ÷ 3 = ___
11. 10 ÷ 2 = ___
12. 24 ÷ 3 = ___
13. 8 ÷ 2 = ___
14. 3 ÷ 3 = ___
15. 14 ÷ 2 = ___
16. 21 ÷ 3 = ___
17. 18 ÷ 3 = ___
18. 12 ÷ 3 = ___
19. 27 ÷ 3 = ___
20. 16 ÷ 2 = ___

Set 36 **Give each quotient.**

1. 8 ÷ 4 = 2
2. 5 ÷ 5 = ___
3. 32 ÷ 4 = ___
4. 20 ÷ 5 = ___
5. 30 ÷ 5 = ___
6. 24 ÷ 4 = ___
7. 35 ÷ 5 = ___
8. 20 ÷ 4 = ___
9. 18 ÷ 3 = ___
10. 27 ÷ 3 = ___
11. 24 ÷ 3 = ___
12. 40 ÷ 5 = ___
13. 36 ÷ 4 = ___
14. 45 ÷ 5 = ___
15. 16 ÷ 4 = ___
16. 28 ÷ 4 = ___
17. 15 ÷ 5 = ___
18. 12 ÷ 4 = ___
19. 25 ÷ 5 = ___
20. 10 ÷ 5 = ___
21. 12 ÷ 3 = ___
22. 21 ÷ 3 = ___
23. 45 ÷ 5 = ___
24. 18 ÷ 2 = ___
25. 35 ÷ 5 = ___
26. 24 ÷ 4 = ___
27. 15 ÷ 3 = ___
28. 32 ÷ 4 = ___

Set 37 **Divide.**

1. 3) 21	2. 5) 25	3. 4) 12	4. 2) 8	5. 3) 9
6. 2) 18	7. 4) 32	8. 5) 40	9. 4) 20	10. 2) 4
11. 5) 15	12. 3) 6	13. 3) 24	14. 5) 35	15. 2) 16
16. 4) 24	17. 3) 12	18. 2) 10	19. 4) 36	20. 4) 32
21. 2) 14	22. 4) 16	23. 3) 18	24. 4) 28	25. 3) 15
26. 4) 32	27. 5) 30	28. 4) 20	29. 5) 10	30. 3) 27

Set 38

1. 3) 17	2. 5) 21	3. 4) 15	4. 2) 15	5. 4) 25
	6. 5) 41	7. 5) 33	8. 3) 14	9. 2) 19
10. 5) 12	11. 5) 27	12. 3) 29	13. 2) 7	14. 5) 8
15. 3) 7	16. 4) 34	17. 3) 25	18. 3) 14	19. 4) 29
20. 2) 15	21. 3) 20	22. 4) 17	23. 3) 17	24. 5) 44

Set 39 **What fraction is shaded?**

1.  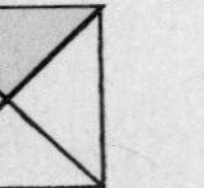 ____

2. ____

3. 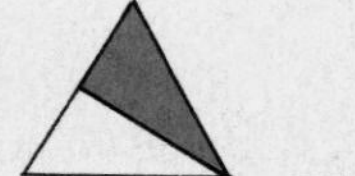 ____

4. 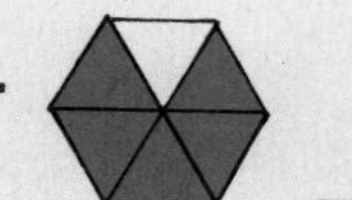 ____

5. 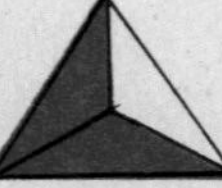 ____

6.  ____

7. 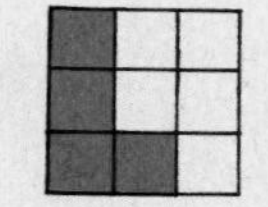 ____

8. 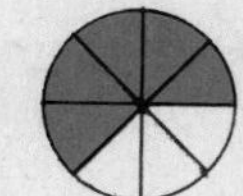 ____

9. 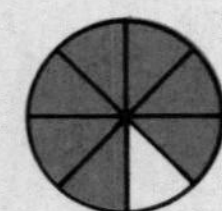 ____

10. 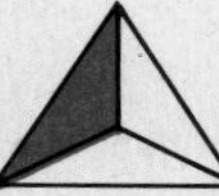 ____

11. 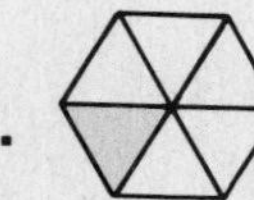 ____

12. 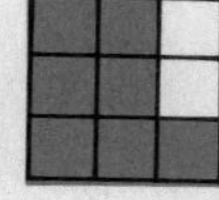 ____

Name *Matin #2*

Set 40 **What fraction of the blocks are blue?**

1. $\frac{3}{3}$
2. $\frac{3}{4}$
3. $\frac{1}{3}$
4. $\frac{1}{4}$
5. $\frac{3}{5}$
6. $\frac{4}{6}$

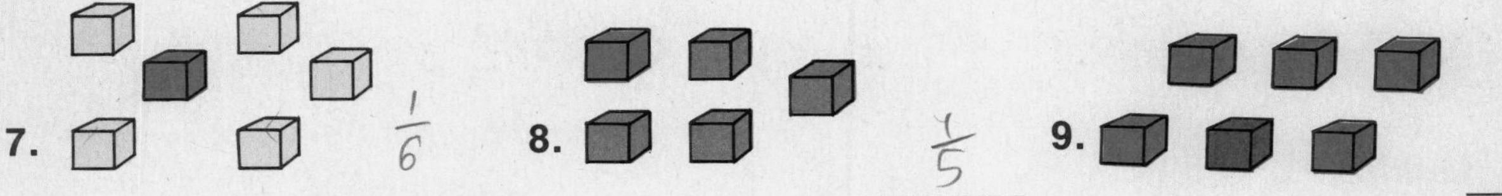

7. $\frac{1}{6}$
8. $\frac{1}{5}$
9. $\frac{5}{6}$

Set 41 **Complete.**

1. $\frac{1}{2}$ of 6 = 3
2. $\frac{1}{2}$ of 10 = 5
3. $\frac{1}{3}$ of 6 = 2
4. $\frac{1}{4}$ of 8 = 2
5. $\frac{1}{2}$ of 12 = 6
6. $\frac{1}{3}$ of 12 = 4
7. $\frac{1}{5}$ of 15 = 3
8. $\frac{1}{4}$ of 16 = 4
9. $\frac{1}{3}$ of 15 = 5
10. $\frac{1}{4}$ of 12 = 3
11. $\frac{1}{3}$ of 24 = 8
12. $\frac{1}{5}$ of 10 = 2
13. $\frac{1}{4}$ of 24 = 6
14. $\frac{1}{5}$ of 35 = 7
15. $\frac{1}{3}$ of 27 = 9

Set 42 **Complete.**

1. $\frac{1}{2} = \frac{3}{6}$
2. $\frac{1}{3} = \frac{2}{6}$
3. $\frac{1}{3} = \frac{4}{12}$
4. $\frac{1}{5} = \frac{2}{10}$
5. $\frac{2}{3} = \frac{4}{6}$
6. $\frac{2}{3} = \frac{10}{15}$
7. $\frac{1}{2} = \frac{5}{10}$
8. $\frac{3}{4} = \frac{6}{8}$
9. $\frac{1}{3} = \frac{3}{9}$
10. $\frac{1}{4} = \frac{4}{16}$
11. $\frac{2}{3} = \frac{6}{9}$
12. $\frac{1}{4} = \frac{2}{8}$
13. $\frac{1}{4} = \frac{3}{12}$
14. $\frac{3}{4} = \frac{12}{16}$
15. $\frac{1}{5} = \frac{3}{15}$
16. $\frac{4}{5} = \frac{8}{10}$
17. $\frac{2}{5} = \frac{6}{15}$
18. $\frac{1}{5} = \frac{4}{20}$
19. $\frac{3}{4} = \frac{9}{12}$
20. $\frac{3}{5} = \frac{15}{25}$

Set 43 **How much is red? Write as a decimal.**

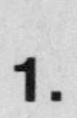 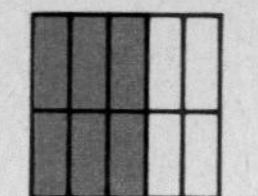  2. 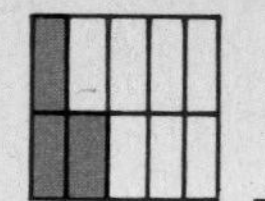 3. 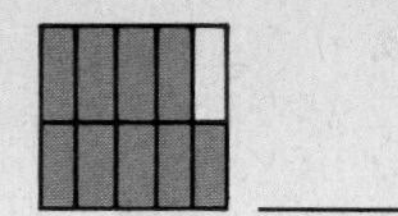 4. 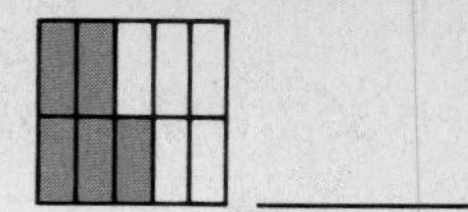

5. 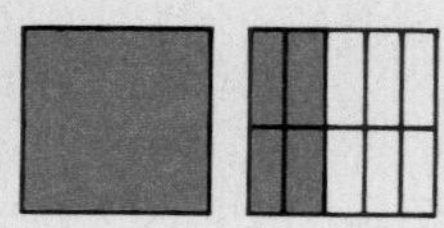 6. 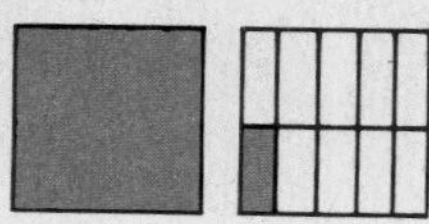 7. 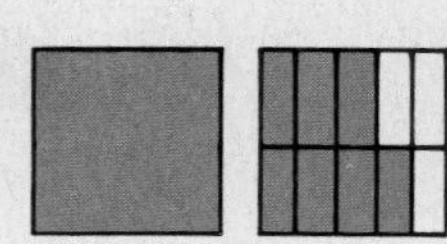 8. 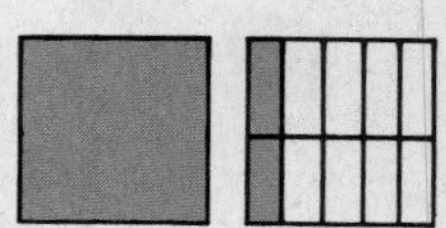

9. 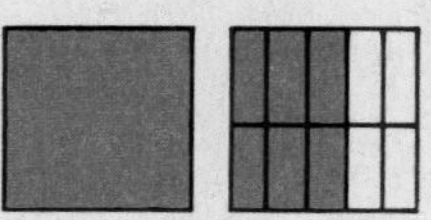 10. 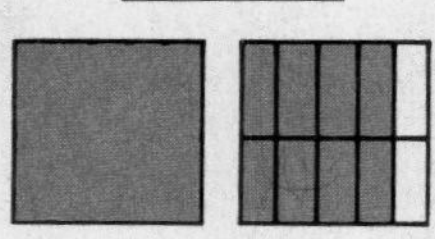 11. 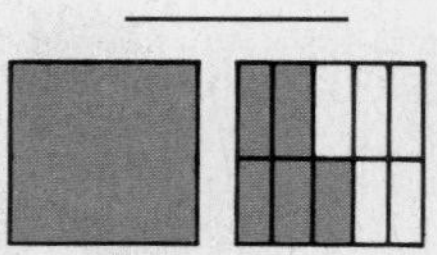 12. 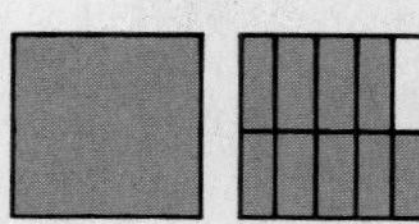

Set 44 **Multiply.**

1. 4×6
2. 6×5
3. 6×9
4. 4×7
5. 6×7
6. 4×9
7. 6×3
8. 8×3
9. 5×6
10. 5×7
11. 6×1
12. 4×8
13. 3×7
14. 5×8
15. 4×1
16. 6×6
17. 5×3
18. 3×6
19. 4×5
20. 5×4
21. 6×0
22. 5×5
23. 3×9
24. 6×9
25. 6×4
26. 3×8
27. 6×8
28. 5×9

Set 45 **Give each quotient.**

1. $3\overline{)24}$
2. $6\overline{)36}$
3. $5\overline{)30}$
4. $4\overline{)36}$
5. $5\overline{)35}$
6. $6\overline{)12}$
7. $4\overline{)32}$
8. $3\overline{)27}$
9. $6\overline{)6}$
10. $6\overline{)42}$
11. $5\overline{)40}$
12. $6\overline{)48}$
13. $5\overline{)25}$
14. $6\overline{)24}$
15. $6\overline{)0}$
16. $4\overline{)28}$
17. $5\overline{)45}$
18. $3\overline{)21}$
19. $4\overline{)24}$
20. $6\overline{)54}$

Name ______________________________

Set 46 Multiply.

1. $\begin{array}{r} 7 \\ \times 5 \\ \hline 35 \end{array}$	2. $\begin{array}{r} 6 \\ \times 9 \\ \hline \end{array}$	3. $\begin{array}{r} 7 \\ \times 7 \\ \hline \end{array}$	4. $\begin{array}{r} 6 \\ \times 6 \\ \hline \end{array}$	5. $\begin{array}{r} 5 \\ \times 8 \\ \hline \end{array}$	6. $\begin{array}{r} 4 \\ \times 8 \\ \hline \end{array}$	7. $\begin{array}{r} 7 \\ \times 4 \\ \hline \end{array}$
8. $\begin{array}{r} 6 \\ \times 3 \\ \hline \end{array}$	9. $\begin{array}{r} 6 \\ \times 4 \\ \hline \end{array}$	10. $\begin{array}{r} 5 \\ \times 9 \\ \hline \end{array}$	11. $\begin{array}{r} 7 \\ \times 2 \\ \hline \end{array}$	12. $\begin{array}{r} 7 \\ \times 8 \\ \hline \end{array}$	13. $\begin{array}{r} 4 \\ \times 9 \\ \hline \end{array}$	14. $\begin{array}{r} 6 \\ \times 7 \\ \hline \end{array}$
15. $\begin{array}{r} 7 \\ \times 3 \\ \hline \end{array}$	16. $\begin{array}{r} 7 \\ \times 6 \\ \hline \end{array}$	17. $\begin{array}{r} 6 \\ \times 5 \\ \hline \end{array}$	18. $\begin{array}{r} 7 \\ \times 1 \\ \hline \end{array}$	19. $\begin{array}{r} 6 \\ \times 2 \\ \hline \end{array}$	20. $\begin{array}{r} 6 \\ \times 8 \\ \hline \end{array}$	21. $\begin{array}{r} 7 \\ \times 9 \\ \hline \end{array}$
22. $\begin{array}{r} 5 \\ \times 6 \\ \hline \end{array}$	23. $\begin{array}{r} 3 \\ \times 8 \\ \hline \end{array}$	24. $\begin{array}{r} 4 \\ \times 7 \\ \hline \end{array}$	25. $\begin{array}{r} 3 \\ \times 9 \\ \hline \end{array}$	26. $\begin{array}{r} 5 \\ \times 7 \\ \hline \end{array}$	27. $\begin{array}{r} 4 \\ \times 6 \\ \hline \end{array}$	28. $\begin{array}{r} 3 \\ \times 0 \\ \hline \end{array}$

Set 47 Divide.

1. $6\overset{2}{\overline{)12}}$	2. $7\overline{)21}$	3. $6\overline{)30}$	4. $7\overline{)14}$	5. $5\overline{)40}$
6. $7\overline{)0}$	7. $6\overline{)6}$	8. $5\overline{)25}$	9. $7\overline{)28}$	10. $5\overline{)30}$
11. $6\overline{)54}$	12. $6\overline{)48}$	13. $7\overline{)7}$	14. $6\overline{)24}$	15. $7\overline{)35}$
16. $6\overline{)42}$	17. $7\overline{)49}$	18. $6\overline{)18}$	19. $7\overline{)42}$	20. $6\overline{)0}$
21. $6\overline{)36}$	22. $5\overline{)45}$	23. $7\overline{)56}$	24. $5\overline{)35}$	25. $7\overline{)63}$

Set 48 Multiply.

1. $\begin{array}{r} 8 \\ \times 6 \\ \hline 48 \end{array}$	2. $\begin{array}{r} 7 \\ \times 5 \\ \hline \end{array}$	3. $\begin{array}{r} 7 \\ \times 7 \\ \hline \end{array}$	4. $\begin{array}{r} 7 \\ \times 9 \\ \hline \end{array}$	5. $\begin{array}{r} 8 \\ \times 1 \\ \hline \end{array}$	6. $\begin{array}{r} 7 \\ \times 6 \\ \hline \end{array}$	7. $\begin{array}{r} 8 \\ \times 8 \\ \hline \end{array}$
8. $\begin{array}{r} 6 \\ \times 7 \\ \hline \end{array}$	9. $\begin{array}{r} 8 \\ \times 3 \\ \hline \end{array}$	10. $\begin{array}{r} 7 \\ \times 8 \\ \hline \end{array}$	11. $\begin{array}{r} 8 \\ \times 9 \\ \hline \end{array}$	12. $\begin{array}{r} 5 \\ \times 8 \\ \hline \end{array}$	13. $\begin{array}{r} 6 \\ \times 9 \\ \hline \end{array}$	14. $\begin{array}{r} 5 \\ \times 9 \\ \hline \end{array}$
15. $\begin{array}{r} 8 \\ \times 0 \\ \hline \end{array}$	16. $\begin{array}{r} 7 \\ \times 4 \\ \hline \end{array}$	17. $\begin{array}{r} 5 \\ \times 8 \\ \hline \end{array}$	18. $\begin{array}{r} 6 \\ \times 4 \\ \hline \end{array}$	19. $\begin{array}{r} 8 \\ \times 7 \\ \hline \end{array}$	20. $\begin{array}{r} 6 \\ \times 5 \\ \hline \end{array}$	21. $\begin{array}{r} 7 \\ \times 3 \\ \hline \end{array}$
22. $\begin{array}{r} 6 \\ \times 6 \\ \hline \end{array}$	23. $\begin{array}{r} 5 \\ \times 6 \\ \hline \end{array}$	24. $\begin{array}{r} 8 \\ \times 4 \\ \hline \end{array}$	25. $\begin{array}{r} 5 \\ \times 7 \\ \hline \end{array}$	26. $\begin{array}{r} 6 \\ \times 8 \\ \hline \end{array}$	27. $\begin{array}{r} 8 \\ \times 5 \\ \hline \end{array}$	28. $\begin{array}{r} 5 \\ \times 5 \\ \hline \end{array}$

Set 49 Divide.

1. $8\overline{)48}$ 2. $7\overline{)28}$ 3. $8\overline{)32}$ 4. $6\overline{)42}$ 5. $8\overline{)40}$

6. $8\overline{)8}$ 7. $8\overline{)24}$ 8. $6\overline{)36}$ 9. $7\overline{)56}$ 10. $7\overline{)42}$

11. $7\overline{)35}$ 12. $4\overline{)36}$ 13. $8\overline{)16}$ 14. $6\overline{)48}$ 15. $8\overline{)48}$

16. $8\overline{)64}$ 17. $6\overline{)54}$ 18. $4\overline{)32}$ 19. $5\overline{)35}$ 20. $8\overline{)72}$

21. $7\overline{)49}$ 22. $8\overline{)56}$ 23. $5\overline{)45}$ 24. $7\overline{)63}$ 25. $4\overline{)28}$

Set 50 Multiply.

1. 9×5 2. 7×7 3. 9×8 4. 8×8 5. 9×6 6. 9×9 7. 9×2

8. 7×6 9. 6×8 10. 8×7 11. 6×9 12. 7×8 13. 9×3 14. 7×9

15. 5×8 16. 6×6 17. 9×4 18. 7×5 19. 6×5 20. 8×5 21. 7×4

22. 5×7 23. 8×4 24. 5×9 25. 8×6 26. 6×7 27. 9×7 28. 8×9

Set 51 Divide.

1. $8\overline{)16}$ 2. $7\overline{)42}$ 3. $8\overline{)40}$ 4. $8\overline{)56}$ 5. $9\overline{)27}$

6. $9\overline{)18}$ 7. $8\overline{)32}$ 8. $9\overline{)54}$ 9. $7\overline{)63}$ 10. $9\overline{)0}$

11. $9\overline{)81}$ 12. $9\overline{)63}$ 13. $7\overline{)49}$ 14. $9\overline{)36}$ 15. $8\overline{)72}$

16. $6\overline{)48}$ 17. $8\overline{)40}$ 18. $9\overline{)45}$ 19. $7\overline{)42}$ 20. $6\overline{)42}$

21. $8\overline{)48}$ 22. $6\overline{)54}$ 23. $7\overline{)56}$ 24. $9\overline{)72}$ 25. $8\overline{)64}$

Name ____________________

Set 52

1. $8\overline{)25}$	2. $7\overline{)45}$	3. $4\overline{)37}$	4. $5\overline{)38}$	5. $7\overline{)60}$
	6. $9\overline{)75}$	7. $8\overline{)37}$	8. $9\overline{)67}$	9. $9\overline{)68}$
10. $7\overline{)51}$	11. $6\overline{)38}$	12. $7\overline{)40}$	13. $8\overline{)60}$	14. $4\overline{)27}$
15. $8\overline{)49}$	16. $4\overline{)34}$	17. $6\overline{)47}$	18. $9\overline{)52}$	19. $7\overline{)30}$
20. $8\overline{)53}$	21. $7\overline{)65}$	22. $4\overline{)19}$	23. $6\overline{)56}$	24. $9\overline{)85}$

Set 53 Multiply.

1. 40 ×2	2. 32 ×3	3. 41 ×2	4. 24 ×2	5. 33 ×3	6. 21 ×4
7. 11 ×6	8. 12 ×4	9. 10 ×7	10. 11 ×9	11. 10 ×9	12. 12 ×3
13. 20 ×4	14. 42 ×2	15. 31 ×2	16. 21 ×3	17. 11 ×7	18. 10 ×8
19. 22 ×4	20. 30 ×2	21. 23 ×3	22. 11 ×5	23. 30 ×3	24. 32 ×2

Set 54 Multiply.

1. 19 ×4	2. 36 ×2	3. 27 ×3	4. 24 ×3	5. 12 ×7	6. 13 ×5
7. 12 ×8	8. 15 ×4	9. 15 ×5	10. 14 ×4	11. 26 ×3	12. 23 ×4
13. 35 ×2	14. 15 ×6	15. 29 ×3	16. 17 ×4	17. 12 ×6	18. 16 ×5
19. 24 ×4	20. 28 ×3	21. 17 ×5	22. 16 ×6	23. 14 ×6	24. 13 ×7

Set 55 Multiply.

1. 48×3
2. 38×4
3. 25×4
4. 46×3
5. 85×3
6. 78×8
7. 64×4
8. 75×2
9. 86×6
10. 57×4
11. 96×4
12. 68×5
13. 56×8
14. 65×5
15. 73×6
16. 82×7
17. 59×6
18. 47×9
19. 68×8
20. 75×7
21. 94×5
22. 83×6
23. 49×9
24. 64×8

Set 56 Divide.

1. $2\overline{)24}$
2. $3\overline{)30}$
3. $5\overline{)55}$
4. $4\overline{)48}$
5. $3\overline{)96}$
6. $4\overline{)44}$
7. $2\overline{)88}$
8. $3\overline{)33}$
9. $3\overline{)66}$
10. $2\overline{)40}$
11. $8\overline{)80}$
12. $7\overline{)70}$
13. $2\overline{)28}$
14. $3\overline{)63}$
15. $4\overline{)88}$
16. $2\overline{)86}$
17. $4\overline{)84}$
18. $3\overline{)36}$
19. $5\overline{)50}$
20. $2\overline{)84}$
21. $7\overline{)77}$
22. $4\overline{)80}$
23. $3\overline{)69}$
24. $6\overline{)66}$
25. $9\overline{)90}$

Set 57 Divide.

1. $4\overline{)64}$
2. $3\overline{)42}$
3. $6\overline{)96}$
4. $2\overline{)96}$
5. $3\overline{)45}$
6. $2\overline{)56}$
7. $3\overline{)72}$
8. $5\overline{)95}$
9. $3\overline{)84}$
10. $8\overline{)96}$
11. $5\overline{)65}$
12. $4\overline{)72}$
13. $2\overline{)74}$
14. $6\overline{)72}$
15. $2\overline{)78}$
16. $4\overline{)60}$
17. $3\overline{)75}$
18. $3\overline{)81}$
19. $4\overline{)92}$
20. $7\overline{)91}$
21. $6\overline{)84}$
22. $5\overline{)80}$
23. $7\overline{)84}$
24. $6\overline{)78}$

Name ______________________________

EXTRA PROBLEM SOLVING

PROBLEM SOLVING Set 1

Name	Arthur	Lauren	Steven	Teresa
Baskets made	5	7	8	4
Baskets missed	7	3	6	8

1. Who made 4 baskets? ______________

2. How many baskets did Lauren miss? ______

3. How many baskets did Lauren and Teresa make? ______

4. How many baskets did Arthur and Steven make? ______

5. How many times did Steven try to make a basket? ______

6. How many times did Lauren try to make a basket? ______

PROBLEM SOLVING Set 2

1. Danny tried to make a basket 14 times. He made 9 baskets. How many did he miss? ______

2. Sonia missed 4 baskets and made 7 baskets. How many baskets did she try to make? ______

3. Mary made 9 baskets and Ellen made 7 baskets. How many more did Mary make? ______

4. Scott made 5 baskets. Bob made 3 baskets. Dave made 6 baskets. How many baskets did they make in all? ______

5. Sarah tried 13 times to make a basket. She missed 6 baskets. How many did she make? ______

6. Don and Ray each made 7 baskets. How many baskets did they make in all? ______

PROBLEM SOLVING Set 3

57¢ 78¢ 96¢ 35¢

1. Leonard bought a ghost and a pumpkin. How much did he spend? _______

2. Darlene bought a hat and a cat. How much did she spend? _______

3. Ricardo bought 2 ghosts. How much did he spend? _______

4. Ellen bought 2 cats. How much did she spend? _______

5. Ben has $1.50. Can he buy a ghost and a hat? _______

6. Deborah has 75¢. Can she buy 2 cats? _______

PROBLEM SOLVING Set 4

1. 18 ghosts in a box
   13 ghosts on a table
   How many more are in the box? _______

2. 24 pumpkins in a box
   17 pumpkins taken out of the box
   How many are left in the box? _______

3. 34 hats for the class
   19 hats for the boys
   How many for the girls? _______

4. 27 big cats
   19 small cats
   How many cats? _______

5. 31 pumpkins for sale
   26 pumpkins sold
   How many are left? _______

6. 24 pumpkins for sale
   7 pumpkins not sold
   How many were sold? _______

Name ________________

PROBLEM SOLVING Set 5

DAY	VISITORS
Monday	128
Tuesday	606
Wednesday	142
Thursday	542
Friday	629
Saturday	837

1. Which day were there the most visitors? ________
2. Which day were there the fewest visitors? ________
3. Were there more visitors on Tuesday or on Friday? ________
4. How many visitors were there during the first two days of the week? ________
5. How many visitors were there during the last two days of the week? ________

PROBLEM SOLVING Set 6

1. Sean saw 18 turtles sleeping. He saw 16 turtles swimming. How many turtles did he see? ________
2. Bill saw 23 sea horses. 9 sea horses swam away. How many sea horses were left? ________
3. Jean counted 86 small fish and 37 large fish in the same tank. How many fish did she count? ________
4. One tank had 534 gallons of water in it. Another tank had 426 gallons of water in it. How many more gallons of water did the first tank have? ________
5. Kate saw 13 adult penguins and 8 baby penguins. How many penguins did she see? ________
6. It cost $3.75 for adults to see the fish and $1.95 for children. How much more did it cost an adult? ________

PROBLEM SOLVING Set 7

1. Driving to the Fair
   43 miles before lunch
   27 miles after lunch
   How far to the fair? ______

2. Lunch
   $.95 for a sandwich
   $.35 for milk
   How much change from $2? ______

3. Buying Tickets
   Adults: $1.25 each
   Children: $.75 each
   How much for 2 adults' and 2 children's tickets? ______

4. Riding the Ferris Wheel
   Tickets: $.65 each
   How much for 2 tickets? ______

5. Taking Pictures
   Small roll: 12 pictures
   Large roll: 20 pictures
   How many more pictures on 2 small rolls than 1 large roll? ______

6. Buying Gifts
   Glasses: 89¢ each
   Cups: 59¢ each
   How much for a cup and a glass? ______

PROBLEM SOLVING Set 8

1. Buying Lemonade
   Lemonades: 45¢ each
   How much for 2 lemonades? ______

2. Riding the Merry-go-round
   Tickets: $.55 each
   How much for 2 tickets? ______

3. Comparing Weights
   Cow: 957 pounds
   Calf: 283 pounds
   How much heavier was the cow? ______

4. Buying T-shirts
   Large T-shirts: $3.95 each
   Small T-shirts: $2.49 each
   How much more for a large T-shirt? ______

5. Supper
   $4.65 for a meal
   How much change from $5?
   ______

6. Time Driving
   Going to the fair: 85 minutes
   Going home: 95 minutes
   How many minutes in all?
   ______

Name ____________________

PROBLEM SOLVING Set 9

$4.00 $2.00 $3.00

1. How much do 4 cars cost?

____

2. How much do 7 airplanes cost?

____

3. How much do 5 boats cost?

____

4. How much do 8 cars cost?

____

5. Peter bought 2 boats and 1 airplane. What was the total cost? _________

6. Kay bought an airplane. How much change did she get from $10? _________

PROBLEM SOLVING Set 10

1. There are 2 boats and 4 cars on each shelf. There are 3 shelves. How many cars are there? _________

2. Each airplane has 3 wheels and 2 doors. How many wheels are on 6 airplanes? _________

3. There are 7 red cars, 2 blue cars, and 3 green cars. How many more red cars than blue cars are there? _________

4. A boat costs $3. An airplane costs $4. How much do 8 boats cost? _________

5. Each airplane has 3 wheels. Each car has 4 wheels. How many wheels are on 5 cars?

____

6. Grace spent $9 for boats. Paul spent $7 for airplanes. How much change did Grace get from $10? _________

PROBLEM SOLVING Set 11

1. Kay and Brad spent $.98 for milk and $1.27 for flour. How much did they spend in all? ______

2. They bought a package of red cherries for $.69 and a box of raisins for $1.15. How much change did they get from $2.00? ______

3. Each recipe made 8 gingerbread cookies. How many cookies could be made with 4 recipes? ______

4. Each recipe called for 2 cups of flour. How many recipes could be made with 16 cups of flour? ______

5. Each cookie sheet held 5 gingerbread cookies. How many sheets would they fill with 30 cookies? ______

6. They put a batch of cookies in the oven at 4:15. At 4:27 they took the cookies out. How many minutes did the cookies bake? ______

PROBLEM SOLVING Set 12

1. Kay and Brad put 3 red cherries on each cookie. How many cookies could they decorate with 24 red cherries? ______

2. They put 4 walnut pieces on each cookie. How many cookies could they decorate with 28 walnut pieces? ______

3. Kay and Brad put 5 raisins on each cookie. How many raisins did they need for 9 gingerbread men? ______

4. They gave 12 of the 48 cookies to their friends. How many did they have left? ______

5. Kay put 3 cookies in each of 5 small bags. How many cookies did she put in bags? ______

6. Brad sold 4 cookies for 9¢ each. What was the total price? ______

Name ______________________

PROBLEM SOLVING Set 13

1. One day Clara worked 28 minutes. The next day she worked 39 minutes. How many minutes in all? ______

2. Julian worked 40 minutes one day and 29 minutes the next. How many more minutes did he work the first day? ______

3. Julian bought a rake for $4.65 and a hoe for $3.79. What was the total cost? ______

4. Clara had $5.00. She bought some flower seeds for $1.69. How much did she have left? ______

5. Clara had 9 flower pots. She planted 4 seeds in each. How many seeds did she plant? ______

6. Julian planted 4 rows of flowers. He planted 8 flowers in each row. How many flowers did he plant? ______

PROBLEM SOLVING Set 14

1. Steve planted 24 flowers. He planted 6 flowers in each row. How many rows did he plant? ______

2. There were 18 rose bushes planted in 3 equal rows. How many bushes were in each row? ______

3. Sonia had 7 flower boxes. She planted 6 flowers in each box. How many flowers did she plant? ______

4. George had 25 seeds. He wanted to plant 5 seeds in each box. How many boxes did he need? ______

5. There were 129 red roses and 176 yellow roses. How many roses in all? ______

6. There were 156 daisies. Jane picked 48 of them. How many were left? ______

PROBLEM SOLVING Set 15

1. Patricia saw a red bicycle that cost $119 and a blue bicycle that cost $105. How much more did the red bicycle cost? _______

2. Patricia bought the blue bicycle for $105 and a basket for $8. What was the total cost? _______

3. There are 481 children in Patricia's school. 137 ride bicycles to school. How many do not ride bicycles to school? _______

4. Patricia took the bicycle safety test. She missed 23 points out of a total of 200. What was her score? _______

5. She got 5 points for each road sign that she got right. How many points did she get for getting 9 road signs right? _______

6. Patricia had to buy 2 new tires for $2.65 each and a bell for $2.19. What was the total price? _______

PROBLEM SOLVING Set 16

1. Each day Patricia rides her bicycle 6 blocks to school and 6 blocks home. How many blocks is this a day? _______

2. If she rides 12 blocks each school day, how far does she ride in a school week (5 days)? _______

3. Each bicycle rack at Patricia's school holds 24 bicycles. How many bicycles can 4 racks hold? _______

4. Handle grips were on sale for $.27 each. She bought 4 of them. What was the total cost? _______

5. She bought a lock for $4.95 and a basket for $7.98. What was the total cost? _______

6. During a 6-day vacation, she rode her bicycle 16 blocks each day. How many blocks did she ride in all? _______

GLOSSARY

addend A number used in an addition problem.

$$\begin{array}{r} 9 \leftarrow \text{addend} \\ +4 \leftarrow \text{addend} \\ \hline 13 \leftarrow \text{sum} \end{array}$$

adding 0 property If you add any number and 0, you get the number.

$4 + 0 = 4$

A.M. A symbol for times after 12:00 midnight and before 12:00 noon.

area The number of unit squares that cover a figure.

1 square centimeter

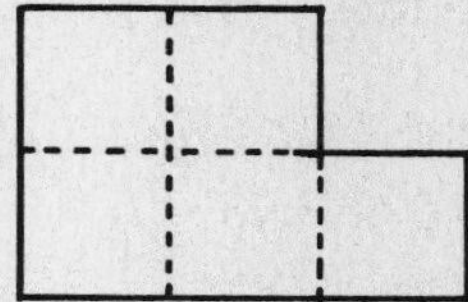

The area of this figure is 5 square centimeters.

centimeter (cm) A unit of length in the metric system. 100 centimeters is one meter.

circle A curved plane figure shaped like this:

computer A machine that can count and keep track of things.

cone A space figure shaped like this:

congruent figures Figures that have the same size and shape.

cube A rectangular solid ("box") with all edges the same length. ← edge

cylinder A space figure shaped like this:

decimal A number such as .4 (four tenths) and 3.2 (three and two tenths).

decimal point A dot written in a decimal between the ones place and the tenths place.

3.2

ones place — tenths place

degree Celsius (°C) A unit of temperature in the metric system.

degree Fahrenheit (°F) A unit of temperature used in the United States.

difference The answer to a subtraction problem.

$$\begin{array}{r} 7 \\ -3 \\ \hline 4 \end{array} \leftarrow \text{difference}$$

digit Any of the symbols 0, 1, 2, 3, 4, 5, 6, 7, 8, and 9.

equation A sentence with an equal sign, such as

$3 \times 9 = 27$

equivalent fractions Fractions for the same number.

$\frac{1}{2}$, $\frac{2}{4}$, and $\frac{3}{6}$ are equivalent fractions.

estimate To use rounded numbers when an exact answer is not needed. For example, to estimate the sum of 47 + 32, add 50 + 30. The sum is about 80.

even number A number that can be divided evenly by 2.

2, 4, 6, 8, 10, and 12 are even numbers.

factors Numbers used in a multiplication problem.

$$\begin{array}{rl} 8 & \leftarrow \text{factor} \\ \times 6 & \leftarrow \text{factor} \\ \hline 48 & \leftarrow \text{product} \end{array}$$

fraction A number such as $\frac{1}{2}$, $\frac{3}{4}$, and $\frac{4}{6}$.

gram (g) A unit of mass (weight) in the metric system.

graph A picture used to show some information.

greater than A comparison of two numbers that are not the same. The symbol is >. For example, **7 > 2**. (Another comparison is *less than*.)

input Information that is put into the computer.

kilogram (kg) A unit of mass (weight) in the metric system.

less than A comparison of two numbers that are not the same. The symbol is <. For example, **3 < 8**. (Another comparison is *greater than*.)

line of symmetry If a figure can be folded along a line so the two parts of the figure match, the fold line is a line of symmetry.

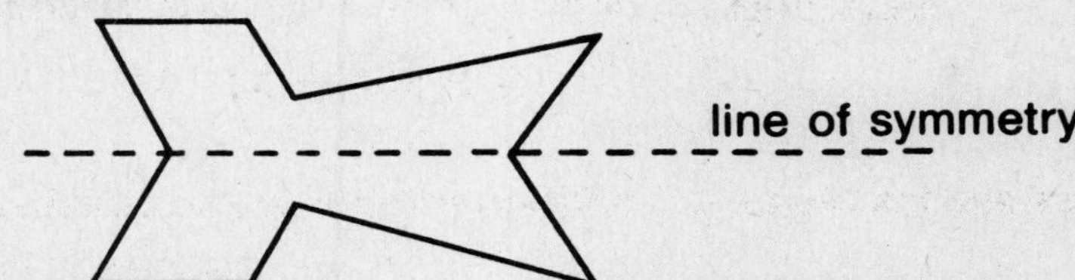

liter A unit of liquid measure in the metric system. One liter is 1000 cubic centimeters.

meter (m) A unit of length in the metric system. One meter is 100 centimeters.

metric system An international system of measurement that uses meter, liter, gram, and degree-Celsius temperature.

odd number — A number that cannot be divided evenly by 2.

1, 3, 5, 7, 9, and 11 are odd numbers.

order property of addition — You can change the order of the addends without changing the sum.

$7 + 9 = 9 + 7$

order property of multiplication — You can change the order of the factors without changing the product.

$7 \times 9 = 9 \times 7$

ordinal number — The numbers *first, second, third, fourth, fifth,* and so on, are ordinal numbers. They tell the place in line or order of objects.

output — Information that is sent from the computer.

perimeter — The distance around a figure. The sum of the lengths of the sides.

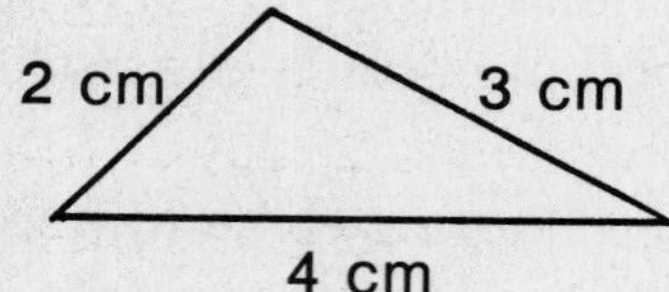

The perimeter is 9 cm.

place value — The value given to the place, or position, of a digit in a numeral.

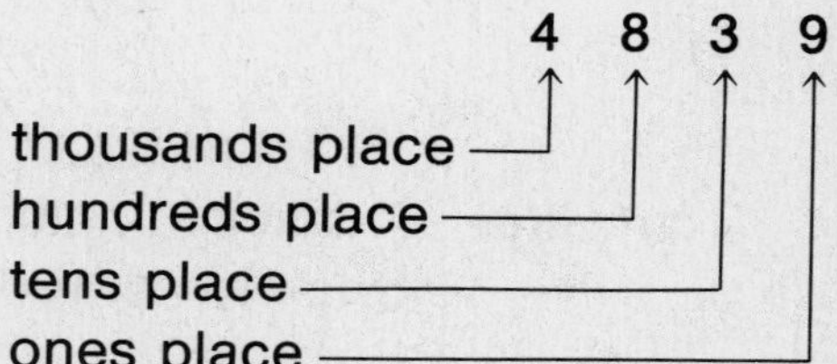

plane figures — Figures that lie in a flat or level surface. Rectangles, squares, circles, and triangles are all plane figures.

P.M. — A symbol for times after 12:00 noon and before 12:00 midnight.

product The answer to a multiplication problem.

$$\begin{array}{r} 7 \\ \times 8 \\ \hline 56 \end{array} \leftarrow \text{product}$$

program A list of directions for the computer to follow.

quotient The answer to a division problem.

$$8\overline{)56}\quad 7 \leftarrow \text{quotient}$$

rectangle A plane figure with four straight sides and four square corners.

← side

↖ corner

rectangular solid Most boxes have the shape of a rectangular solid. A rectangular solid has length, width, and height.

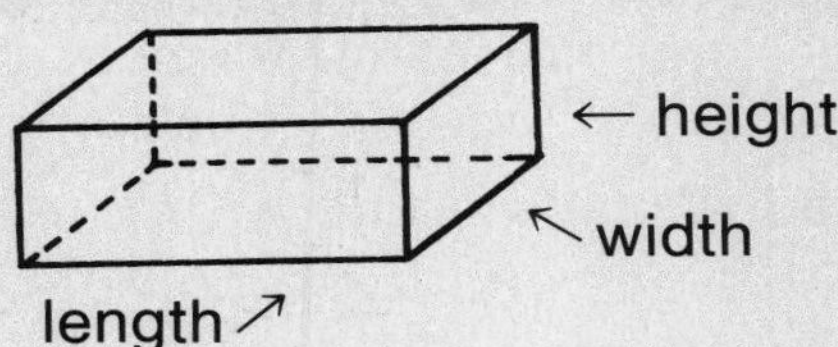

remainder The number "left over" after a division.

$$\begin{array}{r} 5\ \text{R1} \\ 3\overline{)16} \\ -15 \\ \hline 1 \end{array} \leftarrow \text{remainder}$$

round To replace an exact number by another one that is easier to use.

52 rounded to the nearest ten is 50.
278 rounded to the nearest hundred is 300.

When a number is halfway between two numbers, round up.

150 rounded to the nearest hundred is 200.

segment The sides of plane figures are segments. Segments have two endpoints.

endpoints
A B

This is segment AB or segment BA.

sphere A space figure that is the shape of a ball.

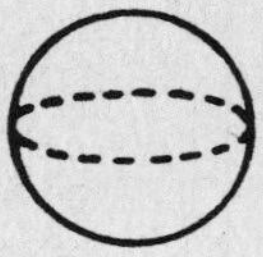

square A plane figure with four equal sides and four square corners.

sum The answer to an addition problem.

$$\begin{array}{r} 23 \\ +58 \\ \hline 81 \end{array} \leftarrow \text{sum}$$

symmetry A figure has symmetry if it can be folded so the two parts of the figure match.

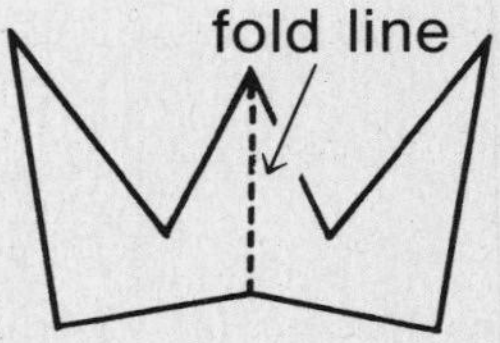

fold line

total Another name for *sum*.

triangle A plane figure with three sides and three corners.

volume The number of unit cubes that fit inside an object.

1 cubic centimeter

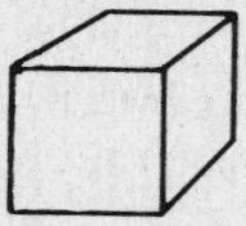

1 cm
1 cm
1 cm

The volume is 12 cubic centimeters.

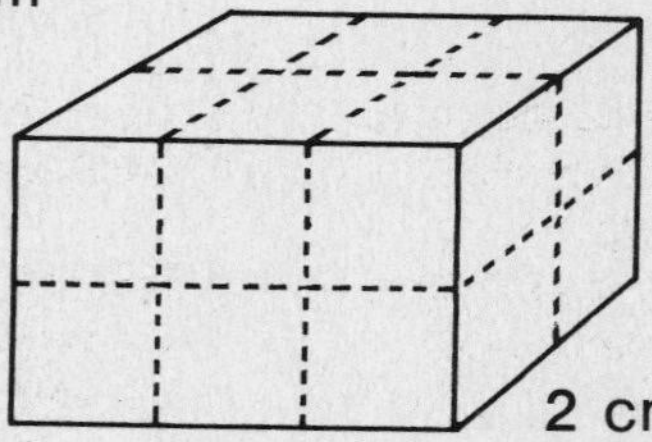

2 cm
2 cm
3 cm

whole number Any of the numbers 0, 1, 2, 3, 4, and so on.

Index